NEO-LATIN LITERATURE
AND THE PASTORAL

NEO-LATIN

LUX
LIBERTAS

THE UNIVERSITY OF NORTH CAROLINA PRESS
CHAPEL HILL

LITERATURE AND THE PASTORAL

By W. LEONARD GRANT

To Kathleen

PREFACE

A number of years ago, when I was starting to study Neo-Latin literature at Oxford, James Blair Leishman, Senior Lecturer in English Literature in the University, asked me whether there were many pastoral poems in Neo-Latin similar to John Milton's poem on Charles Diodati. "I've read a few," I replied vaguely, in total ignorance of how tremendous a vogue the pastoral, in all of its forms, maintained in that literature and in equal ignorance of how often the forms of pastoral that a reader meets in vernacular English or French or Italian originated in imitation of Neo-Latin innovations. I have since tried to rectify my ignorance, and the present book is a fuller reply to Mr. Leishman's question; I suspect that he knew a great deal more of the answer than he let me guess at the time.

Thanks are due to various groups that have assisted me in Neo-Latin studies for a good many years—the Nuffield Foundation, the Humanities Research Council of Canada, the Government of France, and especially the University of British Columbia for a particular grant towards this book. I should also like to thank the Ford Foundation for a grant extended through its program for assisting American university presses in the publication of works in the humanities and the social sciences. Libraries at Oxford, Paris, Siena, Florence, Eton, Harvard, Toronto, and St. Louis have extended me their facilities with generosity and patience. I am especially grateful to my wife, who has had the hardihood to read the entire manuscript more than once.

I should add that throughout the book the verse-translations are my own, but the version of a brief excerpt from Vida's "Art of Poetry" is by Christopher Pitt.

W. LEONARD GRANT

VANCOUVER, CANADA

CONTENTS

NEO-LATIN LITERATURE
AND THE PASTORAL

I

RENAISSANCE LATIN
LITERATURE: PROSE
AND THE DRAMA

ne of the most remarkable phenomena of the Renaissance is the vast original Latin literature produced by a succession of Humanists in Italy, Germany, France, the Netherlands, Portugal, Hungary, Poland, and the British Isles. Thousands of volumes, ranging from duodecimo midgets to folio giants, were devoted to every sort of prose and verse: history, philosophy, theology, biography, the essay, the novel, epic, lyric, satire, elegy, pastoral—all these and many more are represented in staggering profusion.

Some of the authors who appear in this "submerged sub-continent of literature" (as D. C. Allen terms it) wrote only in Latin, as did Giovanni Pontano, Erasmus, and John Owen; others, like Petrarch, Boccaccio, and Giacopo Sannazaro, are major figures of Neo-Latin and vernacular literature alike. The Humanistic Latin literature itself is not the product of grammarians only: its authors are aristocrats, parasites, soldiers, prelates, unfrocked monks, and reformers. Differences of personality existing among the Humanists are as striking as differences of background: contrast the character of Niccolò de' Niccoli, an unregenerate bachelor who avoided marriage lest it impede his studies, with that of Francesco Filelfo, with his three aristocratic wives and his numerous illegitimate children; contrast the saintly gentleness of Giovanni Pico with the savage bitterness of Poggio Bracciolini, the cool elegance of Pietro Bembo with the passionate warmth of Giovanni Pontano, the Presbyterian dourness of George Buchanan with the arrogant ostentatiousness of his friend Julius Caesar Scaliger. Aonio Paleario was burned at the stake as a heretic, but Antonio Beccadelli died rich and respected after producing one of the most obscene books of the age. Connoisseurs of vituperation, too, will appreciate the contrast between the volcanic wrath of Scaliger and the professorial waspishness of Erasmus: a modern analogy would be Mark Twain and A. E. Housman.

What we are confronted with is a vigorous international literature: books written in Latin in Rome were published in Lyon, sold in Madrid, and read in Basel. There was no reason why a Hungarian living in Lisbon should have been ignorant of English history—he had only to read the Italian Polydore Virgil's *Anglica historia*. But if the Latin literature of the Renaissance had done no more than this, it would have been simply a continuation of medieval tradition. As it is, this new literature employed Latin not merely as a convenient and indeed indispensable tool of communication but also as a medium for the creation of works of art. It is not only an international literature using a common language but an international literature forming a unified whole informed by a common ideal, despite differences of race, nationality, and religion among its authors.

It would be easy, but totally wrong, to think of Renaissance Latin literature as endless imitation of Cicero and Livy, Virgil and Horace—a uniform succession of dutiful, labored centos. But the course of the Latin literatures of the various countries in which they flourished shows a normal progression: in Italy, to go no further, we can chart progress from the pre-Humanist age of Francesco Petrarca, Giovanni Boccaccio, and Coluccio Salutati to the empiric age of Poggio Bracciolini, Lorenzo Valla, and Leonardo Bruni, the Golden Age of Giovanni Pontano, Angelo Poliziano, and Giacopo Sannazaro, and the neo-classical elegance of the last stage of Italian Humanism, represented in verse by Girolamo Vida, Andrea Navagero, and Marcantonio Flaminio and in prose by Pietro Bembo, Giacopo Sadoleto, and Paolo Giovio, until Humanistic Latin literature in Italy virtually came to an end with the disastrous sack of Rome in 1527.

i

Renaissance Latin prose, even more than verse, presents a bewildering mass of material, largely unread since the eighteenth century. There are, it is true, a certain number of seminal works, such as Copernicus' *De revolutionibus,* Bacon's *Novum Organum,* and Newton's *Principia Mathematica,* that are known by name to every literate person; but it is from their ideas and influence, not from their literary qualities, that these are known—the fact of their having been written in Latin is sometimes regarded as a circumstance merely curious, if not freakish. Only a few such works are known generally, and anything even approaching a complete history of Renaissance Latin prose would demand the researches of a dozen scholars and would involve years of extensive reading. The results, however, would be of the highest interest and importance to the student of literary history, to the social historian, to the classical scholar, and above all to the student of the history of ideas.

Historical writing in the modern world begins in Renaissance Latin literature. It is in the Latin historians of the Renaissance that we find, perhaps for the first time since Ammianus Marcellinus (ca. 330 to 400 A.D.), a general realization that history is neither an endless succession of unrelated facts nor a continuous demonstration of heaven's will: historians turned to the study of human motives, the weighing of evidence, the understanding of causes, the evaluation of sources. They also became aware, sometimes all too aware, that history is not only a science but also a branch of literature. As in their essays and letters they had modeled their Latin prose on Cicero, so now they modeled their historical style on Livy for extensive works, and on Sallust for briefer monographs, and from both authors derived that rhetorical attitude which is the greatest blemish on ancient and Renaissance historiography alike.

One of the earliest and best-known of such works is the *History of the Florentine People* (*Historia populi Florentini*) of Leonardo Bruni of Arezzo (1369-1444), papal secretary, and later chancellor of the Florentine Republic. The book traces the history of Florence from 80 B.C. to A.D. 1402 in twelve books running to 288 folio pages in Santini's edition (1926). It is a careful, unbiased account based on judicious and conscientious use of all the source materials available in the Florentine archives, informed with a strong republican feeling, as are many such Renaissance productions, Latin and vernacular alike. Its Latin style is Livian—clear, colorful, fluent, and readable. There is, as in Livy's own history of Rome, a remarkable number of passages of brilliantly executed narrative that could be neatly lifted from the text as historical short stories suitable for some anthology; especially notable are the passages in Book II (the career of Manfred), Book V (a night attack on Pistoia), Book VI (the expulsion of the Duke of Athens from Florence), and Book IX (the exploits of John Hawkwood, the Essex tailor's son turned Italian *condottiere*).

A smaller work is Bruni's *Account of His Own Times* (*Rerum suo tempore gestarum commentarius*), a brief monograph of thirty-five folio pages dealing with the period 1378-1444. The most remarkable passage in the whole book is the gory description of the massacre at the Milvian Bridge in Rome (A.D. 1405). The number of monographs that describe the bloodier episodes of Renaissance Italian history is great: the most outstanding example is Angelo Poliziano's much later monograph on the Pazzi plot to murder Lorenzo the Magnificent and his brother at Mass, one of the minor masterpieces of the Renaissance Latin literature of Italy.

Another historian of Florence was Poggio Bracciolini (1380-1459), who, like Bruni, was a papal secretary and later chancellor of Florence. His *Historia Florentina* is a work of eight books in 384 medium-sized octavo pages recounting the history of the Republic from 1350 to 1455; since it covers only a little more than a century, it is to be compared with Bruni's *Commentarius* rather than with the *Historia populi Florentini*. The style is lively, the narrative rapid and clear, the speeches eloquent. Poggio gives more personal and intimate details than does Bruni and is far less interested either in annalistic completeness or in constitutional development. He is both more and less of an historian.

The Venetians come into their own in the massive but unfinished *History of Venice* (*Rerum Venetarum Decades*) of Marcantonio Sabellico of Vescovaro (1436-1506). This is a work of thirty-three books recounting the history of the city from earliest times to 1475. Sabellico is careful to document his work by constant citation of earlier writers, but is not nearly so discerning nor even so accurate as Bruni or Poggio; he is apt, moreover, to concentrate more on the literary style than on the scientific value of his book. As history it is well below Bruni's and Poggio's level, but it is immeasurably superior to the pedantic, pretentious "history" of Bartolommeo Fazio (ca. 1400-1457), self-styled critic of Lorenzo Valla and boring panegyrist of Alfonso of Naples.

The historians so far mentioned have been either men of action or men of affairs; in Paolo Giovio of Rome (1483-1552) we find the man of letters par excellence. He is a historian whose honesty cannot be impugned, a scholar whose erudition is amazing even for the age in which he lived, and a writer whose style is pleasant and unmannered. His collections of biographies, major and minor alike, are of the utmost interest and use to the historian of the Italian Renaissance; but in his own estimation his masterpiece was the *History of His Own Time* (*Historiae sui temporis*) in forty-five books, describing events from 1494 to 1547. Certainly the book has its merits; despite much superficiality, there are passages that display a psychological insight worthy of a Guicciardini.

An older and more important contemporary of Giovio was the Lombard savant Pietro Martire of Anghiera (1459–ca. 1536), one of the most learned geographers of the day, and a personal friend of Columbus, Vespucci, and John Cabot. As chaplain to Isabella of Spain, he had access to all sorts of information denied to other historians; the result is that his *The New World* (*Decades de orbe novo*) is not only one of the most entertaining but also one of the most important works published in the early sixteenth century.

The best-known Latin history produced in the British Isles is unquestionably that by George Buchanan (1506-1582), greatest by far of the sixteenth-century Scottish humanists and a Latin poet of force and originality. The *Rerum Scoticarum historia,* published in the year of the author's death, is composed in the usual Livian Latin, with a marmoreal elegance that contrasts strangely with the homeliness of Buchanan's Middle Scots writings. Like many another he claimed to write without *odium* or *ira;* but in Buchanan the "perfervid Scottish nature" (the phrase is his own) won out over the scholar's impartiality, and although he proposed to rid the national history not only of "Inglis lyis" but also of "Scottis vanitie," there is a good deal of the latter still adorning the work. The book remained the standard history of Scotland until the close of the eighteenth century, just as Buchanan's Latin verse version of the Psalms remained a standard schoolbook: many a Scottish dominie could quote from Buchanan as readily as from Virgil or Livy.

There is space to mention only one more historian—Jacques de Thou (1553-1617), diplomat, scholar, and man of the world at the court of France during the reigns of Henri III and Henri IV. His

Historia sui temporis is a gigantic undertaking (unfinished), dealing with the years from 1543 to 1584 in no less than 138 books; it is undoubtedly the most important historical work produced in France in the sixteenth century, despite shortcomings trenchantly indicated by Mark Pattison in his life of Casaubon. De Thou's connection with the royal court and with men of eminence in France and elsewhere gave him free access to documents of every sort; of these he made thorough use and frequently followed the excellent practice of reproducing sources in full.

ii

Nearly as numerous as these historical works are the volumes devoted to the various aspects of philosophy. Among philosophers three groups are clearly discernible—those evincing a purely Humanistic interest in philosophy, with a strong or even exclusive emphasis on ethics; those devoted to one aspect or another of Platonism; and those who continued (though with a difference) the medieval tradition of Aristotelianism.

What we call Renaissance Humanism (which is by no means identical with nineteenth-century "humanism") was, as Paul Kristeller has made clear, an educational program based almost entirely on the detailed study of Latin and, later, of Greek texts, the aim of which was not only scholarly but practical. It was only natural, then, that Humanists proper, like Cicero before them, should have been almost wholly uninterested in logic and natural philosophy. They confined themselves to the third and most "practical" aspect of philosophy—ethics. And this Ciceronian practicality displayed itself in an eclecticism that leaned heavily on Stoicism: as in Cicero the animus against Epicureanism was strong.

Most typical of the purely Humanistic approach is Francesco Petrarca (1304-1374), who opposed not only the atheistic tendencies of late medieval Averroism but also the "useless" art of dialectic and the even more "useless" questions raised by natural philosophy with an educational ideal compounded of the eloquence of Cicero, the practicality of a Platonized Stoicism, and the piety of Augustinianism.

But Petrarch was even less of a philosopher than most Humanists; far more original and much more interesting is Lorenzo Valla (1405-1457). Valla was neither Neo-Stoic nor Neo-Platonist nor Neo-Aristotelian nor Neo-Pagan; although his reading in the ancient philosophers was extensive and although his chief interest in philosophy was the practical problems of ethics, his hostility to the Church of his day arose not from any neo-paganism of his own, but from dislike for the neo-paganism of contemporary churchmen.

Rather later than the rise of practical Humanism came the Neo-Platonist movement which we associate with the Medici group of the Florentine Academy. The representatives of this group were repelled equally by the ultra-scientific approach of the Neo-Aristotelians and by the practical aims of the Humanists; it was not the purpose of these men to employ ancient ethics as a tool of education: much of their work was in fact an attempt to create an amalgam of Platonism and Christianity. Their aim was never to produce the Humanists' knowledgeable man of the world but rather the devout intellectual.

By far the most influential of the Neo-Platonists was Marsilio Ficino of Florence (1433-1499). Ficino was convinced that complete harmony existed between Platonism and Christianity and devoted his life to the illustration and elucidation of Christian doctrine by means of Platonic concepts which he regarded as of equal importance and authority with those of the New Testament itself. Ficino quite literally believed that Plato's work was divinely inspired; the study of the Platonic dialogues was not a mere matter of literary interest, then, but a Christian duty—only from a complete study and synthesis of the New Testament and Plato could Christianity be thoroughly understood. These two were for Ficino the chief source for attaining understanding of the Divine; but he further believed that, as Christianity is a true and universal religion, adumbrations at least of its truths must appear in the works of Hermetic, Peripatetic, and even of Persian and Arabic philosophers. This naturally led to a metaphysical and religious eclecticism, but an eclecticism far different from that of the Humanists, an eclecticism in which Plato and the New Testament were of paramount importance and validity while the others were supplementary sources from which one might accept only so much as seemed true.

The Aristotelianism of the Renaissance descends from that of the Middle Ages, but performs a quite different function. In the medieval University of Paris, Aristotle had formed the basis for the study of logic, natural philosophy, and theology; but in Italy, especially at the Universities of Bologna and Padua, Aristotle was the basis for the study of the natural sciences and especially of mathematics and medicine. It is significant and characteristic that Ales-

sandro Achillini should have been equally famous as an anatomist
and as an Aristotelian.

But as Neo-Platonism grew in strength and as its attacks on
Neo-Aristotelianism grew ever more powerful, there developed, from
the time of Pietro Pomponazzi of Mantua (1462-1524), a tendency
to concentrate upon the ethical implications of Neo-Aristotelianism,
to build on the basis of a traditionally anti-clerical and scientific point
of view an original philosophy which should emphasize individual
values, yet be in accord with the emerging natural sciences. The
purpose was clearly to fight the Neo-Platonists with their own
weapons without relinquishing any of the positions fundamental to
the secular approach. The result was that Italian Neo-Aristotelianism, far from adopting an inferior or defensive attitude, went on
from strength to strength all through the sixteenth, seventeenth, and
eighteenth centuries.

iii

Among all the forms of prose in this abundant literature, one of
the most interesting and important is correspondence. Renaissance
Humanists corresponded with friends in their own and other countries with an energy and persistence that almost passes belief. Hun-
garians corresponded with Italians who corresponded with Englishmen who in turn corresponded with Frenchmen who in their turn
sent floods of letters to Dutchmen and Spaniards. Nothing in all
the literature of Europe gives a clearer indication of the cosmo-
politan nature of Renaissance culture than these collections of Latin
letters; nothing gives a clearer picture of the unity resulting from a
common training, common interests, and the use of a common international language. The subject matter of the collections is exceedingly varied: the latest political news was passed from one country
to another by this means; news of discoveries of manuscripts or of
new publications of printed books was sent from Florence to Rome
and from Rome to Basel; discussions of literature and philology were
carried on with zest and vigor between one center of Humanism and
another; controversy raged on the correct use of Greek particles or
Latin reflexive pronouns. But many letters dealt with the ordinary
ups and downs of private life: A has just married, B's wife has
presented him with twins, C's father died yesterday, and D has just
(to the malicious amusement of E) been awarded the academic
appointment for which F has been intriguing for six months.

In this field the earliest collection is at once one of the largest and one of the most important—that of Francesco Petrarca (1304-1374). Petrarch himself appears to have retained a copy of every letter he ever wrote from 1348 (the year of the Black Death and of the death of Laura), intending to publish them in groups—the *Familiar Letters,* the *Various Letters,* the *Letters of His Old Age,* and the *Untitled Letters.* Petrarch himself tells us that he burnt over a thousand letters that he considered below standard; even so the total number of letters in the forty-three books far outnumbers Cicero's.

Petrarch was the first man since the fall of the Roman Empire to leave in this way a detailed account of his own life and times. And certainly some of the best-known passages in all of Petrarch's Latin works occur in the letters—his famous description of his home and garden at Vaucluse (fifteen miles from Avignon), for instance, the narrative of a visit to Mount Vesuvius, and that of an ascent of Mount Ventoux along with his brother Gherardo. The first of these is often quoted to prove Petrarch's modern love of natural scenery, and with full justice; the other two are also so quoted, but with less reason: in scaling Mount Vesuvius, Petrarch saw himself as another Pliny the Elder, and the account of the ascent of Ventoux is an Augustinian allegory of the soul's ascent to God (it was addressed, by the way, to an Augustinian professor of theology). Hundreds of the letters could be used as source materials for the history of Humanism in trecento Italy; almost as many are of great importance for the political and social history of the times; all are important for the revelation, often unconscious, of the contradictory and not wholly attractive character of one of the greatest poets of modern times.

The mantle of Petrarch the Humanist fell not on Giovanni Boccaccio, prolific though he was as a Latin writer, but upon Coluccio Salutati (1331-1406), chancellor of Florence. Salutati's letters are not nearly so numerous as Petrarch's; even so, they run to twenty-five books, and while they are even more important than Petrarch's as source materials for political and social history, they are on the whole less interesting, whether as unconscious character-revelation or as literature. They often have an official ring about them even before Salutati became Florentine chancellor, and they have, especially in the earlier books, a decidedly medieval style.

The historical work of Leonardo Bruni (1369-1444) has already been mentioned; his letters are also extant in ten books. These were famous during the fifteenth century for the excellence of their Latin style and are still well worth reading. A great many of the letters are semi-official, a great many are philological; but there is also a very large number which would still be examined with interest by the most general and desultory reader: descriptions of cities and country-seats, acute and often amusing comments on custom and character, and narratives of travel. Even apart from content, Bruni's letters are far better written than Salutati's: urbanity makes its first appearance in the Latin literature of the quattrocento.

We find much narrower interests in the correspondence of Gasparino Barzizza of Bergamo (ca. 1370-1431), professor of rhetoric at Padua, widely famed and extravagantly praised in his own day. He was the author not only of 109 *Epistulae familiares* (real letters) but also of 165 model letters for imitation, arranged in pairs (one reply is missing).

All the *Epistulae familiares* belong to the years 1410 to 1429 and almost all deal with literary matters of one sort or another: Barzizza delightedly tells Danielis Victurius that he has just acquired a manuscript that contains seven orations of Cicero he had never seen before; he asks Joannes Cornelius if he can buy Donatus Casentinus' Livy for him and send it to Padua, and tells the same correspondent that a priest, Bartolommeo, has lent him Cornelius' copy of Pliny— Barzizza promises to have it transcribed and returned as soon as possible. On another occasion he sends a fellow professor at Parma copies of Cassiodorus' *Institutes* and Petrarch's Latin eclogues— for transcription, no doubt; again, he begs a German friend to return his copy of Cicero's *Letters* at once, as he needs it desperately in his work, and requests even more vigorously (not for the first time) the return of his copy of a commentary on Cicero's *De officiis* from Antonio Fantasselli. No other collection of fifteenth-century letters shows more plainly the desperation of the Humanist parted from the tools of his trade. Other letters are more purely personal: in one he patches up a quarrel with Andrea Giuliano; in another he describes to Francesco Barbaro a day in the country with his wife and children; in others he worries whether he will ever have enough money to educate his family properly—the thought of seven dowries for seven daughters appalls him.

Still extant are nearly a thousand letters written by Guarino of Verona (1374-1460), professor of rhetoric in the University of Ferrara, where he trained some of the best-known classical scholars and Humanists of the early fifteenth century: "totam Italiam litteris humanitatis ornavit," wrote Timoteo Maffei. A high proportion of the letters are philological and for that reason are chiefly of interest to the student of the history of classical scholarship, but, as with Bruni's correspondence, there are still many letters that could attract the modern general reader interested in literature and social history. The most pleasant letters are those in which Guarino allows his sense of humor (a quality rarer than wit among Renaissance Latinists) free play.

Even better than Bruni's or Guarino's letters are those of Poggio Bracciolini (1380-1459), the most striking figure in Latin literature during the first half of the fifteenth century. These are certainly the liveliest and best-written letters so far mentioned, and some of them are well known to everyone who has read at all in the Latin literature of the Renaissance—the letter in which Poggio describes in gruesome detail the burning of a Hussite heretic, the description of baths in Germany, the letter in which he turns up his elegant Italian nose at German drunkenness, another in which he intercedes with Cosimo de' Medici for a young man named Girolamo de' Bardi. Many of the letters describe Poggio's discoveries of classical manuscripts mouldering in the still medieval monasteries of Germany: in his expeditions into the savage wilds of Germany, Poggio rescued many a Latin author from the *ergastula* ("slave-dungeons"), as he called the monasteries. The entire collection is, in fact, conspicuous for a liveliness and vigor quite unparalleled in the earlier period of Humanism; a translation, at least in selection, is much to be desired.

Antonio Beccadelli (1394-1471), nicknamed from his Sicilian birthplace *il Panormita,* was in all probability one of Barzizza's students; it would be interesting to know the teacher's opinion of the pupil's *Hermaphroditus,* a collection of elegiac poems and epigrams that contains some of the most scabrous stuff conceivable. After a restless youth he became court poet first of the Visconti family and then of Alfonso of Aragon, King of Naples. We have two collections of his correspondence—"Northern Letters" (*Epistolae Gallicae*), written from Padua and Milan, and "Southern Letters" (*Epistolae Campanae*), written from Naples. So many collections of Renaissance letters describe poverty, plague, frustration, worry, and personal disaster that it is a relief to turn to the uncomplicated Latin of the *Epistolae Gallicae* and there read invitations to friends to spend an afternoon on the River Ticino, descriptions of flower-covered meadows outside Padua, notes on entertainments at court, and comments on Beccadelli's reading. The *Epistolae Campanae* belong to the period after 1434. The tone is more settled, yet the content is similar: Beccadelli describes the happiness of his second marriage and the pleasure he takes in the company of his wife Laura, writes to old friends in the north, discusses new books he has acquired, praises (rather fulsomely) the undoubted generosity of King Alfonso, and reports on the progress of whatever book he is writing at the time.

One of the most extensive collections (thirty-seven books actually published; ten more books are extant in manuscript) of letters written during the fifteenth century is that of the man "who combined the accomplishments of a scholar with the insidiousness and the brutality of a brigand," Francesco Filelfo (1398-1481), least humane of the Humanists, a man whose entire life was a constant quarrel. The letters cover the period from 1427 to the end of Filelfo's belligerent life. For the history of Italian Humanism they are of the very first importance; Filelfo taught (at enormous salaries) at almost every major center of learning in Italy and described his own experiences and those of his contemporaries in tremendous detail. He knew everyone worth knowing and expressed his opinions with libelous freedom. There are fewer letters dealing with literary matters than one would have expected; instead, there are hundreds that discuss Filelfo's hopes for new appointments, the amount of his salary in each successive post, the financial difficulties caused by the size of his family and the almost princely manner in which he often lived, whether he could afford it or not, his troubles with patrons (he firmly believed that he had been ambushed by the agents of Cosimo de' Medici after one unusually spectacular quarrel), his flattery of the great or at least the wealthy, his insolent demands for money, his difficulties with his eldest son (Giovanni Mario), and much more. Filelfo may not be the most attractive of the Renaissance Latinists, and the extent of his correspondence may intimidate, but there can be no doubt of the vitality and variety of his letters—violent and crude they may be, but never dull or sanctimonious.

We can well afford to ignore the few extant letters of Bartolommeo Fazio of Genoa (ca. 1400-1459), even though they do connect that dullard with Poggio, Barbaro, and Enea Silvio Piccolomini, turning instead to those of the last mentioned. After a busy life spent in the public service of the Holy Roman Empire and in an equally devoted pursuit of pleasure, Piccolomini (1405-1464) eventually turned to the Church in 1447, reaching the papacy, as Pope Pius II, in 1458. His Latin writings fill a large folio volume; to the modern reader the most interesting are the *Commentarii* (an account of his own times), a history of Bohemia in the style of Livy, a comedy (*Chrysis*) in the style of Terence, and above all the letters (1431-1454), which fill four volumes in the *Österreichische Geschichtsquellen*. The earlier part forms an indispensable source for the history of the struggle between the Council of Basel and the Papacy and for the long period in which Piccolomini was successively attached to the chancelleries of the Anti-Pope Felix V (Count Amadeus VIII of Savoy) and the Emperor. But besides this there are almost innumerable passages in which this remarkably cynical observer describes the character and motives of highly-placed personages in a manner that would have infuriated the dignitaries in question.

The letters of the Florentine Neo-Platonist Marsilio Ficino (1453-1499) run to 357 folio pages and fill twelve books—there are nearly one thousand letters all told. Many are brief notes accompanying the gift of a copy of Ficino's latest book; others report the progress of some other work or the slowness of the printer. Many others are letters on the nature of friendship: these *epistulae amatoriae* are exceedingly common in nearly all Renaissance Latin collections of correspondence and almost form a distinct literary genre of their own. Those of Ficino are a little unusual: in VII, 9, his friendship for one correspondent is expressed in a complicated metaphor derived from air, fire, and earth; in IX, 3, we find an equally complicated astrological metaphor. Ficino spoke and wrote (e.g., in IV, 18) against the pseudo science of astrology, yet in VII, 22, tells us that he is continuing to practice it. His attitude is ambiguous, to say the least—he was clearly fascinated by astrology, and even went so far as to cast Plato's horoscope in IV, 17.

Ficino was one member of a famous trio at the court of Lorenzo the Magnificent; the second was Angelo Ambrogini, from his birthplace called Poliziano (Politian; 1454-1494): with him the Renaissance Latin literature of Italy reaches its highest point. His letters, covering the period from about 1487 to 1494, fill twelve books of 212 large quarto pages and shed a fascinating light upon the most brilliant period of his career. Among the letters we find the great variety we should expect from such a man: there are flowery compliments to Marsilio Ficino and modest refusal of the praise of Giacopo Antiquario, letters of consolation, essays, and answers to the innumerable requests and inquiries of friends, fellow scholars, and mere strangers. Many letters describe the writing of his own works. In one he promises Pope Innocent VIII that he will undertake the famous translation of Herodian; others, naturally, are on literary subjects: in I, 1, Poliziano presents his views on Latin epistolary style, and in V, 1, holds forth on diction; in VII, 31, he answers Guarino's inquiries about a technical point of scholarship. VII, 16, is famous: Paolo Cortese had criticized Poliziano for not being a Ciceronian purist: "I'm not Cicero," comes the instant reply, "*I'm* Poliziano!" Many are friendly letters to scholars: one is a complimentary reply to Ermolao Barbaro, who had expressed a desire to associate himself with Poliziano in the glorious work of Humanism; one (written in 1489) is a charming letter, completely free of condescension, to a precocious young lady named Cassandra Fedele (1465-1558; a collection of her Latin letters is still extant), who had steeled herself to write to the great man.

The third member of the Florentine trio was the brilliant Neo-Platonist Giovanni Pico della Mirandola, Count of Concordia (1463-1494), of whom Poliziano once wrote, "Upon this man—demi-god, I should say—Nature bestowed every gift possible. He was tall, well-made, and remarkably handsome. Endowed with a mind as acute as his memory was prodigious, he was immensely studious as well. It is a question whether he was famed more for his talent or for his virtue"; it is little wonder that such a paragon was nicknamed "the Phoenix of the Renaissance." Forty-seven of his letters are extant, covering the years from 1484 to 1492, but, like much of Pico's writing, they are rather a disappointment. The Latin style is not nearly so good as Poliziano's and few of the letters are intrinsically so interesting: no doubt this is largely owing to the fact that they were carefully censored by Pico's nephew, Gianfrancesco.

The most notorious purist of the early sixteenth century was Cardinal Pietro Bembo (1470-1547), who was in addition true founder of the literary phenomenon called Petrarchism. It was said of Bembo in his own day that he never once used a word that does not appear in Cicero's works, and the statement has been repeated from that day to this. But, although Bembo is not so free as, say, Paolo Giovio, in using words like *scloppus* and *scloppettarius* and *bombarda,* nevertheless words like *cataphractus* do appear on his chaste pages now and again; *omnis* is occasionally used for *totus,* and the supine of purpose is much commoner than in Cicero. Nevertheless Bembo *is* a Ciceronian in syntax: he once advised Giacopo Sadoleto (1477-1552)—himself later a Cardinal, whose letters are also extant—to avoid reading "the rubbishy Latin" of the Vulgate; no doubt both would have approved of the Huguenot Sébastien

Châteillon's Ciceronian version of the whole Bible. No other collection of sixteenth-century letters gives a clearer picture of the elegance of the *Roma Ciceroniana* of Leo X; but even the great Bembo will write (III, 7) that the mice have been after his Aristotle again, and will Vincenzio Quirino kindly send a cat? Bembo's best-known mistress (Maria Savorgnan) was said to have been one of the most beautiful women in Italy; his affectionate letters to her and to their son are still extant. Perhaps Bembo has been called a frozen pedant too long.

Like Ovid, Bembo found the times precisely suited to him, and he spent a happy and successful career within the Church. On the other hand, Antonio della Paglia, commonly called Aonius Palearius and hence Aonio Paleario (1502-1574), ended his life at the stake as a heretic. His attack on Rome, cast in the form of a Catilinarian speech (*Against the Popes and Their Followers*) is as violent as anything that ever came out of Germany; it is also as Ciceronian as anything in Bembo or Sadoleto, both of whom Paleario knew well and who had encouraged him to write (before his conversion) his Lucretian poem *The Immortality of the Soul* (*De immortalitate animae*) between 1532 and 1538. The four books of letters fill 210 octavo pages. Outside of ordinary friendly notes in which Paleario gives news of common friends, returns thanks for favors done, or sends reports on his reading, the most characteristic letters are those in which he gives us information on the administration of Lucca (a strong center of the Italian reform movement) or discusses with Bartolommeo Ricci the question of the use of Latin vs. that of the vernacular: even after his conversion Paleario was as much pro-fessional Humanist as reformer. The whole correspondence of Aonio Paleario needs more careful study and in particular exact dating of each letter.

Much more extensive, much more conventional, and much less dramatic is the correspondence of the scholarly Paolo Manuzio (1512-1574), whose twelve books of letters cover the years from 1544 to 1572. Manuzio is typical of the sort of man who replaced the Humanists in the period after the Sack of Rome (1527) and the rise of Protestantism: the greatest period of Renaissance Latin literature is at an end in Italy and the professional philologian takes the place of the thinker and creative writer. The days when Filelfo lectured to audiences of four hundred are over; scholarship has retired quietly to the library and the seminar room.

iv

A field of Renaissance Latin literature which appeals far less to modern tastes but which is nevertheless extensive is oratory; the spoken word will invariably be important when books are rare and newspapers practically nonexistent. Latin speeches abound during all periods of the Renaissance but are particularly common during the fifteenth century: there are complimentary addresses to visiting prelates or princes, university addresses at the beginning of a course on Aristotle, congratulations to a pope on his accession, set discourses on philosophical topics, public harangues at celebrations, funeral orations, marriage orations, orations published as open letters, and the like. A few of these are important for historical, literary, or other reasons; the vast majority, however, are occasional and ephemeral, and it will be sufficient to describe only a few main types.

A common form of speech was the one delivered *honoris causa;* it would be published in pamphlet form as a sort of souvenir, apparently, or might form one of a collection of a dozen similar speeches. A typical collection appears in the first third of the *Orationes clarorum virorum* published in Venice in 1559. In the first fifty-three *folia* are fifteen complimentary addresses; none is of much importance, to be sure, but all are well written and fairly interesting to read—the style is, naturally, rhetorical but not so inflated as one might have expected. An excellent example is the speech delivered by Bernardo Giustiniani of Venice (1408-1489) before Sixtus IV on his accession (1471). The speaker remarks that on such an occasion he must avoid *exempla profana* and use a Latin similar to the Church Fathers': the speech is in point of fact a piece of extremely good classical Latin prose; it has, moreover, a good deal of historical interest, since it describes in detail the political and military position of Europe before Sixtus' accession.

The remainder of the same volume is devoted to sixteen very lengthy funeral-orations, a form of oratory even less suited to our tastes than the type just described. It is true that the scores of Latin *laudationes funebres* that have come down to us contain much biographical and historical information that would be hard to find elsewhere; it is also true that so far as style is concerned they are usually irreproachable; but the eulogies pall and grow wearisome. A typical group are the five funeral orations of Poggio Bracciolini; these are constructed on a conventional pattern which over several hundred years varied only in matters of detail. Poggio's third, for instance, runs as follows: (a) introduction; (b) the birth and early training of Niccolò de' Niccoli; (c) general panegyric; (d) specific panegyric (much subdivision); (e) cause of his death; (f) peroration. The same scheme appears in Giambattista Giraldi's oration on the death of Pope Innocent VIII, Marcantonio Sabellico's on Zaccaria Barbaro, and Celio Calcagnini's orations on Queen Beatrice of Hungary, Cardinal Ippolito d' Este, Alfonso d' Este, and Ercole Strozzi.

The speeches of Francesco Filelfo (1398-1481) consist of four funeral orations, eight marriage orations, and eight miscellaneous speeches. A typical example of the structure of an *oratio nuptialis* is found in Filelfo's third, delivered at the Ferrarese court on the occasion of the marriage of Beatrice d' Este to Tristano Sforza in 1455: (a) a panegyric of the honorable state of matrimony and its antiquity; (b) famous wives of antiquity, whose virtues will be surpassed by the bride's; (c) panegyric of the bride's family, with as much genealogical detail as the audience can endure; (d) panegyric of the groom's family, again with much genealogical detail; (e) peroration—in this case, with much rejoicing that Borso d' Este of Ferrara and Francesco Sforza of Milan were now to be connected by marriage. Details vary, but all the marriage orations extant are constructed on this model. Very few are of any interest at all.

A far more important speech is Giovanni Pico's oration *On the Dignity of Man* (*De hominis dignitate*); as Paul Oskar Kristeller puts it, this work is "not merely . . . rhetoric; it contains ideas that are of major importance in the thought of Pico and in the thought of the Renaissance"—Pico would in fact have been a major figure of the Renaissance if he had written nothing but this one brief speech, the introduction to the public discussion and debate of Pico's nine hundred theses intended to take place in Rome in 1487. The fundamental doctrines of Pico, as expressed in the *De hominis dignitate* and elaborated in his subsequent works are four: (a) Humanism does not imply a repudiation of the thought of the Middle Ages: there is nothing in the nine hundred theses or the *De hominis dignitate* that contradicts scholasticism; (b) knowledge, as Plato and Cicero had contended, is a unity—hence not only the works of Plato and Aristotle but those of all philosophers must be combined with the Bible in a vast effort of syncretism in order to attain truth— Pico went even further than Ficino, pushing syncretism to its logical extreme; (c) each philosophic or religious doctrine (including Christ's) has a secret, enigmatic, esoteric teaching—this is elaborated at great length in the *Heptaplus*; (d) all earlier religions and philosophies merely adumbrate Christianity.

Equally worth considering are the large number of speeches by various authors urging a crusade against the Turks; for a different reason it would be worth devoting a page or two to the *Self-Defence (Pro se ipso)* of Aonio Paleario; and as a curiosity it is worth mentioning the practice of having Latin speeches of greeting declaimed in town-squares, at the visit of some prince, in the piping tones of precocious ten-year-olds, with private tutors swelling with pride in the background; far more important than these showpieces are the orations delivered at the beginning of an academic year in universities—Philip Melanchthon's and Giambattista Vico's are well worth the attention of the most modern of pedagogues.

v

So far we have glanced at history, philosophy, correspondence, and oratory. But there are at least a dozen other highly-developed forms of Renaissance Latin prose, and these can be only mentioned. There are extensive works of invective (a favorite manifestation of the Humanists' *verve injurieuse*) like those of Filelfo, Valla, and Scaliger; philosophical dialogues such as Giacopo Sadoleto's; satirical dialogues like Leon Battista Alberti's brilliant series; biographies, such as those by Paolo Giovio or Pietro Bembo; autobiographies, like Hieronymus Cardanus'; prose fiction, like Piccolomini's novel *De duobus amantibus,* John Barclay's enormously successful *roman à clef, Argenis,* and Poggio's famous collection of short tales, the *Facetiae*; innumerable essays, pamphlets, and broadsides, often anonymous, on a wide variety of subjects; works of literary history, criticism, and theory like Lilio Gregorio Giraldi's, Vivès', or Heinsius'; treatises on political, legal, and monetary theory, as those by Jean Bodin, Hugo Grotius, and Juan de Mariana; works on pedagogy, like those of Vergerio the Elder, Maffeo Vegio, Filelfo, Erasmus, Budé, Vivès, and (the father of modern pedagogy) Comenius; works on every aspect of physical science, as those of Copernicus, Brahe, and Kepler; antiquarian treatises, such as those of Flavio Biondo and Raffaele Maffei da Volterra; and encyclopedic works from Guglielmo da Pastrengo's in the fourteenth century to Daniel Georg Morhof's in the seventeenth. Even to list all the material available for study in these fields would take another two hundred pages; we must now turn to a brief consideration of Neo-Latin drama.

vi

The first real plays written in modern Europe were the Latin comedies and tragedies of the Renaissance Latinists. The tradition of Latin drama was not nearly so important nor so continuous in Renaissance Latin literature as that in other genres, to be sure, but the amount produced was still impressive.

The earliest Humanistic comedy was the *Philologia* of Francesco Petrarca (1304-1374), no longer extant. Petrarch refers to it in a letter (1331) to Cardinal Giovanni Colonna and again in a letter (1348) to Lapo da Castiglionchio, calling it a work of his extreme youth. It had probably been modeled on the Latin comedies of Terence, but beyond that one can say little about it; it is not even certain that it is Petrarch's only play—Giovanni Boccaccio mentions a comedy called *Philostratus,* but this is most probably an alternative title for the same work.

Some time later Pier Paolo Vergerio (1370-1444) tried his hand at comedy (in about 1390) with a play of university-life, conceivably autobiographical, called *Paulus.* Vergerio himself describes the play as being written "to improve the character of the young" (*ad iuvenum mores corrigendos*), and this aim he achieves by displaying all too specifically the conduct one should avoid: the students are no better than they should be, their servants cheat them right and left, and the "heroine" is a prostitute who is passed off as a virgin most pure.

Better-known in its own day than the *Paulus* was the *Poliscenê* of Leonardo Bruni (1369-1444), written about 1395. In this play a young man named Gracchus falls in love with the surpassingly beautiful Poliscenê; his slave Gurgulio, well-meaning but inefficient, fails to achieve a happy ending for his master, so the services of an old woman called Taratantara are called in. Taratantara approaches first the girl's mother Calpurnia and then, mendaciously, the girl herself, with complete success. This bare summary hardly does justice to the play, which does display good Latin style, a certain amount of comic suspense, and much wit.

Better known today is the *Philodoxus* of Leon Battista Alberti (1404-1472), if only because this tour de force was attributed by its youthful author to a nonexistent writer of antiquity called Lepidus; it was not until much later that the hoax was uncovered. The plot is the standard "boy-meets-girl" story in its ancient form; there is a good deal of grossness, and a good many situations for which the kindest word would be "ambiguous."

Another comedy of the period is the *Chrysis* of Enea Silvio Piccolomini (1405-1464), the future Pope Pius II. The play, written in 1444, is no more likely than any other of these cynical comedies to improve the character; but, then, it is intended to amuse the cultivated Humanist who has read Terence and Plautus and is aware that life is not always conducted on the principles of a Sunday school. The risqué tone of the *novella*, already present in Piccolomini's *De duobus amantibus*, is notable, but is understandable enough, since the scene of the play is a brothel.

Perhaps the most original and certainly the most representative of the Latin comedies of the early Renaissance is the *Philogenia* of Ugolino Pisani (1410?-1460?), written shortly before 1435. The action of the play takes place in the amoral world of Greek and Roman New Comedy (to say nothing of contemporary Italian life), in which seduction is normal, rape commonplace, and unexpected endings only to be expected. As in Plautus' *Amphitryon*, the only character who is not wholly devoid of humane and generous feelings is the wronged heroine: after being seduced by the hero and raped by his friends, the wretched girl is finally married off to a loutish tenant farmer, who intends to put her to work in the fields.

So far the plays mentioned have been individual *jeux d' esprit*—the authors in question tried their hands at a single play, as much from curiosity as anything else, and then passed on to other interests. But Tito Livio de' Frulovisi (ca. 1400–ca. 1460) wrote no less than six comedies and may therefore be called the first modern playwright. Frulovisi began his career as a schoolmaster in Venice, and it was in connection with his schoolwork that he wrote his first three plays (*Corallaria, Claudi Duo,* and *Emporia*), presented in 1432 and 1433. The author permitted himself a great deal of satirical comment on eminent living Venetians; this brought indignant protests by the score, and a Dominican priest named Fra Leone preached vigorously against Humanists who corrupted manners, morals, and religion; to Leone, Frulovisi was a heathen radical. His *Symmachus* (1433-1434), a satire on the arrogance of the patrician families of Venice, caused even more trouble; Frulovisi did not wait to observe the results of his *Oratoria* (1434-1435), a violently satirical attack on his old Dominican enemy. After travel in Crete and Rhodes, Frulovisi turned to England and became attached to the household of Duke Humphrey of Gloucester in 1436. The comedies *Peregrinatio* (the scene is laid in Crete, Rhodes, and England) and *Eugenius* (which contains much panegyric of Duke Humphrey) belong to the period from 1436 to 1438. For some reason Frulovisi fell out of favor with his employer. He left England and hopefully searched for patrons in Milan, Toulouse, Barcelona, and elsewhere, turning at last, apparently, to the practice of medicine in Venice, where he died after 1456 (perhaps in 1462-63).

The plays of Frulovisi are the first wholly secular plays, derived from ancient models but drawing their themes entirely from contemporary life and character, known to have been actually performed on a stage: they were not designed merely for a reading public. In all except the *Peregrinatio* the unity of place is maintained; the unity of time is preserved in none. The language, style, situations, and modes of characterization are modeled upon those employed by Plautus and Terence, with tolerable success; and the standard of Latinity shows a definite improvement from the *Corallaria* to the *Eugenius*. The last two plays are uninteresting, chiefly, perhaps, because in these Frulovisi had no enemies to attack.

In the sixteenth century *comédies à l' antique* with contemporary settings, themes, and characters continued to be written and staged in Italy, as the *Stephanium* (1500) of Harmonius Marsus and the *Dolotechnê* (1504) of the mathematician Bartolommeo Zamberti. But the Italian Humanists of the sixteenth century turned more and more to exact imitation of classical models, and the writing of plays with Plautine situations but contemporary themes and characters passed quickly into the hands of vernacular writers in Italy and France.

However, Latin comedy with contemporary themes flourished elsewhere in Europe. In the first half of the sixteenth century the main center was Germany and the Low Countries. Here the most famous name is that of Macropedius (i.e., Georg van Langeveldt; 1475-1558) in whose twelve plays—the plots of which are often derived from folklore—are displayed sharp observation of human ignorance, frailty, and conceit, bourgeois realism (characteristic of many Teutonic Neo-Latinists), and much animated *vis comica*.

In the second half of the same century, the chief center for Latin comedy was the University of Cambridge. The Cambridge comedies, not all of which have been printed, are almost formidable in their number. All display the plot of intrigue characteristic of ancient New Comedy and Neo-Latin comedy alike, and the characteristic stock figures of irascible father, tricky servant, erratic hero, and virtuous heroine appear again and again. More important elements are, first, the characteristically English and insular flavor of these

comedies, and, second, the influence of Italian vernacular plays—
Abraham Fraunce's *Victoria* (1582), for instance, was adapted from
Pasqualigo's *Il Fedele*. Some of these plays have an interest that is
more than merely historical—Fraunce's *Hymenaeus* (1578) shows
real dramatic talent, and the anonymous *Laelia* (1594)—a Neo-
Latin *Twelfth Night*—is a first-rate play; the political satire of the
anonymous anti-Spanish and anti-Catholic "The Spaniard" (1598)
is biting and effective, as is the personal satire of John Wingfield's
Pedantius (1581), an attack on Gabriel Harvey.

It should be added that satirical comedy is not confined to England. Long before the days of Fraunce and Wingfield and Hawkes-
worth, Jacob Wimpheling (1450-1528) had attacked ignorant and
corrupt clergy in a play called *Stilpho* (1480) at the University of
Heidelberg, and Heinrich Bebel (1472-1518) had similarly attacked
scholasticism in 1501 at Tübingen; later on, polemical comedy became an instrument both of the Reformation (as in Simon Lemnius'
Monachopornomachia, "The Battle of the Monks and Whores")
and of the anti-Lutherans (as in the play presented before Henry
VIII in 1528). By far the most important author of such propaganda comedies was the Lutheran clergyman Thomas Kirchmeyer,
commonly called Naogeorgus (1511-1578), who attacked monks,
images, indulgences, and the cult of the saints.

Before leaving the subject of Neo-Latin comedy, I should at least
mention the moralizing and often allegorical *comoedia scholaris*, a
form of "drama" in which the language is Terentian and Plautine
enough but plot and characters are drawn straight from the vernacular morality plays of the Middle Ages. These plays reached the
height of their popularity in the first half of the sixteenth century
in France, Germany, and the Low Countries. Among French writers
the outstanding name is that of Ravisius Textor (1480-1524), whose
collected playlets were published under the title of *Dialogi* in 1536.
Each "play" consists (like the prose dialogues of Leon Battista
Alberti) of a single dramatic scene or sketch about four hundred
lines in length. Textor's scenes, however, are all in verse—hexameters or elegiacs. None is impressive as drama; they are all merely
sketches, written in a highly moralistic vein—many of them are
barely distinguishable in content from some of the *Colloquia* of
Erasmus. More interesting is such a work as Macropedius' *Hecas-
tus* ("Everyman"), which was presented with vast success at Utrecht
in 1538; this is a lively, realistic, and often amusing morality, as is
the same author's *Asotus* (1537), a farcical treatment (with a contemporary setting) of the story of the Prodigal Son.

Neo-Latin tragedy is not, as a rule, successful. Having said as much, I should then add that modern tragedy in the vernacular did not develop until the late Renaissance and even then in only a few literatures. The Neo-Latin tragedians at least prepared the way and anticipated the models, the themes, and the mistakes of vernacular dramatists.

The first modern tragedy is the *Ecerinis* of the soldier-historian Albertino Mussato (1261-1329), a work for which the author was crowned *poeta laureatus* in 1314, when Petrarch was still only ten years old. Like all Neo-Latin secular tragedies the play is modeled on Seneca: rhetoric, declamation, blood, and horror reign supreme. The stock characters, the commonplace thought, and the typical exaggerations of Senecan tragedy are all present; so also, however, is the Senecan skill in construction and care for unity of effect. The play is constructed on the familiar five-act pattern, is provided with a Senecan chorus, permits only three actors on the stage at one time, and its declamatory speeches—no doubt delivered *ore rotundo*—are as long, as elaborate, and as rhetorical as any in French neo-classical drama. The *Ecerinis* is based on the life and incredible cruelties of Ezzelino III, tyrant of Padua, and in this is the precursor of many Neo-Latin tragedies based on contemporary events and personalities: in the fifteenth and sixteenth centuries there were tragedies written in Latin on such themes as the capture of Granada, the career of the Italian *condottiere* Niccolò Piccinino, the campaigns of Louis XII of France, and the like.

The golden age (1564-1636) of Latin academic drama at Cambridge produced tragedy as well as comedy. One of the most notable plays here is the *Ricardus Tertius* (1579) of Thomas Legge (1535-1607). Like Shakespeare, Legge used Holinshed, but he produced a typically Senecan *pièce de théâtre* filled with violent passions, sensational events, and bloody crimes. Marlowe and Greene almost certainly knew this play, and it is possible that Shakespeare had also read it: the brilliant wooing-scene of *Richard the Third* has no source in Holinshed but is anticipated in Legge's play.

A better-known name is that of William Gager (ca. 1560-1621) of Oxford. One of the best of his plays is the *Ulysses Redux* (1592). Even if such plays as this are not read today, one should at least point out that a very considerable number of educated and intelligent men in England looked for achievement in the drama not to Shakespeare but to such men as Legge, Gager, and Fraunce.

A remarkable phenomenon of Renaissance literature is the sudden emergence of a Latin Biblical drama in the sixteenth century, a movement that was at its height from about 1540 to 1560, especially in the Low Countries and Germany. It is worth mentioning that the great majority of these plays were written by Protestants and that almost every Protestant religious drama was propagandist.

There are two names here that are especially memorable—those of the Scottish George Buchanan (1506-1582) and the German Nicodemus Frischlin (1547-1590). In the 1540's Buchanan was teaching at the Collège de Guyenne—among others, one of his pupils was the youthful Michel de Montaigne. In addition to much lyric poetry (written for the admiration of his peers), Buchanan here produced (for the edification of his pupils) a Latin drama (1542), Senecan in tone but Greek in its arrangement of choruses and *epeisodia*. Here the Greek form is highly appropriate, since the story of the sacrifice of Jephthah's daughter shows a close resemblance to the story of Iphigenia. As for the quality of the play, it can be best indicated by saying that Renaissance Humanists felt that it was their duty to present examples of every form of literature, the easiest and the most difficult, the most innocent and the most obscene— Buchanan did not first ask himself whether he had the inborn dramatic talent of such a man as William Gager.

It is rather different when we turn to Nicodemus Frischlin (1547-1590), one of the most important and arresting figures of the Latin literature of the sixteenth century. As a controversialist he was as choleric (though not so foulmouthed) as Filelfo, Valla, Poggio, and Scaliger; as a scholar he was as industrious as Erasmus, of whom it was said that "to be awake" was synonymous with "to be working"; in addition Frischlin is undoubtedly the most representative writer of *comoedia scholaris* and *tragoedia scholaris* in the sixteenth century. His plays should, however, be regarded as vivid dramatic sketches or as dramatic scenes capable of being presented upon the stage rather than as full-blown *pièces de théâtre*. But his characterization is lively, his dialogue has verve, and his structure is neat. All of the playlets are anti-Catholic, all are intended for the edification of his pupils, and nearly all concentrate on women as protagonists—Ruth, Rachel, Susanna, Salome, the Virgin Mary, Catherine of Alexandria (a favorite figure in Renaissance Latin religious literature), and many more; the Protestant playlets were answered by Catholic playlets dealing chiefly with the lives of the saints.

II

RENAISSANCE LATIN

LITERATURE: POETRY

hen we turn from Renaissance Latin prose to Neo-Latin poetry, we are almost overcome by sheer bulk of material. Much, of course, of this Latin poetry can be dismissed at once as so much verse composition, as is true of the poetry of any litera-ture; even so there remains a mass of verse which is remarkable alike for variety and quality—if we find a Caspar van Baerle, we also meet an Angelo Poliziano. It is noticeable that, in every European country affected by the resurgence of classical Humanism, the period in which Neo-Latin poetry flour-ished most brilliantly is the early one in which scholars, poets, and men of affairs read their newly-discovered Latin authors, and, having finished models to follow, proceeded to emulate them. In Italy, it is true, Dante and Petrarch had already, before the great age of Hu-manism, shown what could be achieved using the Tuscan form of the Italian vernacular; but Dante and Petrarch were followed by the "century without poetry," *secolo senza poesia*. Vernacular Italian poetry suddenly stopped still for a hundred years, while Neo-Latin forged ahead in a manner that can be described only as spectacular. In the other European countries the vernacular was, in general, in an undeveloped state so far as highly formal literary composition was concerned, or was split up into dialects that changed so rapidly

and radically from one generation to the next in forms and pronunciation that a poem written in, say, London in 1350 might well lose (for example) all its rhymes if read aloud in 1400 by a man from York; there is ample evidence to show that a hundred years after Chaucer's death, his decasyllabics were read, even by Londoners, with so clipped and hurried a pronunciation as to produce a line of only four beats. Neo-Latin verse held the center of attention on the Continent until the vernacular overtook and finally supplanted the "foreign" idiom.

Of course there are reasons other than increasing linguistic efficiency (if that is the right term) for the rise of the vernaculars. Poets who directed their work to women as well as to men, or who had in mind those members of the nobility and their courts whose knowledge of classical idiom could not be taken for granted, or who were virtually directed by their dukes or kings to employ the vernacular for nationalistic purposes (a policy which began as early as the 1370's in France), would naturally use the appropriate medium, as would any poet who chose to employ conventions (extravagant, ultra-romantic, or wondrous) that did not sit comfortably in Latin verse. And it is a curious fact, too, that powerful countries gave up the widespread use of Latin far sooner than did countries like Poland and Hungary.

The innumerable Neo-Latin poets and versifiers of the Renaissance and Baroque periods confined themselves almost exclusively to the forms of poetry devised by the ancients; there were, naturally, experiments aplenty within the limits of these forms; but there is no example of any major, entirely new development. These poets confined themselves to lyric in various forms, to the many varieties of occasional verse developed by the Latin poets who had used the elegiac couplet, and to various types of heroic (i.e., hexameter) verse. And in all these forms the care devoted to style and versification was enormous: even those versifiers whose content is least important are almost always admirably clear—in a word, they are a pleasure to read.

i

Today the term "lyric" is used of almost any expression of personal emotion; among the Greeks and Romans, however, the word often refers more to form than to content and involves three separate styles—choric, personal ("melic"), and elegiac. Choric lyric is represented in Greek by the elaborate odes of Pindar: these poems, tremendously complicated in style, syntax, and rhythm, were sung by choirs to the accompaniment of music. The choric odes of Greek tragedy were composed in the same manner, growing less important and less complicated in the plays of Euripides. This sort of lyric does not appear at all in classical Latin literature except in the choruses of early tragedies and then again in the Senecan trage-dies of the Imperial Age, where they follow the simplified pattern of Euripides. Personal lyric—to us the lyric par excellence—appears in Greek in the fragments of Alcaeus and Sappho of Lesbos, then modified and adapted to suit the different rhythms and sounds of the Latin language in Catullus and especially Horace. Finally, there appears a more reflective sort of lyric written in the elegiac distich ("Ín the hexámeter ríses the foúntain's sílvery cólumn / Ín the pentámeter áye fálling in mélody báck"), a form which has an effect (particularly in Latin) rather similar to that of the English neo-classical rhyming couplet. In Greek this form appears at its best and worst in the *Greek Anthology*; in Latin it reached its zenith in the vigorous Propertius, the melancholy Tibullus, and the ultra-sophisticated Ovid. The Neo-Latin writers followed the practice of the classical Latin poets: choric lyric on the grand scale appears (with a few experimental and unsuccessful exceptions) only in drama, personal lyric is well represented, and elegiac poetry is enor-mously popular.

One of the earliest collections of personal lyric is contained in the posthumously published *Odes* of Francesco Filelfo of Tolentino (1398-1481), whose startling arrogance led him to believe that his Latin style was superior to that of the ancients; his facility was indeed remarkable, but all his work, despite its vigor, exhibits much bombast and not a little awkwardness of syntax: Filelfo displays force but is sadly lacking in polish.

Of the eight books of poems by Giovanni Antonio Campano (1429-1477), the shepherd-boy who became a classical scholar, professor, bishop, and intimate of three popes, the vast majority are elegiac and occasional; even so, the slighter personal lyrics would by themselves make up a pleasant enough little volume of minor verse: the hendecasyllabic poems, for instance, include discreet praise of the undoubted virtues of Pius II, a poetical note to the Cardinal of Pavia (a close personal friend of long standing), some self-examination, an astonishing bit of Humanistic vulgarity in the manner of Martial, and a few lively and good-humored addresses to a probably nonexistent mistress.

At the beginning of the true Golden Age of Italian Neo-Latin poetry, we find personal lyric brilliantly represented in the work of Michele Marullo (Tarcaniota; 1453-1500). In his *Epigrams* a great many poems are addressed to an early sweetheart, probably real, called Neaera. Many of these poems are elegiac in meter; but we can examine here some of the eighteen hendecasyllabic and two iambic poems. These form a most attractive lyric sequence of light, cheerfully amatory poems in which matter and manner are admirably adapted to one another. The poet assures Neaera that he cannot possibly live without her, laments her cruelty, assures her again of undying love, juggles briefly with the rhetorical device called *adynaton,* swears undying love yet again, indulges in a series of elegant antitheses, praises Neaera's lovely eyes, prays for her favor, laments momentarily the days when he was free, discusses life and love with a sympathetic Cupid, describes—a favorite theme of Renaissance Latin poetry—a portrait of his lady, and longs for sleep when she is absent on holiday. Whether Neaera was real or not does not matter in the least, any more than it does in some of the most attractive Elizabethan love-songs; the poet is playing at being in love, is enjoying his command of tuneful verse, and is incidentally giving a great deal of pleasure to the reader.

Equally attractive are the brief poems in hendecasyllabics, Asclepiadeans, and iambics addressed to friends and enemies. To his uncle, Paolo Tarcaniota (Pavlos Tarchaniotes), Marullo writes in Asclepiadeans: cease to deafen me with your complaints about my preoccupation with my mistress; you have had your day, my avuncular relative—devote yourself to study and leave the ladies to me. In Catullan hendecasyllabics he delightedly welcomes to Florence Francesco Scala, a learned member of the Neapolitan Academy and friend of Giovanni Pontano and Giacopo Sannazaro. In nine neat hendecasyllabic lines, he writes a letter of introduction to Alessandro Cortese for an unidentifiable friend:

> Receive the bearer of this verse
> As 't were myself, or no one worse.
> Well-born is he, and lettered, too,
> Urbane, refined, and good (like you).
> Receive with favor such a man,
> Who merits every grace you can
> Bestow; my note is at an end,
> And I remain, your faithful friend.

To the Florentine Platonist, Giovanni Pico, who had evidently urged him to give up amatory trifles for more serious studies, he replies with mock ferocity: if you insist on carping, sir, you will find that you have to deal, not with the dead and defenseless Plato, but with ME.

With Giovanni Pontano of Naples (ca. 1424-1503) we come to one of the greatest names in Italian Neo-Latin prose and poetry alike. No one who has read even part of his extensive Latin works could ever doubt that Pontano thought in Latin as readily and naturally as he did in his native Italian. He was completely bilingual. Angelo Poliziano tells us that he himself wrote not to be another Cicero but to be Poliziano; of Pontano it is equally true that he wrote not to be a second Catullus or Ovid but to be Giovanni Pontano. His Latin verse, modeled though it is on classical genres, has a characteristic flavor all its own, especially in the hendecasyllabic poems—the themes are lush and voluptuous, the diction free and natural, especially in its constant use of Catullan diminutives and of neologisms coined by analogy with classical Latin words or with contemporary Italian words or phrases. The occasional inaccuracy in detail (metrical or syntactical) is more than compensated for by the life and vigor of almost every poem Pontano ever wrote.

The brief personal lyrics are of three sorts—amatory poems of a freedom of expression downright startling (almost always in hendecasyllabics), formal literary odes (usually in Sapphics), and poems on Pontano's friends or family (almost invariably hendecasyllabics); these are found in the *Parthenopaeus,* the *Hendecasyllabi,* the *Iambici,* and the *Lyra.*

In the erotic poems of the *Hendecasyllabi,* in particular, we get a vivid picture of the freedom of manners at the holiday resort called Baia; its reputation was licentious even in Cicero's day. Highly characteristic is the second poem of Book I of the *Hendecasyllabi:* the poet addresses some girls at Baia, advising them of bathing proprieties; a partial version will give a hint of what the Latin poem is like:

> You have gone to the springs
> And are swimming and playing,
> But playing so wrongly!
> You've *gone* to the springs;
> Why abandon your lovers
> While swimming and playing?

Abandon dull care—
Turn to swimming and playing
And love and caresses.
You've *abandoned* dull care;
Why abandon your lovers
When swimming and playing?

Grant love and caresses
(While swimming and playing)
And loosen your tresses.
You've *granted* caresses;
Why must you refuse,
While swimming and playing?

Even more typical (and a little less innocent) is the fourth poem of the first Book, where the elderly poet urges Hermionê bathing to be more careful to keep her breasts covered—Tithonus himself would become young again at such an invitation:

an vis dicere "basia papillas
et pectus nitidum süaviare"?
vis num dicere "tange, tange, tracta"?
tene incedere nudulis papillis?
nudo pectore ten' deambulare?
hoc est dicere "posce, posce; trado!"

But although Pontano's Latin Muse can be decidedly wanton, it is seldom lascivious; one could readily imagine what Martial or Antonio Beccadelli could (and would) have done with themes like these. There are surely few readers who could take real offense at any of Pontano's hendecasyllables; despite the *papillae* and *morsiunculae* and *linguae luctantes* the atmosphere is that of a sunny beach, not of a rococo brothel.

Of the formal odes a half-dozen appear in the *Parthenopaeus*; all sixteen of the poems of the *Lyra* are such, and all are written in the Sapphic stanza. In the *Lyra* numbers 7 and 10 are panegyrics of Alfonso of Aragon, number 6 is an eloquent panegyric of Naples, and numbers 3 and 4 are lyric versions of a theme dear to Pontano and Sannazaro alike—the praise of nymphs who represent various well-known beauty-spots around Naples. In the third poem, for instance, Pontano evolves a "modern" myth of the birth of Antiniana, daughter of Jove and Nesis, and prays for her constant aid and favor, in the manner of Horace's adaptation of the Greek *kletikon*. Antiniana represents Antignana, the Neapolitan suburb where Pontano himself lived, and what might at first sight appear a frigid exercise in an obsolete genre reveals itself as a loving description of home, while a pleasantly domestic touch is added in the affectionate mention, at the close of the poem, of Ariadna: this is not the Ariadnê of Greek myth, but Pontano's own wife, Adriana Sassone.

The poems addressed to Pontano's friends are almost all hendecasyllabic. They are, naturally, highly miscellaneous in content, although all are alike in their light, pleasant, and often bantering tone. In one the poet sympathizes with Pietro Compatre on his advancing years: the girls of Naples run from a greybeard—but not if he is wealthy. In another poem Pontano welcomes the return of the Neapolitan Francesco Elio from Rome; in another he advises Giacopo Sannazaro: no more should he write pastoral poetry; it is easier and pleasanter to go on writing about lovers at Baia. At one time he invites his friends to dinner on St. Martin's Day—no doubt the poem in question actually was sent as an invitation; teases a fellow-poet (Gabriele Altilio) on his taste in a mistress; congratulates another (Marullo) on gaining the affections of a girl to whom he gives the Catullan name of Septimilla; or pleasantly flatters Andrea Contrario on his youthful poems.

A descendant of an old and famous Florentine family was Ercole Strozza or Strozzi of Ferrara (b. 1481) who succeeded his even more famous father Tito Vespasiano Strozzi (1425-1505) as *capo de' dodici giudici* under the Este rule. He was murdered under mysterious circumstances on the night of June 6, 1508; the Latin funeral oration, written and delivered by Celio Calcagnini, is still extant. Tito's poems are all in hexameters or elegiac distichs; almost all of Ercole's are the same, but six poems are extant in hendecasyllabics, five in iambics, three in Sapphics, and one in Asclepiadeans. Ercole died at the early age of twenty-seven; the quality of some of his poems is extraordinary—if he had lived he might well have far surpassed his father.

Few of the hendecasyllabic poems are of great importance, although all are pleasant in their minor way. To the Neo-Latin poet Luigi Pittori (1454-1520), Strozzi addresses a few lines, praising the artfulness of Pittori's Latin epigrams and introducing incidentally a neat compliment to Lucrezia Borgia, now married to Alfonso d'Este. In another such poem he invites Calcagnini to send a copy of his verses; in still another he calls on all men of learning to unite in crushing a *malus poeta*. A couple of erotic-insulting poems appear—in one Glycerê is told that she is neither beautiful (as she thinks) nor a virgin (as others think); in another Gellia's promiscuity is the opportunity for a typical bit of Humanistic obscenity. Much more interesting than any of these ephemeral bits and pieces is a sequence of eight religious odes (five iambic and three Sapphic) on the Virgin Mary and Christ—on the Presentation of the Virgin, the Nativity, the Epiphany, the Presentation again (this poem has a curious resemblance to "I Sing of a Maid That Is Makèles"), the Resurrection, the Ascension, and Pentecost; the series is brought to a close by a fine Sapphic poem *in gloriosam Virginem* that is a most joyous hymn of praise.

Giano Anisio of Naples (ca. 1475–ca. 1540), one of the earliest writers of Neo-Latin biblical tragedy, was also a prolific and extremely skillful versifier. His *Varia poemata* (1531), dedicated to Cardinal Pompeio Colonna, contains nine "books" of miscellaneous verse, most of it occasional: it is highly correct, it is highly allusive, and it is highly important for the student of the literary and social history of the times; Anisio seems to have known everyone worth knowing in central Italy and to have addressed poems with cheerful impartiality to all. Much the same can be said of the Latin poems of Celio Calcagnini (1479-1541) and Giambattista ("Cinzio") Giraldi (1504-1573), both of Ferrara, and of those of Giambattista Pigna of Ferrara (1530-1575) and Elio Giulio Crotti of Cremona (d. after 1564).

Like Anisio, Giovani Cotta of Vangadizza near Legnano (1479-1510), was an excellent writer of minor verse (*er ist der echte Minnesinger,* says Ellinger) although not nearly so prolific: his poems were highly esteemed in their day, however, by such excellent judges as Giacopo Sannazaro, Girolamo Fracastoro, and Marcantonio Flaminio. Cotta wrote some attractive Catullan hendecasyllabic poems to a young lady whom he called Lycoris. The first of these is remarkable for its freshness and innocence—it seems so little an imitation as to persuade us that Lycoris really existed.

There are many other excellent Italian Neo-Latin poets whom we might mention, such as Francesco Maria Molza (1489-1544); but we should now make belated reference to a handful of the scores of Latin poets outside Italy: Johannes Secundus, George Buchanan, Paulus Melissus, and Jakob Balde.

In Johannes Secundus (Jan Everaerts) of Malines (1511-1536) we come to the Low Countries' major Neo-Latin poet. At the moment we are concerned with only two of his works—the *Odes* and the cycle of erotic poems called *Kisses* (*Basia*).

Of all the poems of Secundus, the Horatian odes are, quite undeservedly, the least known—undeservedly, since there is the occasional striking phrase or well-knit stanza not unworthy of Horace himself. The formal odes, like the Alcaic first (on the coronation of Charles V) or the Alcaic sixth (on Charles's entry into Ghent, March, 1531) are elaborate, resounding, and dignified, without the pomposity and turgidity that Filelfo would have thought suitable to the occasions. The reflective lyrics—these are especially Horatian—are best represented by the Alcaic ninth, addressed to Pierre Bausan, when poet and friend alike were in Spain: heaven favors the man who is a true friend; neither envy nor care can attack him, no matter where he may be living:

> Thus, friend, amidst the Muses' charms,
> Embraced between the Graces' arms,
> We'll laugh and love, and jest and play,
> And dream of friendships far away.

Perhaps the best way to describe the poem is to say that Secundus is suffering from cheerful homesickness.

These excellent poems are overshadowed (as are the equally excellent *Elegies*) by the famous lyric sequence called *Kisses,* a work which has found a huge number of imitators among both Latin and vernacular poets—Pierre Ronsard, Lazare de Baïf, Joachim du Bellay, Scaliger the Elder, and Casimir Sarbiewski imitated individual poems, and Rémy Belleau, Jean Dorat, Gasparo Murtola, Jean Lernout, and Gervais Sepin wrote whole cycles called *Kisses, Glances, Sighs,* and the like.

The collection—addressed to Neaera, a blonde courtesan whom Secundus met in Spain in 1534—consists of nineteen brief poems in a variety of meters. The cycle describes all varieties of kiss from the most chaste to the most voluptuous, avoiding monotony and (as the poet himself points out in number 12) salaciousness alike. The whole collection is marked by much delicacy, in fact, and this, combined with the gentle melancholy that marks nearly all of Secundus' work, makes it seem as though the *Basia* were the work of Tibullus writing in the meters of Catullus. In 2, Neaera clings to the poet as the vine to the elm; in 4 she gives him a kiss that is nectar, dew, nard, and honey all in one; in 5 we have a description of Neaera's most voluptuous embrace—she is his New Found Land; in 8 she has bitten him; in 14 she is cold to his desire, and in 16 he begs for even a single kiss although in 6 he had said, like Catullus, that no number of kisses would satisfy him; in 9 he wishes for the lightest kiss of all, while in 13 he has entirely recovered from his momentary pose of artful innocence.

The popularity of these poems was immediate and lasting, not only among Neo-Latinists everywhere, but also among vernacular poets; and their influence was even more extensive as a result of a steady spate of verse-translations in French, Italian, English, Dutch, and German. For three hundred years Secundus was read, enjoyed, and imitated as a classic; it is only now, after four hundred years, that his imitators are better know than he is.

With George Buchanan of Stirlingshire (1506-1582), teacher at Paris, Bordeaux, Coimbra, and St. Andrews and tutor of Mary Queen of Scots, and of her son, James VI and I, we come again to Scotland's greatest Neo-Latinist. His Livian *History of Scotland* we have already mentioned; his work on political theory achieved the distinction of being publicly burned as subversive, on Charles I's orders; his Latin version of the Psalms was a lasting influence in Scottish education; his *Jephthah* and *John the Baptist* place him among the Neo-Latin tragedians; his brilliance as a Latin poet has made more than one critic describe him flatly as a literary genius. Even Samuel Johnson regarded Buchanan's Latin poetry as one of the great achievements of Renaissance Latin literature; earlier, Scaliger the Younger had called him the greatest Latinist in Europe; and Wordsworth considered one of Buchanan's lyric poems "equal in sentiment if not in elegance to anything in Horace." Such judgments are not lightly to be put aside, and modern prejudice or misunderstanding should not permit us to regard the Neo-Latin poet of the Renaissance as the idle singer of an empty hour.

Buchanan's attention was devoted almost exclusively to matters of Scottish religion and politics after 1561; the majority of his poems belong, as a result, to the period from 1529 to that date. They include amatory verse, nature-poetry, patriotic verse, didactic poetry, satires, and occasional verse of various kinds.

The amatory poems addressed to Phyllis, Amaryllis, Neaera, and various other imaginary beauties are elegantly finished specimens of Latin verse composition; that is not to say, however, that they are mere exercises, for they are exceedingly graceful, witty, and attractive. Of the nature poems by far the best known is *May Day*

(*Kalendae Maiae*), probably written in Bordeaux, of which Wordsworth's opinion has already been quoted. One is not to assume, however, from the Lake Poet's approval that *May Day* is a forerunner of the Romantic Revival; on the contrary, Buchanan's enthusiasm was aroused not by the bleak beauties of his native Scotland but by the neatly shaved lawns and cultivated farms around Bordeaux. The iambic poems contain much violently satirical verse; but even a Renaissance Humanist had his gentler moments, and we find here some pleasant compliments directed towards such friends as Scaliger the Elder, Guillaume Budé, and many another.

A huge amount of Neo-Latin poetry was produced in Germany in the sixteenth century; much is trivial, vapid, or frigid; but we can find some excellent writers, in particular the satirist Jacobus Micyllus (1503-1558) and the elegiac poet Peter Lotich the Younger (1528-1560). Among writers of lyric one of the best known is Paulus Melissus (Paul Schede), of Franconia (1539-1602), whose collected poems were published at Frankfort in 1574.

Of the lyrics there are two collections. The first, entitled *Emmetra,* is almost unique in Neo-Latin literature as one of the very few attempts outside of tragedy at choral (Pindaric) lyric on the grand scale; it is even possible that the poems were intended to be performed by choirs, for Melissus was himself an amateur musician of some skill. Some of Melissus' seven Pindarics are impressive in both diction and architecture. Three are epithalamia, one is a choral dirge (on the death of that worthy patron of humanists, Prince Joachim of Anstalt), another is a panegyric of a fellow scholar. The two most interesting are the first, which is an elaborate antiphonal panegyric of Elizabeth of England, and the second (*Ad Rosinam*), which attracts our startled attention because of the fact that it is a courageous attempt to employ choral lyric for amatory poetry.

The second collection, *Melica,* consists of the more conventional forms of personal lyrics—Alcaics, iambics, Sapphics, and (of course) Catullan hendecasyllabics. Melissus' Alcaics and Sapphics tend to be rather heavy, and he never attains in his hendecasyllabic poems the lightness and sureness of touch characteristic of Marullo, Pontano, and Secundus; yet occasionally—as in the ironical little poem in which he sends roses to Rosina and receives nettles in return—he comes very close indeed to the standard set by these masters.

Finally, we should at least mention the Jesuit poet Jakob Balde of Alsace (1604-1668), a true baroque virtuoso. His technical skill is equally incredible in hexameter, elegiac, and lyric forms: as a pyrotechnic display of virtuosity his work can have had few equals in Neo-Latin literature. Like another Horace, he published four books of *Odes* and one book of *Epodes* in 1643. The meters are Horatian and the themes equally so—the golden mean, rational enjoyment of the present, the imminence of death appear repeatedly in Christianized form. He is at his best in such a reflective lyric as "The clear conscience" (*Bona mens*) in which the form and diction are Horatian and the theme an obvious echo of Horace's *Integer vitae*; but the poem, far from being a priggish canto of pious platitudes, is an honest statement of firmly-held personal belief—from this one poem of twenty-four lines one can derive a pretty exact notion of Balde's character.

The third form of lyric (as opposed to choric and melic) is elegiac. Here the elegiac distich can be employed as a vehicle for a whole sequence of poems in which the poet narrates the course of a real or imaginary love affair—the poems describe the series of amatory situations from the first meeting with the beloved to the eventual surrender. The situations are conventional: the lover is struck dumb at the first sight of the beloved; he goes out of his way to meet her accidentally; he scrapes acquaintance with her and is eventually invited to have dinner at her home (where he attempts to deceive her husband) ; he is encouraged and repulsed, is in raptures or despair; he sings a serenade before her locked door; at dawn he is discovered still asleep on her door step; he enjoys a day in the country with his sweetheart, he quarrels with her, scratches her face, tears her clothing, laments his hasty temper; he employs her maid as a go-between for messages, and sometimes seduces the maid if disappointed by the mistress; often the sequence ends with a triumphant seduction-poem along the lines of the fifth of Book I of Ovid's *Amores*. Obviously, any such sequence could be treated with ironical wit and urbane sophistication or coarsened to the point of nausea.

Antonio Beccadelli (1394-1471) is notorious for his *Hermaphroditus,* written while he was a law student at Siena. This volume forms, in its way, an erotic sequence, but of a special sort: many of its eighty poems deal with modes—and, as often as not, perverted modes—of sexual satisfaction, and present the most startling images with an obscenity of imagination rivaled by Martial and the painters of some Greek vases, but exceeded by the unsavory Latin works of Pacificus Maximus and Nicolas Chorier. There is, it is true, the occasional poem that is worth reading and remembering—two epitaphs on two sisters who died of the plague at Siena; a rather pretty poem describing the beauty of a girl named Elisia; an epitaph on a girl called Catherine:

> Slimmest beauty, fairest face,
>   Brightest nature, sweetest grace;
> Lovers languish, all forlorn,
>   Venus sorrows, night and morn.

Here, however, follows a much more characteristic product of Beccadelli's lubricity—an abbreviated and expurgated version of a poem called "To his little book, to visit a certain brothel in Florence":

> Hear my words, my little volume:
> Seek the streets of Florence fair,
> There's a spot within the city
> I would have you visit there.
> Find the Church of Reparata,
> Or the Duomo, rich and rare;
> Keep on south and soon you'll travel
> To a handsome city-square.
> Here's your goal—a lofty mansion
> (You can never fail to see):
> Enter straight and meet its inmates,
> Greet them one and all for me.
> All the girls of Florence city,
> All the girls so fancy-free,
> Will be glad to greet your coming,
> Since you bring them news of me.
> You'll be greeted, you'll be welcomed,
> For they know me well of old:
> You'll be kissed by little Ursa,
> Who has oft her favors sold,
> Peitho, too, and comely Thaïs,
> Who is from a different house
> (Which, to let you know its nature,
> Has a sign, with cat and mouse). . . .
> Janet's pretty, Anna's lovely—
> Both can raise your pulse's beat;
> Helen's blonde and Margaret's darker—
> Both can raise your passion's heat. . . .

Naughty words and naughty pleasures
Are these ladies' specialty:
You will never be embarrassed
By refusal to be free.
What you seek and what you fancy
You will find in plenty here:
Be the doer and receiver
With the girls I hold so dear.

In Cristoforo Landino (1424-1504) we meet a member of the Florentine school of Neo-Platonists. Besides works on ethics and literary criticism, there are still extant a large number of poems, of which some form an elegiac sequence addressed to a woman called Sandra. Landino first saw her in Rome in 1443 and duly described how he was forthwith overwhelmed by her beauty. The rest of the sequence develops along conventional lines, often in a frigid manner; at no time does any of the poems overstep the bounds of the strictest propriety, for Sandra was in all probability the wife of a prominent member of the Medici family, and Landino's pose of the adoring lover was a courtly gesture only. Some idea of Landino's starchy manner may be gained from this partial version of ii, 4:

The candid charms of Lydê, though conceal'd,
   Callimachus, with Grecian harp, reveal'd;
The wanton grace of careless Cynthia, view'd,
   Propertius' Roman lyre at length renew'd;
The learnèd muse of Petrarch could rehearse
   Fair Laura's beauty in our native verse. . . .
Though from the Grecian harp, the Roman lyre,
   And native verse I strike no answ'ring fire,
My Sandra now, resolv'd to hear her praise,
   Commands my laggard muse commence her lays.
'Twere shame, 'twere shame indeed, to leave unsung,
   Those locks that might from Juno's head have hung. . . .
If she to graver thoughts her mind applies
   You'd swear Athenê's self were not more wise;
If then to jest she turns and jollity,
   Not Momus' self reveals a wit more free;
Her voice, so tuneable, could well conspire
   T' accomplish more than ev'n Apollo's lyre.
The Graces' selves admit defeat at last,
   And swear they cannot dance so far so fast!

Yet still a maiden blush her cheek reveals,
  A blush far redder than the rose conceals. . . .
When, pray, is Sandra ever proud of mien?
  When garrulous, when surly does she seem?
Such gifts the very beasts and stones would praise:
  So I shall sing her beauties all my days!

In Ugolino Verino (1438-1516) we find another poet attached to the Medici circle. His cycle of erotic elegies is contained in the first book of his *Flametta* (i.e., Fiammetta). The situations of this sequence are closely modeled on those of classical Latin elegy; but Fiammetta of Florence was as real as Sandra of Rome, for all that. The only unusual element in the cycle is the tendency to satire: number 8 on the avarice of prostitutes is conventional enough, but the satire (17) on a woman who had compared herself with Fiammetta is better, as is the warning to Fiammetta (18) against excessive pride, and numbers 27 to 30 are excellent if occasionally a trifle unsavory.

Yet another Florentine poet was Alessandro Braccesi (1445-1503), whose elegiac poems, called *Amores* (ca. 1485?), were dedicated to Guido di Montefeltro of Urbino. The love-cycle here revolves about a Florentine girl named Flora and is similar to, but considerably more elaborate than, Landino's *Xandra*. In thirty poems, many rather too long and some over-classical, Braccesi tells us the usual tale of ups and downs, from the lover's first sight of his lady (number 4) to the final separation (30). A few poems, however, show a certain amount of originality. In number 12—briefest and best of the poems—the poet is tormented by his own weakness of will; Ovid's "video meliora proboque deteriora sequor" is applied neatly and with some psychological subtlety to an erotic situation. Number 17 is notable, if for nothing else, for its voluptuous language; but Braccesi cannot achieve Pontano's balance between lush and lewd.

Outside Italy, although we find numberless poets—some of them, like Peter Lotich the Younger, of brilliant talents—who wrote elegiac love-poems, the only important elegiac cycles are those of the German Conrad Celtis or Celtes of Hesse (1459-1508) and the Belgian Johannes Secundus of Malines (1511-1536), author of the *Basia*.

The four books of Celtes' *Amores*—they could be called "The Four Winds of Love"—constitute four distinct cycles with four distinct heroines; these cycles were written at various times between 1480 and 1502. Book I is devoted to an affair with a Polish girl named Hasilina of Cracow, apparently real, like the subsequent three. After an elegiac hymn to the power of love, and a description of his journey to Cracow, the poet tells us of his first sight of Hasilina. This is, of course, followed by the usual peripeties and formulae of erotic elegiac verse. The usual lover's pangs are here followed by dark thoughts of suicide and hopes for a lonely burial in the Carpathian Mountains:

> Here beneath this rocky earth
> Poet, luckless from his birth,
> German poet, German sage
> (Sought the wisdom of the age),
> Lies released from earthly care,
> Victim of the cruel fair.

All this is obviously taken not only from classical but also from Italian Neo-Latin sources, especially from Tito Vespasiano Strozzi; yet Celtes' work is not wholly professor's poetry: there is enough of the genuinely personal to redeem it from banality; but the self-consciousness of professional Humanism appears when the poet, accused by Hasilina of preferring books to herself, defends his studies. And Celtes, like a good many German Neo-Latinists, is more than a little inclined to coarseness, as when Hasilina—a married woman of accommodating morals—entertains a priest in her bed while the shivering poet waits on her doorstep; it is not so much the situation as its manner of presentation that repels.

In Book II the poet—in actual life a constant traveler—is in Nuremberg, where, after a few dutiful backward glances at Hasilina, he turns to the equally soft arms and equally venal heart of Elsula. True, he had intended to have no more to do with women, to devote himself wholly to learning, when Amor appeared to him and sternly ordered him back to such a life as he had enjoyed at Cracow. His experiences repeat themselves—Elsula even commits adultery with a priest, and the poet again indulges in a comprehensive curse involving all womankind. Gradually Little Elsa convinces the poet of her love for him; but by now Celtes is ready for chapter three.

In Book III Celtes abandons Elsula for Ursula, southern for western Germany. In Mainz he attempts—for only the briefest interval, it is true—to remain faithful, but soon falls victim to a third courtesan, with the full approval of Venus, who appears to the lover and advises him in Ovidian terms to win his lady by extravagance. The affair runs its normal course until Ursula's death from plague, the signal for more thoughts of suicide; but in a dream Ursula's spirit assures the poet of her happiness in the after-world and thus releases him to travel once more.

This time the poet finds himself in the north of Germany: Book IV is devoted to the mature charms of Barbara of Lübeck. But here the poet's increasing interest in a more serious sort of elegiac poetry intrudes itself more and more: Celtes was a professor, philosopher, student of natural science, and in fact a typical Renaissance "universal savant." Even in the first three books such interests tended to push the love affair aside; in the fourth book, we hear far more of philosophy and theology than we do of Barbara.

The last elegiac love-cycle that we shall mention is that by Johannes Secundus (1511-1536); this brief sequence comprises the fourteen poems of Book I of the *Elegies*. It was either just before he left for France (1531) or just before he left for Spain (1534) that Secundus met and fell in love with a brunette beauty of Malines whom he calls Julia; she belonged almost certainly to the upper middle class (as did Secundus himself), although some romantically inclined Gallic critics suggest noble birth. There can be little doubt of Julia's effect on the poet's feelings—the *Elegies* show a truly astounding advance in every way over such poems as he had written previously. The situations described in the cycle are the conventional ones; but Secundus writes with a fervor and sincerity that carries conviction: the third poem, as notable for its Propertian as is the first for its Ovidian flavor, is one of the poems that anyone doubtful of the intrinsic value of Renaissance Latin literature should most certainly read; so, for that matter, is the fourth, a lighthearted and wholly attractive panegyric of the "only pretty ring time."

ii

It would extend this chapter unduly to examine in detail the uses of the elegiac meter for occasional poetry. From the earliest days of the fifteenth century to the latest of the seventeenth, the printing presses of Europe poured forth an endless succession of volumes of miscellaneous verse of this character, usually entitled *Poemata, Carmina, Elegiae,* or, more often, *Sylvae.* Individual love-poems appear by the bushel, as do poems on the poets' life, feelings, circumstances, and hopes. An author may send a friend birthday greetings in half-a-dozen lines, may attach a few verses to a basket of fruit (or to the collar of a puppy, a very common gift), discourse on nature, describe a work of art, describe a dinner with friends, muse on religion, or, more and more commonly as the sixteenth and seventeenth centuries progressed, gradually build up a collection of epigrams, usually of one or two elegiac distichs each, in the manner of Martial. Of the thousands upon thousands of such squibs produced by scores of poets and versifiers, some are mediocre, some brilliant, some good humored, some biting, some priggish, some obscene. Some poets achieve a sparkling wit worthy of the best of Martial's poems, and there are two names which are especially outstanding—in Italy, Giambattista Cantalicio (1450-1515); in England, the Welshman John Owen (1560-1622), one of the last authors to use Latin exclusively, of whose epigrams F. A. Wright says, "The success of Owen's poems was immediate and complete, and in a few years they were known and widely read, not only in England but all over Europe. They were the delight of men of letters and of the cultivated society which existed then in most European capitals, united far more closely then than today by common standards of taste and mutual knowledge."

iii

The two Latin meters most useful to the Neo-Latinists were the elegiac distich, for elegantly informal compositions, and the "heroic" hexameter, which, although *de rigueur* for epic, was sufficiently flexible to be employed for a large number of different sorts of serious poems. We shall examine epic, epyllion, various occasional forms (which could as readily have been composed in the elegiac distich), poems of travel, verse-epistles, philosophical poems, didactic poems, and verse-satires, concluding with a reference to pastoral poetry.

In epic proper—least successful of all forms of Neo-Latin poetry —we first meet Francesco Petrarca (1304-1374), whose poem (entitled *Africa*) on the Roman Scipio's defeat of the Carthaginian Hannibal is more often adversely criticized than read. It is true that its Latinity and versification are alike faulty, that the style is often pedestrian or pompous, that Petrarch himself had misgivings as the work progressed, that the poem was forgotten by Humanists a generation after its author's death. But there are episodes—the death of Mago, for instance—that read well in excerpt, and, as Settembrini points out, there is a certain grandeur and dignity in Petrarch's conception of Scipio's character—a grandeur and dignity,

one might add, that we can scarcely observe if we continue not to
read the poem. Even so, it is quite true, as more than one critic has
remarked, that the most characteristic passage is that in Book IX
where Petrarch prophesies his own birth and the consequent renaissance of classical studies:

> At last the exil'd Muses he'll recall,
> At last restore the Sisters from their thrall;
> Despite alarms, the arts of peace shall rise
> And praise the name of Petrarch to the skies.
> The deeds *you* witness'd shall he tell at length—
> The Libyan War, and Spain, and Roman strength—
> These shall he tell, in swelling accents grand,
> Until the fame of Petrarch fills the land!

The indefatigable Francesco Filelfo of Tolentino (1398-1481)
chose to flatter his patron, Francesco Sforza of Milan, with a distinctly pedestrian "modern" epic called *The Sforziad* (*Sphortias*)
for which, as it lumbered on from book to book, the irascible poet
was richly rewarded until Sforza's death in 1465. At this point the
patronage came to an end and so did the epic: the *Sforziad* breaks
off abruptly after eight books and sixty-four hundred lines.

A far better poet than Filelfo was Maffeo Vegio of Lodi (1406-
1458), half of whose verse output belongs to the epic genre. As a
young man of only twenty he wrote a startlingly Virgilian supplement to Virgil's *Aeneid*. It would of course be nonsense to criticize
it by the same canons as Virgil's own work; the fact remains, however, that it is a remarkable tour de force by one of those youthful
literary prodigies which the Renaissance produced in such numbers.
More extensive is a brief epic, dedicated to Pope Eugenius IV, the
Antonias, on St. Antony; the four books of this work amount to
only a little over five hundred lines, no longer than a single book of
the *Aeneid*. Within this brief compass Vegio accomplishes very
satisfactorily indeed the limited aim he set himself—to describe
Antony's conversion to the life of a hermit. Identical in extent is
the *Vellus Aureum* (*The Golden Fleece*), written considerably before the appearance of the first printed edition (1474) of Valerius
Flaccus' *Argonautica*. Naturally the classical element is all pervasive; in the *Antonias,* on the other hand, Vegio had achieved a fine
fluent hexameter and a convincingly Virgilian manner without classical allusions or the intervention of classical deities. If Renaissance

Latin epic poets had in general modeled their work on Vegio's, this genre would be more rewarding to examine.

Far less capable than Vegio was Basinio de' Basini of Parma (1425-1457), whose virtually unreadable *Hesperis* (6,948 hexameters in 13 books) relates the life and exploits of the poet's patron, Sigismondo Pandolfo Malatesta, of Rimini. The poem is badly marred by constant intervention in the narration of recent Italian history of every god and goddess in the classical pantheon; similes and the like are sometimes well-managed, but descriptions tend to get out of hand; as for Latinity and versification, the quality of both is abysmally below that of Basinio's contemporary Giovanni Pontano, but is still preferable to the less-inspired passages of Mantuan. Astonishingly, however, Basinio's elegiac poetry (*Liber Isottaeus*) is well worth reading.

The six books of the *Alfonsus* of Baptista Mantuanus (1448-1516; Shakespeare's "good old Mantuan") form a seemingly interminable "theological" epic. The spirit of the youthful Alfonso, nephew of John II of Aragon, is escorted after his death in Naples through Purgatory and Hell by the Blessed Audentius. Alfonso is moved to ask a series of twelve questions on theological subjects which are answered by his guide in a manner that almost places the *Alfonsus* among didactic poems. Alfonso's spirit is eventually escorted to Heaven, where the young prince learns of the future greatness of Spain under Ferdinand II of Aragon: the poem was written shortly after Ferdinand's capture of Granada in 1492. Mantuan's *The Victory of Gonzaga* (*Trophaeum Gonzagae*) is a five-thousand-line "little" epic in five hastily written books celebrating the defeat of the French at Fornovo in 1495 by Francesco Gonzaga. The most remarkable passage is the dream of Isabella Gonzaga, in which she sees her husband placed in Heaven with Caesar, Hannibal, and Pyrrhus, and her awakening to meet the returning Francesco and their triumphal entry into Mantua at the close of the campaign. Mantuan's *Agelaria* traces the history of the family (Aguilar) to which belonged Hernando Consalvo of Cordoba (*el gran capitán*), the Spanish conqueror who drove the Aragonese dynasty from Naples. The work is a highly unsuccessful attempt to compress two thousand years of history into 5,176 lines.

Hernando Consalvo is again the hero in the *Gonsalvia* of Giambattista Cantalicio (1450-1515), an epic in four books running to over four thousand lines: we know that Consalvo hankered after such poems, although he himself apparently could not read Latin.

The narrative is better read in Paolo Giovio the Elder's biography of Consalvo, for this poem is episodic and ponderous, its one virtue being the avoidance of Minerva on a modern battlefield. The best passage of the *Gonsalvia* is the narrative of the famous battle (February 13, 1503) of eleven Spanish and eleven French champions.

The *De Partu Virginis* ("The Virgin Birth") of Giacopo Sannazaro of Naples (1458-1530) is the first epic so far mentioned that is truly worth reading in its entirety for its own sake. This work was published, after twenty years of revision, in 1526, although a pirated edition had appeared at Venice between 1520 and 1523. This is again a "little" epic, being arranged in three books and extending to only 1,443 lines. In Book I, we begin with the Almighty's pitying man's sin and determining to offer redemption. He announces His plan to the Angels and names the Virgin Mary as its instrument. In a passage to be imitated later by Tasso, Sannazaro describes the flight of the heavenly messenger to earth. There follows the Annunciation and a pathetic picture of Mary's bewilderment until she accepts the Miraculous Conception. The spirit Fama descends to the after-world and tells the ghosts of the dead to hope for the eventual triumph of Christ; the spirit of King David prophesies the main events of Christ's life and ministry, while Hell's foundations quiver and the demons shriek in hideous chorus. The second book describes the decree of Caesar Augustus, the arrival at Bethlehem, the Birth, and the Adoration of the Child by Mary and Joseph; it closes with a truly lovely hymn of praise in Joseph's words to the Infant Christ—Joseph, incidentally, is represented as a far older and feebler man than the hale and hearty Joseph of Vida's *Christiad*. In Book III, the angels are sent to announce the Birth to the shepherds, who then bring their gifts to Christ. The news spreads through all the land and is received with paeans of praise by the tutelary deity of the river Jordan. As the poem ends, the Nymphs of Naples receive the glad tidings and add their voice to Jordanes'.

Even from a brief summary it is obvious what it is that has made many a reader uncomfortable: Sannazaro's inveterate paganism. It is true that this poet writes the most limpid and technically proficient verse of any of the Italian Neo-Latinists; his gentle hexameters are almost invariably flawless. But the constant use of pagan elements is frequently incongruous in a biblical setting: Sannazaro's Hell contains Cerberus, Tisiphonê, and the other horrors of ancient mythology; Vida's has the Devil himself.

The accusation of paganism has frequently been leveled at the

Christiad of Marco Girolamo Vida of Cremona (1490-1566). The poem begins at a point quite late in Christ's ministry, shortly before the triumphal entry into Jerusalem, and follows the New Testament story closely up to His appearance before Pilate; before the trial Pilate asks Joseph and John, the beloved disciple, for details about Christ's life and work.   In Book III, Joseph tells him of the birth and childhood of Christ; in the fourth book, John describes the Saviour's miracles and teaching.   Book V is devoted to the Trial and Crucifixion; the last book describes the Ascension and closes with the determination of the disciples to preach the gospel to every creature.

It has become traditional to criticize Vida's Virgilianism; perhaps it is time to reconsider those criticisms.   In the first place, we must judge Vida, to some extent, at least, by the standards and practice of his own century (and of almost every century except the twentieth); moreover, we cannot condemn him for imitation of Virgil in one breath and in the next excuse or praise Milton for even more palpable imitation of Virgil and even of Vida himself. In the second, an actual reading of the *Christiad* reveals the fact that the "imitation" of Virgil is not what the literary handbooks maintain it to be.   True, there is a council in Heaven as in Virgil (and in Milton), there are epic similes as in Virgil (and in Milton), there is a demonic army (as in Milton) described in a Virgilian manner.   All this is only the standard equipment of epic and is perfectly permissible if used successfully; what we do *not* find (literary historians to the contrary) is detailed verbal imitation or the employment of pastiches.   Not one single line of the 6,012 hexameters of the *Christiad* is lifted *in toto* from the *Aeneid,* but only groups of two or three words; often the choice of a single noun or adjective, characteristically Virgilian in a certain context, is all that lies behind the oft-repeated charge of literary servility.   Vida's epic similes are certainly Virgilian (like Milton's) in tone and flavor and manner; yet not a single one is derived directly from any of Virgil's poems, either in matter or diction or in the application of the figure.   In short, Vida's reminiscences of Virgilian language and style are much more subtle than critics would have us believe.

A word or two should be said about the presentation of Christ as an epic hero; Vida does actually use the word *heros* of Christ, as Milton uses "hero" in *Paradise Regained:* Milton, in fact, represents Christ almost as a medieval King Arthur sending out fearless knights to conquer evil.   Both poets had ample precedent, for the concept of Christ as the youthful hero had already appeared in medieval Latin poetry and was to reappear later in a number of seventeenth-century English vernacular poets. But Vida will not go so far as to represent the Infant Christ as the Infant Hercules, as do Milton, Cowley, and Donne. Vida, in short, will add to or embellish the New Testament record when narrating the doings of devils, angels, Jewish priests, or Christ's friends and also when describing the background against which the story develops; but he never does so when describing Christ's own acts or personality.

As to the positive merits of the poem one can point, for example, to the splendidly imaginative description of the cloud that surrounds the Virgin Mary at the moment of the Immaculate Conception; there is real magnificence in this scene and a real pathos in Joseph's telling of it. The horror of the angels at the Crucifixion and their near-revolt in heaven is an excellent piece of invention presented with skill and strength. Book IV is, I feel, a little flat; but the fifth book is in all ways admirable and indeed moving. The lament of Mary is pathetic in the extreme and the closing scenes of the book achieve a horror that is not merely the result of skillful manipulation of dactyls and spondees. And the conclusion of the sixth book is very far indeed from being an anticlimax; it does not peter out after the splendor of the Ascension scene—quite on the contrary, it concludes brilliantly as a cross between Virgil's vision of a brave new world and the muscular Christianity of "Onward, Christian Soldiers."

The *De Partu Virginis* and the *Christiad* are certainly the two most important works in Neo-Latin epic; but it is also worth mentioning—if only for its possible influence on Tasso—the *Syriad* of Pietro Angelio of Barga (1517-1596). This poem, dedicated to Henri III of France, narrates in twelve books the events of the First Crusade and the final capture of Jerusalem (1099) by Godfrey of Bouillon. More worthy of mention is the three-book *Syphilis* of Girolamo Fracastoro of Verona (1478-1553), dedicated (since no social or moral stigma attached to the disease) to a Prince of the Church—Cardinal Pietro Bembo. This poem, which in its imaginative passages and in its narratives of Spanish voyages contains much of special interest, has urged commentators to unearth much curious medical lore of the fifteenth and sixteenth centuries. Returning for a moment to religious epic, I should at least mention the *Sarcotis* of Jacobus Masenius (1606-1681), which appears to have influenced John Milton considerably.

Epic flourished elsewhere than in Italy. In France the two

poems most worth mentioning are perhaps the *Herveïd* (1513) of Germain Brice and the *Joan of Arc* (1516) of Valerand de la Varandière; but the first suffers from a heavy sediment of mythology and the second is little more than versified history. Even more pedestrian are such German epics as the *Bellum Ditmariscum* of Hieronymus Osius (*floruit* ca. 1550) and the *Austriad* of his contemporary Joachim Mynsinger. Of the annalistic epics still being ground out in the mid-eighteenth century, it is only Christian charity to say nothing at all.

The brief hexameter poem known as the "epyllion," usually of a heroic or romantic cast, is common in Neo-Latin literature, but it will be sufficient merely to mention a few typical instances and then pass on to a third type of hexameter poem. In the late fifteenth century we find a good example of the epyllion in the poems of Marcantonio Sabellico of Venice (1436-1506). His eleventh poem (493 hexameters), called *The City of Venice* (*Venetae Urbis Genethliacon*), traces the history of the city from the days of the Trojan War to Sabellico's own times; it is competent, but unimportant. Of greater intrinsic interest—although its Latinity is mediocre—is the *Georgius* (984 hexameters) of Baptista Mantuanus (1448-1516), in which the life of St. George is briefly told as a preliminary to the encounter with the dragon; outside of the eclogues and the *Fasti Sacri* this poem is the best introduction to Mantuan as the *Alfonsus* is the worst.

A splendid example of paganizing purism at its best is the *Benacus* (200 hexameters) of Pietro Bembo of Venice (1470-1547). The gods assemble at Lake Benacus (i.e., Lago di Garda) and with them the tutelary gods of every river in North Italy. After an *al fresco* dinner served by Nymphs, Poseidon tells all present to rejoice, for the flower of Italian youth is now reaching his prime, and rehearses as though in prophecy the achievements of Bishop Matteo Giberti. This epyllion is typical of Bembo's work; his poetic output is small—only ninety small octavo pages in the 1568 edition—but exquisitely finished.

One poem by Ercole Strozzi of Ferrara (1471-1508) falls within this category. Among the many poems Strozzi addressed to members of the Borgia family is an epyllion of 966 hexameters called *The Hunt* (*Venatio*) addressed to Lucrezia Borgia, who later was to marry Alfonzo d'Este of Ferrara in 1502. From internal evidence the poem was originally written in 1494. The young nobles of Ferrara and their friends set out on a hunting party at dawn. Various quarries are hunted and killed until a huge bear (*ursus*) appears; after an Homeric *aristeia,* it is finally killed by Cesare Borgia. A violent storm now breaks out and the hunting party takes refuge in a peasant's cottage, where they are served dinner by a cheerful old woman; at nightfall they finally arrive home and are welcomed by the Ferrarese courtiers. No doubt this is a reflection of an actual expedition; but fact, myth, and symbol are at times almost indistinguishable.

One of the liveliest of Neo-Latin epyllia is a poem of 425 hexameters in which Naldo Naldi of Florence (1436–ca. 1513) describes the knightly combat fought by Giuliano de' Medici and others at Florence in 1475. In the jousting a general melee of smashing spears, fallen men, and neighing horses eventually leads to the first prize being awarded to Giuliano, the second to Giacopo Pitti. The reader may judge the general tone from this version of the conclusion:

> Thus equal blows are dealt, with equal chance:
> By turns they quit the ground, by turns advance;
> Victors and vanquished, in the dubious field,
> Nor wholly overcome, nor wholly yield:
> These with success are fired, and those with rage,
> And each on equal terms at length engage.
> Heaps of spent lances fall and strew the ground,
> And helms and shields and battered arms resound.
> The combat thickens, like the storm that flies
> From westward when the stormy Pleiads rise.
> Mars then bestrode a low'ring, looming cloud
> To view the feats of arms, the fighting crowd.
> No rest, no respite: quiet could not fall
> Till Medici be victor over all,
> And Pitti, second still in arms and grace,
> Right gladly followed in the second place.
> Now was it ended, and applause burst out:
> All Florence greets the victor with a shout.

Many more epyllia of various sorts could be mentioned from Italy and elsewhere; it will be enough merely to mention the *Dutch Truce* (*Indutiae Batavicae*) of the famous jurist Huig de Groot (Hugo Grotius; 1583-1645). Like many another Dutch epyllion on various aspects of the history of the Netherlands, this poem is capable, worthy, and a little dull.

Of the various "occasional" ("commemorative" is perhaps a better word) uses to which the hexameter was put by the Neo-Latinists, we shall mention four: epithalamium, genethliacon (birthday-poem), dirge, and panegyric; the first three offer many obvious opportunities for panegyric, too, and, since the Renaissance Humanists admired rank, money, and genius, such opportunities were seldom missed. Few of these poems, naturally enough, are important in themselves, but their historical interest is often great. Many Italians, incidentally, and most Germans preferred to use elegiac distichs here.

A typical epithalamium—and a very good one indeed—is a 260-line poem by Gabriele Altilio of Naples (ca. 1440-1501), written for the wedding of Giangaleazzo Sforza of Milan, and Isabella, daughter of Alfonso II of Naples. Altilio is not an excellent poet like Pontano or Poliziano, but he stands high in the second rank—he displays skill, good taste, and refinement; his command of Latin idiom is extensive and exact, and his diction is precise if a little affected. The mythological trappings of this poem are perhaps excessive for some readers, yet it is vivid, certainly, and expressed in hexameters that are light and rapid.

Sixty-seven youthful Latin poems are still extant by Ludovico Ariosto (1474-1533), all written during his stay at the Este court of Ferrara. The fifty-third is a fine epithalamium written for the wedding of Lucrezia Borgia and Alfonso d'Este, arranged as a series of antiphonal songs for two choirs of young men, one from Ferrara, the other from Rome, allegedly sung as the bride-to-be made her spectacular entrance into Ferrara on January 2, 1502, escorted by Ippolito and Ferrante d'Este, to be met by the waiting bridegroom and his father, Ercole d'Este.

Obviously, the opportunities for rhetorical amplitude are limitless in such a structure as this poem possesses; not only is there a golden opportunity for much anaphoric repetition of key words and phrases from stanza to stanza, there is as great an opportunity for variety in expression and for contrast. Ariosto takes ample advantage of his opportunities and achieves a bravura performance. Vivid, colorful, elaborate, crowded with piquant and suggestive detail, it is court-poetry at its elegant best. Some readers have thought it a pity that all this should have been wasted on Lucrezia.

There is one epithalamium among the poems of Basilio Zanchi of Bergamo (1501-1558), written for the wedding of Girolamo Quirino and Isabella Foscara of Venice. After calling on the Nymphs of the Adriatic to attend Isabella's wedding on the next day, the poet launches first into a panegyric of the bride's beauty and then into equally fervent praises of her domestic abilities:

> No maid on earth more skilled than she:
>   None plies the loom more merrily;
> None faster sews a finer seam
>   Or neater threads the 'broidered theme.

Then comes a description of dawn breaking over Venice and of the arrival of the Adriatic Nymphs, borne by dolphins, of old Proteus from Egypt, of Palaemon and Glaucus, of Phorcus and Triton, and of the god of the river Po (Eridanus) and his attendant Nymphs, to say nothing of the gods of Mincio and Lago di Garda and the like; but by now the poem has become over-elaborate.

The German Neo-Latinist Johann Stigel of Gotha (1515-1562) composed in hexameters a very long (576 lines) and very elaborate epithalamium for the wedding of Johann Friedrich II, Duke of Saxony, and Elisabeth, daughter of Friedrich, the Rhenish Count Palatine. The poem begins with a lengthy panegyric of the institution of marriage, in which the poet reminds us at wearisome length that it stabilizes society and assures the individual's happiness. With all this in mind (he says) the Duke of Saxony, disapproving of a celibate life, bethought him of Count Friedrich's daughter; he was further urged to matrimony by a crowd of personified virtues, especially *Pietas*. And so it goes on and on, with much panegyric of each family involved and of the heroic ancestors of both bride and groom. It is in painful contrast with the courtly elegance of the poem Ariosto wrote for Lucrezia Borgia, but it is quite characteristic of the more pretentious efforts of the German Neo-Latinists. We should add that some German poets composed whole collections of epithalamia (as also of funeral laments); Christopher Schellenberg's various congratulations on wedded bliss extend to more than six thousand lines all told, few worth a second glance.

The third book of the *Sylvae* of Hugo Grotius (1583-1645) is called *Nuptialia* and contains five hexameter epithalamia. All are rather too long and elaborate; but one of them—a poem of 282 lines—is interesting if only because it is addressed to the brilliant

Neo-Latin poet Caspar van Kinschot (1622-1649), on his wedding to Marie Brouxaux. Its most remarkable feature is the diction of the conclusion, which is outspokenly similar to that of erotic elegy, as in a good many Italian marriage songs. German epithalamia are highly moralizing, if not downright priggish; but here as elsewhere Dutch (and even more so, Belgian) Neo-Latin poetry is more akin to Italian and French than to German.

Among the many genethliaca of Neo-Latin poetry, we should glance briefly at one German example, after noting that here, as in most other types of occasional verse, elegiac distichs were commonly used for this sort of poem: a fine elegiac example is the poem written by Ercole Strozzi on the birth of Lucrezia Borgia's son in Ferrara.

A characteristic hexameter example of the genre is a poem of 251 hexameters addressed by Johann Stigel (1515-1562) to the infant son of Johann Friedrich II of Saxony and Duchess Elisabeth. It is far more worth reading than the overblown epithalamium addressed to the child's parents two years before; it is elaborate, certainly, but lacks, fortunately, the pompous solemnity of its predecessor. After an invocation of the humbler muses, the poet congratulates the parents of the child, describes the christening ceremonies and christening feast, the knightly combat (*Teutonicus lusus*) celebrating the birth, and the rustic celebrations in the villages of Saxony. He then prophesies the Golden Age that will ensue when the child comes of age, trained by his father and uncle in the duties of war and peace; the poem ends with an imaginative picture of little Johann Friedrich grown to manhood, dispensing justice to his loyal peasants.

The epicedion, or dirge, is common in Neo-Latin poetry. Usually it is written in elegiacs, as in the collection of such pieces by Elius Eobanus of Hesse (1499-1540), called *Funebria*; but the hexameter was often enough used, as in the two epicedia by Ercole Strozzi of Ferrara (1471-1508), on the deaths of Cesare Borgia and his own father. There is no good reason why we should linger over this far from inviting topic after pointing out what is obvious, that these epicedia are almost always lugubriously panegyrical. Occasionally they are historically important, when they provide us with information not available elsewhere; as poetry they are of little account.

The panegyric proper is usually more interesting and certainly more lively. There are scores from which one might choose, but it will be enough to mention a few characteristic examples.

In the poems of Christoforo Landino of Florence (1424-1504) we find an hexameter panegyric of Cosimo de' Medici and of Angelo Acciaiuoli that lacks the frigidity that is characteristic of most of this poet's work. Landino begins by addressing Giacopo Acciaiuoli: you have often urged me to more serious verse, my friend; even though I am unequal to the task, I cannot refuse, if only the Muses will assist me to praise Cosimo. In lines 18 to 29, the poet turns to restrained and neatly turned praise of Cosimo's achievements in war and peace. In 29 and 30 he adds that second only to the Medici family in his esteem will be the family of Angelo Acciaiuoli, who by his diplomacy gained assistance from France for the Duke of Milan when he was hard pressed by the *condottiere* Braccio, and who later proved a loyal supporter of the Etruscan lion—Cosimo (strictly, I suppose, the lion is Florence; but many Florentine Latin poets refer it to Cosimo, Piero, and Lorenzo de' Medici).

Among the Germans I might mention Albert Voigt (*floruit* 1580), a Prussian, whose panegyric called *Mauricius* extends to no less than 2,467 hexameters. This is a violently anti-Catholic piece of work, dealing largely with the Spanish conquest of the Netherlands. Much of the vituperation in this ill-proportioned and sometimes incoherent poem derives from Juvenal, and the work is as much hymn of hate as it is panegyric of Prince Maurice of Nassau. Much is crude in versification, much is incredibly coarse in expression; but Voigt's *saeva indignatio* makes the poem worth reading.

A fourth class of hexameter verse, common enough, is the *hodoeporicon,* a record of travel or description of a country. Typical is the highly uninteresting *Description of the German Rivers* (*Descriptio fluminum Germaniae*) of Felix Fiedler of (?) Königsberg (d. 1553). Of this and many poems like it one can do no better than quote L. A. Mackay:

> No alley-cat so well his back-yard knows
> As we the Northern Lights, th' eternal snows,
> The sombre forests and the mountains grand,
> The flashing streams, the golden farming-land;
> And, still unask'd, unwearied bards rehearse
> Unglorified topography in verse.

Far more important than all this "unglorified topography" is the verse epistle, modeled on the *Epistulae* of Horace. Much the most interesting here are the *Epistulae metricae* of Francesco Petrarca (1304-1374), of which one critic has said that if they had been written in Italian they would have been recognized long ago as one of Petrarch's most important works.

The three books of the *Epistulae metricae* contain sixty-seven verse letters addressed to thirty-six different people; those most frequently addressed are Petrarch's generous patron Cardinal Giovanni Colonna of Rome; the *littérateur* and courtier Marco Barbato of Sulmona and Naples; the soldier Giovanni Barrili of Naples; Cardinal Bernard d' Aube or d' Alby; and the polymath Guglielmo da Pastrengo of Verona; curiously enough, only one letter is addressed to Giovanni Boccaccio. The epistles total 4,834 lines; some are as brief as eight hexameters, while a few extend to more than two hundred.

In the first poem (written about 1350) of the first book, Petrarch dedicates the whole collection (some poems of which had been written as much as twenty years previously) to Barbato, whom he had known well long ago at the Neapolitan court of King Robert of Sicily and with whom he maintained close relations until Barbato's death in 1363:

> Had fate preserved, my dearest friend, that noble King,
> No missive now, no faithful message of the heart,
> Through sea and land would urge its dubious course:
> In Naples now myself would see your living eyes;
> In Naples now yourself would hear my living voice. . . .
>
> Both from the gentle tenor of our ordered lives
> Are now withdrawn; by deepest seas, by highest Alps
> Both sundered live; and ev'n when favoring fate permits
> A glimpse of Italy, our paths can never cross,
> By rivers still, by mountains sundered still:
> The farthest south your constant home remains;
> Below the northern bound I may not pass. . . .
>
> Your last and dearest plea, my friend, I yet can hear:
> Some part, then, send you of my various Latin verse,
> Some trifling relic of my youth, my life, my love. . . .
>
> These read; and from them learn my various heart's affects,
> The assaults of jealousy; and mark the empty cares
> My rude, unlettered pen records in youthful verse;
> These read; and from them learn what wound the wingèd Boy

Inflicted in his anger on my youthful heart;
All this then see consumed and dead with time:
By living do we die, and staying, may not stay. . . .

Actually, the themes of the *Epistulae metricae* are wider than the above would suggest, and are in fact identical with those of Petrarch's vast collections of prose letters—public affairs, a large number of traditional themes (many of them ethical), discussions of poetry, and personal letters. As is to be expected from Petrarch, the largest and most important group consists of poems of psychological and autobiographical interest: *ogni scritto del Petrarca è . . . una confessione* (Sapegno).

A fair number of Latin philosophical poems, written in the manner of Lucretius, are extant, and some are of more than antiquarian interest. Especially noteworthy is the *Zodiac of Life* of Marcellus Palingenius (i.e., Pier Angelo Manzolli; ca. 1500-1543), a near crypto-Protestant of Ferrara who produced this remarkable work in the years 1528 to 1530; when it was posthumously published in 1549, the poet's body was promptly exhumed and burned as a heretic's. Palingenius' pessimism led him to deny not the existence but the beneficent activity of God, just as he denied not the existence but the eternal happiness of the soul. But to most readers today the most interesting parts of this long poem—it extends to twelve books—are those passages of virulent satire directed against contemporary life and manners.

Far more orthodox in content but even more consciously Lucretian in style is the *Principles of Nature* (1546) of Scipione Capece of Naples (d. 1562), which extends to 1,754 hexameter lines of such elegance that not only did Pietro Bembo consider the poem equal to the *De rerum natura* itself but Paolo Manuzio even went so far as to prefer it. Its orthodox Christianity is intended as a stinging rebuke to Lucretius.

Equally orthodox is the "Garden of Philosophy" (*Hortus Sophiae*; 1550) of Basilio Zanchi (1501-1558), a work of 1,006 hexameters dedicated to Pietro Bembo. The first book describes the fantastic journey of the poet to the garden of God's wisdom; the second, modeled in part on Mantuan's description of the Earthly Paradise in the *Alfonsus*, describes the poet's wanderings through the garden, his seeing Moses and the Prophets, and his hearing from the lips of Virgil a prophecy of the life and ministry of Christ: the choice of poet is appropriate, since the reader meets Virgilian reminiscence in every other line of the poem.

Among other European Neo-Latinists the philosophical poem maintained a struggling existence throughout the sixteenth and seventeenth centuries; but few of the works produced repay study—typically dull is the *De philosophia* of Wilhelm Holzmann (*floruit* 1560). Its two thousand lines and more are fluent, certainly, and sometimes quite readable; but Holzmann has no ideas of his own and contents himself with expounding the traditional divisions of philosophy—Cicero would have called it a poetical *partitio,* and indeed it is so academic in approach as to merit being called a purely didactic rather than a philosophical poem.

In didactic verse the Neo-Latin poets—especially the Italians—achieved a standard of excellence seldom achieved before the Renaissance and probably never approached since. No subject, certainly, was too unlikely or too unpromising for these venturesome poets, and, although some of the resulting works are so much "library dust," there are others that should not be brushed aside without a careful and sympathetic reading.

The earliest author I shall mention in this field is Lorenzo Buonincontri of San Miniato (1410–ca. 1492), the voluminous historian of Sicily. After a brief career as a soldier under Francesco Sforza of Milan, Buonincontri lectured on astronomy from the text of Manilius at Naples. His Manilian studies bore fruit in the shape of a three-book didactic poem on astronomy, dedicated to Ferdinand of Naples, entitled *Res Naturales et Divinae, sive de rebus Caelestibus* (first printed 1526), a work of which even the hypercritical Scaliger spoke well; Tiraboschi's comment is, "lo stile non è incolto, e talvolta ancora è elegante."

Buonincontri's pupil, Giovanni Pontano (1424-1503), is a far more important figure here; three of Pontano's major works are didactic. The *Urania, sive de stellis* (five books) deals with the heavenly bodies, their influence on the earth, and their alleged influence on human affairs. The diction of the whole work is naturally Lucretian, the rhythms Virgilian. The poem as a whole is far from dry; its unexciting subject is enlivened by digression and myth, simile and metaphor, and a large number of contemporary references, allusions, and applications. The *Meteora* (one book) is a sort of pendant or sequel; it deals with the unlikely subject of the vagaries of weather and their causes. The style is more Manilian than in the earlier poem, and the didactic approach is more noticeable. Both of these poems are dedicated to the poet's son Lucio; the *Garden of the Hesperides* (two books on the growing of oranges and lemons) is dedicated to Francesco Gonzaga of Mantua. The manner is similar to that of the *Urania:* the poem is composed in smooth, elegant verse, with passages of strictest didacticism alternating with narratives of attractive myths suggested by the context. It is certainly the most pleasant of the earlier Italian Latin didactic poems.

The same cannot be said for the *Astronomica* of Basinio de' Basini of Parma (1425-1457) : this is the least successful of Basinio's works. Giovanni Aurelio Augurelli of Rimini (ca. 1454-1537) better deserves mention as a didactic poet. His *Manufacture of Gold* (*Chrysopoeia*) professes to teach all the secrets of alchemy; Pope Leo X, it is said, replied to a gift copy by sending the author an empty purse, with the remark that the poet could no doubt fill it himself without difficulty. Yet Augurelli could write occasionally with real fervor, and no fool would for long have remained the close friend of Marsilio Ficino and Ermolao Barbaro.

Without a doubt the most attractive didactic poems ever produced in Italy are a group by Marco Girolamo Vida of Cremona (1490-1566). The early *Game of Chess* (ca. 1513) is a witty and entertaining poem describing a game between Hermes and Apollo at a banquet of the gods; it is a brilliant tour de force, but Reuben Fine is a better guide to the game. More thoroughly didactic are *The Silkworm* (1524?) in two books and *The Art of Poetry* (1527) in three. The first, dealing with the care and housing of silkworms and the manufacture of silk, is a pleasant work, and it is a pity that Samuel Pullein's verse-translation (1750) sounds as little like Vida as Hobbes' *Iliad* sounds like Homer. Fortunately the *Ars poetica* found a brilliant translator (1725) in Christopher Pitt. "No student of the history and criticism of poetry," writes George Sampson, "should fail to read Vida, and will lose very little of him in the version of Pitt." Pitt's version of iii, 15-31, gives a good notion of the tone of the whole:

> In chief avoid obscurity, nor shrowd
> Your thoughts and dark conceptions in a cloud;
> For some, we know, affect to lose the light,
> Lost in forc'd figures and involv'd in night;

Studious and bent to shun the common way,
They skulk in darkness and abhor the day.
O! may the sacred Nine inspire my lays,
To shine with pride in their own native rays;
For this we need not importune the skies;
In our own power and will the blessing lies.
Expression, boundless in extent, displays
A thousand forms, a thousand several ways;
In diff'rent hues from diff'rent quarters brought
It makes unnumber'd dresses for a thought;
Such vast varieties of ways we find
To paint conception and unfold the mind.
If e'er you toil but toil without success
To give your images a shining dress,
Quit your pursuit and chuse a diff'rent way,
'Til, breaking forth, the voluntary ray
Cuts the thick darkness, and lets down the day.

Didactic poetry flourished vigorously elsewhere in Europe all through the sixteenth and seventeenth centuries; it will be enough to mention only a few of the most outstanding names. In 1573 the astronomer Tycho Brahe (1546-1601) produced his *Urania,* the first literary work based upon the findings (1543) of Copernicus; it was soon answered in 1586 by the posthumously published *Sphaera* of George Buchanan (1506-1582). More pleasant than either of these works is the "Education of Children" (*Paedotrophia*) of Scévole de Sainte-Marthe (1536-1623). In Germany we should note the work of Nathan Chytraeus (*Mundus*), Martinus Praetorius (*De principatu salubriter administrando*), and in France again that of Nicolas du Fresnoy (*Geographia*). And we should not forget that, like Ovid in his *Art of Love,* the German Vincentius Opsopaeus used the elegiac meter to burlesque didactic in his "Art of Drink" (*Ars bibendi*), as did his compatriot Matthaeus Delius in his "Art of Jest" (*Ars iocandi*). But the elegiac meter could here be used seriously also, as in the first two books of Abraham Cowley's five-book didactic poem on plants.

Considering the *verve injurieuse* of the typical Renaissance Humanist, one might have expected satire to have bulked far larger in Neo-Latin literature than it does. Wherever it does occur, its themes are almost always the same—the folly and vice of mankind in general, the immorality of monks, and the moral worthlessness of women; these three topics are liberally represented in the work of the two authors we shall mention here—Francesco Filelfo (1398-1481) and Thomas Naogeorgus (i.e., Kirchmeyer; 1511-1578).

Filelfo's *Satirae* were published in ten "books" of ten poems apiece, each poem being precisely one hundred lines in length; they were completed by 1448 and reached print first in the Milan edition of 1476. The first poem of the first book (or decade) is like Juvenal's first satire, a string of pictures of all the villains infesting Florence and the conclusion that " 'tis difficult to be no satirist"; it is a raucous declaration of war against all the cruelty and fraud in the world. The second poem is a violent attack on the Florence of Cosimo de' Medici and concludes with nine pieces of advice to the Florentines. The fifth is a bitter sneer at a Florentine would-be critic of Dante and Petrarch whom Filelfo calls Nicholas Nobody (i.e., Niccolò de' Niccoli), a poem not nearly so virulent, however, as those attacking Niccolò's friend Poggio (e.g., II, iii and V, vii), in which scurrility reaches its nadir. Juvenal's sixth satire (on women) finds an echo in I, ix, and his second (on male homosexuals) in IV, ii. Attacks on priests and monks assail their ambition (V, iii), superstition (III, iv), or immorality (II, v). Some of the satires are ethical, as I, iv, on true nobility; IV, vii, on self-control; and IV, viii, on the avoidance of anger (a curious theme for Filelfo). Many of the later satires are of interest historically—the civil disturbances in Bologna, Genoa, and Milan are vigorously portrayed, and we learn much about the rise of Francesco Sforza, successor of the Visconti dynasty of Milan. A real curiosity is a passage in VI, iii, written in Lent after Filelfo had been living on a vegetarian diet for rather over a year. Like many faddists, Filelfo regards as immoral, if not downright criminal, anyone who happens to disagree with his fad of the moment; in this poem he sounds almost as crotchety a crackpot as J. E. B. Mayor, whose preface to the second volume of his edition of Juvenal is a classic of addled zeal.

J. A. Symonds, a Victorian Christian gentleman of the most charming type, called Filelfo's *Satires* "the outpourings of a filthy fancy," being, like Henry Nettleship, incapable of understanding that the standards of his own age and social class were not universal; he was certainly not the man to understand the violently outspoken, belligerent individualism of Filelfo. Filelfo undoubtedly had (as J. E. Sandys puts it) the brutality of a brigand; he was hectoring and overbearing, hard and unforgiving. He loved money passionately and doted upon extravagant display; but he really believed himself an honest man who practiced the cardinal virtues. This we can see in II, vii, the sort of evidence that Symonds either does not mention or misinterprets.

The *Satirae* (five books, extending to more than 2,400 lines) of Thomas Naogeorgus (1511-1598) while far better written than Filelfo's are not nearly so exuberant. The first poem of Book One satirizes the scribblers of the sixteenth century: all babble in verse, and the most unendurable of all are those who insist on producing versified translations of the Psalms. This is a readable and amusing piece of verse, but Naogeorgus is content to sneer rather than flay. The third poem of Book Four is an ethical satire of a familiar sort: mankind is never so stupid as when it pursues the mirage of wealth. The commonest theme, however, is anti-Catholic propaganda; the vilest work in Naogeorgus' vocabulary is *Papista,* and terms like *detestandus Papismus, grex Satanae, Stygia turba,* and the like abound. But Naogeorgus, too, must needs produce a satire on the perennial theme of Latin satirical writing—sexual misconduct (IV, iv).

In pastoral poetry, largely modeled on the *Eclogues* of Virgil, we come to one of the most popular literary vogues of Renaissance Latin poetry: between 1300 and 1700 over two hundred Neo-Latinists wrote anywhere from one to twenty eclogues apiece—a complete collection would fill well over three thousand octavo pages, and a reasonably full discussion of the genre is the theme of this book.

The abundance, vitality, and variety of Neo-Latin literature is truly astounding. There are three points we should note: from the beginning of the fifteenth to the end of the seventeenth century in, for example, Portugal, there were actually more books published in Latin than in Portuguese; second, the best of the Neo-Latinists are not merely inoffensive pedants, but men who took an active part in the development of political, religious, philosophical, and literary ideas all over Europe; third, the number of literary genres represented is tremendous. The Neo-Latin literature of Europe should not be relegated to scattered footnotes in the various histories of the individual vernacular European literatures—this prevents one from gaining a general impression of the very abundance, vitality, and variety that these two chapters are intended to emphasize—but should be viewed as a whole, as an international literature the history of which is continuous from the early fourteenth century to the end of the Baroque age.

III

THE CLASSICAL
BACKGROUND OF PASTORAL

he beginnings of pastoral in ancient Greece are obscure. Ancient and modern critics alike have tried to establish a religious origin; but pastoral is almost certainly derived ultimately from the actual piping and singing of shepherds: the recurrent refrain, the rustic but elegantly polished love-song, the singing-match in single lines or couplets (with its attempts to cap rhetorically the last singer's words), and many another feature characteristic of developed pastoral all point clearly in that direction.

Bucolic themes—the loves of shepherds and shepherdesses, the quarrels of young shepherds, their laments for a dead comrade, and the like—appear in many forms of Greek poetry, especially during that later age we call Hellenistic. There may even have existed, in the fourth century B.C., a veritable school of pastoral poets in the island of Cos. What the works of these poets may have been like we have no means of telling; but it is conceivable that it was in Cos that bucolic poetry was first combined with a verse form known as the mime, a brief, realistic sort of poem, quasi-dramatic in form, humorous or ironic in tone, precise in its observation of detail. The "urban" mime could describe the gossip of women visiting friends, a trip to a religious festival by two friends in anything but a religious frame of mind, or could be decidedly risqué in expression and content; the "bucolic" mime became what we think of today as the pastoral and attained definitive form in certain of the *Idylls* of Theocritus (ca. 310–ca. 250 B.C.).

i

Of the thirty *Idylls* of Theocritus (not all are genuine), eleven can be classed as true pastorals. Especially interesting, in view of the possible origin of pastoral as written by Theocritus and his successors, is number 7, "Harvest Home." In this poem Simichidas (the narrator; probably intended to represent Theocritus himself) and two friends meet a goatherd named Lycidas (who perhaps represents an older contemporary poet of Cos). After Simichidas and Lycidas have complimented each other on their skill in verse, they take part in a rustic contest in song in order to pass the time on their walk. Their ways eventually part; Lycidas disappears from the story, while Simichidas and his friends go on to a farm where a festival is taking place. The form of the poem (introduction, two songs, conclusion), the atmosphere of literary rusticity, the use of conventional shepherd names like Lycidas, and the tendency to *mascarade bucolique* are all features which became fixed in bucolic poetry and which recur times almost without number in later European pastoral.

In number 5 appears a "plot" which will become more and more familiar as we examine later pastoral. In this poem two southern Italians—a goatherd named Comatas and a shepherd called Lacon—meet each other as they pasture their flocks. Each accuses the other of theft, and they indulge in an acrimonious quarrel. Eventually Lacon challenges Comatas to a singing-match to be judged by another rustic, Morson, who had been cutting heather nearby. The singing-match turns out to be a series of attempts to "do the other down": in line 22, Lacon says, in effect, "I will cap couplets with you until you can think of no more."

In the sixth *Idyll* we have a singing-match of a different sort. Two young herdsmen, Damoetas and Daphnis, meet near a spring and Daphnis suggests a contest in song. But this is not a capping-contest as in number 5; here Daphnis sings a song of fourteen lines on the love of the Cyclops Polyphemus for the Nereid Galatea, and Damoetas replies with twenty lines on a different aspect of the same subject. Gow (in his commentary on Theocritus) well remarks that the theme, with its combination of the pathetic and the grotesque, is one that would naturally appeal to Hellenistic taste.

In other pastorals we have not a contest but a single song, provided with an introduction and conclusion either in dialogue or in narrative form. In number 1, an unnamed goatherd persuades the shepherd Thyrsis, by promising him a cup (the decoration of which he describes in loving detail), to sing to him of the sorrows of Daphnis. The story of the death of Daphnis, fabled to be the Sicilian inventor of bucolic song, is one that the reader of later pastoral will meet again and again.

Other types of pastoral appear in numbers 4, 3, and 2. In the fourth poem we have not a song or pair of songs or series of couplets or stichomythic lines (as in number 27) but a rambling conversation between the goatherd Battus and the cowherd Corydon, a conversation interrupted at one point when some calves stray into an olive grove and Battus, in trying to drive them out, runs a thorn into his foot.

The third poem is humorous or satirical in conception. In the song of a goatherd before the cave of his obdurate sweetheart Amaryllis, we have a burlesque of what appears to have been an actual custom among young bloods of rank and wealth. After a symposium, a lover (drunk or sober) might serenade his mistress, beat on her doors for admission, hang a garland on the lintel, bewail his misfortunes, and perhaps even spend the night asleep on the doorstep. Theocritus achieves a fine piece of fooling in this poem, even though a full appreciation of its humor requires today a full commentary on the literary parallels.

The second poem introduces a theme familiar to generations of readers of Virgil's *Bucolics*. Here a young woman, poor and an orphan, prepares a magic spell to recall her forgetful lover. After the mystic preliminaries, she sings an incantation in ten four-line stanzas, each of which has its recurrent refrain.

In such "bucolic mimes" as these, as well as in idylls either of a heroic or an urban type, Theocritus reveals himself as the most attractive by far of the Hellenistic poets. He has an understanding of human nature and a love for the gentler aspects of external nature that would immediately place him in the forefront of Greek writers even apart from the undoubted excellence of his verse. His characters are not lay figures, as are the shepherds of many a later pastoral poet, but real inhabitants of a real countryside.

ii

In the sixteenth century (1531), Elius Eobanus of Hesse published a translation of Theocritus' *Idylls* in Latin hexameters which clearly influenced some writers of Humanistic Latin pastoral; further, many Italian poets, like Sannazaro, were familiar with the Greek text, and perhaps even more Germans knew it, for after 1545 Theocritus was a required author for all Greek students at the University of Wittenberg. But for all that it was not Theocritus' *Idylls* but Virgil's *Eclogues* that were the chief influence upon the scores of Neo-Latin poets who produced a steady stream of pastoral poetry from 1300 to 1700 and even later.

Virgil's ten eclogues—his earliest known published work—were composed between 42 and 37 B.C. The order of their composition is known with a fair degree of exactness, and the order is not that of the conventional printed texts, which have maintained Virgil's own arrangement, alternating poems in monologue with poems in dialogue. For convenience, their approximate dates are here listed: *numbers 2, 3 and 5: 42* B.C.; *numbers 7 and 1: 41?*; *numbers 9 and 6: 41? 40?; number 8: 39; number 10: 37.*

In the second (i.e., earliest) eclogue, we are told that the shepherd Corydon loved and admired the youthful Alexis, but in vain, and so could only wander disconsolately through the woods, lamenting his ill-fortune. In his song Corydon warns Alexis not to trust overmuch in his good looks, reminds him of his own easy circumstances, and promises generosity. The Nymphs and Naiads (he continues) will offer bouquets of flowers, and he himself will bring choicest fruits. Then at last Corydon realizes that he will never win Alexis back from Iolas with gifts; why not, he concludes, set about something useful and forget Alexis? Derivative the poem may be, but there are signs that better is to come.

The third eclogue reproduces two easily recognized features of Theocritean idyll—the elegant banter (ill-natured, in this instance) of shepherds and the equally elegant contest in song, in this instance a series of amoebaean (i.e., alternating) couplets. The poem is as imitative as any in the entire collection, for the characters (Menalcas, Damoetas, and Palaemon the "umpire") belong to the most conventional form of pastoral, and in expression there are no less than twenty-seven palpable reminiscences of lines in various poems of Theocritus.

The second eclogue had shown us the lament of a single shepherd, the third the amoebaean interchange of capped couplets; the fifth poem (called "Daphnis") illustrates further aspects of pastoral. Here the shepherds Menalcas (Virgil?) and Mopsus (Aemilius Macer of Verona?) sing of Daphnis, the legendary shepherd of Sicilian song already celebrated in Theocritus' first idyll. In a song of 25 lines, Mopsus laments Daphnis' death and Menalcas replies in a song of exactly the same length, describing Daphnis' deification. This is undoubtedly the finest of Virgil's earlier eclogues. The alternation of dialogue in the introduction is cleverly managed, the illustrations of Menalcas' courtesy and Mopsus' touchiness are made with tact and humour, and the exactly corresponding "subdivisions" of the two songs are maintained with unobtrusive skill.

In the seventh eclogue (the fourth in order of composition and the last of the purely Theocritean poems), Meliboeus listens while two shepherds called Corydon and Thyrsis engage before Daphnis in a series of amoebaean quatrains. The two shepherds boast of their poetic prowess, pray to Diana on the one hand and Priapus on the other, praise first the beauty of the seasons and then that of their sweethearts. In all this the general appearance of the scenery, as every commentator points out, is Arcadian and Sicilian, while the details are drawn from Virgil's own northern Italy, where the Mincio "fringed its green banks with tender reeds": the effect is that of a golden Never-Never Land described in verse "languorous in its suggestion of leisure and music and love" (Duff).

When we turn to the first eclogue we find a poem that is still Theocritean in expression, but inspired by the misery caused to Italian rustics by the confiscations and allotments of land in 41 B.C. to the veterans of Octavian, the later Emperor Augustus. Virgil's own father, we know, had been ejected from his farm at Andes, near Mantua, and the poet was forced to appeal for help, first to Gaius Asinius Pollio and then to Octavian himself. In this poem, Tityrus is shown lying at his ease under a spreading beech tree, when Meliboeus, who has just been evicted from his farm, enters, driving before him his weary, dejected flock. Here and there in the poem Tityrus expresses Virgil's own personal feelings, no doubt; but the identification of shepherd and poet must not be pressed too far. There is not the slightest attempt to make Tityrus' circumstances parallel Virgil's: Tityrus is represented as a slave who had earlier gone to Rome to purchase his freedom; at the same time he is regarded as the owner of his land, and, although well-advanced in years (Virgil himself was not yet thirty), makes the woods resound with praise of the fair Amaryllis like any of Theocritus' most youthfully ardent swains. Rather than prowl about the exegetical outskirts of this eclogue, we should admit with W. Y. Sellar that "the truth of the poem consists in the expression of the feelings of love which the old possessors entertained for their homes" and observe that "Virgil's feeling for the movement of his age, which henceforth becomes one of the main sources of his inspiration, has its origin in the effect which these events had on his personal fortunes, and in the sympathy awakened within him by the sorrows of his native district."

The ninth eclogue was written at about the same time as, but perhaps a little earlier than, the first and turns upon the same unhappy events; the fact that the form of the poem is based on Theocritus' seventh idyll is of no great importance. Here we appear to have a record of an earlier appeal (to Alfenus Varus) on Virgil's part and perhaps an allusion to Virgil's own alleged misadventure at the hands of the centurion who had evicted the poet's father. The poet has ruefully learned that an appeal to personal friendship has proved useless to save the Mantuan district; later he was to find Pollio and Octavian more accommodating, and his "Tityrus" poem could then fittingly form an introduction to the whole collection. The candid reader must admit that the ninth eclogue, despite individual excellences, is not by any means the most rewarding; there are too many obscurities which tend to make him read the work not as a poem but a a puzzle. But it is worth pointing out that, despite resemblances in form, the content is growing less and less Theocritean: the scene of the poem is now not a conventional Sicily or Arcady, but the road between Andes and Mantua; there is no poetic mingling of Italian vine-dresser and Sicilian shepherd, as in the second and third eclogues: Lycidas, Moeris, and Menalcas, for all their Greek names, are now real Italian peasants living in an age of cruel and violent events: the same can be said for those bucolics of Joachim Camerarius that have as background the Peasants' Revolt in Germany.

The remaining poems are almost wholly Roman and non-Theocritean: numbers 2, 3, and 7 had been early derivative work; numbers 1 and 9 are transitional; but numbers 6, 4, 8, and 10 represent Virgil's transformation of the pastoral form and his emancipation from Greek influence.

The sixth eclogue, which bears no trace of the language of Theocritus, is not so much pastoral as a mythological and semi-philosophical idyll; the introduction, however, reads like a rural fairy tale. Two shepherds, Chromis and Mnasyllus, accompanied by the lovely water nymph Aeglê, discover the drunken Silenus asleep in a cave. Egged on by their companion, the two boys bind him hand and foot with wreaths, while Aeglê smears his face with mulberry juice. At this point Silenus awakes, pretends grief at his undignified predicament, and agrees to sing the song for which the shepherds have been teasing him for days.

The major part of the poem now follows, in which the poet tells how Silenus gave an account of the Creation, in the Lucretian manner, and continued with a summary narrative, almost a catalogue, of some of the oldest mythological traditions—the story of Deucalion's Flood, of the Golden Age when Saturn reigned on earth, of Prometheus' theft of fire, and the like. This is followed by ten lines in praise of Virgil's friend Gaius Cornelius Gallus; and then Silenus, we are told, sang of various tales of metamorphosis—how Scylla, Tereus, and Philomela had all been turned into birds.

The source of unity within all this is a famous problem depending on the still uncertain purpose of the lines on Gallus. Skutsch, Leo, Rose, and others have examined it, so far without reaching convincing or even probable conclusions. It seems possible that no formal unity was intended at all and that the lines on Gallus (to modern readers a structural blemish) did not seem in the least out of place to Virgil's contemporaries, whose views on poetry were not necessarily identical with our own. And it is perhaps significant that the classical Humanists and Latin poets of the Renaissance, whose feeling for Latin verse was at once simple and subtle, found no difficulty in accepting the poem as it stands, and, like Matteo Maria Boiardo, writing others which follow it closely.

Virgil's fourth, or Messianic, eclogue—often referred to as "the Pollio"—is one of the best known in the entire collection. It was written during or immediately before the consulate (40 B.C.) of Gaius Asinius Pollio—orator, tragedian, poet, historian, literary patron, soldier, and diplomat. Reversing the Hesiodic pattern of a series of ages successively degenerating from Golden to Iron, Virgil pictures his own age as one of Iron that looks to a golden future. In 40 B.C. the century-old Roman Revolution was not yet over; traces of evil still exist, writes the poet, but soon will come the Argonauts (a naval campaign against the still-dangerous Sextus Pompeius?) and another Trojan War (against Parthia?). This means that the present troubles and uncertainties of the Iron Age will be followed by a new Heroic Age as the rulers of the Roman world, Octavian and Antony, struggle towards their goal; then at last shall come the Golden Age for which all pray, a brave new world in which the lion shall lie down with the lamb: this is the loftier theme to which Virgil alludes in the first line of the poem, addressed to the pastoral Muses.

So far all is clear, provided that we do not insist on forcing a contemporary allusion into every imaginative detail Virgil has seen fit to introduce. But Virgil speaks of a child who will some day actually see this Golden Age of peace and prosperity. There has been debate on this child's identity at least since the day when Pollio's own son, Asinius Gallus, allowed his friends to understand that the poet had been writing of him. There are many other candidates for the honor, of varying degrees of unlikelihood. But it is most probable, and most Virgilian, to suppose that the poet, who did not, after all, write in order to confuse his readers, intended the child to symbolize future generations.

The eighth eclogue, the "Pharmaceutria" (*Enchantress*), is modeled on Theocritus' second; more properly, it is *suggested* by Theocritus' poem, for Virgil does not give us any mere imitative reproduction. The whole poem is strongly Italian, despite the Greek names of the actors: one passage (admired alike by Voltaire and Macaulay) describes a country lad falling in love with a girl at first sight as she picked apples; the picture of boyish innocence is Virgilian, not Theocritean, and the whole passage recalls the cultivated farms of northern Italy rather than the craggy beauties of central Sicily.

Of Virgil's collection of pastorals the last in order of composition is the tenth. This eclogue describes, in *mascarade bucolique*, the grief of Virgil's friend Gaius Cornelius Gallus (an ambitious soldier and man of affairs who was also well known as a capable poet) for the loss of his mistress Cytheris, a famous actress and courtesan whose real name was Volumnia: she appears to have deserted Gallus for some officer on the staff of Agrippa. Gallus is conventionally represented as surrounded by Arcadian shepherds who listen to his plaintive song of unrequited love. None of the poems is so patently artificial in conception; yet none of the poems "is more rich in beauty, and grace, and happy turns of phrase" (Sellar). The whole poem is indeed one of remarkable virtuosity, and shows us Virgil at the peak of his early manner.

It is easy to indicate instances of artificiality in the pastorals of Virgil and obvious contrasts with the reality of Theocritus' idylls, but it is as pointless to do so as it is unjust. No one complains because a harpsichord is not a massive Baroque organ, or because Scarlatti is not Beethoven, or because Sèvres china is not Gothic masonry. The *Eclogues* do not make the slightest attempt to give a realistic picture of rural life; they are intended as finished examples of a sophisticated art-form likely to appeal to urban readers of a highly literate and literary turn of mind.

iii

Other pastoral poets flourished in Virgil's day, notably Gaius Cornelius Gallus, who is said to have influenced or even inspired Virgil himself. But their productions are no longer extant, and it is not until the early years of the age of Nero (ruled A.D. 54-68) that we again meet Thyrsis and Damon and Neaera and Amaryllis. The first five years of Nero's reign were greeted by contemporaries as a Golden Age of glorious promise—relief at the death of Claudius and confidence in a handsome, brilliant young man trained by the philosopher Seneca combined to produce such a lifting of the spirit as Rome had not felt since Augustus inaugurated his brave new world.

A group of seven bucolic poems can be assigned to this period, written by Titus Calpurnius Siculus (*floruit* A.D. 50-60). Very little indeed is known about this author, but it is clear from his work that he was a writer of skill and talent if not of force or originality. Of the seven poems, four are conventionally rural in theme (numbers 3, 6, 2, and 5, probably written in that order before A.D. 54) and three are courtly eclogues, examples of *Maskenpoesie* in which panegyric masquerades as pastoral—numbers 1 (A.D. 54), 4 (about A.D. 55), and 7 (A.D. 57). These we shall examine briefly in their probable chronological order, after observing that the traditional order of the poems in the manuscripts is *courtly,* rustic, rustic, *courtly,* rustic, rustic, *courtly,* the pattern arrangement being clearly intentional.

In Calpurnius' third eclogue we see his earliest, least finished work, which the elder Scaliger, always an impatient critic, considered immature (*puerilis*) and lacking in charm (*inficetus*). The shepherd Iolas, searching for a missing heifer, falls in with his friend Lycidas, who tells him how jealousy of a rival had caused him to lose his temper and give his sweetheart Phyllis, temporarily faithless, a sound beating. Lycidas is terrified that he has ruined his prospects entirely, and rehearses a love-song, pretty enough, with which he hopes to regain Phyllis' regard. Scaliger's censure of the poem is just, but we should remember that "it has redeeming touches of delicacy and chivalry" (Duff).

The sixth of Calpurnius' eclogues describes a quarrel followed by a contest in song. Calpurnius has enough originality to vary the material somewhat, but not enough to impress us. Here the shepherds Astylus and Lycidas fall to quarreling over their respective abilities in poetry: the stylized insults hurtle back and forth in three-line stanzas until Lycidas suggests letting the newly arrived Mnasyllus act as judge. After describing their sureties at rather too great length in rather bombastic verse, the two shepherds are ready to begin: in balancing quatrains they discuss the proper spot for their contest, and Mnasyllus makes his selection. So far all is conventional; but now, as the contest is about to begin, the insults are started all over again, and the disgusted Mnasyllus makes his exit, announcing that some more patient umpire must decide between these two hotheads. The unexpected conclusion is an effective piece of pastoral theater; but the insults grow boring; Duff more mildly describes them as "not very entertaining."

Calpurnius' second eclogue is much more attractive; we should also note that the appearance of a gardener as one of its characters is a hint for the garden-ecologues which are a pretty feature of Renaissance Latin pastoral. After a brief introduction, two young men named Idas and Astacus, one a shepherd, the other a gardener, sing of their love for Crocalê; they sing in quatrains until a change to a three-line stanza apiece signals the end of their amoebaean song. Throughout, the most careful parallelism is maintained in the matching songs, with, of course, much graceful variety in the expression. It is obvious that verse on such a pattern requires a light and knowing hand—when badly done it is wretched; but when well done it can fairly sparkle with rhetorical verve, and Calpurnius has conned his Ovid with too much care to be wholly unsuccessful.

The fifth poem—last of the four rural eclogues—introduces a new form of pastoral, the didactic. After a few introductory lines, the aged shepherd Micon begins to instruct his foster son Canthus on the care of flocks. These sheep and goats (he begins) I now make over to you and will tell you how they must be tended. Here follow precepts on care during spring (lines 14-48), summer (49-65), autumn (66-94), and winter (95-118). The verse runs along with grace and charm, and Calpurnius exercises much tact in the choice and in the amount of didactic detail employed; the poem is in fact by far the best of the four rustic eclogues: the poet has skillfully combined the leisurely tone of Virgil's *Eclogues* with the more serious mood of the *Georgics*—no mean accomplishment.

Among the courtly eclogues the first poem clearly belongs to the first year or so of Nero's reign (A.D. 54). It is modeled loosely on the fourth (Messianic) eclogue of Virgil and like it looks forward to a coming Golden Age of peace and prosperity. Two shepherds, Corydon and Ornytus, take shelter under a beech tree from the oppressive heat of noon. Ornytus discovers a prophecy carved by the pastoral god Faunus on the bark of the tree and reads it aloud (33-38) to his friend: "I, Faunus, foretell the future: rejoice, all! There shall be security under a young prince. Wars shall cease, peace shall return, bringing with it a new age of Saturn. Law shall rule: rejoice, all! The sky's omens are favorable, for our new prince is a very god (*ipse deus*)." The poem closes with two three-line stanzas from Corydon and Ornytus. Panegyric is not a form of verse attractive to modern tastes; but ancient poets, like those of the Renaissance, were not considering the tastes of the twentieth century when they wrote: of its kind this poem is well done.

The tone of panegyric reappears in the fourth eclogue. In responsive verses Corydon and Amyntas hymn the praises of Nero at great length before Meliboeus (Seneca?). Corydon (the poet himself, presumably) hints strongly that he would be delighted to receive such a gift as Horace had received from Maecenas and begs Meliboeus to see to it that His Imperial Majesty learns of his loyal verses.

The last poem of all, the seventh, is modeled loosely on Virgil's first: the rustic Corydon has been to Rome and returns to his friends in the country with his mouth full of news, particularly of the amphitheater built by the Emperor for beast-fights. Corydon describes the appointments of the amphitheater, the animals, and the appearance of the Emperor himself, whom he had seen at a respectful distance. The poem is unusual for its special archaeological interest and also because of the slight elements of mime which appear when an elderly Roman points out the sights to the young countryman. Naturally, Calpurnius has a golden opportunity for panegyric in this poem.

In this poem the echoes of Virgilian thought, diction, and construction are easily perceived and, although they may occasionally annoy a modern reader, were counted a virtue by Calpurnius' contemporaries, as were, too, the much less pervasive influences of

Ovid, Propertius, and Tibullus. Certainly Calpurnius is an excellent minor poet, and his skill in (for example) dialogue is considerable. For our present purpose he is next in importance to Virgil himself, for his influence can be seen quite clearly in the Latin pastoral of the Renaissance, especially in the work of the Italians Publio Fausto Andrelini, Baptista Mantuanus, Naldo Naldi, Girolamo Fracastoro, and Giacopo Sannazaro, and in the French poets Jean Arnoullet, Gervais Sepin, and Jean Dorat.

iv

Exactly contemporary with Calpurnius Siculus' three courtly poems (A.D. 54-57) and clearly belonging to the same artistic environment are two fragmentary pastorals, known as the Einsiedeln eclogues from the Einsiedeln manuscript in which they were discovered in 1869 by the German classical scholar Hagen. The first eulogizes Nero's literary enthusiasms, the second heralds the new Golden Age of the *quinquennium Neronis,* and neither is of much intrinsic interest. Since both appear to have been unknown to the Neo-Latin poets, we can turn to the four brief pastorals of a later imitator of both Virgil and Calpurnius, Marcus Aurelius Olympius Nemesianus (*floruit* A.D. 285). His diction and meter are careful and indeed precise; he is an unoriginal but agreeable poet who occasionally lapses into fatuity.

In Nemesianus' first poem Timetas sings to the aging Tityrus a eulogy of Meliboeus, lately dead. Meliboeus may or may not refer to some friend or patron of the poet; in any case the name is intended to recall that used for Calpurnius' patron just as "Tityrus" comes from Virgil. If there is little to which we can take exception in this poem, there is equally little to praise; it is adequate.

The second poem draws heavily on Calpurnius' second and third pastorals: Idas and Alcon both love Donacê and sing her praises. The structure is neat and careful: introduction (lines 1-19); song of Idas (33 lines); transition (53-54); song of Alcon (33 lines); conclusion (88-90). Both young men lament the continued nonappearance of Donacê, unaware that she is being held virtually as a prisoner by her parents, who rightly suspect that she is no longer a virgin.

The third poem is equally derivative, being closely modeled on Virgil's sixth eclogue. Here three youthful rustics, Nyctilus, Micon, and Amyntas, find Pan sleeping under an elm, on which he has hung his pipes.   They attempt to play the pipes, with such cacophonous results that Pan awakes and promises to sing them a song himself. The song proves to be a panegyric of the god Bacchus and of his greatest gift to mankind; it concludes with an undignified picture of drunken satyrs pursuing nymphs and a comic description of the results of Silenus' first experience with wine.

The fourth eclogue recalls Calpurnius' third in its use of exact responses.   Lycidas and Mopsus lament the pain of unrequited love; each sings a six-line stanza with refrain and each tries to outdo the other.   The poem has at least the virtue of being easy to read; Nemesianus, unlike Calpurnius, seldom becomes obscure in diction or farfetched in allusion.   The four eclogues as a whole are a distinct comedown after Calpurnius' seven, to say nothing of Virgil's ten; still, they were not without influence during the Renaissance.

V

Among Christian poets of the late imperial and medieval eras, the eclogue in one form or another maintained a precarious existence. None of the authors in question appears to have exercised any great influence on the Neo-Latins, and we can afford to dismiss them with a mere mention.

The *Tityrus* of the fourth-century poet Pomponius is the earliest Christian Latin pastoral.   This poem was unknown to the Neo-Latins (it was not discovered until 1878) and is extant today only in fragments.   It is an example of the deplorable form of verse called the cento or pastiche: Pomponius industriously stitches together lines and half-lines from Virgil and thereby produces a dialogue between Tityrus and Meliboeus on Christian topics.   It is true that cento-eclogues were written during the Renaissance by Lelio Capilupi, but Pomponius was not his model.

A superior poet of the fourth century was Paulinus of Nola (born ca. A.D. 353), pupil of Ausonius.   He produced a number of hexameter poems on Christian subjects in which the classic forms and conventions of pagan eclogue maintained their vitality; in the one eclogue of Paulinus' friend, the rhetorician Endelechius (born ca. 395), the pastoral becomes lyric.   In a pleasant idyll of thirty-three Asclepiadean strophes the poet tells how Tityrus had warded off plague from his cattle by the sign of the Cross: this poem was at least known to the Neo-Latins and may conceivably have influenced Antonio Urceo.

Much later (tenth century?) is the anonymous pseudo-eclogue *Theodulus* (*The Servant of the Lord*) and the twelfth-century bucolics of Marcus (?) Valerius, none of which need concern us at all: the Neo-Latins turned to Virgil, Theocritus, Calpurnius, and Nemesianus for models; they were aware of late Christian and medieval literature but made little or no use of it.

IV

PRE-HUMANIST PASTORAL: I

he tradition of pastoral, virtually extinct with Nemesianus in the late third century, was not to be wholly revived until the first stirrings of classical Humanism in the Italian fourteenth century, the period often called Pre-Humanist. In this period it was Dante who revived the eclogue as a living form: his "epistolary" eclogues inspired a small but enthusiastic school of poets that flourished for a generation, until it was replaced by a literary coterie, inspired by Petrarch, that proved of equally brief duration. The content of the pastoral poems written during the Pre-Humanist period is often of great interest and even importance; in expression, however, these poets had much to learn: they wrote a Latin full of medievalisms, Italicisms, unintentional obscurities, and intentional purple patches, and were accordingly ignored by the more fastidious Latin poets of the fifteenth and later centuries.

i

In 1319 Dante Alighieri (1265-1321) was living in exile in Ravenna. In 1316 the Guelfic (i.e., anti-Imperial) ruler of Ravenna, Lamberto da Polenta, had died, to be succeeded by his nephew, Guido Novello da Polenta. Fortunately for Dante, who for years had been moving in uneasy exile from one neutral or Ghibelline (anti-Papal) stronghold to another, Guido was far more interested in poetry than in politics. Dante accordingly turned to Ravenna, entering the diplomatic service of Guido Novello and lecturing on rhetoric at the University. What leisure was left was devoted to the completion of the *Divina Commedia*.

To this last period of Dante's life belongs the poetical correspondence (1319-1321) with Giovanni del Virgilio of Cesena (ca. 1270?–ca. 1330?), professor of poetry at the Guelfic city of Bologna. This correspondence reveals a more genial side of Dante's nature than many a reader might suspect, from the *Inferno*, to have existed at all.

The correspondence began in early 1319 when Dante received a metrical epistle (fifty-one Latin hexameters) from Giovanni del Virgilio. For all his admiration of the *Inferno* and the *Purgatorio*, Giovanni del Virgilio was not at all reconciled to Dante's use of Italian in the *Commedia*. It is not that Giovanni had a pedantic contempt for the vernacular. He would have agreed, however, with that later Humanist (Francesco Filelfo) who complained that even the cultivated Tuscan dialect was not spoken by all Italians and would have understood why the Sienese monk, Matteo Ronto, very soon (ca. 1329) translated the *Commedia* into Latin, to make it available to all educated Europeans. Giovanni felt that since Lovato had written in Latin on Iseult, and Mussato had written his tragedy *Ecerinis* in the same language, Dante was merely being perverse in insisting on using the vernacular, and a form, moreover, of that vernacular not universally understood even by his own countrymen. Such a poet as Dante, he felt, should use the international language. The subject matter, moreover, of the *Commedia* did not strike Giovanni as suitable, and his suggestions show the turn of his mind.

The point of the poem comes when Giovanni urges Dante to come to Bologna, in order to be presented to the University and to receive at his hands a laurel crown of poetry, such as Albertino Mussato had received in 1315 (lines 35-46). At the end (47-51) even Giovanni begins to feel a trifle embarrassed at his own temerity.

Giovanni need have felt no embarrassment, for his letter evidently reached Dante when he was in a mood for cheerful badinage. In his reply Dante ignored the topic of language entirely, thanked his new friend heartily for the invitation to Bologna (a Guelfic city, closely allied, since 1318, to King Robert of Naples and now ruled by Ranieri di Zaccaria da Orvieto, the very man empowered by Florence, since 1315, to execute any male member of the Alighieri family), and as heartily refused it, adding that, even at so late a date, he still hoped to return to Florence, to receive the laurel crown there. But he was clearly pleased by Giovanni's invitation and promised to send him "ten pails of milk" (i.e., the first ten cantos of the *Paradiso*) when they should be ready.

The poem (sixty-eight Latin hexameters) is expressed throughout in pastoral terms; the cipher would have been immediately obvious to Giovanni del Virgilio and is in fact readily comprehensible even by the casual modern reader.

Evidently Dante could see the humor and pathos of the amiable pedant's request. His refusal to visit Giovanni is gently expressed, and, in ignoring the matter of language, he shows that he hopes that the *Paradiso* will be its own justification. But he humors Giovanni's predilection to the extent of composing his reply in Latin verse, that to the student of Dante is a precious and revealing document.

On receipt of Dante's poem at the hands of Dino Perini, Giovanni was clearly transported with delight and threw himself into the game of pastoral cipher with enthusiasm. In his reply (ninety-seven hexameters) he sympathizes warmly with Dante's hope that Florence will at last relent, drops, as impertinent, the suggestion that he present Dante with the laurel crown at Bologna, and says no more on the use of Latin. But he implores Dante to visit him: the dangers are imaginary, and he can hold out the prospect of meeting the great Mussato, expected in the autumn of 1319. How fortunate if Giovanni could entertain both Dante and Mussato under the same roof.

Dante's reply to Giovanni's epistolary eclogue was not written, according to the scholiast, until at least a year later, which puts it in late 1320 or even in early 1321, the year of Dante's death. There is considerable doubt, however, whether this poem is actually from Dante's hand or not. It is kindly enough in tone, to be sure, but is distinctly inferior in expression and interest to its predecessor.

We lose sight of Giovanni del Virgilio for several years. It is known, however, that in 1321 and 1322 many political exiles, supporters of Romeo dei Pepoli, were driven from Bologna, and that Giovanni was one of them. In 1324 we find him teaching at Cesena; he had changed not at all—he still yearned for recognition as a poet, still revered the memory of Dante, still longed for intimacy with Albertino Mussato.

At this time one of the most influential citizens of Cesena was Rinaldo dei Cenci, who, as Podestà of Padua, late in 1324, had met Mussato there and had praised in his presence Giovanni's merits as teacher and poet; it seems that Mussato was much impressed with what he heard and agreed that the exiled Giovanni also deserved a crown of laurel. On his return to Cesena, Rinaldo strongly urged Giovanni to write to Mussato, a suggestion that must have been met with more than eagerness.

Giovanni's letter to Mussato (summer of 1325) takes the form once more of an epistolary eclogue; under the circumstances it is understandable that it is a long (280 Latin hexameters) and elaborate showpiece. After Giovanni had completed the first 252 lines, he received word of the banishment of Mussato (September, 1325) and delayed sending off the poem to Chioggia: political changes could be extremely rapid in fourteenth-century Italy, and no doubt Giovanni hoped that the great Mussato would soon return in triumph to Padua. No such reversal of fortune occurred, however, and Giovanni, after adding a 28-line postscript (in which he refers to the treachery and downfall of Rinaldo in 1326; he was eventually beheaded in March, 1327), dispatched the poem. We lose sight of Giovanni entirely at this point; we do know, however, that he never did receive his laurel crown. He was a learned man for his time, gentle and upright, vain yet modest, pushing yet retiring, innocently pedantic, but not wholly devoid of poetic imagination. Nor was he entirely without influence; it was probably Giovanni del Virgilio's example that impelled Cecco di Mileto to continue the pastoral tradition, and it was friendship with Cecco that aroused Giovanni Boccaccio's interest in bucolic poetry.

ii

It is quite possible that one of Giovanni del Virgilio's pupils at Cesena was Francesco de' Rossi of nearby Forlì (*floruit* 1320-1356), commonly known as Cecco di Mileto, secretary of Francesco degli Ordelaffi of Forlì and Cesena, and friend of Petrarch and Boccaccio. It is certain that Cecco knew the pastorals of Dante and Del Virgilio; direct reminiscence of the poems is frequent in his two extant eclogues. But the style of these two poems tends to be a little obscure; moreover, the content of neither is of such intrinsic interest as that of Dante's or Del Virgilio's epistolary eclogues.

In 1347 Giovanni Boccaccio paid a visit to Forlì, where he was Ordelaffi's guest. It was no doubt now that he learned from Cecco of the recent revival of pastoral in the form of letters. In any case, before his return to Naples, Boccaccio wrote a short epistolary eclogue addressed to Cecco, urging him to continue to write eclogues. This poem is painful to read, for Boccaccio can scarcely be said to have a Latin style at all; all his work, prose and verse alike, is marred by the grossest Italicisms: a schoolboy who said "je suis marchant" or "sum scribens epistulam" would achieve a similar effect.

Cecco replied with a full-blown epistolary eclogue of fifty-eight hexameters, in which Moeris and Menalcas represent the author and Boccaccio; pastoral cipher, however, is scarcely present at all. In the introduction we are told how Moeris had, at midday, herded his sheep and goats to a shady spot by a river and then, after idly resting for an hour, suddenly realized how much of the day had passed. Here follows Moeris' soliloquy, which we can briefly paraphrase as follows: Foolish Moeris, why are you thus wasting your time? Return to your duty, and either care properly for your flock or sing, as Menalcas has urged you to. Yet nothing is less valued than verses. That was true in the past and is even more true today. Every field is ablaze, the trees give no shade, the animals are neglected; even the birds of the air know that the times are out of joint. If you were to sing, as Menalcas advises, what profit would there be? Who would listen? At this point, writes the poet, Menalcas himself arrived, took Moeris by the hand, and sadly suggested that they seek fairer pastures.

Sometime later, in mid-1348, Boccaccio returned to Naples, almost certainly in the suite of Francesco degli Ordelaffi; he apparently served his "splendid master and dear patron of the Muses" as a sort of traveling secretary, while Cecco remained at Forlì. Boccaccio was also to be historian of the military campaign against Naples in which Ordelaffi was about to take part. In late 1347, while Boccaccio was still at Forlì, the Angevin King Lewis I of Hungary entered Italy at the head of a small but efficient army. Like many another invader of Italy, he was welcomed by an astonishing number of cities—Udine, Cittadella, Vicenza, Bologna, and all the cities of the Romagna except Imola and Faenza. Francesco degli Ordelaffi, Bernardino da Polenta, and Pandolfo Malatesta all received him as a conquering hero and entertained him in the most elaborate manner. Ordelaffi left Forlì in the spring or early summer of 1348 in order to overtake King Lewis, already arrived in the Campagna.

It was at this time, probably after reaching the Campagna, that Boccaccio composed in reply to Cecco's eclogue a long and to us disappointing pastoral of 186 hexameters. It is uninspired, ill-written, and even more artificial than one would have expected; since this bucolic correspondence was initiated as self-conscious imitation, so melancholy a falling-off was perhaps inevitable.

After a brief introduction, Boccaccio tells how one day Menalcas had been startled to hear Testilis (this figure may represent Ordelaffi's wife, Marzia [Cia] degli Ubaldini; more likely the name is a personification of Forlì) lamenting the absence of her husband Faunus, who was hunting in the mountains (we know from one of Boccaccio's prose letters that Ordelaffi was in actual fact extremely addicted to the chase, like many Renaissance nobles; but of course this refers in the pastoral cipher to his absence from Forlì with the army of King Lewis). Testilis reproaches him with neglect of her and of his home and warns him of possible attack by wolves (considering the political climate of Italy, this might refer to attack by almost any northern city or group of cities; in point of fact, Ordelaffi returned from the Campagna after only one month). Menalcas, who had been gathering flowers for Mopsus (i.e., composing a poem, real or imaginary, in honor of Petrarch) is puzzled by the lament, and later, on meeting Moeris, asks for an explanation. Moeris, after assuring Menalcas, at inordinate length, that his earlier remarks on the rewards of poetry are not to be taken too seriously, proceeds to expound what has been happening. He explains that long ago there was a wise shepherd named Argus who ruled over all Sicily and most of southern Italy (the Angevin King Robert the Wise of Naples and Sicily, the Polyphemus of Dante's second eclogue, is meant here; he died in 1343). This passes into a panegyric, expressed in a pastoral cipher that is obvious to the most casual reader. Argus died, however, continues Moeris, lamented by satyrs, fauns, dryads, and the very animals themselves; but on his deathbed he left all his possesions to the gentle shepherd Alexis (this name refers to the Hungarian Angevin Andrew, brother of King Lewis, who had married Giovanna I, granddaughter of King Robert; the statement that Robert had left half of Italy and all of Sicily to Andrew instead of Giovanna certainly represents Hungarian Angevin claims only) who, while hunting down a pride of lions (the reference is to the turbulent barons of Naples) had been killed by an enraged she-wolf (the reference here is to the brutal assassination of Andrew in 1345, in which Giovanna was suspected of complicity; the word *lupa* means "harlot" as well as "she-wolf": many of her contemporaries regarded capricious sensuality as Giovanna's chief characteristic); when Tityrus (King Lewis) heard of this disaster he set out from his home by the river Ister (the Danube) accompanied by all his shepherds and dogs, meaning to destroy the lions and especially the she-wolf that had killed his gentle brother.

But what, interrupts Menalcas, has all this to do with the laments of Testilis? Moeris explains that many of "our own shepherds" had joined Tityrus, among them Faunus himself. Thus, abruptly, the poem comes to a halt.

If Cecco replied to this poem, his answer is lost or else is still lying in manuscript in some Italian library; but the correspondence was to be revived five years later. In 1353 Boccaccio was at Ravenna as the guest of Bernardino da Polenta; we know that in this year he wrote an epistolary eclogue to Cecco—the poem seems lost beyond recovery, but Cecco's reply is still extant in a difficult poem of forty-two hexameters in which little of true pastoral exists, although it is true that Menalcas and Moeris again make their appearance and that a rather outlandish pastoral cipher is employed. It is possible that Boccaccio never did receive this eclogue.

iii

Over the next twenty years (ca. 1350–ca. 1370) Boccaccio completed a group of sixteen further pastorals to which is given the collective name *Bucolicum carmen*. The first two of these were completed at Florence in 1350 or 1351; numbers 3 to 6 form a connected group of poems describing the collapse of the Neapolitan Angevins in 1347 and their restoration in 1348; 7 through 16 are a separate series of ten poems (to be discussed after Petrarch's *Bucolicum carmen*) written under increasingly strong influence of Petrarch's eclogues. Numbers 1 to 6, although in their final form belonging to a period after the meeting (1350) with Petrarch, can best be examined here, since they display a strong affinity with the earlier pastoral "school" of Dante, Giovanni del Virgilio, and Cecco di Mileto.

The first two eclogues appear to have reached their final form after Boccaccio's arrival in Florence in 1350; almost certainly, however, they go back to his Neapolitan experiences—the third poem is the final form of a pastoral written in 1348; the first drafts of 1 and 2 appear to antedate the visit to Ravenna in 1346. Boccaccio spoke slightingly of both 1 and 2 in a letter addressed in 1374(?) to Fra Martino da Signa; but he thought well enough of them in their final form to permit their circulation as part of a finished corpus of pastoral. Neither, as a matter of fact, is of the least value as poetry, and we may give both correspondingly brief treatment.

The first poem is a bucolic dialogue of 138 hexameters, the speakers being two shepherds, Damon and Tyndarus; its central portion is a pastoral lament by Damon over the obduracy of his rustic sweetheart Galla. The second, a poem of 159 hexameters, is a similar lament by Palaemon over Pampinea's hardheartedness. Both poems are literary exercises only, both show rather more skill in employing Virgilian tags than do the poems addressed to Cecco di Mileto, both, by making reference to the river Arno, to leaving Naples, and the like, make it quite clear that their present form belongs to the Florentine period.

It is rather more interesting to turn from the academic frigidities of these two poems to the group of four eclogues that deal in retrospect with the sufferings of Naples during the Hungarian occupation. Even though the influence of the Petrarchan type of eclogue is clearly visible (as a result of later revision) in these four poems, it is more convenient to discuss them here than later.

The third eclogue is a revision of one that we have already met and analyzed—that second poem to Cecco di Mileto in which is described the grief of Testilis at Faunus' absence with Lewis' army in the Campagna. In the revision the management of dialogue among a larger number of speakers shows considerable skill; the poem has otherwise changed very little—it has ceased to be epistolary, but it is still more Dantean than Petrarchan.

The fourth poem of the *Bucolicum carmen* is entitled *Dorus,* and this name is derived, Boccaccio tells us, from a Greek word *doris* (actually nonexistent) meaning "bitterness": the shepherd Dorus represents Louis, Prince of Taranto, Giovanna I's second husband; Montanus represents a typical inhabitant of Volterra; and the name Pythias stands for the great seneschal of Naples, the Florentine Niccolò Acciaiuoli.

Some further examination of historical background is necessary before discussing the fourth eclogue. Giovanna's first husband, Andrew of Hungary, was assassinated, it will be recalled, in 1345 (September 18). Prince Andrew's brother, the Angevin Lewis of Hungary, entered Naples in a mood of savage reprisal in January, 1347, promptly placed the government of the kingdom into the hands of men of his choice, and then, to avoid the plague raging in Naples, left the city for Barletta in March. Giovanna now married her cousin, Louis of Taranto (August 20, 1347), who took command of the Neapolitan forces. Louis' resistance to the King of Hungary proved far from successful; Giovanna accordingly abandoned Naples by sea for Provence on January 15, 1348, and, a few days later, Louis himself, accompanied only by Acciaiuoli, fled to Tuscany, from which he eventually passed on to Provence, joining Giovanna at Avignon.

When we turn to the fourth poem, we shall expect the above events to appear more or less dimly behind a pastoral veil. The scene of the eclogue is the approaches to the Tuscan town of Volterra (southwest of Florence), and the first shepherd to appear, Montanus, represents the hospitable Volterrans by whom Louis, it would seem, was welcomed and entertained on his northward flight.

Montanus asks Dorus why he is hurrying and suggests that, since it is still early, he should stop and rest; on Dorus' replying that he is afraid to stop and that he is seeking not comfort but safety, Montanus insists that he can provide both. With the help of Pythias, Montanus finally persuades Dorus to rest in a rustic grotto while Galatea prepares a meal and also to explain why he is in flight.

After a brief lament over his ill-fortune, Dorus explains that the territories once ruled by Campanians and Calabrians were until recently in the possession of Argus (once again, Robert of Sicily). His successor, the unhappy shepherd Alexis (Andrew of Hungary) was loathed by his flocks (the Neapolitan barons) and met a hideous death. Then, says Dorus, I was, thanks to Pythias, married to the fair Lycoris, and with her I lived happily until I learned that my own kinsman, the monstrous Polyphemus (even in eclogue iii, Boccaccio had been less pro-Hungarian than in the original draft of the poem, but Giovanna was still the *lupa* and King Lewis was still the handsome youth Tityrus; here Giovanna has become "the fair Lycoris," and King Lewis is shown as the villain of the piece) had left his native river Ister.

Dorus goes on to give a gruesome description of the fury of Polyphemus' attack on Naples, his brutal execution of Paphus (Charles of Durazzo), and the havoc caused in the Campagna, and to describe how many nobles had actually joined forces with "the monster" and how Naïs (Maria, wife of Charles) had escaped with her two children. Montanus asks whether Dorus' closest friends had remained faithful and is told that only Pythias has stayed by Dorus' side. Together, Dorus continues, we fled the hideous savagery of the monster (*infandam monstri rabiem*), first to the shores of Telamon (i.e., Talamone Vecchio) and now to Volterra.

Montanus replies that whatever he owns is at Dorus' service and that an omen now tells him that after more suffering Dorus will eventually return to his home: "Barren hope will often lead you on; yet whatever you have lost you will regain by delaying; the laurel of victory will not be yours until you send one certain head to the shades. But Galatea is calling; the lambs and sheep are returning, and night is darkening the earth with its shades."

The fifth eclogue (*Silva cadens:* "The Ruined Grove"; 139 hexameters) deals with the same subject matter as iii and iv, and here Boccaccio's change of heart is even clearer, for the poem resolves itself into a panegyric of the Angevin dynasty of Naples, especially of King Robert, and a long lament over the misfortunes of the Kingdom of Naples.

The sixth eclogue (*Alcestus*; 66 hexameters) is the last of the Neapolitan or Angevin poems; it deals with the return of Louis of Taranto from Avignon to Naples (late August, 1348; Giovanna returned at the same time, but is not so much as mentioned: the reader may draw his own conclusions). Its central portion (lines 100 to 140) are a paean of praise to the Angevin dynasty and especially to prince Louis. It is a lengthy and elaborate poem, composed wholly in dialogue—in the Petrarchan manner—that is carefully arranged and disposed. It is rhetorical in tone and filled full of nearly every pastoral motif that Boccaccio could think of; it shows a great advance in Latinity over the first epistle to Cecco di Mileto, although it would still have seemed crude and almost medieval to Pietro Bembo or the Amalteo brothers. It is worth noting that a pleasant Virgilian refrain appears in Amyntas' panegyric of Prince Louis ("plaudite iam colles, et vos iam plaudite, montes"); the use of this device was to have a long history in the bucolic poetry of the fifteenth, sixteenth, and seventeenth centuries.

iv

Far different from, and far more difficult than any of the eclogues so far discussed are the mystifyingly allegorical and cryptic pastorals of symbolism written by Francesco Petrarca (1304-1374), who produced a round dozen of the most puzzling poems imaginable: eclogues i-iv and the early part of xii were written hastily at Vaucluse near Avignon in the summer of 1346; the remainder were composed at various times between this date and 1357. These twelve eclogues, composed in a Latin sometimes turgid and obscure, are in addition so opaque in meaning that not only did scholars like Benvenuto Rambaldo of Imola and Francesco Piendibeni of Montepulciano establish critical reputations by writing commentaries that explained the worst difficulties, but even their self-conscious author felt impelled to provide his admiring but deeply puzzled friends with a key. In a letter to Cola Rienzo, the revolutionary tribune of Rome, Petrarch bluntly states that the nature of pastoral poetry is such that it is entirely incomprehensible ("ut . . . omnino non possit intellegi") unless the author expounds it himself. And, in a letter to his own brother Gherardo, Petrarch sets out at some length his view of poetry and especially of bucolic poetry. Cryptic allegory—and this is something far more complicated than any ordinary pastoral cipher—is to Petrarch no mere rhetorical device of style; on the contrary, it is the very heart and soul of poetry: "it is from allegory that all poetry is formed" ("poetica omnis intexta est"). The more allegory, the better the poem; the more cryptic the meaning, the more all pervading the symbolism, the better the poet. (It is only fair to add that Petrarch was not alone in such notions; critics had long been hunting for allegorical and anagogic meanings in the *Commedia*).

Now it is perfectly true that Virgil, in his bucolic poems, employed oblique allusions to personal and contemporary matters; but he did so only to a limited extent, so that his allusions would have been readily understood or at least suspected, by any informed reader of his own day—and even if they had not, the enjoyment of any of the eclogues would not have depended wholly upon catching the allusions. As for the eclogues of Dante, Giovanni del Virgilio, Cecco di Mileto, and the earlier bucolic poems of Boccaccio, a reader unaware of the precise circumstances would still be able to follow and enjoy the poems as they stand; the poems can, in other words, be read on two levels of understanding. But in Petrarch's work the eclogue has become a vehicle for the most medieval kind of riddling; *the allusions are everything, and the classical form is wholly incidental to the mystification.* The paradoxical result is that we can with a good show of reason call the medieval Dante's eclogues classical and Humanist Petrarch's medieval.

The chief importance of Petrarch's eclogues lies in the fact that they tell the modern student an enormous amount about events and personalities of the fourteenth century in France and Italy. Such a poem as the seventh eclogue of Petrarch's *Bucolicum carmen* is a most valuable primary historical source, and when it is subjected to searching analysis by so profound a student of Italian literature as Ernest H. Wilkins the results are anything but negligible. The twelve poems are in addition equally important evidence for the life, thought, and personality (not always attractive) of one of the greatest of European poets. Yet, no matter how great the importance that we attach to the content of Petrarch's eclogues, we can never say of them—as has been said of the *Epistulae metricae*—that if they had only been written in the vernacular they would today be regarded as being among the most important works of Italian literature.

The first eclogue (124 hexameters) is given the name "Parthenias," the reference being to Virgil. At first reading the poem appears to be no more than a rather puzzling dialogue between two shepherds named Silvius and Monicus. But Petrarch's comments on the true nature of pastoral verse—or what he considered the true nature of pastoral verse—remind us that in each of the eclogues the poet presents us with a riddle. Perhaps Silvius is the author himself. If so, what about Monicus, and what is the point of their highly cryptic conversation? The answers are to be found in Petrarch's *Familiar Letters* X, iv, addressed to the poet's brother Gherardo, a Carthusian monk. Sure enough, Silvius is Petrarch himself; Monicus (a disguised form, says Petrarch, of *monoculus,* one who observes the world from one point of view only—the religious) is Gherardo; and in their conversation Monicus' sheltered cave is the monastery to which he belonged; the countryside and the flock are the secular world and laymen in general; *sepulcrum* represents the afterworld—Heaven or Hell, as the case may be; the hill to which Silvius wishes to make his way symbolizes fame; the desert in which he wanders during that journey is profane scholarship, or rather the purely profane approach to scholarship; the crags in the shade of which he rests symbolize support given by patrons, and the moss on those crags represents the patrons' wealth; the exhilarating springs at which Silvius refreshes himself are the inspired writings of the great; the bristling wood at which he shudders is that unlettered, unlearned mob for which Petrarch never felt anything but the profoundest contempt; descent and ascent stand for theory and practice, and the like.

This eclogue as a whole presents to us—as do the *Secretum,* the *De otio religiosorum,* and many of the vernacular *Rime*—Francesco and Gherardo's contrary enthusiasms, the contrast, that is, between human and divine, secular and religious, classical and medieval, literary and theological. Monicus urges his brother Silvius to abandon the vanities of the world; Silvius replies with what amounts to a panegyric of poetry, of fame, of Roman antiquity, and (whether this is intentional or not) implies that it is far more worthy of a man of intelligence and energy to pursue a difficult ideal than to rest in the peace of the monastery, no matter how seductive that peace may seem in moments of failure and dejection.

In Petrarch's second eclogue (*Argus*; 124 hexameters) we have the monologue of a shepherd named Ideus; the setting, to be sure, is conscientiously classical, but here as elsewhere the most important aspect of the work—to Petrarch's mind, at least—is the *arcana significatio* of the shepherds' names and, especially in the first half of the poem, the obscure symbolism attaching to details which at first reading might seem only casual or decorative. The key is given in number 49 of Petrarch's *Various Letters,* in which we are told that Ideus ("he of Mt. Ida," i.e., Jupiter) represents Giovanni Barrili, the Neapolitan soldier and statesman, grand seneschal of King Robert ("Argus"), whose manners were as gentle as the influence of the benign planet Jupiter, that Pythias is Petrarch's old friend, Barrili's successor in office, Marco Barbato of Sulmona, and that Silvius is the poet himself. But for a detailed exposition of the poem one must turn to the fourteenth-century commentaries on the *Bucolicum carmen* published by Antonio Avena in 1906.

The interest of the first eclogue is mainly psychological; that of the second is historical and literary (if by "literary" we mean that the poem illustrates the strange notion that the more recondite and obscure the symbolism the more effective the poem); the third poem is again important chiefly from a psychological point of view. This ecologue (*Amor pastorius*; 164 hexameters) deals with the nature of sacred and profane love—the love of woman being contrasted with that of fame. The shepherd Stupeus ("hempen," hemp being notoriously inflammable; the implication is that the shepherd was as susceptible to sexual love as to the love of glory) represents the poet himself, and his lover Daphne ("laurel") represents the two aspects of love—at one time she is Laura de Noves (1307/8-1348), wife of Hugues de Sade of Avignon, at another a symbol of the laurel crown of poetry that Petrarch had always coveted so ardently. The laurel crown is not to be taken literally as the actual crown awarded to Petrarch at Rome, but to poetic fame generally.

The reference in eclogue ii to the sun's love for the cypress was derived from Ovid's *Metamorphoses*; so here Petrarch adapts from the same poem the well-known story of Apollo's pursuit of Daphne, who escaped divine *amor* only by being metamorphosed into a laurel. Now it is the poet himself who pursues a sweetheart who at the end is transformed into or revealed as his passport to fame; the allegory can be taken as an extended Latin example of the *petrarchismo* of the vernacular poems. We have passed beyond the cryptic puerilities of the second eclogue to what Carrara rightly calls "la bella poesia del trionfo, che ripete immaginosamente l'eterna storia dell' animo del poeta." It should be further noted that throughout this poem Petrarch's diction is so artfully contrived that it is quite possible to equate Daphne with poetry from the very first line and at the same time to regard her figure as gradually changing in the course of the poem from Laura to poetry. Donato degli Albanzani (who had discussed the poem with Petrarch himself) laboriously explains each *double-entendre* in his practically line-by-line commentary; it is excruciatingly long-winded, but useful as proof that I am not attempting to read more into the pastorals than was actually intended by their author.

In the much briefer fourth eclogue (*Daedalus*; 75 hexameters), the subject of poetry as a basis for an outlook on life is continued from the first and third poems. Here we have a dialogue between two shepherds named Gallus ("French") and Tyrrhenus ("Florentine"): the latter is obviously Petrarch; in the commentaries Gallus is identified as a French soldier of some education or as a French musician, who had admired Petrarch's literary gifts and had asked him to train him as a poet; it appears that his Christian name was Philippe. Petrarch replies, in a poem in which quite ordinary pastoral cipher replaces cryptic symbolism, that such a gift as poetry comes only from inventive nature (Daedalus). It is certainly one of the more immediately attractive poems of the *Bucolicum carmen*.

The eclogue is an affirmation of Petrarch's belief that poetry is a divine gift, that no amount of training can ever make up for lack of inborn talent; if some lines seem arrogant, it was at least a sincere arrogance, aroused by a request that seems stupid to us but perhaps not so stupid to some of Petrarch's contemporaries who looked on versification as a diverting technical skill that could be acquired by good (i.e., efficient) teaching and diligent practice.

The fifth eclogue (*Pietas pastoralis*; 141 hexameters) is political, like the second. Here the shepherds Martius and Apicius discuss ways and means of assisting their mother in her decrepit old age; while they talk, the third brother, Festinus, acts. The earliest key to what seems on the surface a purely literary composition with puzzling overtones of allusion appears in a letter (number 42 of the *Various Letters* of Petrarch) addressed to Cola Rienzo:

This poem, sir, I send to you as a relaxation from your many cares. However, since the nature of this type of composition is such that it cannot be understood at all unless the author himself expounds it, . . . I shall briefly explain my fundamental intention.   The two shepherds represent two sorts of citizen who live in the same community but have widely differing political ideas: the one is Martius (that is, "warlike" and "restless" [by this name Petrarch clearly means the Colonna faction in Rome, although he does not say so]), . . . who is dutiful and compassionate towards his mother, who is the city of Rome; the other brother . . . is Apicius, . . . by whom the reader can understand those who devote themselves to pleasure and sloth [the name is derived from that of a notorious Roman gourmet who lived under Augustus and Tiberius; Petrarch clearly means the Orsini family; again he avoids being explicit, perhaps because (as Cicero once remarked) he was afraid that someone might lighten the letter by reading it].   Between these two there has arisen a difference about the duty each owes to their aged mother, especially in regard to restoring her one-time home (by that I mean the Capitol) and the bridge over which she used to go to her country home (that is, the Milvian Bridge) over a river (namely, the Tiber) that descends from the lofty summit of the Apennine range. . . ."

And so this letter goes on, in more and more detail: the pastoral shepherd, for instance, who had once killed marauding thieves [i.e., the Catilinarian conspirators] on the bridge is explained as Cicero, the Roman consul of 63 B.C., and his flock as the Roman people he once ruled.   While Martius and Apicius still argue over their duty, a bird appears; this is Fama (Rumor), who tells them that their mother has disinherited and abandoned them for the youthful Festinus (the derivation of the name from *festinare* "to hurry" is obvious), who has already rebuilt her home (the reference to the exciting events in Rome in 1346 and 1347 is equally obvious) for her: "That brother," writes Petrarch, "is your own self."

All this may seem pedantic and frigid; but Cola Rienzo's short-lived revolution seemed to Petrarch the greatest and noblest adventure of the age.   There is no question that this eclogue is the expression of a deeply-felt enthusiasm, difficult as it may at first be for the twentieth-century reader to understand Petrarch's choice of medium.   Two considerations were probably paramount in his mind: in the first place, the choice of Latin, to Petrarch the most splendid of tongues, was the only appropriate one in addressing the man who was to revive the grandeur that was Rome; in the second, the allegorical obscurity inseparable (in Petrarch's view) from pastoral made it one of the most impressive vehicles possible. And while this eclogue, unlike the fourth, will probably strike the modern reader as one of the least attractive of all the poems in the *Bucolicum carmen,* it is worth reading with care as being wholly characteristic of the developed fourteenth-century pastoral.

The sixth eclogue (*Pastorum pathos;* 210 hexameters), like the seventh, obscures with a veil of cryptic pastoral a theme which is common in Petrarch's *Untitled Letters*—detestation of the Papal court at Avignon. Two shepherds appear—Pamphilus, who represents St. Peter, and Mitio, who represents Pope Clement VI. The poem begins with Pamphilus' lament, *solus,* over the state of the farms of the countryside (i.e., over the state of the Church); the glades and wood are ravaged, disease is destroying the crops and herds, and so on. Mitio, overhearing him, mutters to himself that this idle fellow with his stone and his keys is forever complaining, and then, for all the world like a character in Plautus or Terence, remarks to an imaginary audience that he will approach Pamphilus and use all his blandishments on him.

Pamphilus, himself like an angry old man in New Comedy rounding on an impudent slave, calls Mitio "gallows-rogue" (*furcifer*), marvels that the earth has not yet swallowed him up, and describes in more detail the pitiable state of the flock that has been entrusted to Mitio. Mitio shrugs his shoulders and replies that these reproaches are only what he might have expected. It is easy to talk, he adds; if *you,* Pamphilus, were the shepherd, would the wolves be less fierce, the winter less bitter, the spring less unpredictable, the summer less hot, the autumn less dangerous to health?

I was myself once the shepherd of this flock, replies Pamphilus, at the time when Nereus (Nero) was at his most savage. Quite so, answers Mitio, and as a result the flock was slaughtered, as were you; I wish to experience nothing of this sort. Yet, insists Pamphilus, from the dead members of the flock I could send purest white fleeces (souls) to the city (Heaven) of my Master; what can *you* send to him?

Mitio's reply is most imprudent. I have stored up, he says, vast quantities of gold from the sale of young lambs (presumably this is intended to call up hideous visions of simony); I am dressed with the utmost splendor; my wife (the Church) is as magnificently clothed, and rests at her ease with me here in the shade: she is a very queen, unlike that ill-clad, ill-nourished wife of yours (the Apostolic Church).

The allegorical reply of Pamphilus requires no comment. He insists that it is madness to court danger thus, for such wealth will attract thieves, and a wife of such easy virtue will never prove faithful; Mitio will find that she has been committing adultery with those he considered his closest friends. More, if he will but raise his drunken face, he will see that wolves and thieves are about to attack his sheep-folds: the reference here may be a general one to heresy or may, as Benvenuto Rambaldo suggests in his commentary, refer specifically to the King of France; the latter is more likely.

Mitio ignores the aspersions on his wife's chastity, replying that he has already made a compact with the Devil to protect him from wolves and thieves: the compact was even signed in pig's blood. He insists that no matter what happens to his flocks, *he* will always be rich.

Pamphilus exclaims at this abominable pact. At least Mitio should return from this forest (Avignon) to his ancestral home (Rome); he may rest assured that the "notorious harlot" will follow, bringing with her all her suitors and especially those stinking goats (cardinals) that so loved the lush fodder of a foreign marsh (if the reader thinks Petrarch's language strong, let him read some of the *Familiar Letters* and the *Untitled Letters*).

Mitio assumes an injured air: after leaving him in peace for so long why does Pamphilus now assail him? On receiving further reproaches, Mitio loses his temper and accuses Pamphilus of having abandoned his own flock in the days of "Nereus" and being stopped only by a vision of Apollo (Christ). Pamphilus angrily replies that anyone can be afraid, but that Mitio had no such reason to flee from Rome as he had had. Shall I then, asks Mitio, return to become the slave of a poverty-stricken fold? I have found a lovely sweetheart, cool caves, wealth; boast as you will of your unknown loves (i.e., the virtues). Pamphilus replies that Mitio is as bad as his predecessor Epycus (Pope Benedict XI), who had pursued the same woman as was now wed to Mitio; while Mitio seeks to adorn his person with roses and admires the effect in a mirror given to him by Corydon (i.e., the Byzantine Emperor Constantine), all goes to rack and ruin.

In a passage which must have been added to this poem after 1352 (the date of Clement's death and Innocent VI's succession), Mitio ironically suggests that his successor may be worse, but is promptly told that it is nonsense to excuse crime with crime. Let Mitio recall what their Master had himself once endured. Their Master, says

Mitio, was a fool, greedy for sheep; more, he insisted on the hardest possible methods even for sheep that were not worth the trouble of saving; better to keep the easily-herded sheep with a minimum of effort, to allow the few unruly ones to escape, and to enjoy a reputation for clemency. This speech of Mitio is long and elaborate; the symbols are many and are dutifully explained in Rambaldo's commentary.

The pastoral comes to an end with two couplets: "Unhappy man," cries out Pamphilus, "is it thus that you understand our Master? While you think that you stand there safely in the shade, He will come, and will change your joy to sorrow." Mitio, his arrogance unabated, replies, "Do you try to terrify me with words? The brave despise present dangers; distant ones can terrify only fools."

The seventh eclogue (*Grex infectus et Grex suffectus*; 143 hexameters) again deals with the Roman *curia* at Avignon; the speakers are Mitio (Pope Clement again) and Epy (his *amica*, i.e., the Church, or, more properly, the Papal court at Avignon). The poem is undoubtedly of great historical importance; but (as Carrara remarks) any aesthetic judgment of the poem can only be unfavorable: it is full of a confused and cryptic symbolism, it lacks dramatic interest, and above all its very fame later encouraged among other poets "a vast series of symbolic flocks, starting with Boccaccio" ("un' ingente seguito di greggi simbolici, a cominciar dal Boccaccio"). It stirs, in fact, no emotion higher than the urge to delve below the surface meaning in order to identify the various cardinals whom the poet attacks with such venomous freedom; this has, as a matter of fact, been carefully done by the scholar best qualified to do so—Ernest H. Wilkins, in his *Studies in the Life and Works of Petrarch*—and it is to his essay that the reader should turn for details.

The present-day reader will find more to interest him in the eighth eclogue (*Divortium*; 126 hexameters written in eleven days), in which we again find a poem of much personal and psychological interest: it is an explanation of the reasons for Petrarch's abandoning Avignon and a justification of the poet's extremely shabby return for the invariable generosity, patience, and understanding of his patron, Cardinal Giovanni Colonna, written (like number vi) at the time of Cola Rienzo's bloodless revolution in Rome. In this eclogue the shepherd Ganymede represents the Cardinal, Amyclas the poet. The choice of names is explained by Rambaldo: just as the obscure shepherd-boy Ganymede had been snatched up to Heaven from Mount Ida by Jove's eagle, so also was Colonna raised to the cardinalate from the obscurity of Praeneste; the original Amyclas was a character in the fifth book (line 520) of Lucan's *Pharsalia,* where he is shown to be as poor and as happy as Petrarch loved to portray his own self.

In the conversation between Ganymede and Amyclas we have not, of course, the record of any actual exchange, but a *pièce justificative* in which Petrarch does his best to exculpate himself from a charge of ingratitude. It is not an edifying piece of work: Petrarch shows little appreciation of the benefits, financial and otherwise, that he had received from 1330 to 1347; he charges that his patron had grown harsh and unsympathetic and that he himself had entered the Cardinal's service (which he actually calls "slavery") poor and was leaving it poorer still, statements which are quite untrue. The conclusion of the poem, in which Ganymede dismisses Amyclas angrily, is remarkably tactless, as is Amyclas' retort that troubles await his one-time friend. The only part of the poem, in fact, that corresponds to the truth is that passage in which the poet insists on his love of independence in Italy and his dislike for Avignon.

Petrarch left Avignon in 1347 and, after a short stay at Verona, passed on to Parma to enjoy the hospitality of Azzo da Correggio. Within a year Giovanni Colonna and Laura de Sade were both dead of the plague: 1348 was the dreadful year of the Black Death. The first eight eclogues are connected with Petrarch's life at Vaucluse, his political views, and his attitude to the Babylonian captivity of the Papacy; the next three poems, "the eclogues of sorrow" (*le egloghe del dolore*) as Italian critics (e.g., Benfenati) call them, all refer to the Black Death and, in greater or less degree, to Laura.

The ninth eclogue (*Querulus;* 100 hexameters) is a lament over the disastrous results of the Black Death and an affirmation of the poet's belief in God and hope of Heaven. As usual, the interlocutors are two in number—Philogeus ("Earth-lover," i.e., any lover of the material) and Theophilus ("Lover of God," presumably the poet himself; perhaps the names merely represent the two sides of anyone's nature—neither of the commentaries on this poem and none of the glosses attempts any identification). The first countryman laments the desolation caused by the plague throughout the whole countryside: the rustic population is decimated, animals wander masterless and starving, crops rot everywhere, and all this is the direct result of the greed of traders who have brought the disease back with them from the Orient. Theophilus, who has spoken scarcely at all throughout the long tirade against fortune, now gives Philogeus the advice which Petrarch would have given himself (lines 87-96 and 99-100) : turn your eyes upward to the path which leads straight to Heaven, difficult though it is and trodden as it is by only a few.

This, of course, is a far easier poem than any of the first eight; so, in general outline, is the tenth eclogue (*Laurea occidens*; 413 hexameters), although its elaborate (and, to the modern reader, unnecessary) display of classical learning makes it heavy going. Here the shepherd Silvanus (Petrarch himself) tells his friend Socrates (as constantly in the *Familiar Letters* and the *Epistulae metricae* this name stands for the German Ludovicus Sanctus of Beeringen, an associate of Cardinal Giovanni Colonna and a close friend of the poet) of his early life—as we should expect, the narrative is throughout intentionally obscured by pastoral allegory. The poet tells how he was raised amid quiet meadows (i.e., Carpentras), left these and traveled widely (this at least is not allegorical, for Petrarch's constant changes of residence still present difficulties to a student of the poet's life), met many great authors (this refers to Petrarch's vast reading in classical and patristic Latin literature), and on his return discovered that a fearful tempest (the Black Death) had destroyed the beautiful tree (Laura de Sade) that grew by the stream near his home. So much is easy; but for the interpretation of specific details referring to contemporary matters, one must turn to the commentators and glossators. And how many of us today could instantly identify the sources for Petrarch's references to such Latin poets of the Augustan Age (now lost) as Fontanus, Carus, Dossennus (not in fact a writer), Melissus, Passienus, Largus, Votienus, and so on? Of course the versified list of authors (many of whom are, incidentally, referred to only allusively) is of considerable historical importance, since it tells us how much was known about Latin literature in the mid-fourteenth century as opposed to the early Middle Ages; yet, like many of the more elaborate of the *Familiar Letters,* the poem would be greatly benefited aesthetically by drastic abridgment of this interminable catalogue. Petrarch evidently did not think so, however, for it seems that, long after the poem was written, he continued to revise and expand the catalogue as his knowledge of Latin poetry was extended and deepened. But the tenth eclogue is worth reading, if only for the lament over Laura's death contained in lines 353-97; and the words with which Socrates attempts to comfort Silvanus (400-8) are particularly interesting to the modern student, summing up as they do the dominant theme of the second part of Petrarch's *Canzoniere*.

The eleventh eclogue (*Galatea*; 102 hexameters) is again directly concerned with Laura, elaborating the theme of lament and consolation that had already appeared in the tenth poem. This theme, which became extremely common in the pastoral of the Renaissance proper, is worked out in precisely the same manner as it is in many of the *epistulae consolatoriae* of the *Familiar Letters*.

The twelfth and last eclogue (*Conflictatio*; 160 hexameters) is political; part was written as early as 1346 or 1347—other passages must on internal evidence be assigned to 1356 at the earliest or 1357 at the latest. There are two speakers—Multivolus, representing the common people, and Volucer, a stock figure of a messenger. In their conversation, the woman Faustula is the Papal court of Avignon, Pan is Philip of France, Arthicus is Edward III of England. The earlier part of the poem, describing events to the Battle of Crécy (1346), is marked by bitter hostility to the *curia* and Philip; the conclusion, dealing with the course of history from 1350, when King John succeeded Philip, until 1356 (the date of the Battle of Poitiers) is marked by a considerable mellowing—Petrarch's diplomatic work for the Visconti court, his embassies, his closer relations with cardinals earlier called "stinking goats," and, in particular, his being invited to Paris by the French king all have a share in accounting for this change of heart. Carrara's comment on the phenomenon is well worth quoting: "ma noi sappiamo troppo bene quanto il cuore degli uomini, nel raffreddarsi dell' età, ami il tepore del sole cortigiano"; it is also worth suggesting that the reader examine the twenty-sixth of Petrarch's *Various Letters* for purposes of comparison.

v

Now that we have examined all twelve of Petrarch's eclogues, we must revert to the *Bucolicum carmen* of Giovanni Boccaccio. It will be recalled that the first six eclogues of this collection, while full of pastoral cipher, were never so cryptic as Petrarch's; Boccaccio began his pastorals under the influence, in other words, of Dante. But after meeting Petrarch in Florence (1350) he came to regard poems of earlier eclogists, including himself, as *ignobiles* and accordingly turned from mere pastoral cipher to pastoral cyptogram: eclogues vii-xvi are quite as difficult as anything in Petrarch.

For the moment we shall postpone discussion of the seventh eclogue, which is closely connected with the ninth, and begin our examination of the Petrarchan poems of the *Bucolicum carmen* with the eighth (*Midas*; 160 hexameters), which, although written in Florence after the meeting with Petrarch, still deals with the lamentable history of Naples and is therefore closely associated in content with eclogues i-vi.

In the eighth poem Niccolò Acciaiuoli, once presented as the faithful Pythias, the one true friend of Louis of Tarentum, is now displayed as Midas, a very monster of ignorance and greed: his greed is as insatiable as that of King Midas himself, and his stupidity and ignorance merit the ass's ears that appear in another form of the Midas legend.

In brief, the eclogue describes how an honest shepherd named Pythias had been lured by false promises into Midas' realm, but is strongly advised by his old friend Damon to leave while the opportunity is still open to him. These circumstances so closely parallel Boccaccio's invitation to Naples in 1361 (1362?) and his subsequent (1362 and 1363) disillusionment that it is hard not to interpret the poem accordingly, especially since the one document describing this episode in Boccaccio's life—a translation into Italian by some unknown of a Latin letter (the original, except for a small fragment, has been lost) of Boccaccio—is clearly genuine.

In 1361, Zanobi da Strada, a close friend of Petrarch living as a protégé of Niccolò Acciaiuoli at Naples, was appointed apostolic secretary, and duly left Naples for Avignon. To fill the vacancy in his household, Acciaiuoli invited Boccaccio to leave Florence and once more settle in Naples. After a brief visit to Petrarch in Padua, Boccaccio packed up all his belongings and proceeded happily to the Regno di Napoli, certain that he would now achieve comfort and tranquillity under the protection of the Great Seneschal.

His welcome did not come up to his expectations. The lodging provided for him was verminous, his bed dirty and uncomfortable, the food unattractive, the dishes filthy; as the author of the *Decamerone* and the *De casibus* he felt himself worthy if not of honor at least of cleanliness. After two months of this, Boccaccio accepted the hospitality of a young fellow-Florentine, Mainardo dei Cavalcanti. On receiving an invitation to stay at Acciaiuoli's own villa at Tripergoli (near Baia), Boccaccio became more hopeful, but discovered that the accommodation now provided for him was as lamentable as at first; worse still, when Acciaiuoli finally returned from Sicily to Naples, Boccaccio, far from being invited into the great man's presence, was left to kick his heels, and, when he complained, received an unmistakable hint that he would be well advised to return to his first lodging. At this point he not unnaturally departed in wrath to Venice, there to meet Petrarch, and, incidentally, to receive an astoundingly impertinent letter from Francesco Nelli (one of Petrarch's dearest friends) chiding him for excessive impetuosity: Boccaccio's reply to Nelli contains the whole history of the unfortunate venture and a virulent attack on Acciaiuoli. All this may well explain the background of the eighth eclogue.

Eclogues vii (*Iurgium*; 138 hexameters) and ix (*Lipis*; 198 hexameters) form a pair, both dealing with relations between Florence and the grandson of Henry VII, Charles IV of Luxemburg (King of Bohemia, King of Germany, and Holy Roman Emperor) in early 1355. At this date the Emperor, soon to be crowned at Rome (April 2, 1355), was in Pisa (January, 1355), where he received ambassadors from Guelfic (i.e., anti-Imperial) Florence. Unlike his predecessors, Charles realized that times had changed and that the notion of a universal Christian empire could no longer be entertained. He was ambitious, however, for the actual title of Emperor, and readily made his peace with the Pope, even going so far as to leave Rome on the evening of the very day of his coronation: he was anxious to give no one the opportunity of even hinting that he considered Rome his capital. But he was eager also for gold, and, on leaving Rome, proceeded to visit city after city to squeeze out as much money as possible; as Matteo Villani remarked, he was successful in returning home with a full purse ("colla borsa piena di danari").

In January, 1355, Charles received ambassadors from Florence at Pisa. The ambassadors cynically expressed contemptuous devotion, and after much hard bargaining the Emperor gained what he wanted (100,000 gold florins and the promise of an annual tribute of 4,000) in return for more, probably, than he had intended to grant: he confirmed all franchises, privileges, and liberties of Florence, revoked all condemnations and sentences ever pronounced against Florence and the Florentines by earlier Emperors, and promised never to interfere in the internal government of the republic.

Before leaving Pisa the Emperor invited the Florentines to make common cause with him against the Visconti of Milan. This, however, they refused to do, "being anxious, just then," says the historian Scipione Ammirato, "to have peace abroad in order that they might have leisure to fight with each other at home."

In the seventh eclogue (*The Quarrel*; 138 hexameters written between January 18 and April 2, 1355), we have a lengthy dialogue between Florida (Florence) and Daphnis (the Emperor Charles: it is worth noting that Boccaccio's name for the Emperor is not a reminiscence of Virgil, as Carrara supposes, but, as Boccaccio himself tells us elsewhere, of Ovid, who had said that Daphnis was "son of Mercury and first among all shepherds"). The first half of the poem (lines 1-77) consists of insults and recriminations on both sides, ending with Florida's claim that she is at least a free and honorable woman.

Here Daphnis bursts into a lengthy piece of vituperation: you are no free woman, but the veriest strumpet; your guards are German and other mercenaries (this was the age of men like Count Lando, Fra Moriale, and Sir John Hawkwood), the lowest of the low: such men as these I will not compliment with arrows, but will beat with sticks (the Emperor was later to suffer a shattering defeat in 1368 at the hands of Sir John Hawkwood). As for yourself, Florida, do not concern yourself with matters of political moment; rather, gather flowers, make garlands for the effeminate, over-dressed young men of your city, and encourage them to indulge in their famous sports.

At this Florida voices her loathing for all barbarous Germans: the passage expresses most eloquently the hatred and contempt felt by all Italians for that ever returning incubus, the German Emperor. In reply Daphnis asks indignantly if he must contend with frogs: let me commend you to your sons, he says, who can deck you in the finery you love so well. Florida, however, succeeds in having the last word: contemptuously she offers the golden apples of the Hesperides (the 100,000 florins) as a cure for Daphnis' madness.

In the ninth eclogue (*Anxiety*; 198 hexameters written in May, 1355) the same theme is continued. The title refers to the anxiety felt by Florence over the coronation of Charles; of the interlocutors the woman Batrachos ("frog") represents Florence itself and more particularly the allegedly garrulous nature of the Florentine people ("loquacissimi enim sumus, verum in bellicis nil valemus," says Boccaccio elsewhere) while Arcas ("the Arcadian," i.e., some pastoral shepherd) represents any non-Florentine. The far from complimentary name given to the figure representing Florence is odd but characteristic of the author. Boccaccio is strongly Guelfic, it is true, but his attitude to Florence is far different from Dante's or Petrarch's: Dante is the idealistic lover of Florence, Petrarch is Italian in sentiment rather than Florentine, while the realistic Boccaccio takes a cynical look at his fellow citizens and sums them up as "quegli ingrati meccanici, nimici di bene adoperare."

We come now to a group of nonpolitical eclogues: after i-vi (Neapolitan) and vii-ix (anti-Neapolitan and anti-Imperial), x-xv are "mystic" and religious or deal with the nature of poetry—they are even more strongly Petrarchan than vii-ix; they belong to the period 1355-1362. Eclogue xvi dedicates the whole collection to Donato degli Albanzani; it was probably written about 1365 or 1366, and revision of the entire *Bucolicum carmen* was probably completed by 1369: for over twenty years, then, Boccaccio had occupied himself, off and on, with pastoral themes.

The tenth eclogue (*Vallis opaca*; 175 hexameters) contains a number of specific reminiscences of Dante; in addition, the general *mise-en-scène* seems intentionally modeled on the passage in the *Divina Commedia* in which the dead Brunetto Latini converses with Dante—Carrara is right to call this eclogue "a bucolic *Inferno.*" Of the two speakers in this poem, the shepherd Lycidas, whose spirit has returned to earth from the "Shadowy Valley," represents a contemporary prince of wolfish character (Boccaccio connects "Lycidas" with the Greek word *lykos* "wolf"). Unfortunately, it is as impossible to identify the man in question as to explain the many historical and contemporary allusions that the eclogue contains—their elucidation depends in large part on the identity of Lycidas. As for the other speaker Dorilus (his name, like that of Dorus, is derived by the poet from a nonexistent Greek word *doris,* "bitterness"), various attempts have been made to identify him with Francesco degli Ordelaffi (so de' Hortis), the Duke of Athens (so Carazzini), or an unknown informer (so de' Rossetti); it is not impossible that Dorilus represents the author himself (Boccaccio had many reasons for bitterness in 1355).

In the introduction of the tenth eclogue Lycidas approaches the shepherd Dorilus and asks why he is constantly in tears. Dorilus' answer, already obscure from the veil of pastoral symbolism which we may almost call normal, is rendered impossible to interpret in detail through our ignorance of the true identity of Lycidas and of Dorilus' cruel master Polypus. The substance of the reply is that Dorilus himself has lost his sweetheart Phyllis and that Jupiter has struck down a magnificent beech tree in the nearby woods, as a result of which all the shepherds are living in terror in whatever caves they can find.

Then the tale that Menalcas brought me *was* true after all, replies Lycidas. At these words Dorilus looks more closely at his visitor, realizes who he is, and invites him to share his cave, uncomfortable though it may be. Lycidas then tells him that he is no more than an unsubstantial ghost. Yet he can comfort and encourage Dorilus: instead of lamenting his poverty (and it is quite possible that "Polypus" is no more than a personification of Dorilus' poverty), he should increasingly devote himself to poetry; the *bella scienza*, noblest of all pursuits, depends not on externals, but on the world of the imagination.

Dorilus thanks Lycidas for his advice and goes on to ask where his spirit now dwells. Lycidas' reply (lines 76-171, with three horrified interruptions from Dorilus) is a gruesome description of Hell, expressed in what is intended as an imitation of Virgil's manner in the sixth book of the *Aeneid*. The only point of real interest here is Lycidas' answer to a question from Dorilus: he says that he has been condemned to everlasting torture because of his thefts from Micon (a possible hint as to Lycidas' identity) and because of his inclination (like Brunetto Latini's) to homosexuality. Lycidas closes with an assurance that Polypus will soon die; Dorilus glumly hopes that that day may soon dawn, and then, as the cock crows, Lycidas' spirit vanishes into thin air.

In the eleventh eclogue (*Pantheon*; 239 hexameters) appears the poet's account of the words of two speakers—Myrtilis (a woman), and Glaucus, the first representing the Church, the second St. Peter. Boccaccio's comments on this poem in the famous letter to Fra Martino da Signa are as follows: "The eleventh eclogue is called *Pantheon,* from the Greek *pan* 'all' and *theos* 'deity,' for this reason, because it is *all* about *deities.* In this poem alone does the author himself speak, recounting a certain conversation held by two interlocutors, Myrtilis and Glaucus. By Myrtilis I mean the Church of God, which I name after the myrtle, because the myrtle has leaves of two colors; on the under side it is blood-red, on the upper it is green: by these colors we see figured the persecutions and tribulations suffered by saints and, on the other hand, the hope of a heavenly reward promised them by Christ. By Glaucus I mean the apostle Peter; Glaucus was a fisherman who tasted grass and, on suddenly throwing himself into the sea, became one of the deities of the sea. So also Peter was a fisherman who tasted the teachings of Christ and, on throwing himself into the waves (I mean, into the menacing terrors arising from Christ's enemies), became a deity—a saint, that is—among those who love God in Heaven (*in caelis*)." Petrarch himself could scarcely have produced a more medieval sounding piece of symbolism; even the use of the non-classical plural of *caelum* (regular in the Vulgate and in medieval Latin generally) is significant.

Two points are worth noticing, the first being a real curiosity of literature, at first sight a little puzzling. In lines 136-228 appears a bucolic version of the life, ministry, death, resurrection, and second coming of Christ. Now in all of this passage, each time that Christ is actually mentioned He is given a completely different name, each name save two being taken from Greek mythology—first Codrus, then Lycurgus, Nathan, Asclepius, Pales, Actaeon, Hercules, Hippolytus, Phoebus, Codrus again, and finally, King Arthur. The intention of this seems to be to insist that Christ is the sum and more than the sum of all the virtues belonging to the heroes of antiquity; further, it is noticeable that in each case the name is chosen as appropriate to the event being described at the time. Christ is Codrus (the legendary king of Athens) when He invades in royal wrath the kingdom of Plutarchus (i.e., Satan; the name has nothing to do with the author Plutarch: it is intended to recall the alternative name of Dis, ruler of the afterworld—Pluton—and the Greek word *archo* "I rule") to rescue His lost cattle (i.e., the saints and prophets of pre-Christian times); He is Lycurgus (the Spartan law-giver) when as a child He expounds the Torah to the doctors in the temple at Jerusalem; He is Nathan (Hebrew for "priest") when He baptizes converts; He is Asclepius (god of medicine) when He cures the sick; as Pales (deity of agriculture) He feeds the multitude; when He is hurled to dogs to be torn to death, He is Actaeon; in a second reference to the descent into Hell, He is referred to as Hercules recovering the cattle from Cacus; at His resurrection He is called Hippolytus, who in one form of the myth was resurrected to life as the deity Virbius (Boccaccio derived this detail from Virgil, *Aeneid,* vii, 765 ff.) ; it is as Phoebus Apollo the sun-god that Christ, in a blaze of glory, ascends to Heaven, as Codrus that He returns in majesty to judge the quick and the dead, and as King Arthur that He sends forth the knightly Apostles to preach the gospel to every creature.

We can also note the importance of the poem in the history of pastoral in the Renaissance. Lines 136-76 narrate the birth of

Christ, the rejoicing of all living beings at the birth, and the arrival of shepherds, guided by the Star of Bethlehem. Francesco Patrizi took the hint and later wrote a whole Christmas pastoral on this theme, and he was followed by a score of Latin poets in Italy and elsewhere in the fifteenth, sixteenth, and seventeenth centuries, with varying success. Further, Antonio Geraldini later wrote a cycle of eclogues on the life, ministry, death, resurrection, and the second coming of Christ. His twelve eclogues correspond precisely to the divisions of the second part of the present eclogue of Boccaccio and it is difficult—especially when we observe the close verbal parallels— not to believe that Geraldini was directly influenced by the *Pantheon* and in due course passed on this influence to others.

The twelfth eclogue (*Sappho*; 202 hexameters: it is noticeable that Boccaccio's eclogues increase in length as the subject grows more abstract and serious) reverts in form to the dialogue normal in fourteenth-century pastoral. Like xiii, it is a good deal more interesting (once the heavy layer of allegory has been cleared away) than either x or xi, since it reveals Boccaccio's own aspirations.

The glorification of poetry—*alma poesis, la bella scienza*—had been a topic of Dante in canto xxv of the *Paradiso,* and we have already seen from his pastoral correspondence with Giovanni del Virgilio how he had hoped to win through his poetry a tardy recognition from his fellow citizens of Florence. The glorification of poetry is likewise a favorite topic of Petrarch, the despiser of the *mobile vulgus,* the self-conscious artist whose vanity would at times be insufferable were it not so marvellously justified. In Petrarch the laurel of poetry and the Laura of the mythos created by the poet himself coalesce in the third and tenth eclogues: in invoking the figure which is at once Laura and *la bella scienza* Petrarch uses the language of the adoring lover. To Dante poetry was a pledge of reconciliation; to Petrarch it was both a vision of beauty and, characteristically, the key to that glory which he so ardently desired.

The glorification of poetry is similarly the topic in Boccaccio's twelfth eclogue, and the contrast with his predecessors is noticeable. Boccaccio is all too well aware of his own deficiencies as a poet— especially as a Latin poet; he is, he implies, a lowly practitioner of an art which is the essence of wisdom and truth expressed in the loftiest of diction. But any poet, however unworthy, is a *vates*— a quasi-sacred custodian of all that is true and beautiful, whose first duty it must always be to preserve the almost sacred majesty of poetry from contamination.

The thirteenth eclogue (*Laurea*; 150 hexameters) presents us with the first use in Neo-Latin poetry of a useful device of classical pastoral—a contest in amoebaean song between two shepherds (here Daphnis and Stilbon), with a rustic judge or umpire (Critis, a phonetic spelling of the Greek *krites,* "judge"). The tricks and devices employed show how sedulously Boccaccio has modeled the externals of this poem upon Virgil's third pastoral; but the purpose of the eclogue is Petrarchan, and its content is typical of the fourteenth century in its glorification of *la bella scienza.* The theme is the superiority of poetry over the pursuit of wealth (a topic which appears in Boccaccio's vernacular *Corbaccio* and in many of his Latin works) and, as the poet himself informs us, is based upon an actual argument which he had had with a wealthy merchant at Genoa: we know that, in the course of a mission to Avignon in 1354, Boccaccio stayed twice at Genoa. As for the name "Stilbon," Boccaccio points out in his letter to Fra Martino that this is a title of Mercury, god of trade and commerce (actually it is an alternative name not of the god but of the planet Mercury).

In classical pastoral such a contest has no overtones of allegory; the shepherds are supposed to be describing real women. Under the present conditions the reader's attention is constantly drawn into other areas as he prowls about each quatrain searching for implications. Furthermore, the occasional quatrain can get badly out of hand and attain a curiously comic effect as when Stilbon solemnly announces that, as a result of Crisis' favors and his own vigorous pursuit of her, even Scandinavia now knows the products of Morocco. Perhaps this is intentional on the poet's part, for there are equally odd lines from Daphnis. At the same time it is true that Boccaccio here and there does show far more ability in rhetoric and epigram than has so far appeared in the *Bucolicum carmen.*

The best, the most famous, and by all odds the most effective poem of the collection is the fourteenth eclogue (*Olympia*; 285 hexameters), "dans laquelle le poète évoque le souvenir de sa fille Violante, morte depuis plusieurs années" (Hauvette): the most probable of the dates suggested for her death is 1348; the poem itself may be as late as 1358 or even 1362—in any case it must be later than 1355. Boccaccio's children, like Petrarch's, were illegitimate; that fact, however, did not prevent either author from feeling the liveliest affection for his sons and daughters: Petrarch's grief over the behavior of his only son and, in the present eclogue, Boccaccio's sorrow over the death of his favorite daughter are equally sincere. How many children Boccaccio had we do not know (nor do we know if they were all by the same mother) ; in this poem, however, Violante speaks of two brothers, Mario and Giulio, and of an unspecified number of sisters—there must have been five children at least.

In the introduction (1-39) of this eclogue, Silvius (the name is Petrarchan; Boccaccio tells us that he gives himself this name because he conceived the notion of writing the poem while walking in the woods) is awakened long before dawn. He says that something strange is going on in the woods, wonders why his dog Lycos is so excited, and orders his servants to investigate. One servant, Camalus (the name is allegedly derived from a Greek word meaning "lazy"), grumbles at being expected to get up when it is still practically night; he is silenced by Silvius, who sends off a more obliging servant named Terapon (Boccaccio tells us in 1374 [?] that he has forgotten just what *arcana significatio* he had attached to this particular name; it is merely the Greek *therapon* "servant") to find out what is wrong. After a few moments Terapon comes rushing back in fright: the wood, he says, is on fire. But Silvius realizes that it is not fire but a miraculous light that is turning darkness into day. He becomes aware, too, of strange perfumes, of heavenly voices singing, and then, suddenly, of the presence of a beautiful young woman; he does not at first realize that she is a spirit.

With line 40 begins the first main division of the poem (40-90) : the spirit of Olympia ("the heavenly one") greets Silvius, who at first thinks he must be dreaming, and tells him that she has come to comfort her father's grief. What, he asks, has detained you so long? What are these clothes you are wearing? Who are these who accompany you? Olympia replies that she has been all this time with Parthenos (Greek for "virgin"; Silvius does not understand until much later that Olympia means the Virgin Mary), who had given her these clothes, and adds that Silvius should surely recognize in her companions his own children: "non Marium Iuliumque tuos, dulcesque sorores/noscis, et egregios vultus? tua pulchra propago est": (72-73).

Silvius exclaims in a delight that is obvious even today from lines that were written six hundred years ago. Still not realizing that the figures before him are only wraiths, he calls on Terapon to prepare a feast: let there be celebrations, games, feasting, prayers of thankfulness, and let each of his children receive garlands and pastoral pipes and join in the songs of thanks. Olympia smiles and tells her father that they know such songs as his world has never heard.

This leads up to the second section of the poem, where Olympia sings a hymn (91-111) constructed in four quatrains with a recurrent refrain ("vivimus aeternum, meritis et numine Codri"). Despite the fact that Christ is referred to as Codrus and Satan as Plutarchus, despite the fact that saints and prophets are called shepherds and the true believers flocks and herds, despite the rhetorical tone and the rather noticeable striving after epigrammatic expression, the hymn is a distinctly attractive and effective piece of writing.

The hymn is followed by a passage of dialogue (third main section: 112-69) between Olympia and Silvius. Not even the Greek and Roman poets, exclaims Silvius, not even the Muses, not even Apollo himself could match such song as this. Silvius invites Olympia and the others to enter his home and share such entertainment as he can offer; but Olympia, in some quite impressive lines (141-44), warns him that she must soon return to Heaven. On Silvius' exclaiming in grief, Olympia comforts him and reminds him that the separation will not be forever. Silvius then asks her to describe those "Elysian fields" of which Virgil had been vouchsafed a partial vision.

The fourth section of the poem (171-271) is devoted to a description (interrupted by occasional questions from Silvius) of Heaven, a description which owes a good deal to Virgil, but even more—as might be expected—to Dante. Olympia tells her father that far to the east is a wooded mountain, constantly flooded with light and bathed in the most delicate perfumes. All about are gardens of flowers and fruits, streams, deer, cattle, lambs, "gentle lions, gentle griffins," and birds of every sort. This vast area has a sun, moon, and stars of its own (like Virgil's Elysian Fields); there is perpetual spring, there is no death, old age, want, or disease. On Silvius' interrupting, Olympia tells him that this blessed spot is ruled by Archesilaus (i.e., the Almighty), whose nature cannot be described; but He bears in his arms the snow-white Lamb that brings salvation. All about Him are satyrs (*stat satyrum longaeva cohors hinc undique supplex:* 213), crowned with garlands of red roses (these satyrs are intended to represent the angels), a venerable line of men crowned with laurels (the martyrs of the Christian faith), and the blessed, among whom, Olympia adds, Asylas is to be seen (this must refer to Boccaccino, Boccaccio's father). It was Asylas who had taken Olympia to the Virgin Mary (Parthenos) on her first reaching Elysium. The passage closes with an ecstatic hymn—much cluttered, it must be admitted, with references to nymphs and fauns—to the virtues of Parthenos and a Virgilian description of the joyous life of the blessed in Paradise.

In the conclusion (272-85) Silvius asks his daughter how he, too, may merit Paradise; feed your brother's hunger, she replies; give milk to the weary, help the heavy-laden, and clothe the naked: "Deo monstrante viam, volitabis in altum" (279). The spirits gradually disappear, leaving Silvius to lament, until he realizes that the sun has now more than risen and that it is high time that he and his helpers were at work.

This poem attracts a modern reader's attention for more reasons than one. Its domestic tone is unusual in the Neo-Latin literature of the early Renaissance: such a tone scarcely reappears until we reach the poems of Giovanni Pontano and Girolamo Fracastoro. The obvious sincerity of religious feeling is significant for the student of Boccaccio's inner life; it is further proof, too, of the strong influence that Petrarch had on his friend's conversion. The Latinity of the eclogue, though very far indeed from the elegance of the later Neo-Latinists, is considerably superior to that of the earlier poems. The hymns to Christ and the Virgin Mary anticipate the Latin hexameter hymns of Girolamo Vida in particular; in the pastoral hymn to the Virgin her beauty is emphasized strongly but (*pace* Carrara) not sensuously—the erotic Mary-poem is a much later product, both in Latin and in the vernacular literatures.

The title of the fifteenth eclogue (*Phylostropos*; 221 hexameters) is another example of Boccaccio's curious Greek; it means or, rather, is intended to mean "the friend who converts," i.e., from profane to sacred love, and it refers to Francesco Petrarca, one of the interlocutors of the poem. Boccaccio is given the name Typhlus ("blind") for obvious reasons, and in the poem is gradually converted to a religious life by Phylostropos as he was in real life by Petrarch. In this connection it is instructive to read Petrarch's *Epistulae seniles* V, iv, a letter of religious exhortation addressed to Boccaccio shortly before this eclogue was written, at a time when the younger man was depressed and haunted by sorrow over the death of his children and by fear of death—a priest of Certosa named Ciani had prophesied that he would die unexpectedly. The poem contains a number of echoes of the letter and no doubt also contains reminiscences of conversations held with Petrarch a few years earlier in 1359. Phylostropos experiences considerable difficulty in persuading Typhlus to turn from the world's temptations and this is probably no more than the truth, for we know that Boccaccio's conversion was a prolonged and painful affair. The poem, despite its artificiality of form and the excessive number of learned allusions to historical characters (all decked out in pastoral costume), is vivid and striking; it is particularly and unusually effective in its characterization, for the quiet, insistent imperturbability of Phylostropos is maintained throughout as a most effective foil for the sheer fright eventually felt by Typhlus when finally induced to change his life: this again is in all probability no more than actually occurred— Boccaccio was clearly aware of what Carrara calls "sua natura passionale, esuberante, fantastica."

The road to salvation is represented as long and acutely painful— as a sort of purgatory on earth, in fact. In a sense, then, the tenth, fourteenth, and fifteenth eclogues form a *Pastorale commedia:* in the tenth poem, a *revenant* terrifies the shepherd Dorilus with a gruesome description of the torments of Hell; in the fourteenth, a spirit gives a vision of the joys of Paradise; in the present eclogue, a friend offers himself as guide through the Purgatory of conversion to the Paradise of a changed and dedicated life. It would, of course, be unwise to lay too much stress on this correspondence with the themes of the *Inferno, Purgatorio,* and *Paradiso,* since the three pastoral poems were clearly conceived quite separately from each other; although all three are evidence of the direction Boccaccio's inner life had taken, there is no indication that they were intended to be considered a unity.

The final poem (*Angelus,* "messenger"; 144 hexameters) is a dialogue between Appenninus (Donato degli Albanzani, to whom the completed *Bucolicum carmen* was dedicated; in at least one Paris manuscript this poem is appropriately placed first in the collection) and a shepherd who drives a gift of fifteen limping sheep (i.e. eclogues i-xv) to him. The poem was written about 1366, but, like the rest of the pastorals, was not finally revised until 1368. It is not especially interesting, or difficult, either.

This completes our survey of Boccaccio's twenty years of endeavor in pastoral poetry, begun as imitation of Dante, continued as imitation of Petrarch, and ending with reminiscence of Dante's vernacular poems and (if we are to regard xvi as epistolary), Petrarchan imitation of Dante's Latin poems once more. Their style is frequently wretched, yet not so much so that they are not characteristic of Boccaccio's remarkable personality—"sua natura passionale, esuberante, fantastica." As with Petrarch's eclogues, these poems, cluttered though they are with allegory, cryptic allusions, and medieval artifice, are interesting and valuable because of the light which they cast upon the psychological development of the author; for the student of Giovanni Boccaccio and in particular for the student of his difficult and confused biography, the sixteen eclogues are invaluable.

V

PRE-HUMANIST PASTORAL: II

n the latter half of the fourteenth century there existed a fair-sized group of pastoral poets, or at least a fair-sized group of writers who at one time or another tried their hand at the pastoral genre. The majority of their efforts are lost; but, to judge from the comments of Coluccio Salutati of Stignano (1331-1406), the loss is not greatly to be deplored. We do know something, however, of at least four minor bucolic poets who flourished during this period, all deeply influenced by Petrarch.

i

First appears a collection of ten ill-written eclogues, from internal evidence clearly later than 1350. The unknown author, possibly a native of Treviso (near Venice) and probably born about 1315, was a protégé ("parasite" might be a better term) of the Visconti family, in particular of Galeazzo II and Bernabò. The strongest literary influence at work in his poems is naturally Petrarch's: the theme of the first eclogue, for instance, recalls that of Petrarch's first very clearly, and in all the poems there are innumerable verbal reminiscences. Perhaps the anonymous Venetian actually met Petrarch at the Visconti courts of Milan and Pavia and just conceivably may have had the hardihood to submit his earliest poems to the man then regarded as the prince of Neo-Latin letters. Of course the Venetian also knew, as a *sine qua non,* the pastoral poems of Virgil; more unusual is his knowledge, betrayed in the tenth eclogue, of the poems of Calpurnius Siculus. Two of the eclogues are incomplete; in their original form they had undoubtedly been, like the other eight, precisely one hundred lines in length. All of the poems are frigidly allusive, enigmatic, and riddling, and it is probable that many of the puzzles they present are insoluble.

Simplest is the tenth and last eclogue (*Apotheosis*), which brings back the two shepherds of the first, Fuscus and Gorgulus, who appear walking through a wood, which here seems to symbolize poverty and its frustrations. As they proceed through its darkness, Fuscus catches a glimpse of the stars (this would appear to symbolize achievement, more specifically the award of a lucrative secretarial appointment at the Visconti court) and insists that he must reach them. Gorgulus, the older shepherd, dispiritedly says that he doubts whether that is possible, but is told rather sharply that capability (*virtus*) can raise a man to Olympus. Fuscus offers a long list, self-consciously learned in tone, in the manner of Petrarch and Boccaccio, of the ancient heroes who reached Heaven through their *virtus*. Gorgulus watches while Fuscus gradually disappears from the fields of pastoral to assume his place among the demi-gods in a sort of self-apotheosis that must be unique in European literature. The poem is of little intrinsic value as literature—all ten eclogues, in fact, make as melancholy reading as one could find.

ii

Later in the fourteenth century we find yet another group of ten pastorals, written between 1381 and 1395 by a Tuscan exile named Giovanni de Bonis, from Arezzo, near Florence. Like the Venetian, De Bonis is a hopeful court-poet whose aim is a lucrative appointment from the Visconti family, this time from Galeazzo's son, Giangaleazzo, who became Lord of Milan in 1378 on the death of his father and Duke of Milan on that of his uncle in 1395; like the Venetian, too, De Bonis is an industrious imitator of Petrarch and, perhaps even more, of Boccaccio; unlike his wretched predecessor, however, he had the decency to provide marginal notes to explain his poems—but his allegories and symbols are easy enough, and for once we could have done without help.

The tenth and last poem, entitled with grim brevity "Death" (*Mors*), leans heavily on the ninth and tenth eclogues of Petrarch. Here a shepherd describes a plague to his rustic friend, in gruesome detail; the afflicted city is not identified in the poem nor in De Bonis' notes, but it is almost certainly Arezzo. The date of the poem is problematical; it is known, however, that the city was visited with plague in 1383 and again in 1390, and the general tone of the poem favors the earlier date. This eclogue has no aesthetic importance whatever—as indeed is true of its nine predecessors; its historical importance lies in the fact that it demonstrates clearly the degeneration of fourteenth-century pastoral.

iii

The next eclogist we meet at this point is Coluccio Salutati of Stignano (1331-1406), later chancellor of Florence and the greatest scholar and Humanist of the late fourteenth century. Salutati spent two unhappy years at Lucca, at one time, waiting for the Florentine appointment that was not to come until 1374. His time was not wasted, however: he corresponded vigorously with a wide circle of friends and acquaintances in letters that not only instructed his contemporaries on ethics and philology but served later as models of Latin style in more than one chancellery. He read omnivorously, too, in Latin literature, specializing in the poets and historians. And he began at this time a series of eight cryptic, Petrarchan eclogues that were no doubt intended to form part of a *Bucolicum carmen* of ten poems.

The eclogues were later destroyed, probably in Salutati's old age; all we possess today is a letter, dated January 21, 1372, and addressed to Giovanni Boccaccio: Salutati sends a copy of the first eclogue, *Pyrgis* ("The Burning Earth"). It is obvious from the letter that the poem must have been highly cryptic. Behind all the bucolic mystification lies a discussion of the nature of the operations of the Divine Grace, which in the poem takes on the form of the rustic Caristes. As with Petrarch, cryptic allegory—in which incidental details are forced to bear a hidden meaning in a manner that can be described only as arbitrary and capricious—seems to have been carried to an extent which strikes the modern reader as almost ludicrous, and it is no great assumption if we suppose that the other seven poems were composed in the same manner. These pastorals circulated among Salutati's friends—Filippo Villani read them, we know, and described them as *lepide e gravi*—and the possibility still exists that diligent search in the libraries of Italy may produce a manuscript containing a fair copy.

Such a search would almost inevitably produce examples of

pastorals written by perhaps as many as a dozen other humanists of the fourteenth century—those, for instance, of Tommaso Rigo of Perugia (mentioned by Salutati as an acquaintance whose eclogues were notably cryptic and mysterious), Domenico Silvestri of Prato (praised highly as a writer of eclogues by Villani), and Giaccobbe Allegretto of Forlì (much admired by Flavio Biondi), associated, like the earlier Cecco di Mileto, with the Ordelaffi family: it would be interesting to learn whether Allegretto's one known eclogue was Dantean and epistolary.

iv

We can now turn to the six pastoral poems—all extant, all ultra-Petrarchan, all extremely difficult—of Giovanni Quatrario of Sulmona (1336-1402), a younger contemporary and close friend of Coluccio Salutati. Quatrario's Latin is remarkably bad, even for the fourteenth century: sentences sprawl as loosely as they do in Boccaccio and are expressed in a style that is obscure, unidiomatic, and occasionally incomprehensible. The one manuscript in which the poems are extant is provided with a series of notes (possibly added by Quatrario himself) that are of considerable practical assistance to the reader of the second and sixth poems; even so, there remain many passages even in these two eclogues in which the power of divination is even more essential than a knowledge of bad Latin. An added embarrassment is the large number of neologisms in Quatrario's lumpish and frequently unmetrical hexameters. But however unsuccessful Quatrario may have been as a poet, there is no doubt about his success as a careerist: he became papal secretary to Urban VI in 1383, and it is clear from his last will and testament (written in 1399) that he prospered famously.

The six eclogues are associated with events at the Angevin court of Naples and in particular with the domestic affairs of Queen Giovanna. Quite apart from the ostentatious obscurity of the poet's manner, it is most difficult to understand many of the allusions, made as they are to quite personal matters, which Quatrario may have learned directly while at Naples or (especially in regard to earlier events) from conversation with his fellow citizen, Marco Barbato of Sulmona, chancellor of Naples at the time of King Robert's death in 1343. Quatrario's purpose was to narrate as allusively as possible past and present occurrences as part of a nexus of stock pastoral situations, at the same time illustrating and amplifying various political, religious, and ethical ideas—most of them as conventional as the pastoral situations themselves. Like the *anony-mus Venetus,* Giovanni de Bonis, and many another Humanist, Quatrario hoped that this major literary work would bring his merits to the attention of the dispensers of patronage; unlike his two contemporaries, he proved eminently successful in this aim. His salary and position once assured, Quatrario no longer devoted himself to literature.

VI

THE ART-PASTORAL OF THE

RENAISSANCE: I

he history of fourteenth-century pastoral is plain. First appeared the epistolary eclogue, introduced by Dante and Giovanni del Virgilio and continued by Cecco di Mileto and Giovanni Boccaccio. In the middle of the century, the enormous literary prestige of Francesco Petrarca drove this form of pastoral from the field and established the cryptic eclogue as standard. The distinguishing mark of the Petrarchan variety of eclogue was an allegorical treatment that went far beyond any simple bucolic masquerade and frequently turned the poem into a downright riddle, incomprehensible if the author himself were not to supply some sort of key.

In the fifteenth century Humanism proper appeared in Italy. This came to be regarded not as an ornament or a way of life or a philosophy but, as Paul Oskar Kristeller has frequently pointed out, as a means to an end: more and more as the century progressed Humanism became a method of educating a man toward a social and professional ideal. The Latin classics were studied in a new spirit; Greek was becoming far more widely known: men like Francesco Filelfo of Tolentino (1398-1481) could not only read and write classical Greek with ease but could also speak its contemporary Byzantine form with fluency. Long before the fall of Byzantium in

1453, scholars like Filfelfo and Giovanni Aurispa had already brought back scores of Greek manuscripts to Italy. And it was in the fifteenth century that the tremendously influential discoveries of Latin manuscripts were made in German and other libraries. Men like Poggio Bracciolini made repeated hunting trips through German monasteries in order to rescue classical authors (many of them unread for centuries) from dust-covered shelves and forgotten laundry baskets. By 1450 the enthusiasm for the rediscovered classical authors was at its height: men read their authors by day and imitated them by night.

Among many Neo-Latin authors of the fifteenth century and later, the aim was not merely to rival classical authors but actually to outdo them, by introducing new uses and forms of literary genres, based upon the classical exemplars. In bucolic poetry there arose three distinct types of eclogue—the purely *classicizing pastoral* (described in the heading of this chapter as "the art-pastoral") in which a poet, if he was of the first class, attempted not to produce a mirror image of the Virgilian pastoral but to compose a poem that was independently valuable as creative genre art; it is only to be expected that many lesser authors missed so lofty a mark completely and produced work that was imitative and derivative. At the same time the Neo-Latin poets went far beyond Virgil's occasional contemporary and personal allusions to develop a whole series of *new uses* of pastoral. The pastoral poem became for generations a standard medium to express the poet's thoughts and feelings on almost any topic: this form of poem was used to celebrate greatness and excoriate vice, to satirize folly and attack incompetence, to celebrate victories and mourn disasters. The appearance of shepherds in the Christmas story naturally led to a pastoral treatment of Christ's birth, which in turn led to the development of pastorals based on Old Testament themes and, much later, to whole sequences of devotional and liturgical eclogues in praise of the Virgin Mary. There was in fact no theme to which the Neo-Latin poets were not ready to adapt pastoral verse: they were as ready to use the form to celebrate a friend's wedding as to turn it into a didactic poem on the raising of dogs or on the problems of ethics. But besides the art-pastoral and these new uses of pastoral there appear also *new forms* of pastoral: midway between a purely classicizing form of eclogue and the "modern" Neo-Latin pastoral are eclogues of fishermen, hunters, sailors, gardeners, vine-growers, and the like.

It was among the Neo-Latin poets associated with the Este court of Ferrara that the new tradition of the Virgilian art-pastoral took shape in the 1460's; and this tradition, once established, maintained itself in a steady succession of eclogists in Italy and the rest of Europe for the next 250 years; pastorals—some of them good—still continued to be written in quite considerable numbers after 1700, but on the whole their day was past by them.

The three eclogues (published in 1496, but written about 1460) of Battista Guarino (*floruit* 1460-1500) can scarcely be called anything but exercises in verse composition. It is true that his intentions were good; but his performance fell short of his aim, and the three poems are best described as correct but colorless imitations. Unimportant as they are as poetry, they are nevertheless significant as the first appearance of that new art-pastoral that was to occupy Neo-Latin men of letters for generations.

Far more interesting as man and as poet is Tito Vespasiano Strozzi (1422-1505), descendant of the famous Florentine family. Born in Ferrara, Tito had the good fortune to be educated by the elder Guarino. From the beginning he displayed not only high classical attainments but also a remarkable bent for financial administration—he was in fact precisely the sort of alumnus on whom Guarino prided himself most. He passed rapidly through the *cursus honorum* at the court of three successive Este rulers (Borso, Ercole, and Alfonso), reaching the highest civil rank (i.e., as *giudice dei dodici Savî*) in 1497, a post which he held until his death in 1505. Sheer financial necessity forced him to tax the city and her dominions heavily in order to fill and refill Ferrara's hard-pressed treasury; he left to his successor—his son Ercole (ca. 1473-1508), like his father equally able as Neo-Latin poet and as administrator—a situation far from easy to control that may have been the cause of the younger man's still unexplained murder.

Of Tito's three eclogues (published at Venice in 1513), the first two form a pair: in number i (150 hexameters), on the invitation of two young shepherds, the nonagenarian Chronidon describes first the joys of spring, then those of summer; in number ii (189 hexameters), the same shepherd sings the pleasures of autumn and those of winter, again before the same youthful pair. The two contrasting poems, each with its pair of contrasting pictures, reflect patterns and themes familiar enough, it is true, to any reader of Virgil's *Eclogues* and *Georgics*; but both are well worth reading for their pleasant flow of verse, their clear and easy Latin, their not too obvious reminiscences of Lucretius and Virgil, and the attractive details derived from contemporary Italian life. Genre compositions they are, without a doubt, but they are not necessarily the worse for that; certainly they come as a pleasant relief after the obscurities in content and expression with which fourteenth-century pastoral is riddled.

The first two poems are inclined to be static; the third is more lively. A rustic named Albicus had played a trick (unspecified) on his tyrannical master Cicada and now gloats over it as he walks home after the day's work with another farm-servant named Tribalus. But, says Albicus, although Cicada is querulous, suspicious, and tyrannical, not all old men are so unpleasant: take Chronidon (i.e., Guarino), for instance. At this point the poem turns into panegyric of Guarino, the whole expressed in a simple pastoral cipher that presents few difficulties to a modern reader and no doubt would have offered none at all to anyone in fifteenth-century Ferrara.

It is probable that the first two eclogues of Strozzi were written about 1460 and that the third was written shortly after the arrival in Ferrara of Gaspare de' Tirimbocchi, who wrote under the name of Caspar Tribrachus (Il Tribraco). Tirimbocchi's own eight eclogues, which have never been printed and are extant in only two manuscripts (one at Ferrara, the other at Bologna), were clearly written some little time after 1461. Tirimbocchi enjoyed a high repute as a poet among his contemporaries; from a reading of these eclogues it is difficult to see why—the last two are unpleasantly fulsome pastoral eulogies of Borso and Ercole d'Este; the first six are the lachrymose laments of unsuccessful shepherd-lovers, all expressed in a Latin by no means so expert as Strozzi's.

The ten eclogues of Matteo Maria Boiardo, Count of Scandiano (1441-1494), a courtier, poet, and diplomat, are very youthful work indeed. As courtier and confidant, Boiardo was long held in esteem by the Estes. As poet, he is best known for his *Orlando Innamorato,* the poem continued as *Orlando Furioso* by Ludovico Ariosto; as diplomat and administrator, he undertook missions to Rome in 1471 and Naples in 1473 and governed Modena from 1481 to 1483 and Reggio Emilia from 1487 to 1494. He is described by a contemporary as *cavaliere nobile e cortese.*

Boiardo's earliest original work was all in Latin—occasional poems in a variety of meters (called *De laudibus Estensium*), a number of epigrams of very little but historical interest, and a group of ten hundred-line pastorals (written between 1463 and 1465) that have strong affinities with such courtly eclogues as those produced in France in the Valois period (1515-1589).

Five of the eclogues we shall examine later as panegyrics. The remainder, although containing overtones of contemporary allusion (like Strozzi's), are art-pastorals.

The third eclogue, entitled *Eripoemenon* ("The Shepherds' Contest"), presents three speakers—Hercules (Ercole d'Este, naturally), Silvanus from Sicily, and Poeman from Arcadia. In structure the poem is stylized, formal, amoebaean: Poeman tells Hercules that they have arrived to sing for him, and on receiving permission, the two shepherds sing in alternating and antithetical quatrains (lines 17-80) the joys of the successive seasons, the beauties of their rustic sweethearts, and the power of love. A summary of the quatrains will make the mannerisms of amoebaean verse clear:

P.:   The snows are gone, my ardor increases, I shall sing of Cytheris.
S.:   But I shall sing of Cardelia in every season.
P.:   Summer is more pleasant than winter; come to me, Cytheris.
S.:   Why is *my* sweetheart so slow in coming?
P.:   I could live always with Cytheris in this beauty-spot.
S.:   But I could live with Cardelia anywhere.
P.:   Where were you, Hamadryads, when Phyllirrhoê died?
S.:   The nymphs wept for her and put flowers on her tomb.
P.:   Cytheris loves my songs; she only pretends to hide.
S.:   Cardelia secretly follows me when I hunt rabbits.
P.:   What can Love not do? It first taught me to sing.
S.:   Love teaches the birds to sing.
P.:   Shepherds, keep your goats from the river; there is a snake there.
S.:   Shepherds, bring your flocks over here, out of the wind.
P.:   Here fountains were dry, goats died, and land was sterile when Hercules left for the south.
S.:   The mountains, flocks, herds again rejoice, now that Hercules has returned (i.e., from Naples).

Hercules tells them that their songs are equally good and must be rewarded by equal gifts—two Corsican hunting dogs ("Corsa de matre gemellos/pugnaces catulos"). After a few lines praising Hercules, Poeman adds, "But by now the many stars are beginning to shine in the heaven: let us leave" ("sed iam crebra polo collucent sidera: eamus"); the brief, almost abrupt conclusion is characteristic of all Latin pastorals, ancient or modern. The form of the whole poem, obviously, is ultra-Virgilian; but, as in Strozzi, the details are Italian.

In the second eclogue (*Phyllirrhoê*) the resemblance to Tirimbocchi's sixth seems too great to be accidental; but if Boiardo, as seems most likely, modeled his work on the earlier poem he paid it a compliment it did not deserve. Here two shepherds, Lynces and Bargus, interrupt a leisurely walk when they hear the tearful laments of Tityrus. In reply to their questioning, Tityrus says (lines 22-38) that all nature is at peace; he alone is tormented by grief for his dead sweetheart Phyllirrhoê, and he later bursts into a longish lament in which he threatens suicide:

> But why prolong my tale in accents drear
> To soundless crags, and deserts far and near?
> My grievous care is cured by death alone:
> For no one hears my grief or hears my moan.
> Then hurl your body, shepherd, from the height
> And let the river bear your corpse from sight!
> But you, the cause of all my grief and woe,
> Farewell; farewell, all creatures here below (69-74).

But Lynces and Bargus finally calm their troubled friend, whose final words (line 100) are: "Go on—I'll follow; perhaps a better life awaits me" ("perge—sequar; forsan melior fortuna paratur"). In this poem Boiardo aims at and achieves a sweetly melodious melancholy that escapes sugariness by the gentle irony with which the poet makes Bargus meet Tityrus' insistence that he is more than half in love with easeful death.

The seventh pastoral, entitled *Bucula* ("The Heifer"), displays a considerable number of textual variations in MSS V and C, none of which, however, is so important as to affect the poem's interpretation as an eclogue. It appears that Boiardo himself produced a second redaction of the poem to remove many rather salacious details and several quite pointed allusions to living persons who cannot be identified today but whose identity was no doubt all too readily obvious to Boiardo's contemporaries: satirical overtones are seldom popular in courtly poems. The pastoral itself is simply constructed. Poeman asks if Corydon has seen his lost heifer; Corydon answers in a surly tone that it is not his duty to look after Poeman's herds. Some elegant verbal scuffling ensues (of the "You're a fellow, sir" variety), until the two agree to settle hostility by a singing match with Bargus as umpire. In lines 43 to 90 appears a series of amoebaean hexameter distichs in which Corydon sings of the charms of Cardelia and Poeman of those of Philomela, both incidentally introducing a great many compliments to Ercole d'Este, a good many more, in fact, than most modern readers would care to see.

The eighth pastoral, *Philicodiae* ("Lovers' Songs"), is pleasing in its general effect without displaying any particular outstanding merit in detail.

In the fifth poem (*Silva*) Lycanor and Menalcas appear as they stroll at leisure through a little wood. They comment on its beauty and wish that Bargus and Tityrus could be present to enjoy it: but (says Lycanor) the one is too busy with his sheep, day and night (this would appear to refer to a professor's students in the Ferrara *Studio*), while the other has deserted the woods to turn his attention to the wars of princes (this must surely refer to Tito Strozzi's unfinished *Borsias*). In that case, says Menalcas, since these clever ones despise the woods we must do our best even though we lack their capabilities. Menalcas' song (lines 23-48) is a lament over the faithlessness of his unnamed sweetheart; Lycanor's (60-84) is devoted to the careful specification of the anatomical charms of a shepherdess preparing to bathe in a river: the detail is appreciative and possibly reminiscent but is definitely not lewd; the description of the banks of the little stream, too, has a flavor that is undeniably Petrarchan. At the close of the poem the two exchange gifts and, as the reader will by now doubtless expect, succeed in working in a courtly compliment or two for Duke Ercole.

Before turning to Antonio Urceo and to a brace of poets from Mantua, we can glance briefly at the Genoese (?) Antonio Mario (*floruit* 1450), who probably spent most of his adult life at Florence as a copyist of Greek and Latin manuscripts. Mario wrote a number of pastoral elegiac poems of the sort called *lusus pastoralis* ("pastoral vignette"; so far as I know he was the first in Italy to do so) and composed (if in fact he was—as Cosenza thinks—the writer in question) at least one bucolic. There may well be many more Latin poems lurking in some Italian library but these, I believe, are the only ones that have ever been printed.

Lines 34-81 consist of alternating quatrains, followed by the

usual brief conclusion, in the poet's mouth, in lines 82-84.   Thyrsis
begins the amoebaean verses and sings of Phyllis, Iolas, Orithyia, and
Lycidas; Alcon answers with praise of Lydia, Galatea, Lycoris, and
Varus, as follows:

T. You nymphs, that by the river waters stand,
    And guardian Pan, and Satyrs' hornèd band,
    Receive my song; let Phyllis favor me,
    Or let my life at last from love be free.

A. If ever, Faun, I've sung your love divine,
    Or hung your statue's horns with sacred pine,
    Or set upon your brow a garland fine,
    Make Lydia take my love, and make her mine.

T. You hills, you shaggy hills, and fields below,
    And Rhene, that runs along with gentle flow,
    Has not my Phyllis taught ev'n you to sigh,
    The while she sings, and smiles with merry eye?

A. You springs, you mossy springs, you too-much blest,
    Who bathe my lady's arms and snowy breast,
    Has not my Galatea roused your blood
    Or by the bank or in the glassy flood?

T. Than swans more white, than kids more wanton now,
    Than flowers more lovely is Iolas' brow;
    He comes, and as I sing to lessen care
    He plants a kiss to make the song more fair.

A. As violets lovely, and as roses bright,
    As shadows gentle is Lycoris' sight;
    With me she guards the flocks, the meadow walks:
    Thus clings the vine with ever-closer stalks.

T. See, how the flowers bloom throughout the fields;
    See, how the wood its fruit and blossoms yields;
    See, how the birds make all the meadows ring,
    And, if he smile, for Lycidas will sing.

A. But mark, when chilly Dawn reveals her beams,
    How ice can glisten on the frozen streams,
    How scarlet roses drip with dismal dew:
    Such is the grieving Varus to our view.

T.   Here breezes blow, here trees wave in the sun,
      Here caves invite the weary, rivers run;
      Here may you rest yourself—or hunt the deer,
      My Lycidas, and drive their wild career.

A.   No longer please my heart the mossy rills,
      The grassy meadows, and the gentle hills;
      Yet come, my Varus, and those hills will charm,
      The meadows capture, and the rills disarm.

T.   Would that Iolas never love refuse;
      Would that my Phyllis never spurn my Muse;
      Would that fair Orithyia garlands twine,
      To deck the Faun and say her love is mine.

A.   Would that these streams with whitest milk could flow;
      Would that these shrubs with sweetest honey grow;
      Would that the fleeces shine with purple glow:
      What verses then, my Lydia, would you know! (34-81)

For its date—to say nothing of Mario's youth at the time of writing—this pastoral is astonishingly good; it is only natural, of course, that the young Humanist should have expended quite extraordinary pains on a showpiece intended to gain him advancement from the governor of Verona, and it is a pity that we know little of his career and nothing of what influence the poem may have had upon it.

Let us now—before examining four of the eclogues of Boiardo's very different contemporary, Mantuan—look briefly at the one extant pastoral of Antonio Urceo, nicknamed by himself *Il Codro* (1446-1500). The name Urceus or Urcaeus is derived from the family's native place, Orzi Novi (near Brescia; but Antonio himself was born in Reggio Emilia) and the cognomen *Il Codro* is a wry reference to Juvenal, *Satires* iii, 208 (*nil habuit Codrus*). After receiving a good training in Greek not only from Guarino the Elder but also from Strozzi's friend Luca Riva (almost as famous in his day as Guarino himself), Urceo became professor of Greek at the *Studio* of Bologna, where he became a notorious example of the less attractive sort of Renaissance Humanist—learned, querulous, and irritable: as a result, he complained, "I am called Grandpa by my students" ("*avus a iuvenibus vocor*": he was only forty at the time).

Urceo's works appear in a Bologna volume of 1502 (no title page in the only copy I have ever seen; unpaged, unfoliated); his untitled

ecloga unica is a poem of 118 hexameters, with Tityrus and Corydon
as speakers. Tityrus laments losses among his flocks and the daring
of wolves that now attack the fold despite all precautions taken by
the guards, Damon and Meliboeus. Corydon instructs him how to
keep off the wolves and also how to maintain the health of the animals. Thus far, it would seem, the poem is entirely genre composition. But the melancholy and querulous Tityrus apparently becomes
the melancholy and querulous Urceo himself when Corydon advises
him to marry the shepherdess Galatea, who has already expressed
her willingness ("corpora nostra/pressabit pastor nullus, nisi Tityrus
ipse," she had said frankly) ; Tityrus, however, refuses, saying that
he is too old:

> Seek not, my Corydon to flatter me;
> My life remaining still shall single be,
> So long as life remains within this frame,
> So long as music gives a lasting name.
> Now must we go: my flock I must review;
> But sup with me, and rest a while we two.
> A simple meal awaits of cheese and bread,
> Some fruit, a well-aged wine of deepest red. (111-18)

It is a pretty enough poem, but not nearly so attractive as almost
any of Urceo's *Silvae,* many of which are not only verbally dexterous
but display a quiet but very real humor—a quality less common
among Neo-Latin poets than wit. The poem, by the way, cannot be
dated precisely; but it probably belongs to a year between 1480 and
1485.

Contemporary with these Ferrarese poets is the oldest of a group
of Mantuans, Giovanni Battista Spagnuoli (or Spagnoli or Spagnolo;
ca. 1448-1516), commonly called Mantuan (Baptista Mantuanus).
Eight of his ten eclogues were written at Padua about 1465, while
he was a student; the other two were composed over twenty years
later and published, with revised versions of the earlier pastorals, in
1498 with a dedication to Paride Cereseri, a Mantuan nobleman of
great wealth and considerable learning, called by Matteo Bandello
"nobilissimo, e in ogni sorta di lettere dottissimo." Carducci speaks
of Mantuan as "a cynical, unpolished observer of life, crude-spoken
though not obscene, who speaks in the coarsest way of women and
of love . . . ; no flowers of elegance here, but, rather, coarse vigor
and prolix truth; in some passages he seems to anticipate *commedia*

rusticale, in others the poems of Teofilo Folengo." There is no denying Mantuan's occasional crudity, and certainly a bizarre touch appears in many of the eclogues; but in his own day, and for two centuries more, these poems enjoyed a phenomenal popularity. They were the subject of elaborate commentaries by many scholars, notably by Filippo Beroaldo in Italy and Jodocus Badius Ascensius (Josse Bade) in France (innumerable editions of the latter's commentary were published) ; they were closely imitated by Edmund Spenser and Alexander Barclay in England; at least four editions appeared of George Turbervile's English translation of the eclogues into "four-teeners," in 1567, 1572, 1594, and 1597; the poems were used as textbooks of Latin poetry in European schools (particularly in Germany and Spain) from 1503 to at least the early part (as Dr. Johnson tells us) of the eighteenth century, holding the position in Europe generally that George Buchanan's Latin versions of the Psalms held in Scotland until a hundred years ago. Some teachers, such as Jacob Wimpheling, even went so far as to prefer Mantuan's eclogues to Virgil's—for teaching purposes only, one would assume, although the elder Scaliger and Thomas Farnaby seem to have thought that this meant a real preference.

As a result of familiarity, overt allusions to the eclogues of Mantuan in the literatures of England, France, and (especially) Germany are almost innumerable, while vernacular works, almost wholly based on Mantuan's verse, now go unrecognized as such, owing to the prevailing neglect of Neo-Latin literature: large passages of Alexander Barclay's *Egloges,* for instance, are nothing more than youthful paraphrases of Mantuan.

Giovanni Battista Spagnuoli was born at Mantua about 1448. His father was a Spaniard, born at Granada (hence the name Spagnuoli), and the family name was Modover, a Latinized form of Moduer. Mantuan studied first in his native city under Gregorio Tifernate (i.e., Gregorio da Città di Castello) and the Humanist Georgius Merula, and then at Padua, where his chief interest appears to have been philosophy. In about 1466 he entered the Carmelite order, of which he became Vicar-General in 1483, an elective office which he gained on five further occasions. The *Enciclopedia Italiana* describes him as *uomo di singolare pietà,* and he was in fact beatified by the Church in 1885—hence the odd titles of Gabotto's biographical essay *Un poeta beatificato* and Zabughin's *Un beato poeta.*

Mantuan's unbelievable productivity in Latin prose and verse alike is proverbial and has been since 1587, although H. H. Furness (in the *Variorum Shakespeare*) apparently thought that the ten eclogues constituted his entire works. Mantuan wrote with the greatest rapidity; his twenty-one hundred hexameters on St. Catherine of Alexandria were thrown off casually, as relaxation, during an enforced rest of forty days. For long he was called the second Virgil (from at least 1483) until the choleric Julius Caesar Scaliger dipped pen in vinegar and wrote the famous line "flabby, languid, ill-arranged, unrhythmic, commonplace, not without native ability, but rather without art" ("mollis, languidus, incompositus, sine numeris, plebeius, non sine ingenio, sed sine arte": *Poetics*, vi, 4). After this sentence gained currency, abashed critics were less eager to equate the pagan and Christian Mantuans, and, having once read through all the more than sixty thousand lines of Mantuan's Latin poems, I can readily agree with Scaliger's verdict. For all that, Mantuan's authority in Latin diction was cited in dictionaries until the early nineteenth century. And some of Mantuan's *versus paene innumerabiles* (the phrase comes from Lilio Gregorio Giraldi's readable *De poetis nostrorum temporum dialogi duo*) are still worth study, even by those whose chief interest does not lie in the field of Neo-Latin literature—some parts, at least, of the *Parthenicae*, a great many of the occasional poems in the *Silvae*, much of the *De sacris diebus*, and above all the ten eclogues.

Of these eclogues we shall consider at the moment only the first three; they are genre compositions, being examples of the art-pastoral, literary in inspiration, and largely derivative in content. It should be observed at the start that in expression Mantuan is far from being the equal of Tito Vespasiano Strozzi or of Matteo Maria Boiardo. His Latin is undoubtedly intended to be classical, but, even after revision, displays startling irregularities and crudities of vocabulary, syntax, and meter. Some of Mantuan's linguistic curiosities are ecclesiastical, some medieval; many are Italicisms, and not a few seem to be downright mistakes. His versification is adorned with a truly remarkable number of false quantities. One natural result, too, of his rapidity of composition is diffuseness: Strozzi wrote pastorals of about one hundred lines each; each of Mantuan's ten is about two hundred.

In Strozzi's pastorals, the first eclogue is placed in contrast with the second; Mantuan's first two poems likewise form an antithetical pair: the first is entitled *Faustus: De honesto amore,* the second *Fortunatus: De insania amoris,* and this topic is continued in the third eclogue as well. In the first poem (176 hexameters) the shepherd Fortunatus (beginning with the words quoted by Holofernes in *Loves Labour's Lost,* words as familiar to the Renaissance school-boy as is the date 1066 to the English fourth-former today), asks Faustus to tell him the story of his courtship of Galla and his happy married life.

Three points are worth noticing in the first eclogue. No reader could fail to notice—whether with amusement or with irritation—the sententious comments of Fortunatus as Faustus makes his grad-ual way to the happy ending of this bucolic love-story. When he learns that the mother and married daughter had tried to prevent Galla's marriage, he comments, "Those with a full belly can easily praise fasting" ("qui satur est pleno laudat ieiunia ventre": 61); when Faustus speaks of his love for Galla, Fortunatus ventures the opinion that Love attacks all, high and low (81-84) and that the lover is a slave ("quisquis amat servit; sequitur captivus amantem": 114), and when Faustus (with mild irony?) suggests that For-tunatus is perhaps not inexperienced in love, the latter remarks, "It is a distress common to all: we have all played the fool at one time or another" ("id commune malum; semel insanivimus omnes": 118), the last three words of which became proverbial and on one occasion lost Dr. Johnson ten guineas (Boswell's *Johnson,* London ed. 1890, iii, 266).

Equally noticeable is the homeliness (here as elsewhere) of Mantuan's comparisons. Faustus remarks that, in repulsing his attempts to win Galla, the girl's mother and sister had been like cats: "They opposed wishes contrary to mine as does a cat to a mouse: the one does his best to invade the ham, the other watches the cracks with sharp eyes":

> Sicque repugnabant votis contraria vota
> non secus ac muri catus: ille invadere pernam
> nititur, hic rimas oculis observat acutis. (58-60)

And earlier Faustus had described himself as a fly caught in the spider's web of his lady's charms: "My Galla had overcome me with her beauty as a spider overwhelms a fly caught in its chains":

> me mea Galla suo sic circumvenerat ore
> ut captam pedicis circumdat aranea muscam. (42-3)

A third matter worthy of notice is the strong comic element, characteristic of Mantuan (how J. A. K. Thomson could refer to

Mantuan as a humorless schoolmaster is beyond me) in the description of the bagpiper Tonius at the rustic wedding; Tonius blows out his flushed cheeks (flushed more from alcohol than from exertions), opens his eyes till they fairly bulge, raises his eyebrows high as his fingers fly on the chanter, and his elbow works the bag:

> Et cum multifori Tonius cui tibia buxo
> tandem post epulas et pocula multicolorem
> ventriculum sumpsit, buccasque inflare rubentes
> incipiens oculos aperit ciliisque levatis
> multotiensque altis flatu a pulmonibus hausto
> utrem implet, cubito vocem dat tibia presso. (163-8)

Mantuan's first eclogue was probably the best-known Neo-Latin pastoral ever written in Europe; a full translation follows:

Fortunatus

Here let us rest and sing of love's delight
(Since now the herd is resting 'neath the height),
Yet watch, for fear the wolf may wait to seize
The choicest heifer by the shady trees.

Faustus

This is the very tree, the very shade
Where once I (love-sick) woo'd a tender maid!
Can you with patience hear, while I relate,
This summer noon, the annals of my fate?
Here did I labor in my boyish years,
Here did I toil, here shed my boyish tears;
My grieving heart and aching body knew
How hard the road that Love had led me to.
No dainty can the unwanted taste impel:
All sweet will sicken and all sour repel.
No longer did I dance or play my flute:
My mind was idle and my songs were mute.
My bow was useless, with its string released:
My joys were fewer as my cares increased:
No joy to weave the basket's wicker beam,
No joy to find the nest, to fish the stream,
To look for berries and to pick the best,
To join with comrades in the merry jest.

Just so, the nightingale, returned to nest,
To feed her nurselings in their cradle prest,
Surveys the empty home, the ravished brood,
Laments her offspring, and rejects her food.
Just so (her young removed) the heifer lows,
Refuses comfort, and renews her woes.
But tedious indirection wastes the day:
In fine, my love of life had pined away.
If asked, my ready answer's short and brief:
My Galla's beauty, to my dole and grief,
Had compassed me, as spiders compass flies,
As serpents compass wildfowl with their eyes!
Her cheeks were ruddy, and her limbs were long,
Her eyes (though gleyit) held a promise strong.
She seemed to me, who loved her as she smiled,
As Dian lovely and as Ceres mild.

Fortunatus

Love steals the senses, blinds the one who sees,
Makes weak the strong, and steals our liberties.
The heart once entered, Cupid stirs the flame,
Removes our judgement, and enjoys the game.
Not *Amor,* then, but *Error* is his name,
Not butter-sweet but bitter-sour his fame.

Faustus

Her nods, her becks her equal love foretold,
But fortune does not always aid the bold!
A comrade grim attended as she walked:
Her mother, or her married sister stalked!
They dwindled my desire, they watched the house,
They eyed her going as a cat a mouse:
For when the mouse steals forth on mischief bent,
The cat, though torpid, is the more intent.

Fortunatus

He praises thrift whose purse is stuffed with pelf,
And hunger, when his belly bursts itself.

Faustus

Now came the time to scythe the whitened field:
The stems were nodding with the barley's yield.

The mother came, with daughters, to the ground:
What reapers lost, the patient gleaners found.
That mother knew I sighed, but scorned my name;
She saw my rustic gifts, and knew my flame.

Fortunatus

A foe to honesty, to vice a friend,
Her need made her deceitful in the end.

Faustus

The rustic maiden ever followed me:
Her foot was naked, and her arm was free;
A hat she wore throughout the summer days
To save her features from Apollo's rays:
If face be tanned and features darkly burn,
A maiden sees her love to others turn.
And now behind, beside, with shoulders bent,
She gleaned the stalks I dropped with kind intent;
And, woman-like, she did not fail to show
That love was there, was growing, and would grow.
This much frivolity she let me see;
This much of levity she showed to me.

Fortunatus

Not only maids are such, but those whose mind
Is lauded far above the human kind,
Whose robe is edged with purple's glowing band,
Whose wealth is splendid and whose riches grand.
The girl was silly? *You* were sillier:
The profit that you made you gave to her!
Continue; sleep may overcome my eyes:
So hot the summer sun, the cloudless skies.

Faustus

Enraged, the mother shouted her alarm;
Her spite was kindled and her wrath grew warm:
"Why, Galla, have you thus deserted me?
The shade is cooler by the alder-tree!
Here, by the edges of the barley-field,
The breeze is fresher, and profuse the yield!"
At this my brow grew dark, and swift I prayed,
"You breezes, bring to me your present aid:

Reverse your course and change your path today,
And blow her mother's spiteful voice away!"
Should any lead his flock to meadows fair,
And then forbid the thirsty sheep to drink;
Who then would not condemn this cruel spite,
And save the luckless sheep from such a plight?
That voice as hateful to my listening ear
As thunder and as lightning did appear.
For all I tried, I could not help but glare,
While Galla smiled at me with timid air.
Again the mother called, again she cried;
Again the daughter, hearing, naught replied.
Since Galla's heart and step now followed me,
My duty 'twas to aid her liberty.
No ruse does crafty Cupid e'er forget:
He makes the crafty lover craftier yet.
With noise and clamor filled I then the rear:
The mother thought that Galla could not hear.
Then quick I cleared the prickly thorns aside
To give my love a path both safe and wide.

Fortunatus

See how the lover bears his bondage now,
Endures the goad, and drags the weighty plow!

Faustus

Your words attest a knowledge of the heart.

Fortunatus

I too have loved, I too have felt the dart.

Faustus

This venomed sweet, this joy to harm inclined,
Grew by the hour, and flourished in my mind.
Pale, mute, and sleepless did I senseless lie;
A prey to madness and to love was I.
No need to tell what caused my misery:
My brow revealed my spirit's malady.
No stranger to the god, my kindly sire
Divined my hurt and yearned to quell the fire:
"Unhappy boy, the mark of love you bear:
Reveal your passion and relieve your care!"

Fortunatus

To harshness though a parent may incline
His heart is loving and his aim benign.

Faustus

He asked; I answered; straight he promised true
To win the mother and the maiden too.
So, long before the wintry fields were white,
My courtship prospered and my heart was light.
But though of pleasures I might often dream,
Like Tantalus, I thirsted 'mid the stream.
How oft I left the weary plow to see
If she, alone at home, might welcome me!
How oft I found excuse on her to steal—
A strap, a yoke, a scraper, goad, or meal:
Whate'er was lacking sought I from her store:
What lacked I most, yet must I hunger for.
Yet I did toil: to work the livelong day
My hand was ready, for my heart was gay.
My hunting's booty would I give to her:
The neighbors smiled to see my busy stir.
But once, in secret tryst, at midnight's stroke,
Her father's snoring hounds I careless woke.
Mid lights and din I leaped the garden fence;
Escaped, nor came again, once driven thence.
But now the heavy wintertime had passed:
The spring had come, the wood was green at last.
The grain was spiky 'mid the morning dew;
At night with gleaming wings the beetle flew.
At last arrived the day of promise bright,
At last arrived the longed-for nuptial night;
No need to tell the pleasures of the bed:
The breeze was kindly and the ship was sped.
Two days and nights we feasted 'neath this tree:
An ox was slaughtered and the wine flowed free.
The meats were laid on rustic tables here,
And friends arrived to feast from far and near;
And when they'd had their fill of food and wine,
The village-jester entertained the line.
With bag and drone and chanter then uprose
The manly piper, with his manly pose:

His head is raised aloft, with gesture grand,
His cheeks empurpled swell, his lungs expand,
His eyes protrude, his eyebrows rise and soar;
He stamps his foot, and struts about the floor.
The rustic maidens love the piper's strains,
And tread a lively measure with their swains.
Three years of pleasure have already passed;
The fourth approaches and approaches fast:
The joyful day it is that disappears;
The slowest is the one that's full of tears.

Fortunatus

But, Faustus, see! The cows attack the vine!
Arise and save the grapes—or pay the fine!

In the second eclogue (174 hexameters) the same pair of shepherds discourse on the unhappy course of illicit love. Faustus suggests that they resume the topic of love (*nostros repetamus amores:*
27) and Fortunatus launches forth into a long tale, occasionally
interrupted by the comments of Faustus, of the amatory misadven-
tures of a common friend, a shepherd named Amyntas: Amyntas
had become infatuated with a young married woman and, in the
grip of desire, had become "a raging wanton boy that seemed bereft
of sense."

The poem has its sequel in the third eclogue (*Amyntas: De insani
amoris exitu infelici*; 194 hexameters). Faustus and Fortunatus
discuss the recent hail storm that has done little damage to their
own farms but has had grievous effects on those near Verona (1-46),
after which Fortunatus re-echoes the words of Faustus in the second
eclogue (*nostros repetamus amores:* 47) and launches forth into a
long narrative (50-155) of the miserable end of Amyntas.

The poem ends abruptly, as usual: Weep we must, says Faustus;
but the evening star has already appeared—the sun is setting, and
black clouds threaten rain; it is high time to turn our animals
homeward.

Three aspects of the poem point to future developments. The
didactic tone of large passages foreshadow the moralizing didactic
eclogues of such poets as Gervais Sepin of Saumur; the satirical
attitude anticipates such poems as Mantuan's fourth eclogue and
those pastorals dealt with in Chapter XII; the lament for the unknown poet is a forerunner of scores of full-blown pastoral epicedia

like the younger Janus Dousa's poem on the death of Sir Philip Sidney at Zuetphen.

A younger contemporary and friend of Mantuan was Battista Fera or Fiera (1469-1538) of Mantua, described by Alessandro Perosa as "a physician, a philosopher, and a poet reasonably well known in his day." In the fifth book of his overgrown epyllion *Trophaeum Gonzagae,* Mantuan describes how, after the battle of Fornovo (July, 1495), the wounded Marquess Gianfrancesco III Gonzaga returned home to Mantua, but before reaching the city was met by a convoy, sent ahead by his wife Isabella (daughter of Ercole d'Este), supplying him with food, wine, ointments, and— most important of all—a man to whom the poet devotes a longish and quite eloquent passage of panegyric on his merits as physician, poet, and friend, "Battista, eternal glory of the house of the Fieras." No doubt it was gratitude for such praise that, in part, impelled Fiera to set up in 1514—before Mantuan's death, that is—a terra-cotta portrait-bust of the poet along with busts of Virgil and the Marquess Gianfrancesco; this bust of Mantuan still exists in the Museo Patrio in Mantua.

Fiera's poems were published first in a modest volume in 1515 and subsequently reissued in a magnificent specimen of printing at Venice in 1537. His three eclogues, of which we have to examine only one at the moment, are most easily accessible in Johannes Oporinus' anthology of pastoral (799 pages of Latin bucolic poetry by 38 Italian, German, Dutch, and French authors), published at Basel in 1546.

The first of Fiera's pastorals, *Meliboea* (only sixty-five hexameters in length), is a modest and undistinguished piece of work. There is little in its Latinity or versification at which even Scaliger might cavil (although, being Scaliger, he did, as did Lilio Giraldi), except for the occasional awkward elision; nor is the structure in any way remarkable. The poem is simply a quiet-toned lament by the shepherd Alcippus over the death of his mother Meliboea—the melancholy is sentimental and correct, the due and proper figures of thought and of speech are introduced very much *à la mode de Virgile,* and all nature, as of course it must, mourns. I have little doubt that, if a college undergraduate who had carefully studied Virgil's eclogues were to be given this poem for sight-translation, he would find it pleasantly easy to translate and would enjoy it for its straightforward Latin and its fluent and occasionally adroit use of familiar images. Nevertheless, if this specimen of art-pastoral were Fiera's only eclogue, we might brush it aside as little more than a competent exercise based on much industry, a tenacious memory, and a commendably exact knowledge of Latin. Fortunately, the two garden-eclogues to be discussed in a later chapter prove that Fiera had rather more originality than this little work would suggest.

The next author we meet was not a teacher like Guarino the Younger, a scholarly copyist like Mario, an administrator like Strozzi, an independent nobleman like Boiardo, a churchman like Mantuan, or a physician of literary tastes like Fiera, but that typical phenomenon of the Renaissance, the professional protégé—Pierfrancesco Giustolo of Spoleto (ca. 1450-1529). He accompanied Cesare Borgia on a number of his campaigns, earning his keep by composing no fewer than twelve Latin panegyrics on his patron, of which only three have survived: the others were destroyed in the war with Faenza. Among the poems also appear a few verse epistles, an epicedium on the death of the Roman Humanist Pomponio Leto, a brief didactic poem (*De cultu croci*) addressed to Agostino Geraldini, and three eclogues; the second eclogue belongs to the section on new forms of pastoral, the first to that on new uses.

Giustolo's third eclogue, entitled *Galatea,* runs to 106 hexameters. Corydon prays to Pan for wings like Mercury's as he hurries to the city (in the Never-Never land of pastoral there is always a city, usually unnamed, not too far off) to visit Galatea, whom he has not seen for two weeks while she had been visiting friends. As he speeds along he daydreams happily of her beauty and imagines himself in her embrace: like most Latin and Neo-Latin poets Giustolo becomes distinctly specific and outspoken here. It has sometimes been said (e.g., by Paul van Tieghem) that the Neo-Latinists wrote only for men, as Renaissance women knew no Latin—but the extensive collected Latin works of such women as Isotta and Ginevra Nogarola, Cassandra Fedele, Olimpia Morato, and others are enough to show that the rule has important exceptions.

Corydon catches sight of an old friend, Amyntas by name, and hails him. Amyntas tells Corydon that Galatea has left the city unusually early and is now waiting with her flock in the hills, hopefully expecting Corydon: Amyntas envies the reception he will get. Corydon remarks that Amyntas is far luckier than he, for, since he is always with his Phyllis, he has no idea of the pain of separation—or of suspicion; where precisely *is* Galatea?

Amyntas replies that Corydon must give him a present if he is to know: "My voice will not make you happy for nothing!" On

Corydon's promising to give him dinner the next day, Amyntas torments him no longer but gives detailed information on how to find the shepherdess; as Corydon hurries off at top speed, he calls back over his shoulder:

> So let her burn me with a searing flame
> If but she will not, proud, despise my name.
> Farewell; you see those trees beyond the plain?
> Tomorrow by their shade we'll meet again. (104-6)

The poem has no outstanding faults; it has no outstanding virtues, either, but is at least competent and makes pleasant reading. It is chiefly attractive because of the mild spice of malice in Amyntas' words and the ways in which Corydon's stumbling eagerness is displayed.

So far we have dealt only with northern or (in the case of Giustolo) central Italian authors. With Giano Anisio (ca. 1475–ca. 1540) we meet one of the many Neo-Latin authors of Naples. Anisio was born and died at Naples, where he lies buried in a tomb of his own design at the church of S. Giovanni Maggiore. As a young man he studied classical literature and civil law in his native place, traveled cautiously for a while, stayed briefly at Rome, and then returned gratefully to Naples, where he was happy to take holy orders and quietly enjoy the pleasures of a benefice—not a very exciting or heroic life, but a secure and pleasant one, the quietness of which is reflected in the tone of his poems.

His fame as a writer was widespread in his own day; he was known as a fluent and fertile poet who shared Giovanni Pontano's voluptuous streak but whose verse—stylistically correct though it usually was—was weak in feeling and imagination: Pontano was a poet; Anisio was an exceedingly clever, smooth versifier, with more than a tendency to excessive display of erudition. But his work is almost invariably pleasant to read (in small amounts) and much of it—particularly the epigrams and the elegiac occasional poems—is of great importance for the literary and social history of his time.

Of Anisio's six eclogues—all interesting for one reason or another—only two (numbers v and vi) belong to the present category of art-pastoral, and these, while perhaps the least effective of the six, are not the least interesting as documents. The fifth eclogue, entitled *Ursus* (a personal name) is a pleasant pastoral poem of 123 hexameters. There is nothing really exceptional about it: a few shepherds gather in the heat of noon to rest; they pass the time by retelling various unconnected anecdotes of the sort long familiar to any reader of bucolic verse. The lines trip along very neatly indeed, and the reader well knows what to expect in the next line at any given point along the way. The versification and diction are strongly Virgilian; in content the poem is clearly an imitation and amplification of Theocritus' seventh idyll.

One point is worth notice. Although there is no attempt at real portraiture of actual persons, and although this is not a pastoral of the sort where contemporary events or personal relationships are described (as in the many pastorals written as epithalamia and the like), yet it is clear that Anisio's readers were intended to recognize various members of contemporary Neapolitan society. Coritius, for instance, must be the famous German Humanist Johann Goritz, active at this time in Rome, who usually Latinized his name as Corycius; and this easy identification, along with the fact that the Ursus of the poem is about to be married, would lead contemporaries to recognize without difficulty the personalities hidden behind the other Greek names of this poem, of which Carrara writes "anche qui la società partenopea ci sorride da' suoi amori e dallo splendore delle sue terre e delle sue ville."

In the sixth eclogue (*Coritius*; 143 hexameters), the shepherds Foenius and Peridon, in alternating distichs of conventional but by no means stilted charm, praise the rustic beauties Myrtis and Silvia in the presence of the Spartan Coritius. As reward Peridon receives a goblet and Foenius a flute from the older shepherd.

This attractive pastoral I have included among those literary in form, content, and method, even though (as in the fifth) the personalities are real enough. Coritius, although described as a Spartan, is of course Goritz once more, in which case Foenius is most likely Anisio himself and Peridon is possibly Quinziano Stoa—probably the young ladies who are eulogized are equally real. The number of reminiscences of Greek pastoral is noticeable: no doubt within the pastoral setting this is intended as compliment to the allegedly Greek shepherd; but reminiscence of Greek poetry is common among Anisio's compatriots, particularly in Coriolano Martirano, Bishop of Cosenza.

In Paolo Belmisseri of Pontremoli (ca. 1480–ca. 1547) we meet one of the earliest Italian Humanists to bring the new learning (and the Neo-Latin literature) of the Italian Renaissance to France: Publio Fausto Andrelini of Forlì (1460-1518) had earlier been associated with the University of Paris and the court of Charles VII; Paolo Belmisseri was to be connected with the court and family of François I after he had left his position as professor of medicine at Bologna. His collected Latin verse was published in a volume of 108 folia at Paris in 1534. Eight eclogues are followed by a curious didactic and pseudo-philosophic poem called *Heptas* (on the mystic properties of the number seven), a group of fifteen occasional poems practically devoid of interest, a second group of occasional poems that are rather more sprightly, and the philosophic *conclusiones* that the author debated and defended before Pope Clement VII in Rome in 1532. The whole volume is dedicated to François I—individual poems are dedicated to the Dauphin François, Marguerite of Navarre, François I's two daughters Madeleine and Marguerite, Cardinal Louis de Bourbon, Cardinal Jean du Bellay, and so on.

Of the eight eclogues, two (numbers ii and viii) fall under the category of art-pastoral. The second runs to seventy-four hexameters, preceded (as are all the others) by a neat quatrain addressed to the gentle reader:

> If, still untouched as yet, you bear a heart
> That's fancy-free, nor pierced by Cupid's dart,
> Then read—and learn the power of Cupid's flames,
> The songs of lovers, and their rustic names.

The structure of the eclogue is similar to that of many we have already noted. During the height of summer, a shepherd, Mopsus, and a goatherd, Astacus, stopped for a rest by the river Medoacus: both were of an age, both were equal in looks and singing ability, and both were in love with shepherdesses—Mopsus with Phyllis, Astacus with Leucê. They sing the praises of their sweethearts in six amoebaean groups of five lines each (each group is actually a quatrain with the recurring refrain "o si quis duras haec carmina ferret ad aures"). The poem's virtue is its clear Latin, but it lacks vivacity.

The eighth eclogue (81 hexameters) has no specific faults but is equally lacking in sparkle. Here we have an introductory conversation between Nisus and Maenalus (lines 1-28), followed by the amoebaean distichs of two shepherds, Daphnis and Codrus (29-76), and a brief conclusion (77-81) in the words of Nisus. The two singers praise their sweethearts, the summer weather, the fruits, grapes, and trees of their native countryside; but it all grows tiresome long before we reach line 81.

Lack of vivacity can never be charged against Andrea Navagero (1483-1529), one of the most elegant Latin poets of the Italian Renaissance and one of the very few important Neo-Latin writers produced by Venice (it was less a center of literary studies than of erudition), a man whose handsome, patrician features are well known from the splendid portrait by Raphael, now in the Galleria Doria Pamphili at Rome. He was educated by Marcantonio Sabellico the historian, in Venice, and by Marcus Musurus the philologian and Pietro Pomponazzi the philosopher, at Padua. He was a close friend of Girolamo Fracastoro, who paid him the compliment of dedicating to him his dialogue on poetry (*Naugerius*).

Besides scholarly work, Navagero undertook a variety of public duties. Master of a correct and vigorous Latin prose style, he was appointed by the Venetian Senate to deliver the funeral oration of Caterina Cornaro in 1510, that of Bartolommeo d'Alviano in 1515, and that of the Doge Leonardo Laredano in 1521. In 1516 the Senate appointed him custodian of the library of Cardinal Bessarion; this appointment was a sinecure intended to give him the leisure to complete Sabellico's *Historia Veneta* (it was in fact completed by Cardinal Pietro Bembo). Later Navagero was appointed Venetian ambassador to Madrid, where he took no small part in preparing the treaty of 1526 that freed François I, prisoner since the Battle of Pavia; but he found time for literary pursuits and literary friendships in the midst of diplomatic duties, for he became intimate with Juan Boscán of Granada and influenced him in the adoption of an Italian style of verse. Recalled to Venice in 1527, he was appropriately made ambassador to François I, in order to try to induce yet another French king to interfere in Italian politics. While still ambassador, he died at Blois in 1529.

Navagero's vernacular works are few, slight, and of historical interest only, consisting of a few verses, five letters addressed to G. B. Ramusio, and a few succinct but informative notes on his travels in Spain, France, and elsewhere. His Latin works (first published at Venice in 1530 and later brought out in a splendid piece of eighteenth-century printing at Padua in 1718) are few also, but of far greater interest and significance. These consist of the second and third funeral orations (the first he destroyed himself), four literary letters, about fifty pages of critical *adversaria* on the text of Ovid, and the poems (forty-seven, nearly all in the elegiac meter). Imbedded among the poems we find a considerable number of brief pastoral vignettes (*lusus pastorales*) and two bucolic poems in the conventional hexameter meter and of the normal length.

Only the second eclogue (*Iolas*; 88 hexameters) concerns us at the moment, and it must surely be one of the prettiest—indeed, most elegantly finished—of its type in the long history of Neo-Latin pastoral. Navagero's verse is patrician and perfectionist—not for him the slap-dash methods of Mantuan; the only complaint that the captious critic could make is that the occasional line is too close a reminiscence of Virgil or Ovid. *Iolas* is a poem to which it is a pleasure to return even after reading scores of pastorals by scores of poets; Navagero's skill in selecting or discovering the *mot juste* is a minor triumph of literary tact. If it is a virtue to apply precisely the right adjective in precisely the right place at precisely the right time, it is a virtue that is undeniably his; and if he learned the art from Virgil, he refined it by his prolonged study of Ovid.

In content the *Iolas* is as conventional as it could possibly be. It is all very artificial, no doubt; but it is the artificiality of *haute couture*:

> Now graze, my sheep, throughout the verdant plain;
> Return to wander through the meads again.
> No need to spare the meadows' tender lawn;
> For more will grow before the morrow's dawn:
> Thus swell the udders of the gentle dams,
> More than enough to feed the playful lambs.
> Now, Teucon, faithful guardian of the flock,
> My ready watchdog, perched on yonder rock,
> If wolves appear, arouse the loud alarm,
> And keep the innocent from every harm.
> Myself, beside the mossy cavern's shade,
> Shall now rehearse the song that I have made.
> Thus shall I spend at ease the idle hour,
> Beside the cave, beside the spreading bower:
> My Amaryllis, nothing charms my heart,
> So long as you and I must live apart.
> All nature now prepares to welcome spring:
> Each field will blossom, and each bird will sing.
> At last released, the herds can wander free;
> The sheep and goats can wander on the lea.
> Without your presence none of these can charm:
> As well might winter chill my silent farm;

As well might drifting snow o'erspread the plain;
As well might fall the hail of freezing rain.
As grass to lambs, as blossoms to the bee,
As streams to lawns, so is my love to me.
No gold I seek, nor wealth's deluding charms:
I seek to hold my love within my arms,
To spend my life amid such scenes as these—
The plain, the stream, the hills, the gentle breeze.
Here lies my grotto, 'neath the lofty hill,
Here grows the crocus by the icy rill,
Here grows the olive by the cavern door,
Here vines and ivy shade the space before;
Nearby, the spring, that rises from below,
Delights the eye with never-failing flow.
Below, a fertile valley spreads its fields of grain;
A river waters all that smiling plain.
Here live, my Amaryllis; be my wife,
And spend with me a long and happy life.
With me release at morn the bleating lambs,
With me recall at eve their woolly dams.
Within the forest dense, the open plain,
I'll sing for you, and pipe with might and main;
Then, as we turn and make our way along,
We'll join our voices in a happy song.
This done, we'll rest beside a shady rill,
And kiss, and take our pleasure as we will.
Would Heaven grant my prayer, with Croesus' self
I'd not exchange my joy, for all his pelf.
Once did I see you, in your garden there—
A scarlet rose adorned your golden hair.
I saw, I loved, approached with beating heart,
Confessed to you the pain of Cupid's dart.
Then with a smile the scarlet rose you dropped;
I made as though to follow you, then stopped:
The rose, recovered, stays beside me still;
I keep it ever, and I ever will.
Since then, no blossom dearer is to me;
Since then, my heart belongs alone to thee.
What though Alcippê sends her gifts along?
What though she offers love in tuneful song?

Before I cease to love my Amaryllis so,
Will honey from the sour genista flow;
The rose will blossom on a stony walk,
And darnel flower on the lily's stalk;
The lion and the lamb will frisk and play,
The owl be tuneful, Philomel be gay.
As spring is fairer than the winter's pall,
As apples sweeter than the aloe's gall,
As wool is softer than the lion's hair,
So Amaryll outshines each other fair,
This tree bears witness to my love sincere;
I've carved my verses on its surface here:
When rams exchange their wool for spiky hair
Shall I no more extol my lovely fair.—
But as I sing, the moon appears above;
The sun has vanished while I sing my love.
Though chill the night, yet am I still afire,
And naught can cool my heart from its desire.
Rhipaean frost could not assuage my pain;
The only hope lies in my lovely bane.
But come, my flock, leave now the dewy lawns;
Enough of singing till the morrow dawns.

Navagero's verses have a strongly Ovidian flavor. As strict a
Virgilian in verse as he was a Ciceronian in prose was Marco Girolamo Vida of Cremona (ca. 1490-1566), Bishop of Alba and Cremona, whom Ariosto calls "an inexhaustible vein of lofty eloquence."
Born of a distinguished but impoverished family, Vida was soon sent
from his native city (which, like contemporary Siena, was unsympathetic to Humanistic pursuits, being grimly tenacious of medieval
traditions) to Mantua, the spirit of which was far more congenial
to the budding Humanist: here he pursued not only the customary
studia humanitatis but theology and law as well, studies which he
later continued at Padua and Bologna. While still a very young
man, he proceeded to Rome, where he immediately took orders as a
member of the *Canonici regulares domini Ioannis Laterensis*. Vida's
skill in Latin verse soon brought him to the attention of Pope Leo
X, who had carefully examined Vida's witty and entertaining mock-
epyllion on chess called *De scacchia ludo*. It was Pope Leo—the
tradition seems certain—who all but ordered Vida to write the
Christiad, which was to be the work par excellence of Christian

Humanism. This Christian epic occupied the poet's mind for about ten years, and was completed in 1535, during the reign of Clement VII. Like a true Augustan patron, Leo had presented Vida not only with benefices but also with a pleasant country retreat where he could devote himself wholly to composition. Clement dealt as handsomely with the poet: Vida was appointed Bishop of Alba in Piedmont (1532) and administered his diocese with notable success for thirty years; in addition he was created Bishop of Cremona in 1549 by Paul III. He distinguished himself at the Council of Trent but later was forced by the hostilities that followed the death of Francesco Sforza to retire (he was no iron cleric like Julius II, the hero of his unfinished *Juliad*) to Cremona, where he peacefully worked on the second edition (1550) of the *Christiad.*

The second eclogue (*Corydon*; 75 hexameters) presents us with a young man who sings first of Narcissus, then of Arion, and finally of the Nereids, before an admiring throng of shepherds and fauns. In content it is rather a jumble, like Anisio's fifth eclogue; in form it is (like many other poems of Vida) notable for the frequency of Greek rhythms and metrical licenses (one monosyllabic end, two spondaic ends, four quadrisyllabic ends—more than appear in a whole book of the *Aeneid*): it is the more natural in this particular poem since the reminiscences of Theocritus are especially frequent. But it is by far the least capable of Vida's eclogues; it is hard to know just why the poet felt impelled to write it and why he selected the particular stories he has put in Corydon's mouth—almost any other myths would have done as well. If this is a very early poem (as it probably is), it showed considerable precocity, even though its expression is repetitious, and a command of Virgilian idiom far beyond the reach of, say, Quatrario; if, however, the poem was written after Vida's arrival in Rome—after he had achieved such a tour de force as the *De scacchia ludo,* that is—it is distinctly unworthy of him.

Equally unimportant are two eclogues of Girolamo Angeriano of Naples (ca. 1490-1535), of which the first (*Bianorus*; 112 hexameters) is in form a monody. Here the shepherd Bianorus has been unsuccessful in gaining the love of the shepherdess Neaera and is ready to abandon his flock and leave the country. The second poem is an amoebaean dialogue of the usual type in which Libetrius praises the beauty of Chlora and Daphnis describes the power and universality of love in a long series of quatrains. The schematic parallelism is badly overdone in these quatrains and the mannerisms become irritating: in one quatrain the word *silet* is repeated no fewer than nine times in describing how all nature gazes in silence at Chlora's beauty; in the corresponding quatrain the *canit* duly appears in a nine-fold anaphora to express all nature's joy in love.

Quatrario was incapable of handling the rhetorical tricks of pastoral; Angeriano had learned them all too well. The same is true of another Neapolitan poet, Pomponio Gaurico (1481-1530). Gaurico came originally from the town of Gauro (hence his surname) near Salerno and spent most of his youth at Naples in close association with Giovanni Pontano and Giacopo Sannazaro. From about 1500 to 1510 he was at Padua. After a short stay at Rome he was appointed professor of rhetoric at the *Studio* of Naples. His death in 1530 is unexplained: he seems to have set out with carriage and servants from Salerno for Castellamare to pay a visit to a certain lady of wealth and appears to have been murdered en route by a rival.

Quite a number of his works are still in manuscript; but of those that are known, by far the most important is one in excellent Latin prose, written at Padua, entitled *De sculptura*. Gaurico was himself an artist (like the Flemish Neo-Latin poet Johannes Secundus) and his shrewd comments on ancient and contemporary art form the most significant part of the book.

Gaurico devoted the last ten years of his life to Latin poetry, and his elegiac poems are often excellent, marked as they are by spontaneity and sincerity. It is a pity that we cannot say the same of his first two eclogues—early, almost juvenile work, written during his first stay at Naples. The second (*Orpheus*; 128 hexameters) is of precious little importance, and the song of Orpheus is marked by repetitions as mechanical as those of Angeriano and by the use of a refrain no fewer than nineteen times—the use of the refrain in pastoral poetry can be most attractive, but enough is enough.

The first poem (untitled; 136 hexameters) is noteworthy for its overwhelming rhetorical manner and an almost unbelievable use of anaphora that would almost justify one's placing the poem by itself in a special category of new forms of pastoral. After a brief introduction by the poet, Orpheus and Thamyras praise and blame love in alternating quatrains. No one would have any great objection to this conventional form; but the constant and excessive parallelism is too much for any ordinary reader to bear; a brief quotation will achieve more than a page of description:

O.   *quisquis amat,* duro firmet sua pectora ferro;
     quisquis amat, pulchra componat imagine vultus;
     quisquis amat, dulci praevincat carmine cycnos;
     quisquis amat, doctas suadeat placuisse per artes.

T.   *nil opus ut* duro firmet sua pectora ferro;
     nil opus ut pulchra componat imagine vultus;
     nil opus ut dulci praevincat carmine cycnos;
     quisquis amat, fulvum studeat placuisse per aurum.

O.   *qui cupit* in terris felicem degere vitam,
     qui cupit aetherei cognoscere gaudia caeli,
     qui cupit ambrosia pasci hyblaeoque liquore,
     ille amet, ille suo semper succumbat amori.

T.   *qui volet* infelicem degere vitam,
     qui volet inferni cognoscere tristia mundi,
     qui volet elleboro pasci saevisque cicutis,
     ille amet, ille suo semper succumbat amori. (20-35)

After 136 such hexameters the reader begins to wish that amoebaean verse had never been invented.

Gaurico turned again to pastoral poetry some time later. His third eclogue (a panegyric of Pope Julius II) we shall reserve until chapter eleven; the fourth (*Thyrsis*; 125 hexameters) we need only mention.

Francesco Berni of Lamporecchio near Florence (1497-1535) published, in his late twenties, twelve Latin poems, but, as Ellinger remarks, these twelve are worth more than some two-hundred-page collections. Berni, like Vida, was a friend of Giovanni Matteo Giberti; and, despite his own personal austerity, was long in the service of the by no means austere Cardinal Bibbiena at Rome, and later of Cardinal Ippolito de' Medici in the same city. Berni's name is a famous one in histories of Italian literature: in parody and burlesque he is unequaled, and it was at his hands that the fantastically exaggerated Petrarchism that had long been popular in Italy received a lethal wound; his combination of ridiculous content and incredibly elegant form is still known as *poesia bernesca*.

There is, as far as I know, only one Latin eclogue by Francesco Berni, the *Amyntas* (73 hexameters). This is a fine specimen of art-pastoral: Berni writes very much in the manner of Virgil's tenth eclogue, but he is careful neither to follow too closely nor to excel by ill imitating. In fact one would readily, I think, place this poem on a par with the *Iolas* of Andrea Navagero himself. Both these poets represent the happy mean between the lumbering, prosy hexameters of Quatrario and the overpoweringly precocious bravura effects attained by Pomponio Gaurico—Virgil himself, I feel, would have read the *Antoniad* of Maffeo Vegio, the *De bombyce* of Vida, and the eclogues of Navagero and Berni with approval and pleasure. It is true that Berni's poem is imitative verse; nevertheless Berni might well have replied to a hostile critic as did Virgil himself, who said that to steal a line from Homer was to steal the club from Hercules.

The plot of the poem is simple, as usual. At midday Meliboeus had gathered his flock together under a shady holm oak and passed the time by singing to himself of the sorrows of his dead friend Lycidas—how Lycidas had loved the unresponsive Amyntas, had died of grief, and at last been buried by the sorrowing nymphs:

> At noon the shepherd Melibee reclined
> Beneath a spreading oak; to rest resigned
> His flock still cropped the grassy surface ripe
> The while their master sought, with shepherd's pipe,
> To tell the tale of Lycidas, whose pain
> Was known to every hill, to every plain;
> His plaints made every wood with grief resound—
> From rivers, caves alike, the cries rebound:
> "You woodland nymphs, who saw, who heard the youth,
> You woodland nymphs, reveal to me the truth,
> How Lycidas, with loving grief oppressed,
> Filled all with cries, to ease his swelling breast.
> This Lycidas, this poor, unhappy swain,
> The fair Amyntas loved, but loved in vain,
> And, wandering through these very spots, alone,
> To ease his aching heart, would ever moan.
> The gentle flock, forgotten, roamed the plain;
> The lowing herd, neglected, lowed in vain;
> No fruitful crop the sickly fields can show;
> The weeds now flourish where the grain did grow.
> Ah, Lycidas, ah, poor unhappy swain,
> Amyntas will your homely gifts disdain,
> Nor, should you offer all your little store,
> Will rich Iolas yield, but offer more.

And so, with love unanswered, through the plain,
The lover sought his comfort, but in vain.
The Dryads saw his grief, and wept for long;
The Naiads, too, and plowmen heard his song.
Apollo's self observed his son's distress,
And Cupid came, to cure his bitterness:
'Set limit to your sorrow,' Cupid cried,
'For love with grief is never satisfied:
As grain for breezes, kids for tender leaves,
So love is greedy for a heart that grieves.'
'Why thus,' cried Lycid, 'sing a gloomy strain,
Why thus, relentless, urge the dying swain?
'Twas you, a god, that first impelled desire;
'Twas you who first aroused my burning fire—
No heavy duty for a god of love;
What mortal could contend with gods above?
So on the downs a raging wolf might rend
The gentle sheep and shepherds without end.
One thing remains before my death to say—
Retain my words, and let the hinds obey:
A time will come when Lycidas shall be
Revered by every swain on bended knee.
Farewell, you shady woods and bosky groves!
Farewell, my gentle flocks and lowing droves!
Now perish, Lycidas, not least of swains,
And may Amyntas hear my dying strains.'
He spoke; about his lifeless body wait
The Nymphs, lamenting loud his cruel fate:
His failing limbs they raise in fond embrace,
And kiss the lips that yet recall his grace.
But now the triple Fates had cut his thread,
And Prosperine received, among the dead,
The voice that once, to Muses and to boys,
Had brought the gift of song and music's joys.
No singer with his songs could e'er compete;
None threw the spear so far, or ran so fleet.
The streams and woods bear witness to the thought
How great the loss that love and death have wrought.
The Naiads, grieving for their absent swain,
Lamented seven days and nights again,

And to his tomb they brought, with long regrets,
The yearly gift of purple violets,
And yearly cried aloud to Lycidas,
    'Twas love alone that caused your death, alas!
All you who tend the flocks' Lycaean run
Avoid love's madness and its pleasures shun.
Love is to all a sharp and deadly pain,
To mortals poison and to beasts a bane:
As bullocks fight, so heifers rage in heat;
The herd, grown sickly, neither drink nor eat.' "
    This song did grieving Melibee rehearse
The while he charmed the breezes with his verse,
Till, unperceived, the heavens with stars were hung,
And rustic duties stilled the tuneful tongue.

Tommaso Raggio (Flaminius Rajus or Raiius) of Prato (*floruit* 1510-1530) was a fairly prolific Latin poet contemporary with Giacopo Sannazaro, part at least of whose *Arcadia* he is believed to have translated into Latin. Raggio may have written several eclogues; if he did, all except one (like all of those by Amerigo Corsini, 1452-1501) have disappeared; on such losses Carrara philosophically remarks, "ma in questo caso puo ben dirsi che basta sapere, per la diffusione del genere, che tali poesie furono composte, ben sicuri che non perdiamo molto con l'ignorarle." The one extant eclogue of Raggio is entitled *Mopsus* (127 hexameters); the whole poem is a monody, a lament by a shepherd, with the refrain "pulchra Amarylli, redi; cur Mopsum, saeva, relinquis?" The theme appears in lines 1-6:

> What cause is here to change your love for me?
> Why has your heart been turned to cruelty?
> Why leave this pleasant leafy grove to roam?
> Why seek another's love, another's home?
> Should I not think that love from you is due?
> Should you not know the love I've borne for you?

There is nothing new or unusual in ideas or expression; but we must certainly admit that Raggio is skillful in manipulating language, as in the following:

> seu tenebras vesper, seu lucem ostentat Eous,
> me flentem vesper, flentem me cernit Eous. (13-14)

But he never permits rhetoric to get the better of him as do his older contemporaries Angeriano and Gaurico; this poem is an excellent one of its type.

Among a group of Veneto-Lombard Neo-Latinists appear a remarkable trio of brothers, members of a family of Friuli (originally from Pordenone), that for two hundred years produced a steady succession of Humanists and literary men, many of whom belonged to what is called *l'umanesimo controreformista.* Girolamo (1507-1574), Giambattista (1525-1573), and Cornelio Amalteo of Oderzo (1530-1603?) were among the best and certainly the most celebrated Latin poets of the sixteenth century in Italy. Giuseppe Toffanin writes of Giambattista, "rinfocolava ai fervori della controriforma l'entusiasmo classico dei predecessori"; the same remark could be made of Marcantonio Flaminio of Serravalle.

Girolamo Amalteo, who, after teaching medicine at Padua, practiced it at Ceneda, Serravalle, and Oderzo, was known particularly for his Latin epigrams; these were as widely read in Europe in the sixteenth and seventeenth centuries as were those of the later Welsh Neo-Latin epigrammatist John Owen. Many of Girolamo's poems have a bucolic flavor, but only one of the eighty—number xiv—can truly be called an eclogue. Although it is composed in elegiacs, it is in all but meter (like Niccolo d'Arco's *Galatea* and Arthur Johnston's satirical *Tityrus Fasting*) a real eclogue and not merely (like Pietro Bembo's *Galatea*) an elegiac poem displaying pastoral or idyllic elements. This poem is modeled on Virgil's eighth pastoral (*Pharmaceutria*; "The Enchantress"), in the second part of which a shepherd called Alphesiboeus had told how a woman tried by magic spells to make her lover Daphnis return to her. There are many *Pharmaceutria* poems in Neo-Latin literature; this one is unusual for its meter, for its lack of a recurring refrain, and because the chief figure is not a woman trying to recall a lover who has lost interest in her but the poet, who is trying (unsuccessfully) to rid himself of his overpowering love for Hyalê. At first his spells seems successful, and he feels a certain relief; at last, he says, he will be able to turn from love-poetry and devote himself to manlier verse; but he feels love assaulting him once again—he struggles, give way, and finally concludes,

> te celebrent alii, quibus est mens libera, vates;
> mi sat erit dominae posse placere meae. (77-78)

An editorial note on this poem appearing in the Amsterdam (1728) edition of Sannazaro tells us that Girolamo wrote this poem when he was very young indeed (*admodum adulescens*), in which case the following lines (61-62) seem distinctly precocious:

> gauderem interdum niveas tractare papillas
> et dare compressis oscula blanda notis.

But it is a poem of some originality and of quite unusual verbal dexterity; Girolamo and his Latin teacher had been understandably proud.

Of Antonio Maria Visdomini (*floruit* 1520-1530) little is known except that he was a private tutor in the home of the noble and wealthy Rangone family, that he was the author of a quasi-philosophical dialogue called *De otiis,* and that an eclogue called *Silvanus* (120 hexameters) appears within its framework. After an introduction full of Theocritean echoes, Silvanus tells Thyrsis the story of his unsuccessful courtship of Philomena; the two shepherds decide at last to drive off their flocks, abandoning this countryside forever, but not before Silvanus has carved warning verses on the bark of the beech-tree under which they have been sitting:

> All dwellers in this wood, all men and Fauns,
> Avoid these trees, avoid these grassy lawns;
> If here you stop to rest or sleep in shade,
> Your heart will soon be broken by a maid (117-19)

Thyrsis agrees that the beech, which had once given food to mortals, now yields nothing but bitterness. It is a good enough poem, but there are scores better to be found among Neo-Latin pastorals.

Francesco Vinta of Florence (*floruit* 1550-1560) was a lawyer connected with the court and administration of Duke Cosimo de' Medici and even more with Francesco de' Medici of Florence and Siena. He was an excellent minor poet and littérateur who, like his good friends Benedetto Accolti the Younger, Fabio Sangi, and Benedetto Varchi, modeled his work on that of Andrea Navagero and Marcantonio Flaminio. His best poems are the twenty-three *lusus pastorales* (in elegiacs, hexameters, and Sapphics) that appear in the two books of his collected poems. In his one full-scale eclogue (*Amyntas*; 121 hexameters) the two interlocutors are Maenalus and Alcon. The structure of the poem is quite formal: after a twenty-two-line introduction by the poet, Maenalus and Alcon alternate songs of seven lines each for ten interchanges, then single sets of five lines each (93-102) and six lines each (103-114); the poem ends with seven final lines from Alcon. Their songs form a lament over the death of a shepherd named Amyntas; I suspect that Amyntas was a real person and that this poem should accordingly be included among the epicedia or funerary eclogues that were excessively common in Italy and Germany, particularly in the sixteenth century. A skeleton outline of part of the antiphonal lament follows:

A. All the towns of Tuscany lament.

M. The river-gods of Arno and Tiber lament.

A. Triton, Tethys, and Amphitritê lament.

M. Nereus, Melicerta, and Neptune lament.

A. Galatea, the Muses, and Graces loved him for his songs.

M. Dolphins, swans, and Nereids loved him for his songs.

A. Like sea-birds in a storm, we were terrified by his death.

M. Like a man that steps on a snake we were terrified by his death.

And so it goes on, until Alcon reminds Maenalus that night is coming on apace. The schematic parallelism of the poem is not quite so aridly mechanical as the above abbreviated summary of lines 23-78 would suggest; the chief fault of the poem is rather the excessive number of Theocritean and mythological allusions.

A little younger than Francesco Vinta was another lawyer, Francesco Denalio of Reggio Emilia (*floruit* 1560-1570), who was likewise linked with a ruling house, that of Ottavio Farnese, Duke of Parma and Piacenza. His four books of Latin poems (Bologna, 1563) were written while he was studying literature and law as the University of Bologna; the first is dedicated (very properly) to Duke Ottavio—the remaining three are dedicated to various members (in descending order of importance) of the ruling house of Corregio that had attained prominence in the early part of the sixteenth century under Count Gilbert X and his countess Beatrice. Denalio's vernacular poems were published, again at Bologna, in 1580. There is a tradition that he was crowned a laureate by Charles V, but Tiraboschi casts doubt on it. Among the Latin poems appear a number of *lusus pastorales* and two eclogues, both examples of the purely Humanistic type of pastoral (the third eclogue is not by Denalio).

The first eclogue (*Lucilla*; 103 hexameters) is a monody in which the shepherd Celaenus calls upon his unco-operative sweetheart Lucilla to relent. There is nothing really unusual in the poem; it is common, for instance, for the singer to attempt to arouse his lady's jealousy by pointing out that he could, if he wished, enjoy the gifts (listed) and favors (hinted at) of Neaera or Daphne; Celaenus does, it is true, cite a larger number of girls' names than does any shepherd in any other pastoral I can recall.

The second eclogue (*Tmoleon*; 118 hexameters) is in dialogue throughout, the greater part being a singing-match in amoebaean couplets between Lytius and Macron before Tmoleon, who, as is usual in pastoral, concludes the poem by saying that both have won. A typical passage occurs on p. 178 of the 1563 edition:

M.   How oft, how oft has Lisa clipped me tight,
       And bade me come (her husband gone) at night.
L.   Lelaea, too; she bids me join her soon,
       When that her husband's mother sleeps at noon.
M.   With charms unveiled, my Lisa's soft as silk,
       As gentle as the lamb, as white as milk.
L.   I'll say no more (for fear and modest shame):
       Lelaea yields what she might blush to name.

Clearly these rustic belles have a good working knowledge of Ovid's *Ars Amatoria*.

We turn again to Naples with the name of Giovanni Battista Arcucci (*floruit* 1560-70), who called himself in Latin Arcucius or Arcutius. The 1568 edition of his Latin *Odes* is prefaced by complimentary verses by Bernardino Rota, Angelo Constanzio (who remarks that if Sannazaro was the Virgil of Naples, Arcucci was its Horace), and Gianfrancesco Lombardo. Little is known of Arcucci beyond what is claimed in the preface, that he was "a weighty theologian, an eloquent orator, and an excellent poet." The 1568 volume contains four eclogues, of which we shall here examine the second pair.

The third eclogue (*Amyntas*; 107 hexameters) begins with a complimentary address (1-13) to Placido Sangrio, governor of Camerata, in which Arcucci speaks of himself as the successor, in Latin poetry, of Giovanni Pontano (died 1503) and Actius Syncerus (i.e., Giacopo Sannazaro; died 1530). Arcucci then goes on (14-22): What glade, what shepherd does not know Apollo's favorite, Amyntas, whom the Thespiad Nymphs once crowned with a green garland? (Is this intended as a specific reference to an actual contemporary Neapolitan playwright? It seems likely.) They bathed him in the sacred waters of Permessus (i.e., inspired him with poetry). But a young girl had inspired in him a hopeless love which he dared not reveal (does this conceal a reference to an actual lady of the court?), but confined himself to laments. The remainder of the poem (23-107) consists of the monody of Amyntas in praise of the beauty and kindness of Sylvia—it is not outright cento, but does contain an astoundingly large number of echoes of Theocritus, Virgil, Ovid, and (very noticeably) Tibullus; unlike most of the better Neo-Latin poets, Arcucci is not above transferring a whole line or couplet from a classical poet.

The fourth eclogue (*Lyda*; 71 hexameters) is dedicated to Giulio Antonio Santorio, Archbishop of Santa Saverina, and is in dialogue throughout, with Tityrus and Corydon as interlocutors. In return for Tityrus' song in praise of Cupid (16-29), Corydon says that he will tell him the lament of the shepherdess Lyda when abandoned, much against his will, by the blond Lycotas, summoned home to his native shores: the Zephyrs could not soften her woe, nor the river Sebeto, nor the countryside district of Labulla. The specific reference to Labulla suggests a real situation and the reference to a peremptory summons may suggest a young (and perhaps actually blond) diplomat or ecclesiastic recalled to Castile or Aragon—and in fact in lines 41-42 we do come to a reference to Spain: "Who bade you, sweet lad, abandon the bank of Sebeto and visit again the streams of farthest Iberia? ("a, quis te Sebethi, dulcis puer, amne relicto / extremi fontes invisere iussit Iberi?"). The lament of Lyda appears in lines 41-65. Tityrus ends the poem briefly, as usual, by reminding the younger shepherd that the sun has set and that the night air can be harmful.

This poem is not nearly so full of imitative phrases as the earlier one and is certainly a great deal livelier to read. The most remarkable aspect of it is the rather lubricious description of the couple's love-making in lines 58-65: there is much lubricity (and worse) in Neo-Latin poetry but it is rare in pastoral.

We have already glanced at an elegiac eclogue by Girolamo Amalteo; we can now turn to his brilliant younger brother, Giovanni Battista Amalteo. Giambattista was born in Oderzo in 1528 and died in Rome in 1573. He was widely famed during the cinquecento as a poet, lawyer, philosopher, theologian, and intimate of statesman and authors; he served as secretary of the state of Ragusa (in which

post he was succeeded by his considerably less brilliant brother
Cornelio) and, at Rome, as *segretario ai Brevi* and as what we
should call executive secretary of the *Congregazione del concilio*.
His Italian poems have a sweetness, grace, and elegance truly
Petrarchan; the same qualities appear in his Latin poems, for which
he was chiefly famed during his lifetime, particularly for his elegies
and eclogues.

In the Amsterdam edition (1728) of the poetical works of Sannazaro and the three Amalteo brothers appear seventy-three Latin
poems by Giambattista and one Greek ode; as in the collection of
poems by the eldest brother, the longer and more ambitious hexameter poems (twenty-six of them) come first, and the remaining forty-
seven poems form a separate group consisting of elegies, lyrics, and
epigrammata. According to a prefatory note on page 376, Giambattista's six eclogues are very early work indeed; in that case they
were undoubtedly revised and polished over many years, for in their
present form they are anything but juvenile productions: their frag-
ile, sophisticated grace is on the very razor-edge of decadence. Such
lengthy revision was common among the Neo-Latin poets and
prosateurs: Tito Vespasiano Strozzi subjected his erotic poems to a
lifetime of continuous revision, and Pietro Bembo is said to have
kept no fewer than forty portfolios, through which every page of
Latin verse and prose he ever wrote passed in slow and stately succession, undergoing revision at every step.

Of the six eclogues, four (numbers i, ii, iii, and vi) belong to the
present category. The first poem (*Lycidas*; 93 hexameters) may
have in fact a topical background. After a brief complimentary
address (1-13) to Duke Cosimo de' Medici of Tuscany and a request
not "to scorn the rustic Muses," we are shown Lycidas, who like the
blond youth in one of Arcucci's eclogues "had been bidden to tra-
verse far-off lands," bidding farewell to Italy (17-93). Arcucci's
blond shepherd (if he was in fact an historical personage) was a
Spaniard, for he was described as being summoned "home"—
Lycidas, however, is Italian, for he laments (17-77) having to say
good-by to his own homeland (*patriae fines:* 44). He then turns
and (in lines much more reminiscent of the tone of *lusus pastoralis*
than of eclogue proper) addresses a farewell to the goat that is "the
leader of his flock," and to the laurels under which he has often made
love to Amaryllis (78-93). It is obvious that Lycidas is being sent
to Spain, but there is no hint or allusion in the poem of the shepherd's identity—Carrara believes that Lycidas is Giambattista him-

self, but this is only a guess, and in any case it may not be necessary to look for contemporary reference.

In the second eclogue (*Acon*; 81 hexameters)—a very dainty piece of work indeed—Acon prays to the gods and Nymphs to cure the languid illness of Hyella and promises songs of praise and gifts of roses in return for a speedy recovery. The situation of illness, the name Hyella, the rather sentimental melancholy, the idyllic picture of a countryside covered with flowers and echoing with songs—all these are strongly reminiscent of the *lusus pastorales* of Navagero and Flaminio, and, to tell the truth, some readers may well be inclined to think the poem rather bloodless:

> What god will bear me to the lofty height
> Of Dictê or to Erymanthus bright,
> To gather cyper-rush or panace-leaf
> Or myrrh, to bring Hyella sweet relief?

> Now fails her breath, now labors evermore;
> No physic aids, no cures her health restore.
> Her tears, her grief, her sighs, her bosom's pain,
> Apollo, see, and hear as I complain.

> Almighty Sun, the ruler of the sky,
> Whose warmth enlivens, and whose power is nigh,
> A present help in trouble, lend your aid,
> To comfort Acon, and to cure the maid.

> A lofty laurel by the river's banks
> Shall Acon plant to prove Hyella's thanks:
> Its leaves shall flourish as its boughs extend;
> No cold shall shrivel and no lightning rend.

> Nay, more, Hyella's self, to health restored,
> Shall bring to you her garden's fairest hoard;
> She'll build an altar by the river's edge,
> And keep it ever trimmed with flowering sedge.

> There shall the grateful rustic swains rejoice
> With merry dances and with tuneful voice,
> To tell how once you slew the Python's brood
> And stained unerring darts with serpent's blood.

> You forest-Nymphs, who dwell within the grove,
> And through the caverns' deep recesses rove,

If ever, with due honor, she has brought
The reddest roses to your sacred grot,

If ever she has brought the verben's bloom
Or ivy-boughs to deck the caverns' gloom,
Then bring in turn the Eastern spices rare
That deck the gardens and enrich the air:

To cure Hyella's illness bring the best
Of frankincense from Araby the Blest;
To please Hyella, from the Eastern shore
Bring all the perfumes that the Syrians wore.

Refresh the maiden, and her ills restrain;
Her dolor slacken and relieve her pain;
Restore the blushes to her pallid face;
Renew her voice, her glance, her body's grace.

Just so the hyacinth that blushes 'neath the trees,
Fed by the dew and fostered by the breeze,
If plagued by drought and summer's searing sky,
Will lose its bloom and, like the grasses, die.

Now all the rustic swains their bitter grief confess,
The meadows all reveal their true distress;
No waving blossoms yield their perfumed charm,
But thorn and darnel flourish through the farm.

No painted lilies grace the river's brim,
No lawns, no gardens show their wonted trim;
The very springs contract their watery flow,
And, grieving for Hyella, murmur low.

Now must the sprite familiar of the wave
Withdraw from mossy bank to dreary cave;
No maiden comes to bathe within his stream:
No pliant limb, no snowy breast is seen.

No longer do the songs of maids rejoice
That spirit's heart, with sweet and merry voice;
No longer, at the close of every day,
Do maidens dance the summer hours away.

Now do Hyella's lips yet paler grow;
No more the woods her cheerful presence know.

To Heaven daily do I fervent pray
To spare her frame and drive the plague away.

But see! the Dryads' selves the cures convey,
And bid Hyella put her fears away!
The ready Nymphs now bring their eager aid,
To heal the malady, and save the maid!

Soon shall Hyella tread the leafy grove,
Soon through familiar vistas shall she rove,
The while, with gladsome noise, the rustic train
Shall fill with grateful voice the smiling plain.

The third eclogue (*Corydon*; 90 hexameters) is less likely to
hold the reader's attention, for all its verbal felicity. Here Corydon
envies the breezes that can accompany his huntress-sweetheart Nisa
wherever she goes, and on this conventional thought Giambattista
rings many an elegant change upon many an elegant Virgilian and
Ovidian line; certainly his variety of phrase and his command of
the due epithet are alike remarkable, as in the poems of Navagero.

In the sixth eclogue (*Daphnis*; 74 hexameters) the shepherd
Daphnis calls from the wood to Hyalê to come to him, escaping in
the early dawn from her still sleeping mother. Daphnis is impatient
and urges her not to take time to primp, concluding with the words,

Your mother sleeps: then come to love's delight;
The dewy lawns and shady woods invite.
A thousand kisses wait, a thousand sighs;
A thousand gifts await your startled eyes.
Still glowing, fades from sight the morning-star,
And Venus smiles approval from afar! (70-74)

Some may find this poem a trifle too arty and consider even its
seventy-four lines a trifle too long; of the four eclogues we have thus
far noticed certainly the first and second are the most rewarding.

With Giambattista Amalteo the Humanistic type of eclogue in
Italy reached a pitch of mannered elegance from which we can
observe its decline in Pigna, Marco Publio Fontana, and Giovanni
Antonio Volpi. Giovanni Battista Nicolucci, usually called Pigna
(1530-1577), was born at Ferrara and educated there by Lilio
Gregorio Giraldi, Alessandro Guarino, and Vincenzo Maggi. At
twenty he was appointed professor in the *Studio* of Ferrara and at
this unusually early age found himself welcomed into the court of

Ercole d'Este, Duke of Ferrara. He eventually became secretary, chancellor, and official historian of Alfonso II. His most important work is *I Romanzi,* an acute and original discussion of poetic invention and imagination that aroused lively discussion with Giambattista ("Cinzio") Giraldi. His *Gorgoferusa* is a lively narrative of the celebrations, *divertimenti,* and spectacles presented at the court of Ferrara at the marriage of Alfonso II with Barbara of Austria (1561). A good many of the works attest the versatility, acuteness, and originality of a man who could hold his own at the Este court with Giraldi, Tasso, and Bartolommeo Ricci.

As a Neo-Latinist he is as productive but far less impressive. His poems, published at Venice in 1553, include four books of *carmina* and one of *satyrae.*

Four of the *satyrae* are eclogues and, of these, two require brief notice here. One of these (number xi) is a *Pharmaceutria* poem in seventy-four elegiac couplets: despite the meter we can regard it as a real eclogue, like a poem by Girolamo Amalteo examined earlier. Here a witch named Empusa endeavors by means of incantations to draw her former lover Menippus back from Lycia to Libya, and finally, like Aemê in an earlier poem, realizes from favorable omens that her spells have been successful:

> Siste mihi, Styx atra, meum mihi siste Menippum:
>   ex Lycia tandem Punica regna petit. (147-148)

The second of the *satyrae* (*Galatea;* 67 hexameters) if of very little interest indeed. A shepherd named Sylvanus finds Galatea as she wanders along the seashore and takes this opportunity to urge her to be less cruel to his suit; she casts up to him the number of sweethearts he has deceived in the past and is continuing to deceive in the present. Sylvanus finally gives up and returns gloomily to his home at the foot of the mountains. This poem is dull not only for anyone who has read through all the eclogues thus far discussed in this chapter and the preceding two; it would be dull for anyone who had never read any Neo-Latin pastorals at all—it is so totally lacking in vivacity that even the *Pharmaceutria* (itself far from outstanding) is preferable.

A Humanist little-known today but of considerable repute in Italy and elsewhere from about 1600 to 1750 was Marco Publio Fontana of Bergamo (1548-1609), fellow townsman and friend of Torquato Tasso. Fontana was carefully educated by his father, Gianfrancesco, and by Pietro Rossi, receiving a most thorough training in Greek and Latin literature, especially in the poets (above all, Virgil). For mathematics, philosophy, and eventually medicine, he was sent to Brescia, but continued to study the poets, as he did after transferring his interest to theology and the Church Fathers.

The first collected edition of his Latin poems (Bergamo, 1752) runs to well over three hundred pages. The chief work is the *Delphinis* in three books, a mythological epic of very little but historical interest today. This is followed by five books of *Heroica carmina* (verse epistles, epicedia, and the like). Besides Horatian lyrics, hendecasyllabics, and a hexameter poem on the birth of Christ, there is also the *Pastoralia carmina*—six eclogues and three *lusus pastorales*.

The fifth eclogue (*Doris et Alcon*; 78 hexameters) is by far the least attractive, being a sentimental love-story of little verve. The sixth eclogue (*Caprea,* "The She-Goat"; 103 hexameters) has far more to offer. Much earlier the Neo-Latin eclogue had given rise to a new class of pastoral poem called pastoral vignette (*eclogiola,* "miniature eclogue") or pastoral toy (*lusus pastoralis*). These could be unconnected poems in lyric meters, written as individual pictures of nymphs, satyrs, or shepherds and shepherdesses; they could also be written as connected sequences or cycles telling a continuous story, as in the third book (fourth, in some editions) of the poems of Marcantonio Flaminio of Serravalle (1498-1550). At the close of the sixteenth century and the beginning of the seventeenth the influence began to run in the other direction: the *lusus pastoralis* began to influence the eclogue proper, and we find bucolics which show far more similarity to Flaminio than to Virgil. The second eclogue of Giambattista Amalteo is the first noteworthy example, and the influence of the tone of the sentimental miniature eclogue is especially noticeable in the sixth bucolic of Fontana. At the same time there appears in this poem much burlesque and parody of the stock phrases, stock laments, and stock consolations that appear in the countless epicedia (pastoral or otherwise) in which the Neo-Latin literature of practically every European country abounds from 1400 to 1700 and later.

This poem is a lament over the death of a youthful she-goat of vast charm (*caprea suavissima*) allegedly belonging to Bartolommeo Fino, a gentleman of Bergamo who doubtless had sufficient knowledge of Latin, of pastoral poetry, of *lusus pastoralis,* and of epicedia to appreciate the combination of melancholy elegance and ponderous consolation that pervades the eclogue:

> You lofty crags, remotest ridges steep,
> To which the fleetest goats alone can leap,
> Grant me your stony ears, your rocky mind,
> While I lament the fairest Rosalind.
> Your jagged peaks have mourned her woeful death,
> Your empty caves lament with earthy breath;
> What grief, then, think you, should inspire my friend,
> Whose soul of love and pity is a blend,
> When first he saw that tender goat in pain,
> By Lycidas recovered from the plain?
> Not yet had she to rocky peaks attained,
> Nor fed on Alpine grasses, weather-stained,
> Nor dashed with headlong rush through mountain rill:
> But still must she be mourned on every hill.
> As yet, on dainties fed, she looked her thanks,
> Or drained her mother's never-failing flanks.
> Why should my friend not love so sweet a toy?
> Why should his heart not grieve to lose his joy?
> His true companion, never did she roam:
> Her pretty footsteps echoed through his home.
> His step she followed, sure of tenderness,
> And begged with lifted hoof a light caress. (1-22)

> But now through fields Elysian must she tread,
> Beside the oak, beside the river-bed,
> Where blooms the amaranth with tender grace,
> Where lilies and where violets embrace.
> Can you recall your master and his friend?
> Do sense and feeling with the body end?
> They stay! The gods this favor surely lend.
> Your master cannot lose your memory,
> Or loose his mind from conscious misery;
> What though his powers of poesy remain,
> He still can utter but a grievous strain:
> Here by the cavern's mouth, the chilly shade,
> He still must mourn the goat that died a maid!
> "Alas (he cries), alas, and must you die?
> No healing hands can keep you 'neath the sky?

No dainties drive away the fell disease,
No kindness aid, no gentle comfort please? (40-55)

"Come, father Pan, the country's kindly friend,
Who guard the Satyrs, and the Fauns defend,
Oft have you seen her, at my frugal board,
Approach the table, and salute her lord,
Request a morsel that she could but spy,
Accept the comfit with a melting eye.
Can you not love the memory of this pet?
And can the fields of Hellas charm you yet?
While yet I grieve, while yet I shed my tears,
Will you not come to aid and still my fears?
Let Heaven bring me back my Rosalind,
Or bring a plaything of a different kind. (61-69)

"But sure some god will grant me this request:
She shall appear on heaven's starry breast!
Her light shall glitter in the starry sphere,
Like Caprea brilliant, and like Haedi clear.
When cloud and rain shall threaten to descend,
She'll warn the farmer and inform her friend!
This, Heaven, be your task; let there remain
To build within my home a tiny fane,
A tomb of marble for the corse to rest,
On which now read these words, my cleric guest:
'The darling of her lord this stone conceals;
The measure of his grief this stone reveals.'" (82-93)

At this point Fontana concludes the poem by addressing his friend:

May all the rustic Muses favor bring
To crown my labor: 'tis the last I sing.
Here stands a temple, fanned by breezes mild,
A temple sacred to a Virgin's child;
Hard by, my home provides a life of ease;
My garden nurtures, and my studies please.
You now, your rustic holiday complete,
The city welcomes, and the noisy street:
No leisure now; to urban cares restored,
Pray still recall how sweet our rustic board (94-103).

Many more pastorals from the sixteenth and seventeenth centuries could be cited from minor authors. We may, however, close this chapter by noting one eclogue written by a typical eighteenth-century philologian, Giovanni Antonio Volpi (1686-1766), remembered today as a learned Lucretian scholar and especially as editor of the poems of Navagero and Sannazaro. Volpi's three books of *Carmina* were published at Padua in 1725; besides a number of *lusus pastorales* there appears an eclogue of 183 hexameters (*Carm.,* III, iii), entitled *Charidemus*. Despite its length, it is pretty, attractive, and well written. An old shepherd named Chromis finds Neaera wandering sadly alone and asks the reason for her depression. Neaera heaves a gusty sigh and wonders (at rather excessive length) why it is that when Cupid can overwhelm the most august divinities a young shepherd like Charidemus can ignore both Cupid and her. Chromis in a distinctly pedantic speech tells her that it is by no means out of the question for her to make the first advances—we can observe just such a phenomenon in the animal kingdom, he adds kindly, and lists examples.

Neaera, for all her lovelorn state, is a young lady of spirit, who can tell a hawk from a handsaw and a fool from a falcon. She replies sharply that she is no whinnying mare; nor for that matter does she relish the implied comparison of Charidemus to a stallion. Chromis huffily answers that he is an old, old man and a very, very wise one, which impresses Neaera not at all.

Neaera sits down and pours forth a song on a theme now hackneyed in pastoral—how she first met Charidemus, and how overpowering is the effect of love. She describes her own physical and emotional reactions and expresses her longing to live with him and be his love.

Chromis is delighted with her song and praises her, prophesies that Charidemus will soon change his mind and offers his assistance as a go-between; never give up hope, he adds, for it is always darkest before dawn, and a cloudy sky always clears eventually. And with these tried and true sentiments the poem ends.

It is clear that (despite many ups and downs) the Neo-Latin art-pastoral retained its vitality from 1460 to 1725: this last eclogue still has vigorous, lively and amusing aspects. It is time now to turn to the other countries of Europe and to observe the course of this variety of pastoral in Germany, the Low Countries, France, England, and Scotland.

VII

THE ART-PASTORAL OF THE

RENAISSANCE: II

he extent of German Neo-Latin poetry is immense, and even if one were to read through the four chunky volumes of the *Delitiae poetarum Germanorum* (Frankfort 1612; Volume III alone has 1,515 pages of blindly small print) one would still have made only a beginning. Yet one does not have to read far to observe differences from the Italian poets. For most of the Italians, the composition of this new Latin literature was an avocation: their working hours were devoted to the strenuous pursuit of law, theology, diplomacy, the civil service, the Church, and the like; but only a few betray the amateur's uncertain grasp of technique and material. In general, too, there is an aristocratic flavor to it all, especially in such writers as Navagero and Bembo. The Germans, on the other hand, are commonly priests, schoolmasters, or University professors; in Germany the background of Neo-Latin literature is not a ducal court or diplomatic corridor, but the groves of Academe. And in the eclogue, we find that the art-pastoral is less common than in Italy; the Germans were more interested in using pastoral as a medium for the discussion of contemporary matters and the like. In the present chapter we shall meet three German poets only.

The earliest German pastorals of importance are those of Helius or Elius Eobanus Hessus (1488-1540), whose name represents his birthday (Sunday), his patron saint (Eoban), and his birthplace (Bockendorf or Halgeshausen, in the province of Hesse); his real name was probably Koch, according to the *Allgemeine deutsche Biographie*.

Eoban entered the University of Erfurt in 1504, at the age of sixteen. After a two-year period as principal of the school at St. Severi, he was appointed to the court of Bishop Hiob von Dobeneck at Riesenburg as secretary; he also served as unofficial occasional poet and, unfortunately, as court drunkard. This last proficiency may explain the shortness of his stay at St. Severi; certainly it explains much of his hand-to-mouth existence. In 1513 he turned to law at Frankfort, gave it up, applied himself to literature at Leipzig, gave it up, returned to Erfurt in 1514, and, being penniless and without prospects, married Catharina Spater. His love of drink, his numerous progeny, and his refusal to subject himself to any sort of routine combined to make his correspondence unusually rich in begging-letters.

In 1517, however, Eoban was lucky enough to be appointed Professor of Latin at Erfurt; but this appointment lasted only until 1526. Up to now, the University had been an easy-going spot; but more and more students, inflamed less by love of learning than by a Lutheran zeal that few of their professors shared, deserted the place for Wittenberg while the Lutheran clergy of Erfurt assailed the Humanists as opponents of true religion—it was not long since Catholic priests had done the same. Eoban was ill-advised enough to reply to Luther's preachers in a series of Latin prose satires that guaranteed the loss of the one lucrative position he had ever succeeded in retaining for any length of time.

In 1526 Philip Melanchthon and Joachim Camerarius secured him a position at the short-lived Upper School of Nuremberg; in 1533 Eoban was forced to accept a minor post at Erfurt, but finally received an offer from Marburg, where in comparative happiness he lectured until his death at 48.

Eoban's works are fairly extensive in prose and verse alike. His occasional poetry, like that of many German Neo-Latinists, is adroit and agreeable, but tends to be trivial in subject matter and long-winded in expression. His best original work is without doubt "The Christian Heroines" (Ovidian letters of female saints), as successful an attempt as many during the Renaissance to combine classical finish with Christian content. The seventeen eclogues fall into two groups: the first twelve are very early work, written between 1504 and 1507, but no doubt greatly revised later on; the remaining five were written between 1517 and 1526. Of the seventeen, four are humanistic art-pastorals.

In the second eclogue, *Cantilena Philetae* ("Philetas' Song"; 101 hexameters) a young shepherd named Philetas (representing, according to Ellinger, Eoban's friend, Burkhard Spalatin) sings the praises of music, poetry, and poets, especially pastoral and Christian poets: song is an *immortalis honor,* more precious than rubies, sweeter than roses, and to it he will devote the rest of his life; no doubt it is placed early in the collection as a poetic manifesto. There are some sprightly lines here and there, but the influence of Mantuan is almost as strong as in the eclogues of Eoban's contemporary and friend, Euricius Cordus; all three poets have an intensely irritating habit of writing as many as four or five lines which are nothing but strings of appositive nouns or repetitive phrases, as in lines 20 through 24 of the present poem:

> Vos ego per silvas, valles, iuga, saxa, cavernas,
> per mare, per fluvios, per devia lustra ferarum,
> vos ego per pluvias, per agentes nubila ventos,
> per duras hiemes, laedentesque arva pruinas,
> vos ego per tenebras sequerer noctesque profundas.

I add here a full version of the second eclogue, not because it is excellent but because it is representative:

> When first the Muse inspired my youthful mind,
> And Jove his kindly favor had inclined,
> Then, as I rested by the river's brim,
> I met my friend, and thus I sang for him:
> "A valley once there was, a pleasant sight;
> Its slopes were verdant and its streams were bright.
> To every rustic Muse that spot was dear,
> And Nymphs would gather there from far and near.
> Here once Philetas came, a shepherd swain,
> A youth the fairest of the rustic train,
> Whose heart was ever filled with merry song,
> Whose mind was joyful as he strolled along.
> Besides the rushing stream he paused one day,
> And thus was heard to sing his rustic lay:

'My dearest joy, the Muses all, now hear,
Who lend to Christian song a willing ear,
Turn now receptive to my youthful strains,
And hearken from those far-off, Eastern plains,
Where first our Parents lived in Eden's bower,
Till tempted by the cruel Serpent's power.
Now pluck new blossoms of a different song,
And I shall follow as you move along:
Through woods and valleys, lofty rocks and caves,
Through rushing streams and ocean's sounding waves,
Through drenching rain and roaring wind's alarms,
Through winter frost that scars the fruitful farms,
Through deepest shadow and through darkest night,
I'd follow, ever rushing in my flight.
Had I the soaring power of eagle's wings,
I'd follow swiftly even Tempê's springs.
My dearest joy, the Muses all, now hear:
Immortal are the songs you love so dear,
Immortal is the poet in his fame,
Immortal is his everlasting name.
The gold and silver of the fabled East,
Attract the thoughtless, satisfy the least.
The diamond, and the polished sapphire's sheen,
The ruby, and the verdant emerald's green,
The pearls that decorate a throat so fair—
All these will vanish into empty air.
But when the Muses fill my heart with fire
I scorn the baubles that the mob inspire.
My dearest joy, the Muses all, now hear:
The blossoms spring when Zephyr's touch is near;
As grass in water, elms in marsh rejoice,
So will I glory in the Muses' voice.
Now pluck new blossoms of a different song;
And hear Philetas as you glide along:
No honied cake can ever taste so sweet,
No pear, no cherry in the summer's heat,
No sweeter is the taste of fresh romaine,
Than is the sweetness of your sacred name.
My dearest joy, the Muses all, now hear:
My voice is eager now to please your ear,

My face is comely, and my head is high,
My heart is honest and acute my eye.
Late did I tend my flowing hair at night;
My mother saw, and smiled upon the sight:
Take now the mirror, glance upon your face,
(She said) and see the fairest of your race:
Now will Adonis vaunt his looks in vain
And seek to gain from looks a lasting name.
I owe the Muse (said I) whate'er I own,
I owe it all to them, to them alone.
Now pluck new blossoms of a different song,
My heart is eager, and my voice is strong.
As grows the branch upon the healthy tree,
As bloom the roses on the fertile lea,
So am I yours so long as I shall live,
So long shall I immortal praises give.
My dearest joy, the Muses all, now hear:
Draw near to me and as I sing draw near.
What greater joy, amid the world's alarms,
Than to embrace the Muses' loving arms,
To live with them, to yield the heart entire,
To wait the inspiration of their fire?
No longer now let Beauty's charms inflame,
Or wealth or glory or a famous name!
Far better by the purling stream to lie,
And watch the cooling waters gliding by!
Now pluck new blossoms of a different song:
Pluck all the blooms that to the Muse belong:
The shining lily and the roses fair,
The modest violet, the privet rare,
All crown the poet with the garland's band,
And place the scepter in his willing hand.
May I among the humble take my place
And raise my eyes unto Apollo's face.
In truth the poet's songs can never die,
Nor can the Muses' promise ever lie.
Rejoice, my flock; rejoice, my little herd;
Rejoice, and now attend my every word:
Tomorrow shall we wander to the west,
Where grass is plentiful and water best:

There by an airy hill, a sloping vale,
We'll seek by Gotha's walls a fresher dale.' "
Thus sang the shepherd youth; but he was heard,
For Thrasybulus marked his every word:
Into the alder's bark he cut Philetas' praise
That it might last, and grow through all the days.

In the third eclogue (untitled; 146 hexameters) Cygnus laments his unfortunate love for Chloris, now married to another shepherd although once her embraces (and rather more) had been for him alone. There are many verbal reminiscences of Mantuan here, as in the first poem, but the Carmelite Vicar-General (himself rather coarse on occasion) would probably have been offended at Eoban's frequent grossness.

The seventh eclogue (160 hexameters) is called *Amor Philotae et Narcissi* ("The Love of Philotas and Narcissus"). Here Philotas sings of his love for Callirrhoê, Narcissus of his for Philanthis. The poem, although never so lively as most Italian eclogues, has more life to it than the third.

The tenth eclogue (untitled; 104 hexameters) is by far the best of the art-pastorals; the content holds nothing fresh (save in detail), but the verse is far more competent than in any other of Eoban's eclogues so far discussed. Again we have the situation of a lover, Eurytus, and a friend, Thyrsis, who tries to dissuade him from folly. Eurytus sings a very attractive love-song to his absent sweetheart Canacê, urging her to accept his rustic gifts and to come with him to be his love: this song is far better than anything Euricius Cordus was to write and is in fact about the best-written passage in all Eoban's eclogues.

A close friend of Eoban was the physician Euricius Cordus (Heinrich Solde) of Simsthausen (Hesse; 1486-1535). As a young man Cordus studied at the chief universities of Germany, particularly at Erfurt; but, since his father had twelve children to support, he had to interrupt his studies periodically to teach elementary school— he did well as a schoolmaster, earning the praise of so good a judge and merciless a critic as Erasmus. About 1512 he was at last able to visit Italy and study medicine at Ferrara; after his return to Germany he devoted the rest of his life to the teaching and practice of medicine at Erfurt, Marburg, and Bremen.

Among his hundreds of poems we find ten eclogues, all of which were excessively praised in their day and all of which, like some of

Eoban's, show all too clearly the influence of "good old Mantuan" (whom Cordus did actually meet on his Italian sojourn) on subject matter, syntax, and versification alike. Three of the ten are art-pastorals.

In the third (untitled; 198 hexameters), a youthful shepherd named Thyrsis (Cordus?) has acquired a brand-new pipe from a friend (Eoban) who has just gone away *in Prussos agros* (Riesen-burg?); he describes, to a much older shepherd, Damon, the wood and its elegant carvings, done by Amyntas (perhaps Konrad Muth, who had taught both Eoban and Cordus): the pipe symbolizes pastoral poetry. This is a pleasant enough eclogue, with just enough personal references to keep it from being wholly a verse exercise, but it is far too long and is marred by clumsiness and obvious imitation of Virgil and Mantuan.

The fourth eclogue (again untitled; 184 hexameters) is pure genre composition (a conversation between two shepherds Meliboeus and Moeris about an injured animal) and as such is of scarcely any interest whatever.

In the eighth eclogue (untitled; 148 hexameters) Faunus describes to his friend Daphnis the death of his hunting dog Cilyndus—he describes the dog's dam, her litter, the dog's faithfulness and courage, and, finally, the hunting party at which the dog had been killed by a huge boar. This part of the eclogue reminds one—in content if not in skill—of some of the poems in which Ercole Strozzi describes the aristocratic hunting parties popular with the Estes of Ferrara and their guests.

In the second (and much longer) part of the poem Daphnis tells Faunus of the disease that now afflicts his sheep as the result of the carelessness of a farm hand named Petulcus ("Feckless"). Two things are worth noting: the exactness of Cordus' description of the disease and its remedies (which may or may not be the result of his being a medical student), and the coarse realism of his narrative of the servant's liaison with "rouged (*fucata genas*) Phyllis"—Phyllis is no dainty shepherdess but a heavy-set slut who sounds like a caricature of Mantuan's Galla.

In Joachim Camerarius (1500-1574), whose family name appears to have been Liebhard, we meet a man of letters and universal savant who, as a figure of the German Renaissance and Reformation, is the peer of Martin Luther and Philip Melanchthon, a man whose career in scholarship and public service was distinguished by moderation, energy, and wisdom. Born at Bamberg in 1500, he received his elementary education there, until his schoolmaster, in somewhat desperate admiration, announced that he had nothing further to teach this phenomenal thirteen-year-old. After five years at Leipzig, he was sent in 1518 to Erfurt and in 1521 to Wittenberg, whither he had been attracted by the fame of Luther and Melanchthon. As pointed out before, it is noticeable how much more closely the middle-class German Humanism was associated with universities than was the often aristocratic Italian form; in Italy universities were often hostile fortresses of Aristotelianism, while Humanism was associated with a semi-royal court. In 1525, like Melanchthon and Lotich and many another, Camerarius fled from the disorders at Wittenberg; after a year in Prussia, he returned to teach at the Gymnasium of Nuremberg with Melanchthon. In 1530 both were appointed by the Senate of Nuremberg as delegates to the Diet of Augsburg, where they were largely responsible for the declaration of Lutheran principles known as the Augsburg Confession. In 1534, when asked to become secretary of Nuremberg, Camerarius refused this honorable and lucrative position on the grounds that scholarship needed him more; he was promptly taken at his word, for Ulrich of Wittenberg asked his assistance in the reorganization of the University of Tübingen, and Heinrich of Saxe employed him in similar duties at the University of Leipzig. Yet these academic undertakings did not prevent him from performing still further duties in connection with the Diet of Augsburg in 1555 and the Diet of Ratisbon in 1556, or from advising Maximilian II in 1568 on matters of doctrine and policy. He died at Leipzig in 1574, stubbornly refusing medical attention, although painfully and continuously aware that he was suffering from the stone.

Besides a large number of prose works Camerarius published a considerable body of Latin verse. The only complete edition of his twenty eclogues (two of which—numbers xvi and xvii—were written not in Latin but in Greek) appeared at Leipzig in 1568; almost all show the influence of Mantuan as clearly as do those of Eoban and Cordus. Of the twenty, six are art-pastorals; but, as is true of his two predecessors, Camerarius is more successful with pastoral as medium—his art-pastorals are, however, frequently enlivened by humorous, picturesque, or realistic pictures of German peasants (temporarily masquerading under the names of Thyrsis or Menalcas or Lycidas).

The second eclogue (113 hexameters) is entitled *Dirae* ("The Curses") and can be regarded as an expansion of Virgil's phrase

triste lupus stabulis ("the wolf is a sore threat to the sheep-folds").
Camerarius (in lines 7-8) says that the sheep are in terror in the
folds and that "the enemy" ranges scot-free; in the Bodleian Library's
copy of Oporinus' Basel anthology, line 8 is heavily underscored by
some sixteenth-century reader—would it have been, had that reader
not interpreted *hostis* as Satan?   Almost certainly not; but there
seems no reason whatever to regard the poem as an allegory.

In the third eclogue, entitled *Querela* ("The Complaint"; 161
hexameters), the same shepherd laments that no sooner had he
brought home his few sheep than he discovered the loss of two
carved beechen cups, which he then proceeds to describe in the
familiar Theocritean and Virgilian manner.   I suspect, laments the
shepherd, in fact, I know, who is the thief; but it is of little use to
know, for he is now far away, displaying his trophies and laughing
with his friends.   The next forty lines call down every conceivable
misfortune on the thief.

The fourth eclogue, *Lycidas,* extends to 263 hexameters and is
really two pastorals in one.   After a brief introductory conversation,
Lycidas sings to his fellow shepherd Palaemon of the fate of Moeris.
This song alone runs to 124 lines, which is far longer than any of
Virgil's eclogues (which average 83 lines).   The poem is here a
mythological narrative of the sort one would expect to find in Ovid's
Metamorphoses, written with much verve and dexterity; it is precisely the sort of mythological tale which Sannazaro and others
turned into a special form of eclogue, inventing "new" myths for
the purpose.

The second main part of the poem (which consists of 98 lines)
is a song by Palaemon; this, like Lycidas' narrative, has a recurrent
refrain appearing at irregular intervals.   This section is distinctly
disappointing: Palaemon tells how an unnamed shepherd lamented
the death of his brother Iolas.   The lament is dull because one is
constantly led to expect so much more.   The unnamed shepherd is
constantly hinting at specific details which never become clear: how
the brother died, who was involved, what treachery occurred, who
had deserted the surviving brother after Iolas' death—all this is left
vague, and the reader (today, at least) is left uncomfortably puzzled.
Is all this genre poetry only and is the vagueness intentionally
assumed for literary reasons, or are the two brothers historical
persons and is the vagueness assumed for reasons of prudence?
One's complete inability to answer these questions is the more annoy-

ing since this elaborate eclogue is obviously intended as a major work.

The seventh poem (*Meliboeus*; 128 hexameters) is of a familiar sort: after an introduction of 61 lines, a passage of reported amoebaean verse follows (lines 62-117), and then comes a brief conclusion. The general structure of the poem is based on that of Virgil's third, the argument of which is thus described by John Dryden: "Damoetas and Menalcas, after some smart strokes of country raillery, resolve to try who has most skill at song; and accordingly make their neighbour Palaemon judge of their performances. . . ."

Here Meliboeus tells (1-61) how he had been cutting logs in the hills and had been resting for a few moments after drying off his sweating brow (*sudorifluos vultus*), when he heard the voices of two men quarreling. There is a realistic and lively interchange of dialogue in lines 26 and following: Clausus accuses Perilas of stealing Moeris' club and is accused in turn of stealing from Amyntas the cloak he is wearing. After still more accusations they turn to Meliboeus, announcing that they will "sing each other down" if he will act as umpire. Lines 62 to 117 consist of conventional amoebaean couplets in which Perilas attempts to outdo everything that Clausus has just said:

C.   Tegean Pan has come to see my farm:
       He loves my song and keeps my flock from harm.

P.   But German Nymphs all love my rustic lay:
       They guide my herds along the grassy way.

C.   You sylvan Nymphs, to listening ears rehearse
       The gifts of Pan, the subject of my verse.

P.   Sing, German Nymphs, beside the river's edge,
       The joys you've given and the joys you pledge.

C.   Why from the lofty oak do birds thus wail?
       Is Eunice now the subject of their tale?

P.   Naught gloomy do the nightingales recall:
       My loving Marilê is kind to all!

C.   See, Lycid loves: his Naiad looks with hate;
       Love threatens him with rustic Daphnis' fate.

P.   His Nymph the love of Dorylus returns:
       She sighs with yearning as his passion burns.

C.   Pipe sweetly, Pan, to all my feeding flock:
       A goat I'll offer by your altar-block.

P.   The Nymphs protect my cattle in the lea:
      A handsome heifer shall their offering be. (62-81)

Each couplet presents a tiny picture of rustic life as the conventions
of pastoral poetry show it, as the interchange goes on for another
36 lines. Meliboeus, as is only to be expected, says that both have
won and that neither need relinquish his pledges.

The eighth eclogue (*Rusticus*; 96 hexameters) is a highly stylized
picture of idealized rusticity, in strong contrast with the nineteenth,
which displays a realism as marked as anything in Mantuan. Here
we have the monody of a farmer named Ilus as he awakens his farm
servants before dawn. As the sleepy hands stumble off to feed the
horses, the farmer begins to think of his wife Phyllis and the Darby
and Joan existence they have led since as orphans they had married
twenty-nine years ago. The poem is well written and well managed;
the ideal does not become unreal and the affectionate is not allowed
to become maudlin.

In the nineteenth poem (*Phyllis*; 47 hexameters) we have a
realistic mime, very much in the Theocritean manner. It is a lively
dramatic sketch of a farmer's wife (Thestylis) who seeks advice
from her neighbor Phyllis:

(T.) Phyllis home? (P.) Who's that? Oh you, Thestylis.
Come in and talk. (T.) I haven't time to stay.
My husband wants to grind the grain; I'm taking home
The pestle he forgot to bring back from the shop—
Drunk, you know. If I delay
He'll let *me* have it, not the grain. His temper's vile.
No reason for me not to say it—known to all.
What's your advice? (P.) What do you mean?
Tell me plainer; such as it is,
I'll give you my opinion: I won't let you go
Without attention, if you'll ask me plain.
(T.) Don't tell a soul. (P.) None living in the town
Shall learn a word from me. (T) He's cruel, and he's wild,
Unreasonable, vain, and rough in words and acts,
A nuisance to the district and a plague at home.
For long I've thought to leave him. . . .

The tone is not one of elegance, clearly: colloquial expressions
abound, as do short, jerky questions and exclamations of surprise

or irritation, and the realism extends to the characterization—
Phyllis is cautious and, despite her assurances of assistance, does not
wish to become involved in any matrimonial wars; Thestylis is just
depressed—she says she will leave her drunken ruffian of a husband,
but is too spiritless to carry out her threat; she merely wants unlimited sympathy.   In other poems of this type (e.g., in France)
the diction tends to be like that of Terence and Plautus; on the
whole, however, Camerarius keeps remarkably close to that of Virgil
and Ovid.

Among the poets of the Low Countries, the first we must mention
is Geert Geertsz of Rotterdam (1469-1536), commonly called Desiderius Erasmus—the names mean Geert (Gerard) in bad Latin
and worse Greek—of whom it has been frequently remarked that,
although he had absolutely no creative genius whatever, he attained
to a greater international intellectual influence than did any other
man of his time, and that he was a truer precursor and initiator of
the modern spirit than even Petrarch: the two men were very different personally, to be sure, but both were marked by the same
tremendous range of interests, the same fever of industry, and the
same tenacity.   One might add that they shared the same waspishness of temper; Petrarch's repute as a lyrist and the gentleness of
feature in Hans Holbein's famous portrait of Erasmus tend to make
us forget how exceedingly unpleasant both men could be.

Erasmus' one pastoral—probably his earliest extant poem—was
written when he was only fourteen, as a schoolboy at Deventer.
No doubt thousands of schoolboy attempts at pastoral existed in
copy-books and attics—it was a natural form to attempt, for it is
simple in structure and not too long; further, the pastoral, as written
by Virgil or Mantuan, was often the first imaginative poetry that
schoolboys met in their Latin studies and was read with enormous
attention to detail.   Virgil's own eclogues were early work, so that
it was only natural that, if a budding Humanist were to try his hand
at Latin verse, he should begin thus.   Many a Humanist kept his
youthful attempts at pastoral, revised and polished them out of all
recognition, and then published them: this is no doubt true of
Girolamo and Giambattista Amalteo in particular.

The eclogue of Erasmus we possess both in its original and in
its revised form.   The young student quite clearly followed his
model as closely and as accurately as he possibly could, without
making the least attempt to express any idea or feeling of his own:

artistic originality was not his aim.   And yet the poem is, in its way, an astounding tour de force.   It is quite extraordinary that a boy of fourteen, living under the strain of the most unhappy family circumstances and studying in unbelievably crowded classrooms under junior masters, should have been able to produce a piece of verse that, however immature, is far, far more correct in expression than the eclogues of Petrarch, Boccaccio, Quatrario, and the rest of the Italian Pre-Humanists of the fourteenth century.   There are medievalisms and awkward expressions; but there is no doubt that at fourteen Erasmus had mastered the intricacies of classical verseform.   The poem is of no positive intrinsic merit, but it is obviously a document of the greatest interest not only for the history of Neo-Latin pastoral but also for the history of education.

Petrus Pontanus (ca. 1480–ca. 1540), also called Pieter van der Brugge and Pierre du Pont, was born in Bruges.   Despite his blindness he made his way, after an excellent education received from the monks of St. Omer, to Paris in 1505 as a teacher of Greek and Latin; he spent nearly all the rest of his life in studying, writing, and teaching.   His is an attractive personality: there is no word of complaint over his blindness anywhere in his works—no boast, either, of his courageous and uncomplaining life; there is much, however, to display his downright Flemish character, his cheerfully sardonic good-humor, his kind but deeply ironical nature.

His Latin poems consist of hymns, personal lyrics, occasional poems, panegyrics, invectives, epicedia, and the like.   His ten eclogues were printed in Paris in 1513; they are called "hundred-lined": in fact, number ii has 101 lines, number iii has 99, and all the others have 100 lines each.   Of the ten only one is an art-pastoral; the rest all belong to the categories of new forms and new uses.   In all, content is far more interesting than form—Pontanus' versification is rough and crude, even more so than Eoban's or Cordus'.   Still, there is many a vigorous line in the poems, and the air of elegant boredom that vitiates much of late Italian Neo-Latin poetry is refreshingly absent.

The third eclogue (untitled; 99 hexameters) is, it must be admitted, the least attractive of all.   In lines 1 through 50 a young Norman named Rasculus and an old "Frank" named Hernus quarrel bluntly and bitterly about their poetical abilities.   As usual, they put the matter up to a third shepherd (Olphus)—amoebaean verses (three lines apiece) follow from 51 to 95; then, after a single line from Rasculus, Olphus' words (97-99) complete the poem.   The reader is startled by the very first two lines of the poem; a crashing false quantity in the opening word is followed by a remark whose coarseness might have come from Martial or Rabelais:

> By God, I'm forced to piss my pants with rage,
> For folly holds the center of the stage!

After this far from languid introduction one expects a satirical poem on the stupidity of contemporaries, but Rasculus, it develops, is venting his rage on the untuneful verse of Hernus, who is himself not slow to bring his command of classical Billingsgate into play. After the amoebaean interchange (decorated with many false quantities and several nonexistent Latin forms, such as *sequeret* for *sequeretur*), Rasculus is on the point of actual violence, but is calmed by Olphus, who says,

> I see your crests begin to rise with rage!
> Let each restrain his wrath; respect my age!
> Now let your muse attain a peaceful stage (97-99).

Matters are far different when we turn to the brilliant Johannes Secundus of The Hague (1511-1536), most famous of the Low-Country Neo-Latin poets, described by F. A. Wright as "one of the half-dozen greatest love-lyrists in world-literature, in grace and dexterity of wit worthy to rank with Meleager, Catullus, Heine, and De Musset." Certainly he was one of the finest of Neo-Latin poets; with him we may couple Angelo Poliziano, Giovanni Pontano, Giacopo Sannazaro, Andrea Navagero, Marcantonio Flaminio, Giambattista Amalteo, Peter Lotich, and George Buchanan.

Among his works there appears a single eclogue (*Orpheus*; 164 hexameters). In this poem Lycidas, whose love for the nymph Neaera has caused him to forget everything but her, sings of Orpheus' lament for the twice-lost Eurydice. This poem shows great skill, and its effect is all the more favorable if the reader comes upon it (as I did) immediately after reading the pastorals of Euricius Cordus. More interesting, perhaps, than details of versification and the like is the identity of Neaera. The name, of course, is one that any Neo-Latin poet might use for any imaginary light of love; but to the reader of Secundus' *Elegies* it can refer only to the girl with whom the poet had an affair in Spain. In the eclogue she is called "fair, and white as the doves of Venus," and Janus Dousa the Elder also refers to her strikingly fair complexion (but this may be only a following of Spanish literary convention). Secundus met Neaera in Spain in 1534. She was not a young girl like Julia of Malines, but a blonde courtesan, *femme facile et vénale*: the poems addressed to her are among the most sensual of the *Basia* and the *Elegiae*. The poet's suit was unsuccessful, for she turned from him to favor the Spanish poet Zurita of Saragossa.

Some of the poets of the Low Country are distinctly Latin in spirit, notably Johannes Secundus and the much later Floris van Schoonhoven; but others, like Pieter van der Brugge, are markedly Teutonic and Flemish: this is also true of Jacobus Sluperius (Jakob de Slupere or Sluyper) of Herzele in Artois (1532-1582). After a university training at Loewen, Sluperius became a priest at Boesinghe, near Ypres. Here he devoted his leisure to building up a literary circle, which was scattered in 1566 when religious dissension (its beginnings are described in the seventh eclogue, of 1563) drove him to abandon Boesinghe for Ypres, where he was forced to spend an unhappy two years; the point of view of the non-Protestant Dutch who acquiesced in Spanish rule is paramount in Sluperius' work. In 1568 he was able to resume his church work in Westvlaeter; here, once he had recovered from the news of his father's torture and death at the hands of Dutch Protestant extremists, he was able to spend his life in comparative peace and quiet, from 1568 to 1578, until Ypres came under the influence of a persecuting Calvinistic minority. Once more Sluperius was forced to flee, this time to Arras, where he lived with his friend Anton Meyer until his death in 1582.

Sluperius' Latin poems appeared at Antwerp in 1575 and consist of hymns, eclogues, elegies, lyrics, youthful *lusus pastorales,* verse epistles, and a dream-poem called "The Garden" similar to Basilio Zanchi's "Garden of Wisdom" (*Hortus Sophiae*). There is much, of course, that reflects the bitter religious struggles of the time, and many lyrics of a highly personal character occur. In all of his poems Sluperius' greatest fault is length. He frequently says "to be brief," or "as briefly as possible" or the like; but it is all too clear that he did not know the meaning of the word *brevis*: if the fifth eclogue, for instance, were cut to one third of its present length, it would be an excellent piece of work—as it is, it is very long-winded. His work reads very well, however, in selection, for his vigor and humor are undeniable.

The eight eclogues (two belong to 1563 and the rest to 1574) include two art-pastorals. The first poem (*Amyntas*; 278 hexameters) is one of the best of the whole collection. It begins with a description of a trip (no doubt real) that the author took to Bruges along with four secular friends. Sluperius tells us how in the chilly dawn of a spring morning he rose from his warm and comfortable bed, joined his friends, and set off. He lists the towns and villages they passed (one can easily draw a map of the itinerary, as with Horace's famous trip to Brindisi), and describes the country roads and the cross-road shrines. At noon they stopped at an inn: they spent two hours over lunch and conversation, and then, since his companions showed signs of intending to spend another two hours over the wine bottles, Sluperius tactfully decided to go for a walk in the fields.

The poet describes how he came to a handsome formal garden, with a fountain in its exact center. Being himself an ardent gardener, he promptly walked in and there, he tells us, saw two young men—both were good singers, both were Flemish, both were of an age; one was called Alphesiboeus, the other Damoetas.

In preparation for the purely bucolic part of the poem, Sluperius girds himself up with an invocation of the Muse Calliopê. In line 58 we begin with a conversation between the two young men (58-133; this by itself is longer than Virgil's second, fourth, seventh, or ninth pastorals), in which they describe their friend Amyntas' love for Aeglê, who had deserted him and married Pamphagus ("Greedy"); this is followed with Amyntas' lament (134-253; again as long in itself as many other eclogues), and Damoetas' conclusion (254-63).

When they had finished their songs, continues the poet, the two young men left and made their way home. Sluperius, too, made his way back to the inn. He and his friends spent the rest of the afternoon and all night at the inn, and resumed their journey to Bruges next morning.

The introduction and conclusion of this poem no doubt recall an actual journey to Bruges on a May 3 earlier than 1574—the four bibulous companions certainly sound very real; and even the pastoral section may well be an ultra-literary version of an afternoon's walk through the fields in which the poet really did hear a young man singing. We shall later meet an eclogue by Henri Estienne with an almost identical plot.

The fifth eclogue (*Eucharis*; 326 hexameters) describes how two shepherds, Lycidas and Menalcas, pass the blazing heat of noon by recalling the tale of Iolas and his former sweetheart Eucharis. He courted her for three years, they tell us, but was forbidden by his father to marry her because she came from so poor a family, Iolas gathered together a few lambs and kids and left home, intending to return wealthy and independent some day. But Eucharis, convinced that he was gone for good, allowed herself to be forced into a marriage of convenience with a rich but (of course) old and ugly landowner named Mopsus. The inevitable happens in this pastoral verse-novelette: Iolas returns, discovers the truth, reproaches Eucharis, and brings the poem to an end by a long lament (143-326), the last section of which (275-319) is highly rhetorical and stylized, with a recurrent refrain. This eclogue is drawn out beyond all reason and although Georg Ellinger speaks of it as Sluperius' best, it would be immensely improved if two hundred lines were subtracted.

A far more capable poet than Sluperius was Daniel Heinsius of Ghent (1580-1655), associated for most of his life with Scaliger the Younger at the University of Leyden. A child prodigy in Latin studies, he horrified his father by displaying an invincible antipathy for Greek and especially for grammar, Latin or Greek. In 1595, however, when sent to university classes at Franeker to study law, he suddenly turned to Greek and studied it with such ferocity as this time to terrify his father. Study at Leyden under Joseph Justus Scaliger from 1597 to 1599 convinced him that literature was his field, and for seven years he taught Latin poetry there. In 1606 he became professor of history and then librarian and secretary of the University. In 1618 he was appointed Swedish Historiographer Royal by Gustavus Adolphus, an appointment that was to prove important for the career of his son Nicolaus. His philological works (editions of Terence, Livy, Horace, Seneca's tragedies, Hesiod, Theocritus, Aristotle's *Poetics,* and—his best—Ovid) are extremely uneven in value; Casaubon called him "a lesser Scaliger," and certainly his method of constituting a text is the same—he paid little attention to the evidence of manuscripts but introduced emendations with an extremely free hand. His original Latin works consist of two Latin tragedies (1602, 1632), elegiac poems of great skill and delicacy (1613), orations delivered on formal occasions at the University of Leyden and elsewhere (1615), a philosophical poem *De contemptu mortis* (1621) in four books, and various comic prose works (*Dissertationes ludicrae;* 1638) of a sort for which we have long since lost the taste—professors' jokes are notoriously bad at the best of times.

Among his original Latin poems two eclogues appear—one an

elaborate epicedium (*Thyrsis*) on the death (1640) of Scaliger, the other an art-pastoral dedicated to Janus Dousa (Jan van der Does; 1571-1597) the Younger. This second eclogue is called "Noortwijck, or, Unhappy Love" (*Nordowicum, sive Infelix amor*; 128 hexameters; Dousa was born in Noortwijck). The poem begins with a brief address to Dousa (1-7) in which Heinsius refers to disturbances in Leyden that prevent close attention to study and writing. Since the poem must have been written fairly early in 1597 (when Heinsius was only seventeen), the reference must be to the beginning of Maurice of Nassau's campaign against the Spaniards.

At line 8, without a word of transition, the eclogue proper begins by introducing us to Tityrus and Lycidas and their respective sweethearts, Nisa and Neaera. Then comes a love-song sung by Lycidas (18-67), followed by another by Tityrus (70-126), and a two-line conclusion in the poet's words. Lycidas' song consists of seven six-line stanzas with a refrain eight times repeated; Tityrus' song has a similar pattern: eight six-line stanzas with a refrain repeated nine times. For a seventeen-year-old boy this is an even more startling display of virtuosity than Erasmus' schoolboy poem: here not only is the meter impeccable, but the rhythms are genuinely Virgilian; as for its tone, Lycidas' description of his erotic dream would have raised eyebrows at the Deventer school. The poem's chief fault is an exuberant rhetoric that delights in excessive use of anaphora; a few quotations—whether the reader understands Latin or not—will make it all too clear:

> bis leviter somnum volui defendere solem,
> bis metui mollem pavidus turbare soporem (26-27);

> visus eram blandos compellere montibus haedos,
> visus eram blandae supponere colla Neaerae (30-31);

> bisque "vale" dixi "formosa," locumque notavi,
> bisque iterum saxo volui recubare sub illo,
> bisque eadem optavi mihi somnia. . . . (43-45);

> at tu aversa feroxque meos non cernis amictus,
> at tu aversa feroxque meos non cernis amores (78-79);

> et quoties blandas genitor me misit ad agnas,
> et quoties gratas genetrix me misit ad herbas (120-21).

In any heavily inflected language anaphora is a particularly effective rhetorical device; but it has its temptations, which Heinsius was later to avoid. Lines 78 and 79 quoted above are a horrid example of everything that can be bad about Neo-Latin poetry.

All six eclogues of Floris van Schoonhoven of Gouda (1594-1648) are art-pastorals. After studying law at the University of Leyden and taking the degree of *Iuris utriusque doctor,* he turned Catholic, which automatically barred him from public affairs. He passed the remainder of his life almost exclusively in the study of Latin poetry; his own Latin poems (published in 1613 and 1618) are very early work in which he shows himself a lively, fluent, and frequently elegant poet. Among his poems appears a sequence of forty pastoral vignettes in lyric form (*lusus pastorales*) called *Lalagê* and a group of six eclogues. A preface dedicates these six poems to van Schoonhoven's old headmaster at Gouda, and suggests, in its defensive tone, that the *Lalagê* had met with criticism from respectable Dutch Protestants, who apparently considered most of them frivolous and the rest lascivious. Early work or not, the eclogues are far better constructed and far better written than those of, say, Sluperius. In each of them, van Schoonhoven takes a typical pastoral situation and works it out to his own satisfaction with skill and an air of ingratiating innocence, much concerned with variety of diction and exactness of expression: his Latin is smooth, fluent, and very clear. He has mastered the resources of Latin verse-rhetoric, but does not overwork them. He displays, in a word, all the typical virtues of a very fine minor poet.

The plot of each poem is neatly summed up, a couplet at a time, in a brief elegiac dedicatory poem in the 1613 (Leyden) edition:

> The joys of shepherds and the country's ways,
>   My friend, are painted in my rustic lays;
> The first the grief of Corydon reveals,
>   As to the grave of Lalagê he steals;
> Then Daphnis roses to his love presents,
>   As in the Golden Age of innocence;
> Damoetas, next, laments the cruel fair,
>   His rival's cunning, and his own despair;
> Then Meliboeus, to the city fled,
>   Repents his folly, and reveals his dread;
> With gold the one, with skill the other tries
>   (Both shepherds), to attract a lady's eyes;
> Last, Pterelas reveals his joyless mind:
>   His life is lonely and his love unkind.

With themes so conventional it will scarcely be necessary to examine each poem successively in detail, but we can observe a few small points. Like a good many other poets who wrote Latin poetry in youth, van Schoonhoven is rather fond of introducing naughty details (as in *Ecl.* iii, 49-50; vi, 24); it is perhaps not so very astonishing that his more stolid elders considered his verse a trifle lascivious. The *theme* of the rich rival is common enough in pastoral poetry, ancient and modern alike; but he usually stays in the wings—in the fifth eclogue he actually appears in the person of the arrogant Lycidas: here van Schoonhoven (like Camerarius in the *Dirae*) has taken what was in Virgil a single phrase and built it into a complete, independent eclogue of the Humanistic type. We should also note that in the fourth eclogue there are strong elements of satire; the rhetorical contrast between town and country, a theme constantly under the surface of much pastoral writing, here comes out into the open in the manner of purely satirical poems by Enea Silvio Piccolomini in Italy, Alexander Barclay in England, and Gervais Sepin in France. Only the first (*Lalagê*) and the last (*Amaryllis*) eclogues have titles; the average length of the six poems is 94 hexameters, a relief after Sluperius.

Daniel Heinsius' earliest extant Latin poem was written at the age of ten; Johannes Secundus' elegies were written when he was about twenty; Floris van Schoonhoven's best work was published when he was nineteen; the posthumous Latin verses (1641) of Petrus Stratenius (1616-1640) must have been written in his early twenties at the very latest. We know that he was born at Goesa, studied law at the University of Leyden, became secretary—"chancellor," as the sixteenth-century Italians used to call it—of his native city (a lucrative post), and died suddenly at The Hague at the age of twenty-four. Perhaps through family connections, he was much favored by the famous Dutch jurist (and Neo-Latin poet and philosopher) Hugo Grotius and by the eminent classical scholar Johann Friedrich Gronovius; he was himself an ardent admirer of Admiral van Tromp, the Dutch seaman who sailed up the English Channel with a broom at his masthead and who figures in many a lively Dutch Neo-Latin poem.

Of the five brief eclogues—the longest is seventy-two hexameters —two are art-pastorals, and in these Stratenius shows himself a lesser Floris van Schoonhoven. Where Stratenius is original, he tends to become stilted, and where he is most fluent, one can be sure to find Virgilian or Ovidian cento.

Daniel Heinsius' son Nicolaus (1620-1681) enjoyed a far more spectacular career than did his father. As a youthful prodigy he undertook, from the age of seventeen, scholarly correspondence (still extant) with scholars and public men of the standing of Johann Friedrich Gronovius and Hugo Grotius. For the purposes of research he visited England, France, Italy, Russia, and Sweden. In England he was insulted by provincial librarians; in France, Italy, and elsewhere he was fêted in palaces by some of the most distinguished personages of the seventeenth century: his visit to Sweden was at the invitation of Queen Christina.

At fifty-four he retired from the Swedish and Dutch diplomatic services to a small town (Viane) near Utrecht to devote himself for the rest of his life to his friends (especially Johann Georg Graevius) and to Latin poetry. His Latin verse received the most enthusiastic praise from contemporaries in half a dozen European countries, and merits it.

Only one eclogue appears among Nicolaus' poems, an early work: it appears in Book II of the *Juvenilia* and is entitled *Ecloga amatoria* (115 hexameters). After an introduction of forty-three lines we read the lament of Lycidas over the unco-operative shepherdess Nisa. In form the eclogue recalls the poem that Nicolaus' father wrote in 1597 (*Noortwijck*); in style the son does, it is true, avoid the précieux rhetoric that had proved all too seductive to the father, but he fell victim in his turn to a turgidity that is even more repellent. It is a very capable piece of work from the purely technical point of view but is over-blown, over-learned, and over-repetitive, and a poor introduction to the major body of Nicolaus Heinsius' verse.

Peter de Fransz of Amsterdam, called Petrus Francius (1645-1704) is yet another of the brilliant series of classical scholars that flourished in Holland in the seventeenth century. After a gymnasium training in Amsterdam under the direction of Hadrianus Junius (Adriaan de Jonghe, grandson and namesake of a close friend of Johannes Secundus) and study at Leyden under the elder Gronovius, he traveled widely in England, France, and Italy and was successively appointed professor of Eloquence (i.e., Latin literature) and professor of Greek at Amsterdam. There is a famous anecdote connected with Francius: in memory of Admiral Ruyter, killed in an engagement off Sicily, he was to recite a Latin verse-panegyric in the New Church of Amsterdam; so huge were the crowds that assembled to hear this that the commander of the military guard spoke in Latin to all who tried to enter the church; only those who replied in Latin were admitted.

Besides Latin orations and a selection of his Latin correspondence with such men as Nicolaus Heinsius, René Rapin, the two Gronovii, and Pierre-Daniel Huet, Francius published a large number of Latin poems. The Amsterdam edition of 1697 contains 494 pages (in very small print) of hexameter poems, eclogues, elegies, odes, epigrams, and the like; in 1706 his posthumous verses appeared in a supplement almost as extensive and varied.

Of the six eclogues the first three are religious, the fourth deals with personal matters, and the last two are art-pastorals. The poems all tend to excessive length (they average 147 hexameters) and tend also to be over-rhetorical—not for nothing was Francius a specialist in Ovid from his student days at the Amsterdam Gymnasium; note especially iv, 25-26:

> crebraque per longos ducens suspiria soles,
> crebraque per longos ducens suspiria noctes,
> absentem suspirabo noctesque diesque?

and v, 35-37:

> a, quanto satius foret ignorare quid esses,
> et numquam sentire tuos, insane, furores,
> et numquam sentire tuos, insane, dolores!

and 62-63:

> ipse tuas eadem pecudes in pascua cogam,
> ipse tuas eadem pecudes in flumina ducam,

and 66-67:

> dumque ligo dumque impono, simul oscula iungam;
> dumque ligo dumque impono, simul oscula iunges.

The fifth eclogue, from which the last three deplorable quotations are taken, is entitled *Alexis* (155 hexameters). After an introduction describing the lonely shepherd Alexis wandering in the mountains, we read his lament over the cruelty of Amaryllis and the power of Love (6-155), at the end of which Alexis prophesies his own coming metamorphosis into a river. Most of the stock motifs and stock details of this type of poem appear: in 72 through

76 Alexis warns the haughty Amaryllis that although *she* may despise him there are others who have courted him—Thestylis and Aeglê and Galatea; so also we find in line 130 that Alexis' flocks wander neglected through the fields: "incustoditae pecudes per rura vagantur." The conclusion is overdone, affected, and not a little ridiculous (140-55):

> My eyes shall springs become, my body flow
> And with its tears bedew the fields below.
> Farewell, my Amaryllis, heart's desire:
> Alexis, burned by Amor's raging fire,
> Now to a river changed, a torrent steep,
> Shall weeping flow, and ever flowing weep;
> From mountain rushing to the plain below,
> Through fields once cherished shall he ever go.
> His waters shall be drunk by rustic swains;
> Yourself at times will wander through these plains:
> At noon you'll bring your woolly flock to drink,
> And bathe yourself beside my river's brink.
> Yes, you will bathe within my waters' flow;
> Yes, you will drink and marvel at the glow:
> You'll feel within an unaccustomed fire,
> The final relic of my old desire.
> In vain you'll sigh with soft desire for me,
> In vain you'll sigh for one no longer free.

The sixth eclogue (*Lycoris*; 146 hexameters) is a monody by an unnamed youth for a shepherdess named Lycoris. The themes employed in this poem are all familiar: in the first part the shepherd insists that all nature shares his grief for Lycoris—the woods, the fields, the flowers, the trees, the very birds and animals themselves. He then recalls how he and Lycoris had often tended their flocks together in this very valley, and promises that he himself will now look after her sheep and goats faithfully; he promises, too, that he will tend her grave and keep it decked with flowers and will recall, each time he visits it, how he had first met her when a young boy.

The poem is by no means perfect. In the first part, the theme of the "pathetic fallacy" receives as thorough an elaboration as it ever did in Neo-Latin poetry—Francius is not content to say that every flower mourns; he must, with a decorative abundance that recalls Baroque floral carvings, enumerate every flower known to botany and provide it with decorative epithets and mythological allusions. And amid the mass of rhetoric the reader is pained to discover a couplet (69-70) that reads,

saepe dies primus nostros conspexit amores;
saepe dies serus nostros deprendit amores.

The commanding officer of the Dutch troops on the famous occasion when Peter Fransz presented his Virgilian poem on the death of Admiral Ruyter was Jan van Broekhuyzen of Amsterdam (1649-1707), usually called Janus Broukhusius, Francius' boyhood friend and fellow pupil at the Gymnasium of Amsterdam and an "original Latin poet in his lyric as well as his elegiac pieces" (Sandys). After the death of his father, Broukhusius' uncle apprenticed the extremely unwilling young man to an apothecary. The nephew, after dutifully enduring apprenticeship for several years, enlisted in the army, since there seemed no hope of an academic career, and rose to the command of one of the bodies of troops stationed in Amsterdam. His duties were not entirely decorative: he served with distinction in the campaign of 1672 and in America under Ruyter in 1674. He retired from the army in 1697 with a generous and well-earned pension.

During his military career, Broukhusius never lost his interest in Latin poetry, ancient and modern. De Jonghe had advised Ovid for Francius and Propertius for Broukhusius: the latter's edition of Propertius appeared in 1702 with a second edition in 1727. But he was even more interested in editing Neo-Latin poetry. His edition of the poems of Antonio della Paglia (Aonius Palearius, Aonio Paleario) appeared in 1696 and had been preceded by an elaborate edition of the works of Giacopo Sannazaro and of the Amalteo brothers (1689; second edition, 1728). His tribute to Sannazaro's wonderful verbal felicity of expression is characteristically generous: "If one were to conclude that nothing of greater elegance had been produced since the days of Augustus himself, his judgment would not have gone astray." Being a sensible Dutchman he goes on to point out that since publishers are chiefly interested in making money the frequent reprinting of Sannazaro's poems is proof of their quality; being also a patriotic Dutchman he insists that "our countryman Secundus" is Sannazaro's equal. Most who know both would, I think, agree; some would award a higher place to Secundus.

Of Broukhusius' eight eclogues, six are art-pastorals and are of uneven merit. By the late seventeenth century, the possibilities of art-pastoral had almost exhausted themselves. The Latin eclogue still showed as much vigor as ever in the new forms and new uses; but even men like Francius and Broukhusius came near to idle displays of virtuosity when attempting a purely classicizing eclogue. A time was to come in the late eighteenth century when even the eclogue of new forms and uses was to prove tired to death.

In Broukhusius' second eclogue (*Corydon*; 111 hexameters) we find a shepherd's monody: Corydon tells how he had fallen in love with Galatea and, on being repulsed, had wandered through many countries in the hope of forgetting her. More interesting than this pastoral song is the conclusion (lines 98-111) with its references to Broukhusius' lawyer-friend Jan Seecks, to the author's military duties, and to the exploits of the *bellator Auriacus* (i.e., Frederick Henry of Orange-Nassau) which the poet hoped to narrate in an epic. It is as well that he did not, for it was elegy, not heroic verse, that was his forte.

The third eclogue, "The Unsuccessful Lover" (*Amator ineptus*; 75 hexameters) is again competent but in itself of no compelling interest. Here Lycidas rather noisily bewails his lack of success with a shepherdess named Thestylis; the poet's advice (lines 72-75) is more characteristic of erotic elegy than of pastoral:

> Poor Lycidas, your mind is mazed indeed
> To weep forever, never to be freed!
> If thus your tears and life you foolish waste
> Then die you must; or happy live—unchaste.

Broukhusius' fifth eclogue, called "The Lovers" (*Amantes*; 114 hexameters), is a most attractive art-pastoral of the most formal and stylized variety: the whole poem has a most engaging air of innocent sophistication, and might have come from early sixteenth-century Italy:

> A shepherd once, named Lycidas, I knew;
> His rustic sweetheart Aeglê saw I often, too;
> Both of an age they were, that rustic pair,
> Both loved to sing, and both were passing fair.
> Once, driv'n by heat, they could no longer rove,
> And sought the coolness of a nearby grove;
> In turn they seek the Muse, in turn they sing,
> And thus they make the woodland echoes ring.

L.: Now may the ravening wolf forbear to slay,
     And may he spare my younglings every day;
     From larger herds now steal the lambs away!

A.: Lampurus, guard my flock as now I lie,
     And warn your mistress if the foe be nigh;
     Keep watch, while here we rest, my love and I.

L.: Though Phoebus burns the pasture every day,
     Though Dog-star parches lawns with burning ray,
     Though every field is dry from east to west,
     A fiercer flame now burns within my breast.

A.: As rages fire throughout the summer grain,
     As blazing Auster wastes our fields again,
     As burns the stubble on the fallow-land,
     So burns the flame of love on every hand.

L.: If Venus or if Juno's self should sue,
     Not Juno's self nor Venus could me woo;
     If life extend from now to farthest age,
     No love but Aeglê's shall my heart engage.

A.: If Phoebus' self should seek to win my love,
     If Phoebus' self should come from Heaven above,
     Then (now believe, and trust a simple lass)
     I'd not prefer the god to Lycidas.

L.: My heart dissolves within your gentle arms,
     My heart is captured by your gentle charms;
     Now turn your glance aside, your aspect turn:
     The lover's eyes now see, and, seeing, burn.

A.: By nodding plane-trees, in the vineyard there,
     Your mother bore you in the open air,
     A lovely child, of lovely hope, as fair
     As gleams the rose amid the maiden's hair.

L.: As gleams the violet I saw but now,
     As gleams the ripened apple on the bough,
     As gleams the lily by the garden rocks,
     So gleams the beauty of your raven locks.

A.: Would that yourself could be my brother true,
     That brother, sister we might be, we two;

Then might I safely walk or dance with you,
Nor shame to kiss you in the public view.

L.:   You're like my sister, I your brother dear:
One home, one couch, one love throughout the year;
Both Venus and the wingèd Cupid, too,
Will bid us kiss within the public view.

A.:   Now cease, my comrades, now to seek my home;
No more invite my vacant heart to roam;
Now am I Cupid's, now am Venus' prey,
And Lycid must I love both night and day.

L.:   Thus do I gaze upon your smiling face,
Thus do I hold you in my arm's embrace.
Thus do I lean upon your snowy breast,
Thus do I turn to you at Love's behest.

A.:   And shall I not await your coming nigh?
And shall I not invite you thus to lie?
And shall I not await you here below?
And shall I not embrace your body—so?

L.:   As lovely myrtle at the river's edge,
As gleaming apples by the privet hedge,
As glowing clusters at the vineyard's crest,
So is the beauty of your naked breast.

A.:   The breezes that throughout the meadow sigh
Shall cool my ardent brow as here I lie;
The trees shall murmur as the breezes blow,
And lull my mind to slumber here below.

L.:   Thus on Idalia's height fair Venus lies
And lulls to sleep the little Cupid's eyes;
Nearby the Nymphs reveal their wanton charms,
Yet Sleep still holds him firmly in his arms.

A.:   As hyacinth is stained with scarlet glow,
As scarlet roses in the garden blow,
As gleams the cherry with its scarlet hue,
So gleams your cheek before my eager view.

L.:   As scarlet wool with Tyrian dye suffused,
As grapes with summer's scarlet deep imbued,

As pomegranates at the summer's height,
So gleam your smiling lips with scarlet bright.

A.: As leaves to trees, as lawns to meadows stand,
As flowers to lawns, as vigor to the hand,
As ox to herd, as water to the brooks;
So do your waving locks adorn your looks.

L.: Here once you gathered lilies as a child;
Here, too, I gathered lilies in the wild;
Then first I saw, then first approved your face,
Then first I knew, then first I loved your grace.

A.: Here first we drove our flocks within the dale,
Here first we kissed within this very vale;
Here first I felt the Love-god's cruel dart,
Here first I felt the wound within my heart.

L.: Far sweeter are you than the early dawn,
Than rivers fresher, softer than the lawn,
Than Phoebê brighter, handsomer than vine,
Than meadow warmer, straighter than the pine.

A.: A garden am I—here my beauty grows;
Here blossoms amaranth, and here the rose;
But if you bring not Zephyr's warming breath,
The rose and amaranth will fade in death.

L.: This verse I'll hang upon a lofty tree
That, Cupid, I have written now for thee:
"While I love Aeglê, Aeglê Lycidas,
Your name will never from our mem'ry pass."

A. To Venus shall I consecrate this bough,
And as I pray I'll make this loving vow:
"So long as myrtles bloom, as flowers have scent,
So shall my love for Lycidas augment."

Thus sang the lovers at approach of night
While Hesperus prepared to glisten bright;
Thus did they solace each the other's fire,
And satisfied with song their heart's desire.

The sixth eclogue (*Hyella*; 78 hexameters) is a lament by the
shepherd Dorylas over the death of his wife. It is conceivable that

Hyella represents the wife of a common friend of Broukhusius and Jacobus Servatius, the friend to whom the poem is addressed; but there is nothing in this eclogue that so much as hints at it. The poem is extremely well constructed; but there is certainly nothing out of the ordinary as far as content is concerned. In the introduction, by the way, Broukhusius calls for inspiration on the Nymphs of the Sambre (*Sabiades Nymphae*), just as Scottish poets call on those of the Grampians (*Grampiades*), French poets on those of the Loire, Seine, or Nevers (*Ligerides, Sequanides,* or *Niverides*), Austrians on those of the Danube (*Istriades*), and Portuguese on those of the Tejo (*Tagides*); this sort of thing all sounds much more natural among the Italians, even when they introduce nymphs unknown to Virgil (as Fontana's *Olliades Nymphae*).

The seventh eclogue (*Doris*; 58 hexameters) has all the inevitable artificialities of pastoral situation and all the tricks of rhetoric common in bucolic poetry, but for all that it is as attractive an example of the art-eclogue as is the fourth. The poem is a highly successful evocation of the pastoral world of Virgil; at their best, the Dutch Neo-Latin poets had no superiors in Europe.

The eighth poem (*Lycidas*; 111 hexameters) returns to the lachrymose, and the reader tends to return to impatience, despite all the literary tact and precision which Broukhusius undoubtedly displays in this mannered and ultra-classicizing pastoral. By the banks of the Breda, Lycidas laments the death of his sweetheart Phyllis, who had died just before they were about to be married; the contrast between the joyous spring and Lycidas' sadness stirs the sympathy of Venus and she changes him to a myrtle: the beauty of the shrub would recall the idyllic quality of his love for Phyllis, the bitterness of its berry the unhappy outcome.

The last Dutch Neo-Latinist whose acquaintance we shall make at present is Gerrit Jordens (Gerardus Jordensius) of Deventer (1731-1803). After taking a degree in jurisprudence, he practiced law in his birthplace and became eventually (in 1786) a member of the Dutch parliament; in 1802 he attained his ambition—a seat on the Batavian supreme court. His Latin works include two highly technical treatises (1753 and 1756) on aspects of Romano-Dutch law, the *Carmina* (1763), and a heroic poem on Joseph and his brothers (1795).

The Latin poems include the *Gellia* (a cycle of erotic elegiac poems), a group of *epigrammata* of little interest even to the historian, and three eclogues, two of which are art-pastorals of practically no interest whatever: they are correct and proper but totally lacking in any sort of sprightliness or zest. The best one can say of these poems is that their Latin is correct, their rhythms inoffensive, and their length reasonable.

The Neo-Latin eclogue was introduced into France in the late fifteenth century by Publio Fausto Andrelini (1460-1518) and remained a common form in French Neo-Latin literature from the time of Charles VIII (1483-1498) at least until Napoleon Bonaparte's victory at Marengo (1800). The first art-pastoral did not (as far as I know) appear until 1543; during the preceding half-century pastoral had been used for special purposes of one kind or another by Simon Nanquier, Jean Regnier, Philibert Girinet, Sébastien Châteillon, Gilbert Ducher, and Jacques Gohory, all of whom we shall meet later.

The earliest French Neo-Latin art-pastoral is by Hubert Susanneau or Susannet (Sussannaeus) of Soissons (1512-ca. 1555), of whose life we know a fair amount. His only eclogue (*Sylvius*; 80 hexameters, published in the *Annotationes*) is a rather prosy piece of work in dialogue throughout, with an odd resemblance, in content, at least, to a couple of Italian and German eclogues in which remedies for a flock's diseases form a topic for bucolic conversation. It is likely that the poem is wholly Humanistic; it is conceivable, however, that Sylvius represents some well known physician and professor of medicine whose abilities are thus lauded in pastoral masquerade. The mention of Picardy in particular suggests this.

The next example of the art-pastoral appears in the works of the poet who, after Pierre de Ronsard, is the most distinguished member of the Pleiad, Joachim du Bellay (1522-1560), second son of the senior branch of a noble family of Anjou. Du Bellay was an excellent classical scholar and Neo-Latin poet, and his vernacular work, both in prose and in verse, is strongly influenced by classical doctrines and models. The *Deffence et illustration de la langue françoise* (1549) called for the use of classical Latin verse and the verse of the Neo-Latin Humanists of Italy as models for French vernacular poetry. In 1553 Du Bellay set out for Rome with his uncle, the Cardinal, and on the way composed a great deal of Latin verse (not actually published until 1558); he later illustrated his own critical theories in the vivid elegiac miniatures of *Les antiquités de Rome* and *Les regrets* (1558).

Du Bellay's only Latin eclogue (*Iolas*; 75 hexameters), despite the extreme formality of its structure, lacks the artificiality and padding noticeable in the eclogues of his contemporary Jean Dorat. The Latinity is excellent, and the poem is full of phrases intended to recall well-known half-lines of Virgil or Ovid: in line 3 *placidis pulcherrimus undis* (describing the countryside of Anjou) is obviously intended to recall Ovid's description of his birthplace, Sulmona, *gelidis uberrimus undis,* in tone, phrasing, and rhythm.

In the introduction (1-22) Du Bellay describes, with obvious pleasure and affection, a group of rustics gathering together for a local religious festival. He singles out for particular attention a youth named Iolas, who prays to Pales, Ceres, and Bacchus (23-70). The prayer consists of twelve stanzas of three lines each, each followed by a refrain ("vota Pali et Cereri iam solvite, solvite Baccho"), the liturgical effect of which is especially appropriate here. In the series of triplets, Iolas offers rustic gifts of flowers, grain, and grapes (all appropriate, of course), praises the three deities, praises their kindness to mortals, hopes for good weather, prays that storms may never visit Anjou, promises continued reverence, and so on. The prayer is graceful and pleasant and has not a trace of the padding and repetition that can occur in amoebaean dialogue and stanza arrangement. A reading of Du Bellay's *Deffence,* this eclogue, half a dozen of the Latin elegiac poems included in the *Delitiae poetarum Gallorum,* and all of *Les regrets* would form a sound basis for a university seminar in the critical theory and practice of the Pleiad.

A much less important figure is that of Louis-François LeDuchat (Lucius Franciscus Ducatius) of Troyes (ca. 1530–ca. 1600), friend of Marc Antoine Muret and Jean Antoine Baïf and protégé of Jean Brinon (active as a Maecenas). His Latin verses, published at Paris in 1554 under the title of *Praeludia* ("first efforts"), contain some love-poems (Ovidian elegiacs and Catullan hendecasyllabics) that reveal an agreeable minor talent. Many of his verses hymn the praises of country life or at least of country life as enjoyed by a sixteenth-century gentleman of education and refinement, comfortably provided with a rural retreat near Troyes and a pretty mistress called Lygia (there seems no reason to doubt the lady's reality). Along with these elegiac and hendecasyllabic pieces that often show the influence of conventional pastoral, there are also some pleasantly pagan *lusus pastorales* and two full-scale eclogues written not in hexameters but in elegiac couplets: these last are not *eclogiolae* ("miniature eclogues," pastoral vignettes) but true eclogues in everything but meter.

The first of these elegiac eclogues (untitled; 20 couplets) is, like Camerarius' nineteenth, a semi-dramatic mime, modeled after the Greek of Theocritus, in which appear the naïve shepherdess Mycalê and the enterprising shepherd Licus. At the poem's close, Mycalê weeps, and wonders what is to become of her if she becomes pregnant:

> quid mihi si tumeant inviso lacte papillae?
> et sim famoso nota puerperio? (35-46)

Licus jauntily promises marriage (in that case), and Mycalê hopes that he is telling the truth.

The flippant, Ovidian tone of this narrative (which reminds the reader of John Aubrey's *Brief Lives* of an anecdote about the youthful Walter Raleigh) reappears in the second elegiac eclogue (*Satyrus*; 48 couplets), a rather more ambitious piece of work, closer to idyll than pastoral, a rustic and mythological version of *La ronde d'amour*.

From LeDuchat we turn to one who was primarily scholar, editor, and printer—Henri Estienne (Henricus Stephanus) of Paris (1531-1598), editor and printer of fifty-eight Latin and seventy-four Greek authors and compiler of a Greek dictionary in five folio volumes (*Thesaurus Graecae Linguae,* 1572) that as a lexicon on a large scale is still unsurpassed: like a good many major works of the past, it is obsolete but unreplaced.

His Latin poems include two eclogues (one of which is an art-pastoral) and two brief idylls. The first eclogue (*Chloris*; 207 hexameters) is far too long and has a few technical flaws in meter, but it makes pleasant reading for all that. It is precisely the sort of sentimental love-story that many Neo-Latin poets preferred to break up into a series of half a dozen or a dozen brief lyric, elegiac, iambic, and hendecasyllabic poems to form a cycle or sequence as a *lusus pastoralis*. There is very little indeed in this poem, by the way, that is Virgilian—the whole eclogue is strongly Ovidian in tone, vocabulary, phraseology, syntax, rhythms, and versification.

Of the two idylls the first (*De laudibus vitae rusticae*; 57 hexameters) is a brief panegyric of country life, written, we are told, *in via,* probably on his first journey to Italy in 1547. There is nothing remarkable about this little poem: it scans, it is correct, it served its purpose as a *passe-temps*. The second (untitled; 27 hexameters) is worth reading with much more care: it is a very brief poem that reminds the reader of Sluperius' tale of his trip to Bruges, though it is far less artificial. On the same journey to Italy, Estienne tells us in a prefatory note, he had gone out for a walk from the inn where he was staying overnight and had stopped to listen to some farm girls singing as they worked in the fields nearby. The poem is a sort of pastoral reverie on the happiness of simplicity as contrasted with the worry in the poet's own mind (the reference seems to be to the trouble brewing between Henri II and Charles V).

Little of either importance or interest is known about Estienne Forcadel (Forcatulus) of Beziers (1534-1573). Among his Latin poems appears one very brief eclogue entitled *Amyntas* (32 hexameters), unusual in that it purports to be a letter written by Amyntas to Corydon. It seems likely that Amyntas represents the poet himself and that Corydon is a disguise for Charles de Lorraine (the Cardinal), to whom the entire 1554 collection is dedicated. If this assumption is correct, we have before us the first example of epistolary eclogue since 1321.

Far more important than Forcadel—in every way—is our next author, Scévole (i.e., Gaucher) de Sainte-Marthe (Scaevola Sammarthanus) of Loudun (1536-1623), son of François I's physician and member of a remarkable family of scholars and poets: between the mid-sixteenth and mid-eighteenth centuries this family produced no less than nineteen writers well-known in their day. After a thorough training in the humanities under Marc Antoine Muret, Adrien Turnèbe, and Petrus Ramus, Sainte-Marthe studied law at Poitiers and Bourges, and then devoted himself to a successful career in law, financial administration, and politics at Poitiers, Blois, and Tours, being particularly active in his support of Henri III against the League.

Sainte-Marthe published collections of French verses, very famous indeed among his contemporaries, in 1559, 1570, and 1573 (they include, by the way, a fine alexandrine paraphrase of Marcantonio Flaminio's *Lusus pastorales*). His Latin *Poemata* (Paris, 1575) were many times reprinted—these are excellent: they are correct, precise, elegant, and can almost all be still read with lively interest. Pierre de Ronsard, on first seeing these poems, delightedly cried, "These are the Muses speaking themselves!" and preferred them to those of Pietro Bembo and Andrea Navagero.

Among the Latin poems there appears one eclogue (*Damoetas*; 100 hexameters), dedicated *ad Claudiam Retiorum Ducem,* i.e., to the wife of François de Coligny, Claudia de Rieux, described as "the new light and glory of our era" (*nostri nova lux et gloria saecli:* 8). Many women of the Renaissance were active literary patrons, as Publio Fausto Andrelini and Lilio Gregorio Giraldi had already discovered to their pleasure and profit.

The first twenty-nine lines of the *Damoetas* consist of a complimentary address to Claudia de Rieux (flowery compliments on her literary taste and promises to compose a heroic narrative of her husband's military exploits in northern Italy). In lines 30-96 we have the usual sort of pastoral song sung by a shepherd to his obdurate sweetheart. At this point there is little new that one can say about such an eclogue as this: like all those of the better Neo-Latinists, it is well contrived, polished, and precise, marked by balance and good sense, the work of a man to whom the graces and varied skills of good style have become almost second nature.

With Pierre Mambrun (Mambrunius) of Clermont-Ferrand (1600-1661), we are well into the seventeenth century and for the first time in this survey of pastoral meet one of that century's many Jesuit poets. After entering the Jesuit order, Mambrun taught rhetoric at Paris for four years; he was then sent to the University of Caen to teach philosophy for six years and here his reputation gained him unusually large classes, the most notable member of which was Pierre-Daniel Huet, later Bishop of Avranches and a notable Neo-Latin author. Mambrun was finally sent to teach theology at La Flèche; here he spent the rest of his life in teaching and working on his commentary on Aristotle.

Virgil had written eclogues, the didactic *Georgics,* and an epic poem; Mambrun in conscious emulation wrote nine eclogues, one of them in Greek (La Flèche, 1661), a three-book didactic poem on ethics, and a religious epic on the triumph of Christianity in 323 A.D. called *Constantinus* (Paris, 1658) preceded by a long critical essay on epic technique. Mambrun's Latinity and versification are fluent, correct, even elegant, but he lacked imagination and was more than a little pedantic. The reader is not astonished to discover that Mambrun's third eclogue is as cryptic as anything in the work of Petrarch and his successors.

Four of the eclogues are art-pastorals. The fifth is entitled *Umbra* ("Shade"; 95 hexameters). On January 1, 1568, Jean Passerat had addressed a *jeu d'esprit* called *Umbra* (not a pastoral) to Henri de Mesmes; the present poem is addressed in a dedicatory epistle to Henri's grandson, Claude de Mesmes. It describes how a shepherd, as he drove his flock to pasture, sang the story of the sun-god Apollo's pursuit of the lovely nymph Umbra. She fled him constantly, and whenever the god of light overtook her, she disappeared from his sight. The whole song is an extended paronomasia—the half-punning references to Umbra or *umbra* disappearing at the arrival of Sol or *sol* grow wearisome—in a brief epigrammatic tour de force they are bearable; but this poem runs to ninety-five lines.

The sixth eclogue (*Damon*; 72 hexameters) tells the tale of yet another rejected suitor. After an invocation of the *Leiriades Musae*, Mambrun tells how Damon, rejected by Thaumantis, wandered disconsolate through forests, mountains, and trackless paths, until he reached a desert, where he lamented for three long days.

The seventh eclogue (*Corydon*; 71 hexameters) recalls one of the earliest Italian art-pastorals (one by Strozzi). Here Codrus and Thyrsis contend in amoebaean quatrains before Corydon: Codrus praises morning and the morning-star (*Luciferus*) while his opponent praises evening and the "folding-star" (*Hesperus*). Certainly the poem is inoffensive and even pleasant if one has not already read too many of its type.

In the eighth eclogue (*Delphis*; 91 hexameters) Meliboeus and Tityrus lament the death of their friend Delphis and describe at length the elaborate tomb they intend to build for him. Perhaps Delphis refers to some actual friend of the author. Certainly the description of the statuary and ornaments on the tomb suggest that of an actual memorial in some baroque church or cathedral; the details are so circumstantial and specific that it would not be in the least astonishing if the very memorial could be identified. Mambrun, however, gives no indication in the introduction to his poem that any historical personage is intended.

The last author we shall examine here among French Neo-Latinists (we can omit Gaspard de Varadier of Arles [*floruit* 1679], author of one extremely bad and apparently unfinished eclogue) is in fact one of the most interesting—Jacques Moisant de Brieux (1614-1674), son of a wealthy Huguenot family. After his elementary education at Caen, Moisant studied at Sedan and then at Leyden. He next spent three happy years continuing his studies at Oxford and Cambridge, since at no time in his life did he ever lack for money. The rest of his life he spent at Caen in the peaceful study of literature. He established weekly meetings at his home, and it was from these that the later Académie de Caen developed: members of this Monday group were, among others, Pierre-Daniel Huet (later

Bishop of Avranches and, with Bossuet, tutor of the Grand Dauphin) and Tannegui le Fèvre (Tanaquil Faber, whose chief claim to fame is that he was the father of Mme Anne Dacier). He died (after an operation for the stone) in 1674, leaving a very considerable fortune to his surviving son (a Huguenot clergyman) and daughter.

His writings in French and Latin alike are extensive; for the history of Neo-Latin literature the two most important works are his letters, published at Caen in 1670, and the three collections of Latin poetry, also published at Caen, in 1658, 1663, and 1669: of these three I have seen only the second. The 1663 volume contains a large group of hexameter poems, the chief of which are the three eclogues and an outraged poem on the execution of Charles I of England (a fair-sized anthology of such poems could be compiled, by Italian, French, German, Dutch, Belgian, English, and Scottish Neo-Latinists; so also with the death of Mary, Queen of Scots), a large group of elegiac poems of no particular interest today, and an excellent series of witty and pointed *epigrammata,* e.g., on Louis XIV, Christina of Sweden, Scarron, Mazarin, and a large number of personal friends.

The three eclogues ('Ερωτικά; *sive, Lycidas et Phyllis*; the individual poems are untitled) form a connected narrative. Each has a very brief introduction by the poet, followed by dialogue between the two rustic lovers at different times of the day (this last detail is characteristic of the *lusus pastoralis*). The third poem is clearly unfinished, and there was to have been a fourth (was there, in the 1669 edition?) completing evening, morning, noon, and evening.

In the first poem (141 hexameters) Lycidas and Phyllis pass the time by telling each other sad and unhappy tales of lovers and protest their own undying love for each other. One notable piece of rhetoric (which we might compare to Romeo and Juliet's greeting each other at their first meeting with lines that form a sonnet) appears in lines 114 through 120, of which the following is an inadequate version:

L.	I'll sooner gather shells upon the hills—
P.	I'll sooner gather berries from the rills—
L.	Than to my darling Phyllis be untrue.
P.	Than to my fairest Lycid prove a shrew.
L.	If I do lie, let lighning burn my shape—
P.	If I do lie, for me the earth shall gape—
L.	To die for you would be my sweetest fate!
P.	Then live with me, before it be too late!

The second eclogue (198 hexameters) takes place at dawn on the following day. Lycidas brings a spray of flowers for Phyllis and is prettily thanked; Lycidas assures his sweetheart of the steadfastness of his love and Phyllis replies in kind. But Lycidas wonders if there might not be a blight on the rose of their love: he has been troubled, recently, by puzzling and ominous dreams. Phyllis suggests that perhaps they ought to be more discreet and not see so much of each other. At this point one of the dogs begins to bark and Phyllis realizes that Aegon is approaching: Aegon is a friend and spy of the wealthy Mopsus, who had been influencing Phyllis' mother. Phyllis tells Lycidas to hide until Aegon is gone, and Act II thus comes to an end.

The third poem (76 hexameters as we have it today) forms an unfinished third act: it takes place at noon, some hours after the "action" of the second eclogue. Lycidas is discovered hiding in a cave by the shore, still not sure why Aegon had put in an appearance in the first place—he is just on the point of going back to see for himself, when Phyllis arrives. She tells him that Aegon had waited suspiciously an unconscionable length of time and had then left in irritation, finally convinced that Phyllis had been alone all the time.

In England the art-pastoral is rare—the only important writer here is Thomas Watson of London (ca. 1555-1592), a friend of Christopher Marlowe who traveled rather widely in France and Italy and learned much from the Continental writers of Neo-Latin verse. His first eclogue, the *Amyntas* (1585), is a shepherd's lament over the death of his sweetheart Phyllis, written in decidedly flowery Latin that shows strong influence of both Ovid and Petrarch. In 1592 Watson reverted to the story of Amyntas and Phyllis with the *Amintae gaudia,* producing a sequence of eighteen poems, which I have not seen and for which I must now rely on Leicester Bradner's *Musae Anglicanae.* In the first part of the work we find ten pastoral epistles of Phyllis in which she persists in rejecting Amyntas; in part two appear eight eclogues in which the poet narrates Amyntas' gradual conquest of Phyllis. But here I must refer the reader to pages 44 to 51 of Professor Bradner's work and to an article by Walter Staton (see bibliography).

The Neo-Latin literature of Scotland is extensive and of excellent quality; Geddes and Leask's edition (1892-1910) of the Aberdeen poets alone runs to three large quarto volumes, and, as for quality, it should be emphasized that one of the best collections of Neo-Latin poetry ever made—second in value only to the Italian ones—is Arthur Johnston's *Delitiae poetarum Scotorum* (Amsterdam, 1637). Especially during the reigns of James I and Charles I, Latin was in Scotland, as it never was in England, the accepted, normal, recognized vehicle of expression in poetry. The Scots excelled in two fields of Neo-Latin verse—the epigram and ceremonious poetry. The eclogue also flourished vigorously in Scottish Neo-Latin poetry, and in fact one of the major names in the history of Neo-Latin poetry—John Leech of Montrose and Aberdeen—belongs here. The majority of Scottish eclogues belong to the special forms and special uses: I have met only one real art-pastoral, John Barclay's third—there may be more; I have never, for example, seen the *Pastoria* of Andrew Aidie (*floruit* 1620), published at Danzig in 1610 (referred to in Leicester Bradner's *Musae anglicanae,* p. 184), a volume which may, for all I know, contain half a dozen such poems.

John Barclay (1582-1621), author of the two best-known novels in Neo-Latin literature, was born at Pont à Mousson in Lorraine where his father, William Barclay of Aberdeen, was professor of civil law; his mother was Anne de Malleviller. Though a life-long Catholic, Barclay was apparently not educated by the Jesuits and was in fact at odds with the order most of his life. In 1602 he left France for London. A Scottish king was on the English throne, and the gifted and enterprising youth knew that James VI and I would welcome the likes of him. His rewards did not always measure up to his expectations, however, and in 1616 he left for Rome, where he was assigned a generous pension by Pope Paul V. He spent the last years of his life raising tulips and writing the novel called *Argenis,* completed in the year of his death.

Barclay's Latin verse is fluent and pleasing and rarely aspires to be more. As a prose author he is one of the major figures of European Neo-Latin literature; in his verses, he is a good minor poet whose work can be depended upon to be pleasant and lucid but no better than that of scores of others. Among his poems appear five eclogues, of which only the third is now relevant.

This eclogue (*Daphne*; 106 hexameters) is typical of Barclay—it is well written and is a pleasure to read because of its lucidity and its apt and artful use of the familiar situations and patterns of bucolic verse; at the same time it does not descend to cento. A Thracian shepherd named Corydon sings a love-song (23-87) before the doors of his sweetheart Daphne, for all the world like a lover in Ovid; it is quite possible that Daphne is Louise Debonnaire, whom Barclay married in Paris in 1605.

In Portugal and Spain, even more than in Scotland, Latin was the normal medium for literature, that is, if the authors expected to be able to appeal to the educated readers of all Europe. More books were published in Spain in Latin (the majority being theological) than in the vernacular during the sixteenth century, and the situation is the same in Portugal. Unfortunately, the chief collection of Portuguese Latin verse, Antonio dos Reis' seven-volume *Carmina illustrium poetarum Lusitanorum* (Lisbon, 1745), is far from being all-inclusive, and there may well exist in manuscript a good many Portuguese Neo-Latin eclogues that I have never seen; Antonio dos Reis mentions by name 291 Latin poets of the sixteenth, seventeenth, and early eighteenth centuries in his *Enthusiasmus poeticus*—most of these probably never reached print; the works of those who did are extremely difficult to consult outside of Lisbon, Coimbra, and Madrid.

The only Portuguese Latin poet to be mentioned at the moment is Antonio Figueira Durão or Duram (Durianus) of Lisbon (ca. 1617-1642), a youthful prodigy from the University of Coimbra who distinguished himself not only by his brilliance in public disputation but also by publishing in 1635 a three-book epic on St. Ignatius Loyola that had been written at the age of sixteen. He completed his doctorate in law at Coimbra before he was twenty and was promptly selected by John IV of Portugal to serve as *ouvidor* (magistrate and financial overseer) of northern Brazil. Durão became bored, embittered, and discouraged; in addition, the Brazilian climate aggravated the illnesses he had already encouraged by overwork, and he died overseas at the age of twenty-five.

His *Ignatias* is undoubtedly a work of the utmost precocity; if we are to judge it on its own merits, we can only say that it displays all the vices of the baroque period with few of its virtues: as in much Portuguese literature of the age, Latin and vernacular alike, the style is unbelievably florid, and the mythological element—always awkward in a Christian epic—is overpoweringly omnipresent. In 1750 the Abbé de la Tour put it succinctly when he wrote that St. Ignatius never found himself in worse company.

But Durão can be attractive in his shorter pieces. Of his three eclogues, the third (*Pharmaceutria*; 99 hexameters) is an art-pastoral. Like many incantation-eclogues, it has two sets of magic songs: here Frondosus (19-54) tries to win back the blonde Isbella ("Isbellae rigidos avertite, carmina, sensus") with repeated invocations of Circê and Medea, while Sylvanus (56-99) tries to soften the heart of Chloris ("pectore mitte ferum, iam mitte, ingrata, rigorem"). Frondosus is successful, for he receives a lucky omen at the end of his song; Sylvanus remains as unlucky as before. The poem is at least neat and inoffensive.

The last author we meet here is a Dane—Christian Aagaard of Viborg (1616-1664): Aagaard studied at Copenhagen from 1635 to 1639, became, in 1647, professor of poetry at Soroë and then at Copenhagen, and was eventually appointed rector of the college at Ripen in 1651. His poems, printed in the *Delitiae quorundam poetarum Danorum* (Leyden, 1693), include one eclogue, the only Danish-Latin one I have seen.

Aagaard's poem—which unaccountably makes Olaus Borrichius compare the author with Vida—was written between 1645 and 1650; it is untitled and runs to 109 hexameters, of which lines 6 through 107 are the song of Damon as he prays to the gods in a song that is almost an incantation (it has a repeated magical refrain, like the eclogues entitled *Pharmaceutria*) to aid him in recovering the love of Phyllis. The poem is entirely conventional, introducing nothing even faintly new in content or expression and is included here only for the sake of completeness.

There is one curiosity of word order, however, which I have never seen in any other eclogue, Greek, Latin, or Neo-Latin, a scheme that appears in classical Greek and Latin (Sidonius Apollinaris is the great offender), but is much commoner in medieval Latin and in Renaissance French, Spanish, Italian, and English poetry, called *contraria contrariis*.

Ho! hearts, tongues, figures, scribes, bards, poets cannot
Think, speak, cast, write, sing, number (ho!)
His love to Antony!

is a familiar example, and the *ne plus ultra* is to be found in Sir Philip Sidney's *Excellent Sonnet of a Nymph:*

Vertu, beautie, and speech did strike, wounde, charme
My heart, eyes, ears, with wonder, love, delight;
First, second, last did bind, enforse, and arme
His workes, showes, sutes with wit, grace, and vowes' might;

Thus honour, liking, trust much, farre, and deepe
Held, pearst, possesst my judgement, sence, and will;
Till wrongs, contempt, deceite, did grow, steale, creepe
Bands, favour, faith to breake, defile, and kill.

Then grief, unkindness, proofe took, kindled, taught
Well-grounded, noble, due spite, rage, disdaine.
But, ah! alas! in vain! my minde, sight, thought
Doth him, his face, his words leave, shunne, refraine:
For nothing, time, nor place can loose, quench, ease
Mine owne, embracèd, sought knot, fire, disease.

In lines 37 and 38, Aagaard, in describing the inconsistency of a woman, writes as follows:

odit, amat, pellit, revocat, fastidit, anhelat
tristis, amica, ferox, mitis, inflata, benigna;

at least he has not gone so far as Sidney.

VIII

NEW FORMS OF PASTORAL

n the fifteenth century Giacopo Sannazaro intro-
duced a new form of eclogue in which the charac-
ters were no longer shepherds but fishermen, the
scene no longer the fields but the seashore, and
in which, although diction, manner, and tone remained as in the Virgilian art-pastoral, all details
were so changed as to leave the same taste but a
different flavor. In the sixteenth and seventeenth centuries, other
Neo-Latin poets in Italy, Germany, the Netherlands, France, England, and Scotland more or less consciously vied with one another
in devising such new forms of pastoral. In the present chapter we
shall examine eleven types—eclogues of fishermen, sailors, huntsmen,
gardeners, vine-growers, and plowmen, the humorous eclogue, the
domestic, the dream-eclogue, the epistolary eclogue (a reappearance),
and a type of idyll in which the poet invents a new world of myth
and metamorphosis.

i

Among these eleven forms the only one at all well known today
is the fishermen's or piscatory eclogue (widely imitated in almost
every vernacular literature by a number of minor but competent
poets, such as Phineas Fletcher in English), developed by Giacopo
Sannazaro of Naples (ca. 1456-1530). Sannazaro early became
attached to the household of Alfonso, Duke of Calabria, probably

through the good offices of Giovanni Pontano who had already welcomed him into the Neapolitan Academy, giving him the rather mysterious "Humanistic" name of Actius Syncerus. For a while Sannazaro served in the Duke's army, and seems to have acquitted himself with honor; but, like Pontano himself, he was more diplomat than soldier: he took a notable part, for example, in the negotiations between Naples and Pope Innocent VIII in 1486.

There are five fishermen's eclogues (*eclogae piscatoriae*) and a brief fragment of a sixth. The charm of these poems is great, and they have accordingly had a wide influence on later European literature, both Latin and vernacular; they were, like Mantuan's bucolic poems, read at least as widely and as thoroughly as Virgil's all through the sixteenth and seventeenth centuries. In fact, as Miss C. V. Wedgwood has recently emphasized (in *The King's Peace*), more Neo-Latin than classical Latin poetry was read during the seventeenth century in certain schools in England; one result of this, as J. Max Patrick noted in a review in *Seventeenth-Century News,* was "that most so-called innovations in seventeenth-century English poetry were only the introduction into English of what was already current internationally in Latin."

Since most subsequent attempts to create new forms of pastoral appear to have been inspired by Sannazaro's example, it will not be out of place to offer the reader at this point a complete version of one piscatory (the second: *Galatea*; 86 hexameters):

> Lycon, a fisher-youth, with love distressed,
> A hollow cave had sought, to ease his breast;
> While others range along the well-known shore
> With torch held high, or draw their nets before,
> Or bring the ocean's tribute to his sight,
> The youth this song rehearses through the night:
> "My Galatea, neither gifts nor sighs
> Can serve to make me worthy in your eyes.
> Your pride rejects my words as rocks the wave,
> Nor ever am I loved, your willing slave.
> But now no zephyr stirs; the very deep,
> The heaven itself, the very stars do sleep.
> All others happy, I alone remain,
> And through the waning night must still complain.
> No thought of Lycon ever vexes thee:
> No care regards, no kindness reaches me.

Yet other maids have cared: Amyntas' flame
And others (fairer still) have loved my name.
Ev'n from Aenaria's heights (if you'll believe)
Petitions come; fair Hyalê begs leave
T' admire my youthful Muse; her generous sires
Castilian blood reveal; her beauty's fires
Old Neptune's self could rouse; her judgment grave
Enjoys the wealth that favoring heaven gave.
But what avails all this, if I repel,
Nor all my songs *thy* loathing can dispel?
Misenum's hanging rocks have yielded scores
Of oysters, gifts for you; Euploea's shores
A thousand keep; her sister-island saves
As great a store beneath the glassy waves.
So Nesis' isle, in never-ending store,
Of spiny urchins keeps a thousand more,
Which neither mastic stains with bitter leaves,
Nor hostile moon of fullest growth relieves.
Nay, more, my hand well knows with practiced skill
Beneath the wave the Tyrian fish to kill:
Thus have I learned to seek the purple juice,
Nor have I failed to learn its skillful use.
Ev'n now the wool lies ready to be dyed,
A royal offering for your royal pride—
Robes that are softer than the Ocean's spray,
The gift of Meliboeus' self one summer day:
Myself he'd heard rehearsing by the shore;
Straightway the gift he made, and promised more;
Since then, the princely robes I guard with care—
A gift to cherish, and a gift to share,
Yet you (so that no hope can flatter me)
Must still refuse, and ever cruel be!
This cruelty at last has broke my heart:
Go sadly, Muses: Amor's keenest dart
My Galatea spurns: for sure, her scorn
Is for a simple sailor, humbly born,
A fisher-youth, whose meager wealth is earned
By sailor skill from sailor father learned.
Yet Glaucus' self, upon this very strand,
Ev'n Glaucus, watcher of the watery strand,

Lived thus, a simple fisher, once before,
Now god of swelling wave and pleasing shore.
Let not the tales of Lydê anger thee,
Who boasts of loving presents sent to me.
I call to witness waves and Nereids all:
Her love ne'er tempted me within her thrall!
If now I lie, come, shipwreck, from the sea:
Let waves engulf and Nereids bury me!
Yet what is left? For long my heart is fain
To seek my solace far across the main;
To sail where never fisher sailed before,
Bewailing sorrows on a foreign shore:
Accursèd northern seas, with ice encased,
Or burning Libyan sands, forever waste.
Yet all is vain, since I can never flee,
By haste or distance, Love's sweet agony.
Escape the winds, escape the angry seas:
From Love is no escape to tranquil ease.
Escape is none, though madness bids me leap
From yonder crag into the sounding deep.
Nymphs of the sea, I pray, concede to me
A gentle death, to end Love's ecstasy.
Some day (my tale of woe now known to all)
The coasting sailor to his mate shall call
(His voice resounding as they skim the Bay):
'Hold right, my fellows, to the right, I pray,
Nor hug that coast ill-omened, fair to see:
The crag of Lycon's Leap is on our lee!' "

In vain he sang; in vain the fisher-youth
Rehearsed his woes to breezes deaf to truth.
His vows, his gifts, his love itself once spurned,
His hope now vanished as the day returned,
As now, arising from the eastern verge,
The sun bedecked with red the morning surge.

The first eclogue (*Phyllis*; 130 hexameters) follows the same piscatory conventions. Lycidas, speaking to his fisherman friend Mycon, says that he had been wondering why the sea-birds were making so mournful a din, and why the dolphins had stopped their usual games; then he had realized that this was the anniversary of Phyllis' death. As they walk along the shore they recall the day of Phyllis' death until they come to her grave. Mycon presents gifts—cypress and myrtle-boughs, sea-moss, shells, and corals—and Lycidas sings a lament (44-105) which is freely modelled on the lament for Daphnis in Virgil's fifth eclogue. The poem, like the second, is in every way typical of the piscatory genre; it is also, like all the piscatory eclogues, notable for its excellent versification, its gently melancholy tone, and its highly conventional form. A verse-translation of the lament follows:

> What rocks, what caverns can the Nereids show?
> What herbs, what grasses for the sea-gods grow?
> Can I, like Glaucus, leave the teeming land,
> Transformed by magic on the golden strand?
> Let now my body flash with fishy scale,
> And strike the foaming wave with forkèd tail!
> For why should I, unhappy, hope for life,
> Bereft of her, that was to be my wife?
> What now is left? Why should I further stay?
> Why live, when I have lost the light of day?
> Why, stretched upon the seaweed of the shore,
> Lament beside her grave for evermore?
> Is this my wedlock, this the union dear?
> This, too, the joy Lucina gives my fear?
> Who, dearest Phyllis, tore you from my arms,
> My love, my joy, my hope 'gainst life's alarms?
> With grief my heart is filled, and bitter pain;
> No love my bed confers, but lasting bane.
> Not mine to gain the lover's youthful joy,
> Or live to greenest age without annoy.
> Though none believe, these stones her beauty hide:
> These stones, where sea-birds wail and waters glide.
> Her shade torments my slumbers as I dream:
> Where seek her now—in ocean, or in stream?
> Because of her all lands to me were dear,
> All men I welcomed, or from far or near,
> Now would I journey through the vasty deep,
> Through stormy waves that surge to heaven's steep,
> Past monsters of the sea, past Triton-throngs,
> Past shapeless seals, past woeful mermaid-songs.
> Farewell, these shores, farewell, these happy lands;
> Farewell, my Phyllis, and these golden sands.

Sev'n altars shall I raise, beside the wave,
Sev'n sea-calves sacrifice, before her grave.
Sev'n garlands shall I hang beside her fane,
And oyster-shells, and pearls without a stain.
Here shall Nisaea, and, her tresses free,
That lovely maiden nymph, Cymodocê,
Palaemon's gentle self, and Panopê,
And Galatea, come from Sicily,
Perform before your tomb the mourning dance,
And sing beside your grave the mourning chants
Once sung by Proteus, to afford relief
And cure the goddess Thetis of her grief.
You, Phyllis, if you live in heaven's height,
Or in Elysian fields, 'mid spirits bright,
Or watch the fish in Lethê's placid wave,
Or pluck eternal flowers beyond the grave
(Narcissus, amaranth, or crocus trim),
Or twine the sea-flowers with the violets dim,
Remember us, now goddess of the sea,
A lucky omen now, for such as we.
To Amphitritê and Nereus do we pray:
To you our prayers shall rise both night and day.
Accept this final gift of verses fair,
Which, as he spreads his nets to catch the air,
Each fisher-lad may read, and sigh amain
To think that she is dead, while we remain:
"Here Phyllis in the Siren's bosom lies:
All Naples' grief for both shall ever rise." (44-105)

The third eclogue (*Mopsus*; 101 hexameters) is the fishermen's equivalent of Virgil's seventh: we have the familiar situation in which two lovers sing the praises of their sweethearts in amoebaean verse—quatrains, in this case. One of the attractions of the poem—as with all of Sannazaro's poetry—lies in the easy and affectionate references to the islets and streams and headlands of the Bay of Naples that could all be seen quite clearly from Sannazaro's villa of Mergillina, and of course still can be seen from the modern Piazza di Sannazaro. The wonderfully artful mingling of artificiality and realistic details of setting had been piquant to Sannazaro's contemporaries and is to anyone today who sits down on the seashore of Mergillina and reads the poems amid the very scenes they describe.

The alternating quatrains of Chromis and Iolas run from 47 to 93:

C.   O Nereids, ocean's sacred nymphs, reveal
What gifts will soften Chloris' heart of steel;
Or, if she'll not obey the gods above,
Release me straightway from the rage of love.

I.   My dearest care, the Sirens, Nisa's heart
Must call me back, nor tear my mind apart;
Or let me die, and let her see my death:
And weep to see me draw my latest breath.

C.   Just as the ships on tranquil ocean skim,
When zephyrs gently curl the water's brim,
And safely all delight to sail the main,
Such was my life when Chloris loved my name.

I.   See how the angry winds assail the strand;
See how the winds uproot the deepest sand;
The sea and wind in combat dread engage:
Such fury but reflects my Nisa's rage.

C.   O mighty Proteus, speed my suit for me,
Since pride is hateful to divinity:
See Ischia's isle, and warn fair Hyalê
That even gods will not despise the sea.

I.   The isle of Procida is Nisa's home;
I pray you, Glaucus, hasten through the foam:
If Nisa still disdains my calloused hands,
Say, once *you* piled the fish upon the sands.

C.   Though Lemnos Vulcan, Cyprus Venus holds,
Though Samos Juno, Crete ev'n Jove enfolds,
While Ischia's hills receive fair Hyalê,
Not Lemnos' isle nor Samos coaxes me.

I.   Mars Rhodopê, Cyllenê Hermes loves;
Ortygia Dian, Delos Leda roves;
But Nisa's Procida delights my eye:
Not Delos nor Ortygia's isle can vie.

C.   Here in this cave is wicker, fit for weels,
And myrtles grow beyond, to make our creels:

If Pholoê or Chloris were but here,
The rage of wind and wave I'd never fear.

I.   No spot can smile for me; the sea repels;
The earth, no longer fair, my joy dispels;
If Nisa comes, my heart with love expands,
And would exist with joy in Libyan sands.

C.   The turbot's caught by Sinuessa's stream;
Fair Baia mullet yields, Amalfi bream;
The girls of Naples are the city's pride:
Why seek another shore, another tide?

I.   Some, like the mullet, love the grassy reeds;
The black-tail in the deepest water feeds;
My joy's to wait beside my Nisa's home:
What fairer port exists beyond the foam? (47-93)

The fourth eclogue (*Proteus*; 96 hexameters) is dedicated to
Federico's eldest son, Ferrante, now Duke of Calabria, who had
been only twelve when his father was deposed in 1501. The poet
first announces (1-6), as he invokes the Nymphs of the Bay of
Naples, that he is about to attempt a loftier theme, "the first honorable beginnings of our dear land" ("telluris primos carae dicamus
honores": 5); he then goes on to address Ferrante (7-17), urging
him to not to stay over-long in Spain (under the circumstances the
young man had precious little choice, but it would not do to admit
publicly that he was a virtual prisoner of the Spaniards).

In lines 18 through 27 Sannazaro tells how two young Neapolitan fishermen, sailing home late at night, heard the old sea-god
Proteus singing. Proteus repeats the legends of various places about
the Bay of Naples (one can readily imagine how congenial such a
theme was, not only to Sannazaro himself but also to the members
of the Neapolitan Academy)—Baia, Cuma, the rocks of the blonde
Sirens, Naples itself, Vesuvius, Pompeii, Castellamare di Stabia,
the peninsula of Sorrento. All this leads up to a lament (79-81)
over the exile and death of the last Aragonese King of Naples. The
mingling of classical and contemporary, of antiquity and Renaissance, of artifice and realism, is a feature of this poem as it is of
Neo-Latin poetry generally.

The fifth eclogue, "Herpylis the Enchantress" (*Herpylis Pharmaceutria*; 121 hexameters), is dedicated to Cassandra Marchese,

whom in the dedication of his *Canzoniere* Sannazaro had called "most learned of the lovely, most lovely of the learned." This poem (as Mustard puts it) is an extremely ingenious imitation (I should prefer to say "adaptation") of Virgil's eighth eclogue. There are here, as in Virgil's poem, two songs. In the first (lines 21-73) Dorylas tells how a forsaken girl, Herpylis, endeavored to secure the return of her lover, Maeon, by incantations; but of course, for all the classical background of the poem, the girl is a Neapolitan, the scene is by the stream Sebeto, the poisons and potions are ones derived from the sea—the juices of the sting ray and the "black torpedo" figure prominently. Like all enchantment-poems, Herpylis' song of binding has a repeated refrain. In the second part of the eclogue (lines 76-121), the despairing lover Thelgon expresses his grief at the faithlessness of Galatea: the theme is one familiar and over-familiar to the reader of the art-pastorals described in the preceding chapter; here, naturally, Sannazaro's whole effort is devoted to adapting the details to a form appropriate to a fisherman's lament. In his refrain it is Triton to whom Thelgon appeals for aid; the spot which recalls Galatea to mind is not a meadow or an oak tree's shade but a craggy cliff from which the island of Capri is visible; in Thelgon's sorrow it is not the flocks and herds that go untended but his boats and nets; and when Thelgon urges his abilities they are the abilities of a fisherman, not of a shepherd.

The sixth eclogue (untitled; 42 hexameters) is incomplete, but in finished form so far as it goes. The Vatican manuscript in which it appears contains also an early draft of the beginning, in Sannazaro's own hand; his changes and substitutions can be clearly seen and are as instructive as the scribbled draft of Milton's *Lycidas*.

Except for an inept and wholly uninteresting anonymous poem written some time before 1546 (*Iolas*; 90 hexameters), we do not meet another piscatory eclogue until we come to Girolamo Amalteo (1507-1558), eldest of the three Amalteo brothers, some of whose poems we have already seen. Amalteo's eleventh poem (a very brief one, untitled, of only 26 hexameters) describes the catching of a fish which is being sent as a present to a friend. Unfortunately, the story is an exceedingly silly one; Sannazaro would have been astonished and pained.

A far more interesting poem is the fourth piscatory eclogue of John Leech (Johannes Leochaeus) of Montrose (ca. 1590–ca. 1630), a man born in the wrong century and the wrong place. While it is true that for sophisticated poetry Latin was the normal and accepted vehicle of expression in Scotland, the hard fact remained that Scotland was a poor country and had no place for the man who insisted on remaining purely and simply a *littérateur:* Arthur Johnston, Scotland's finest Neo-Latin poet at this period, was a physician by profession and a poet by avocation and enthusiasm, and the other Scots-Latin poets of the time were all either professional men like Johnston or gentlemen of means like John Barclay. Leech, though a man of excellent family with good connections, was in fact neither, yet wished to hold the position of, say, one of Pope Leo X's favorite poets; he no doubt saw himself as the Marcantonio Flaminio of Scotland. Leech forgot that even so favored a poet as Angelo Poliziano worked extremely hard—any favors he received from Lorenzo de' Medici he repaid with substantial interest. But Leech's failure to get on in the world was also owing partly to his own personal extravagance and dislike of a settled course of life, partly to his venomous attacks on Archbishop Spottiswoode of St. Andrews.

Leech's best verse appears in a volume entitled *Musae priores* (London, 1620). There are twenty eclogues (most of which seem to have been written in France in 1618 and 1619)—five each of Virgilian pastorals (*bucolicae*), piscatory eclogues (*piscatoriae*), seamen's eclogues (*nauticae*), and vine-growers' eclogues (*vinitoriae* or *ampelicae*); Leech prided himself on being the originator of the last-named class.

The four *bucolicae* all belong to the special uses of eclogue; the *nauticae,* on the other hand, are purely and simply seamens' eclogues; the first four *vinitoriae* have no special underlying meanings, but the fifth is a disguised invitation to a friend—an epistolary eclogue, in other words, in which all the characters are vine-growers; the *piscatoriae* all belong to the special uses, except for the fourth, which is composed as a fishermen's eclogue pure and simple, on the model of those of Sannazaro (with which, by the way, Leech was thoroughly familiar, as he clearly was with a great deal of Continental Neo-Latin poetry).

The fourth piscatory eclogue (76 hexameters), entitled *Thaumasta* ("Marvels"), describes "the more extraordinary features of the seas and lakes of Scotland" (its prose subtitle: *quaecumque circa aquas Scoticas miranda magis circumferuntur*). There are notable echoes of Sannazaro, and the same blend of artifice and realism is noteworthy: the framework is classical, but the characters, for all their Greek names, are in reality the "fisher-fowk o' Muchalls" or of Donmouth or Peterhead; and the affection that Sannazaro obviously felt for the Bay of Naples has its counterpart in Leech's equally obvious fondness for the bleak, windswept coast of North-East Scotland. The occasional touch of Caledonian cantiness that appears in Leech's pastorals is also worth mention, the more so as it is rather rare in Scots-Latin poets—these writers, after all, considered themselves European men of letters, members of an international republic of letters, so that the tone of "John Anderson, my jo" is not for them, even though they would have found a precedent in some of the domestic sounding verse of Giovanni Pontano or Girolamo Fracastoro.

Petrus Stratenius of Goesa (1616-1640) we have already met among authors of art-pastorals; the third of his five eclogues is piscatory (*Milcon*; 68 hexameters), similar to Sannazaro's lament for Phyllis. Here a fisherman named Milcon laments by the banks of the Schelde for the death of his father Lycabas. There is nothing at all remarkable in the poem, but it is competent enough.

Among English Neo-Latinists a fairly well-known name is that of Phineas Fletcher (1582-1650), better known to students of English literature as a capable but occasionally grotesque Spenserian poet: *The Purple Island, Brittains Ida,* and the seven vernacular *Piscatorie Eclogues* are his major works. Fletcher was born at Cranbrook, Kent, and educated at Eton and at King's College, Cambridge. After ordination he served briefly as chaplain to Sir Henry Willoughby, who in 1621 presented him to the living of Hilgay in Norfolk; here Fletcher married and spent the rest of his wholly uneventful life.

Fletcher's Latin poems (the *Sylva poetica*) were published at Cambridge in 1633 and consist of thirty occasional poems and epigrams (several of which are extremely good) and four eclogues, two of which are piscatory. In the fourth, entitled *Lusus* ("A Sport"; 65 hexameters), the only real virtues are those of brevity and neat versification. Here a shepherd named Thyrsis and a fisherman called Myrtillus, each surrounded by a crowd of friends, meet in friendly rivalry by the seashore, cheered on by Nymphs on the one hand and Tritons on the other (1-14); in lines 15 through 62 they sing amoebaean quatrains, the one singer praising the woodlands and the farm, the other the sea and the fisherman's life. The obvious rhetorical antitheses are made with great precision, no doubt, but all are in such general terms as to fail to arouse any great interest; the valid, lively details which appear everywhere in a precisely similar poem (translated below) by Niccolò Giannettasio are sadly lacking here—no brightness, no vivacity, no real vigor, except where Fletcher has taken a line *in toto* from Sannazaro or Virgil.

The third eclogue (*Myrtillus*; 101 hexameters) borrows very freely from Sannazaro, so freely as to amount in part almost to a paraphrase of clearly recognizable passages from the first, second, and third piscatories. But it is rather better than the *Lusus,* despite its hackneyed topics.

In the works of Jacob van den Eynde (Eyndius) of Delft (ca. 1575-1614), count of Haemstede, soldier and Latin poet, appears one hexameter poem called a *piscatoria*; this is not, however, in any sense an eclogue or idyll, but simply a poem about fishing. Renaissance terminology can sometimes be misleading: the term *ecloga* (and even more often *idyllium*) can be used, for instance, of any sort of religious or meditative poem, especially among the Italians and French.

There is no question, however, about the piscatory eclogues of that fine Jesuit poet Niccolò Partenio Giannettasio of Naples (1648-1715), two of which belong here, as being piscatories pure and simple, with no contemporary or other undertones. Giannettasio entered the Jesuit order at an unusually early age and, after a brilliant academic career, in which he specialized in philosophy and literature, became professor of mathematics at the large Jesuit college at Naples. Despite the distractions of academic life and despite miserably weak health, Giannettasio never ceased to study and compose Latin poetry. His published verses were so extremely successful that he was actually able to build a church to the Virgin Mary with the proceeds; the history of European Neo-Latin literature holds many surprises, but none, surely, quite so startling as this.

Giannettasio's earliest finished work consists of fourteen piscatory eclogues, of which the majority belong to the special uses of pastoral (two are epinicia, three are epicedia, three are religious, three are contemporary and personal, and one is epistolary). These were so well received that Giannettasio undertook a major work on navigation (in eight books) with such zest that he completed it in six months; Mantuan himself could scarcely have worked faster. The two works were published together in an extremely handsome volume (*Piscatoria et Nautica,* Naples, 1685) illustrated by the well-known painter Francesco Solimene, who appears as one of the characters in the third eclogue.

Giannettasio next turned to a long poem on fishing in ten books (*Halieutica,* Naples, 1689) and two more on the history of war, by land (*Bellica,* Naples, 1697; ten books) and sea (*Naumachica,* Naples, 1694; five books). This was followed by four books of antiquarian verse in the Alexandrian manner called *Annus eruditus:* "Summers at Sorrento," "Autumn at Sorrento," "Winters at Pozzuoli," and "Spring at Ercolano" (*Aestates Surrentinae,* 1697; *Autumnus Surrentinus,* 1698; *Hiemes Puteolani,* 1704; *Ver Herculanum,* 1704). With his *Cosmographia* and *Geographia* all these were collected in the splendid *Opera poetica* (Naples, 1715; three quarto volumes).

Despite the rather alarming themes chosen by this remarkable man, even the prejudiced critic who might feel that Giannettasio wrote and published far too much far too quickly must agree that there are passages of real eloquence in the *Opera poetica,* an admirable clarity, and an enthusiasm for style that is characteristic of the Jesuit poets at their best.

In the third piscatory eclogue (*Antigenes;* 127 hexameters), Antigenes (merely out of compliment) represents Giuseppe Valletta (so the 1715 edition tells us), the Neapolitan lawyer, classical scholar, and bibliophile, and Argilochus stands for the artist Francisco Solimene. Here we have a well-worn plot: two fishers named Milcon and Dorylas first quarrel in a lively bit of repartee and then appeal to Antigenes to act as umpire. The poem is more thickly sown with references to actual places in and about the Bay of Naples and to actual types of fish native to the Tyrrhenian Sea than are the piscatory eclogues of Sannazaro himself.

The seventh piscatory eclogue (*Epaeneteria;* 107 hexameters) is similar: after an introductory conversation a shepherd named Tityrus and a fisherman called Amylcon each praises his own way of life. A verse-translation follows:

> Beside the foot of Pozzuoli's rocks
> The shepherd Tityrus attends his flocks:
> Beneath an oak-tree's leafy branches high
> He plays his flute, and Nymphs come dancing nigh.
> Amylcon chanced to hear the sound one day,
> Who'd late from Baia made his dusty way;
> His burden laid aside, he sank to rest,
> While scoffing Tityrus his scorn expressed:
> "You'll find no joys, my fisher-lad, like these
> Upon your sands; no rest, no tuneful ease!"

His eyes now angry and a-flash with fire,
Amylcon knit his brows and spoke with ire:
"Far better joys, my shepherd-friend, than these
We find, who dwell beside the sounding seas."
This said, while grazing flocks around them rove,
One praised the shore, the other praised the grove.

T.   In early spring, when warming suns appear,
When meadows glisten, and the skies are clear,
When blossoms raise their heads to questing bees,
And buds begin to swell upon the trees,
The tuneful swallow then begins her nest,
The gleaming world is new and shows its best.
We shepherds wander, joyful, far and wide;
We range the plain and climb the mountain-side.

A.   In spring the gleaming surface of the sea,
The pleasant light of day, the Zephyrs free
Invite the fishing boats to leave the sand
And coast along the rocks and past the strand.
Then fishers cast their nets, or set the weel,
Or bait the hook, to fill the bursting creel.
Then homeward turn the prow and skim the main,
To reach the port and see their homes again.

T.   But when the summer's heat begins to burn,
To shady groves and cooling springs we turn.
The longed-for breezes and the shadows dim
Refresh our bodies by the river's brim.
Here, by the shade that beechen boughs diffuse,
We shepherds meditate the sylvan muse;
Our cares we banish with a rustic song,
And watch the river as it glides along.

A.   But when the sun grows fiery, every day
We plunge our naked bodies in the bay;
As dolphins speedy, on the surface rove,
Or dive beneath the surface of the cove:
The ocean's floor we touch, then turn about,
And break the surface, with a merry shout,
Then, cushioned by the perfumed moss, recline
At ease upon a shaded rock's incline.

When mid-day heat makes over-bright the waves,
We fishermen retire to hollow caves,
Where softest myrtle, palest ivy grow,
And icy streams with gentle torrent flow.
Before the caves we make the welkin ring
With Triton-shells, and to our sweethearts sing.

T.   When winds disturb the shade, we shepherds rove
Within the forest and within the grove:
The murmur of the oak delights the ear;
The music of the birds is sweet to hear:
The lively swallow and the gentle dove
Protect their fledglings and display their love.
Beyond the woods, cicadas tune their lay,
And tempt the youths to sleep the hours away.

A.   When winds disturb the ocean's glassy tide,
When waters murmur and the billows ride,
Then breezes swell and rising gusts delight:
The ocean's waves are high and decked with white;
The rocks resound, the myrtle-branches wave,
The fisher hastens to the welcome cave,
Where, lulled by winds and sea-birds' plaintive lay,
He makes his bed and dreams the hours away.

T.   At such a time, on such a summer day,
We watch the dancing Nymphs and Dryads play;
In rustic finery, the shepherd-girls
Perform a lively dance, and toss their curls.
And if we wander past the haunted hill,
When day is done and night grows dark and chill,
At times we shepherds see the Satyrs prance
As Pan himself invites them to the dance.

A.   Amidst the Nereids we can dance as free,
When Doris leads her graceful company.
Beside the shore the Triton sounds his horn,
And Glaucus sings for us at early morn.
The dolphins leap and dash in merry ploy,
And fill the fishers' heart with simple joy.
Our shores with lovely maids are well supplied;
Our shores see Naiads sporting in the tide.

T.   When autumn grapes are bursting on the vine
And apples fill the trees at harvest-time,
We praise the gods and range the fruitful fields,
And pluck with joy what kindly nature yields.
Ripe nuts and fruit and cream are then our fare,
To feed our bodies and remove our care.
Our bleating flock at nightfall never fails
To store our dairies with the brimming pails.

A.   The gods we celebrate are far the best
(As Neptune, Proteus, Glaucus, and the rest),
When that we race our boats in festive sport
Or swim our fastest to the crowded port.
Both sport and nurture come from ocean's stream:
No lack is here of turbot or of bream;
The urchin and the oyster's culled by hand;
The scallop lurks beneath the golden sand.

T.   Now freezing winter spreads across the plain:
Now rivers cease their flow, and hushed remain;
Before the hearthstone of the silent farm
We pile the logs to keep us safe from harm.
The woolly sheep are settled in the barn
To keep them scathless from the wolf's alarm.
The shepherd and the shepherd's wife and boys
Are safe from winter and the world's annoys.

A.   When freezing winters rouse the stormy seas,
In house or smoky cave we take our ease.
All snug, we care as little for the roar
As does the dolphin, or the solid shore.
But, shepherd, let us stop: my way is long,
My path is hard, though lightened by our song.
If you revere the woods, I'll love the shore:
Let each prefer his own for evermore.

ii

Closely related to the eclogue of fishermen is the eclogue of sea-men—the *ecloga nautica*; it required no great effort of imagination to modify the details suitably. We shall meet four authors here, and it is perhaps significant that three are Dutchmen with a fine pride in the achievement of Netherlands seamen of the sixteenth and seventeenth centuries.

Jacob de Sluyper or Slupere (Sluperius) of Herzele (1532-1582) we have already met. Of his eight eclogues the fourth (*Damastor*; 332 hexameters), which reaches the length of an epyllion, is an *ecloga nautica:* it is preceded by an elegiac dedicatory poem (of 112 lines) that settles the date of composition at 1573. The length of the poem would be no objection if only it were livelier and less uneven; as it is, it would be vastly improved by drastic editing and the excision of digressions (notably lines 147-163) and repetitions. Lycabas, home at last from a lengthy voyage, tells his landlubber friend Celadon about the wonders he has seen in Europe, Africa, Asia, and America. This promises well; but the actual description of voyages appears only at the beginning and the end of the poem. The introductory poem of dedication whets a reader's interest but gives no indication of the vast amount of irrelevant detail that separates the two passages constituting the poem's chief attraction today.

Sluperius' poem had the virtue of turning to the theme of strange places and romantic tales of Indian Pygmies and Cuban cannibals, but foundered on the rock of the author's invincible longwindedness. A more mechanical but at the same time more successful adaptation of the conventional eclogue appears in the one *ecloga nautica* of the Dutch poet Franz Mod (Franciscus Modius) of Oudenburg near Bruges (1556-1597).

Among his poems appears one eclogue (untitled; 70 hexameters). A sailor named Grippius is discovered sitting on the top of a cliff overlooking the Adriatic; he laments the cruelty and faithlessness of Beroê and wonders whether he should not hurl himself into the sea. It is all rather lachrymose, and the versification has some rather unexpected crudities here and there—a poem so stylized as the eclogue must, after all, have elegance if nothing else.

The best-known *nautica* (it is often wrongly called the first— e.g., by its own author) is the *Myrtilus* of Hugo Grotius (Huig de Groot) of Delft (1583-1645). Educated at Leyden by the younger Scaliger, Grotius distinguished himself as statesman, diplomat, lawyer, theologian, and classical scholar. While yet in his teens he published an astoundingly learned commentary on Martianus Capella; its frontispiece shows the youthful prodigy arrayed in a gold chain that had been presented to him as a mark of esteem by Henri IV. After taking a doctorate in law, Grotius became an advocate at The Hague (it was here that he wrote the *Myrtilus*). He shortly became historiographer of the Netherlands, advocate-general of Holland and Zeeland, a member of the Estates-General, and author of influential works on international law.

In 1619 Grotius was condemned to life imprisonment for anti-Calvinist sympathies displayed in his support of Olden-Barneveldt (who was at the same time condemned to death by the Synod of Dort). In prison he continued to write, and received a steady supply of books from Gerrit Jan Vossius, packed in a four-foot long box: it was in this box that Grotius was, with the aid of his wife, smuggled out of prison.

The next decade was spent in Paris. Here Grotius completed his "The Truth of Christianity," his "Defense," various technical scholarly books, and above all his classic work "The Law of War and Peace" (*De iure belli et pacis,* published in 1625).

An attempt to return to the Netherlands being met by a decree of perpetual banishment, Grotius entered the service of Sweden under Gustavus Adolphus and later (1630) became Queen Christina's envoy to France, a position he retained to the end of his life. In 1645, while on the way to Lübeck, he suffered shipwreck off the coast of Pomerania and died at Rostock of the effects of exposure.

Grotius' achievements in theology, law, history, and philology make him the Netherlands' greatest scholar. His Latin poems (the first complete edition is that of 1617, frequently republished) influenced Milton (especially the "Adam in Exile," *Adamus Exsul*) and afford ample proof of a wide knowledge of classical poetry and an admirably disciplined taste: "Of the Latin poets of that age Baudius [Domenicus Baudius or Dominique le Bauldier of Ryssel (Lille), 1561-1613] may excel in fancy; Broukhusius [Jan van Broekhuyzen of Amsterdam, 1649-1707] and the elder and younger Heinsius [Daniel of Ghent, 1580-1655; Nicolaus of Leyden, 1620-1681] in smoothness of style; but Grotius surpasses all in the success with which he reproduces the spirit of classical poetry and clothes modern thoughts in ancient forms" (Sandys).

In the *Poemata omnia* appear two exercises in pastoral—Latin verse-translations of two of the idylls of Theocritus—and one original *ecloga nautica* (*Myrtilus*; 159 hexameters), dedicated to Daniel Heinsius, who, like Grotius himself, had been a favorite pupil of the younger Scaliger.

In the introduction (1-11) Grotius claims originality for this eclogue, as Sannazaro (*Pisc. ecl.* ii, 45) had done for his piscatory eclogues and as John Leech was later to do for his vinitory eclogues, and promises Heinsius, in the conventional phrases of the Humanists, that this poem, like Heinsius' own *Auriacus* (1602), will make his name a household word even in the least civilized parts of the world:

> My muse is first to leave the springs and groves:
> Through Ocean's water and the wave it roves—
> The wave, fit subject for Batavian song;
> The woods and pastures have been sung too long.
> The busy farm of Zeeland's dear to me,
> But dearer is the surge of open sea.
> I sing the songs no poet sang before;
> Your honored name, my friend, they'll honor more:
> Soon shall the Libyan, Javan, Indian, too,
> Revere your merit as your comrades do.
> Soon shall the southern stars your praises sing,
> Your drama's pages know, and tribute bring.

With this much as preliminary Grotius then proceeds with his *nautica*. In lines 16 through 158 we have the song of a sailor who has just brought his ship safely home from a long voyage in which, it develops later, he has touched at China, the Dutch East Indies, India, and Arabia. As the ship comes in to land, Myrtilus wonders whether Cochlis will be watching for him as she used to do, but doubts it, to judge from her behavior the last time he had seen her: has she changed (he asks himself), or has he?

At this point the waves become suddenly silent and the winds drop unexpectedly: Myrtilus chooses to regard this as a good omen. He steps on shore and decides to sing a song of invitation to Cochlis by the water's edge; he urges her to board his ship in a distinctly unusual version of "Come live with me and be my love." At this point, Myrtilus realizes that the sun is setting and that this night's stars will soon appear, and the poem comes to a close.

This *ecloga nautica*, the best extant example of its kind, is a fine piece of craftsmanship throughout. The rhythm and diction are as near the faultlessly classical as one is likely to find in any Neo-Latin poet, and the modern references are introduced with such skillful tact that they never jar as they tend to in Sluperius' *Damastor*. The variety of expression and the richness of fresh detail are a constant pleasure in a poem that never seems too long. In all these aspects it affords a noticeable and significant contrast with

Franz Mod's *nautica* in exactly the same way as does Niccolò Gian-nettasio's *Epaeneteria* with Phineas Fletcher's *Lusus*.

The twenty eclogues of John Leech (Johannes Leochaeus; ca. 1590–ca. 1630) contain five *nauticae*, dedicated to Thomas Hamilton, Earl of Melrose; they total 558 hexameters, by themselves a sizable little corpus of Neo-Latin poetry.

The first (*Amyclas;* 128 hexameters) is highly conventional, and, while not the least successful of the five poems, excites only a languid interest. In the introduction (1-22), obviously modeled on that of *Myrtilus,* Leech announces that he is setting sail on a sea first explored by a Batavian seaman (i.e., Grotius); he appeals to the Nereids for their favor, makes a graceful, glancing compliment to Thomas Hamilton, and then, like Grotius, tells us that he intends to abandon the Virgilian beech tree's shade, turning for inspiration to "the threats of Boreas, Eurus, and Notus, the cries of seamen as they vie with each other." And as the reader goes on through the poem he cannot fail to notice the number of verbal reminiscences clearly intended to recall the best and best-known exemplar of this type of eclogue. Of course it would be a mistake to regard these as proof of any lack in Leech's abilities—they are intended as compliments, not weak imitations—although it must be admitted that the present-day reader, however sympathetic, feels that so many indirect compliments are out of place and grows especially impatient (in this particular poem, at any rate) at the overt references to Java and the like, places which the average English or Scottish skipper was not likely to see at this time; the present-day reader is also likely to jib at the pedantic reference to Flavio Gioia's maritime compass, lugged in by the ears at lines 110 and 111.

The second poem, entitled *Tiphys* (117 hexameters), is a dialogue of sorts between Emporus and Aegialeus; this poem is the least successful of the five *nauticae*. Emporus meets Aegialeus on the banks of the river Tay and the two sit down to rest under a Scotch pine. Aegialeus remarks that the shade of such a place is propitious to the Muses; if Aegialeus has anything new, let him sing, "whether the praises of Magellan, or the battles of Da Gama, or the courage of Vespucci, or the mighty exploits of Columbus":

> sive Magellani laudes, seu proelia Gammae,
> Vesputiive animos, vel habes ausa alta Columbi,
> incipe, nam nostras tenet ancora firma carinas.

This sounds promising, but the suggestion is not acted upon. Emporus holds forth himself at some length (32-61) on the daring of the first sailors who had the courage to set out to sea when ships were first invented. The passage is little more than panegyrical commonplace.

The third poem (*Phroura:* "The Night-Watch"; 88 hexameters) consists of an introduction (1-9), an exchange of quatrains (10-81), and a brief conclusion (82-88):

> Now had the lofty ship, her journey done,
> Arrived at port, at setting of the sun,
> Fast held at anchor near the island-chain
> That spreads refulgent on the Scottish main.
> Two sailor-lads (while Cynthia ran her course)
> Kept lonely vigil, and exchanged discourse:
> Their years were equal, and their minds agreed,
> Their sweethearts different, but alike in deed.
> Thus Myrtilus and Phrasidamus sang,
> And round the Firth their youthful voices rang:

P.   My Panopê, than Chrysê's gold more dear,
      Or gladsome breezes that at dawn appear,
      Unknowing, will you dream the hours away,
      And leave my heart to wakeful cares a prey?

M.   The ruin of my soul, my heart's alarm,
      My life, my death, my dearest, fondest harm,
      Come, Chloris, and the sun would soon be near,
      The shadows vanish, and the day appear.

P.   Fine gems I've giv'n, and crystal goblets rare
      I've sent to win the favor of my fair;
      No answer did she deign to send to me,
      Aloof remained, and deaf to every plea.

M.   When I returned from India's fabled shore
      And showed to Chloris all the gifts I bore,
      Such golden kisses did she give to me
      That all the wealth of Ind seemed beggarly.

P.   What change is presaged by the cloudy sky,
      What kindly breezes make our vessel fly,
      What ocean paths to follow, these are clear;
      All doubtful are the humors of my dear.

M.   The Southern Stars and Cross I know of old;
     The Northern Bears for me no terrors hold;
     No constellation hides a mystery;
     Why must you, Chloris, hide yourself from me?

P.   Italian dust with water hardens fast;
     And clay is toughened by the forge's blast;
     My tears are water, and my love is fire:
     The heart of Panopê is stone entire.

M.   Within, cold quicklime bears consuming fire,
     And salt can burn though gathered from the mire;
     Should Chloris love, what flame would then arise!
     What fire would flash and sparkle in her eyes!

P.   All white is Kemnay's stone, a glitt'ring mass,
     And lovely beryl is as hard as glass;
     Though white as marble, still her heart is steel;
     Though fair as beryl, she can never feel.

M.   Though dark, no iron resists the magnet yet;
     Though dark, naught's stronger than our Scottish jet;
     Though dark, my Chloris still attracts my mind;
     Though dark, her love is strong, her heart is kind.

     .   .   .   .

P.   If heaven's favor gave her love to me,
     I'd say that none save her should rule the sea;
     I'd guard her like a tender lover true,
     And sacrifice to her with ritual due.

M.   What god will bring my Chloris here to me?
     The night is silent, peaceful is the sea.
     No sound is there from wind or angry blast:
     Let Chloris come, and let me hold her fast.

P.   Come, Nymphs of Orkney, come from Thulê's shore,
     And make her love me true for evermore,
     And let me kiss her lips beside the sea,
     And plight my troth to lovely Panopê.

M.   You Nereids, swimming by the golden sand,
     Take me to Chloris on the Scottish strand;
     Back to the vessel shall I swift return,
     If but a single kiss I suppliant earn.

P.   While birds are in the air, and crags in sea,
      Stars in the sky, and grass is on the lea,
      While Boreas is wild, and Zephyr bland,
      I'll sing my sweetheart's praises through the land.

M.   The ox shall love the sea, the whale the land,
      The sun at midnight warm the wintry sand,
      The breeze be silent on a waveless sea,
      Before my Chloris shall forgotten be.

      Thus did they fill the air with tuneful sound,
      And now prepared to bring their ship around:
      At dawn, a gentle breeze began to blow;
      They called their comrades from their rest below.
      The breeze now rising ever more and more,
      They came rejoicing to their native shore.

The fourth *ecloga nautica* (*Nereus*; 96 hexameters) is clearly modeled on Virgil's sixth bucolic and, more particularly, on Sannazaro's fourth piscatory. Sometimes Leech's *nauticae* show specific influence of Sannazaro's piscatories more clearly than do his *piscatoriae*.

The early part of the poem is rather disappointing. With line 79, however, the reader's interest quickens: Nereus praises the exploits of Vespucci and Columbus, Da Gama and Drake, and grieves over the tragic death of Cafarus. Their glory will never fade from the minds of men, proclaims the old sea-god, and he ends (87-94) with a really eloquent tribute to the courage of the seaman explorers of the Renaissance.

The fifth and last *nautica* (*Echo*; 129 hexameters) consists of introduction (1-33), quatrains (34-125), and conclusion (126-129), a structure we have seen many times before and will see many times again. In the introduction we are told how a young seaman named Nautilus had fallen hopelessly in love with a girl called Naera (*sic*); Leech does his best to enliven the poem with references to voyages to Nova Zembla, Guinea, and the like; but the poem remains lifeless and *précieux*.

iii

So far as I know, the eight poems of the four authors just examined (along with one other, written in 1566 and dedicated to Basilio Zanchi, by Lorenzo Gambara of Brescia, 1496-1586) are the only *nauticae* ever written, except for a couple, discussed in a later chapter, that were used for special purposes. The hunting eclogue (*ecloga venatica* or *venatoria*) is equally uncommon—I know of only nine poems, written by five authors. But the bibliography of Neo-Latin literature is so chaotic and the amount of unpublished manuscript material extant in the smaller libraries of France and Italy so extensive, that it is impossible to be sure.

The first known *venatoria* is the *Mopsus* (87 hexameters) of Luigi Annibale dalla Croce (Cruceius) of Naples (*floruit* 1490), about whom practically nothing is known: he is not so much as mentioned in Tiraboschi's history of Italian literature. A good many of his poems are printed in Gruter's *Delitiae poetarum Italorum* (Frankfort, 1608) and the *Carmina illustrium poetarum Italorum* (Florence, 1719-1726). He was an exact contemporary of Giacopo Sannazaro and, about the time that that poet was composing his piscatories, produced what appears to be the first hunting eclogue. In this poem a hunter named Mopsus leaves his bed at dawn, driven by unrequited love for Galla; he arms himself with bow and quiver and sets out with his hunting dogs. He starts a stag and stalks it until by accident he comes to the very spot where he had first seen Galla: this all reads very much like something out of Ovid, and the verbal resemblances are in fact to the *Metamorphoses* of Ovid rather than to the *Ecologues* of Virgil. Mopsus halts and, in a highly conventional lament, describes the agonies of unsuccessful love. At this point rhetoric gets the better of the writer:

> o quam saepe meo crevistis, flumina, planctu;
> o quam saepe meo viruistis, gramina, planctu;
> o quam saepe meo gemuistis, robora, planctu.

The effect of the anaphora and the similarity of sound not only in the three *-istis* verbs, but also in the nouns *flumina, gramina, robora* is impossible to reproduce in any sort of English version; the literal meaning is "how often have you increased, rivers, with my lamenting; how often have you grown green, grasses, with my lamenting; how often have you groaned, oak-trees, with my lamenting." The notion of grass growing lush with Mopsus' floods of tears is a conceit that would be hard to tolerate in a better poem.

The next hunting eclogues are two by Luigi Alamanni of Florence (1495-1556), one of the best known names in the history of the Italian vernacular literature of the Renaissance. Both, unfortunately, are extremely wooden, and we had better turn to a far more competent Latinist than Alamanni, Pietro Angelio of Barga (Petrus Angelius Bargaeus, often simply called Bargaeus; 1517-1596). After the usual training in Latin and Greek, Angelio studied law at Bologna for a time, but eventually returned to the humanities. Much of his subsequent life was a series of adventurous ups and downs, but Angelio has tricked out the tale so elaborately in his poems that it is difficult to decide how much is truth and how much fantasy.

Angelio's Latin poems appear in a handsome volume, *Poemata omnia* (Rome, 1585; two volumes in one). His most important work (mentioned earlier) is a twelve-book epic, "The Syriad" (*Syrias*), begun in 1561 and published in Florence in 1591. Besides this there are four eclogues, of which the first three are *venatoriae;* of these three, one is an epicedium and will be discussed in a later chapter. In the first, an extremely skillful poem called *Damon* (92 hexameters), we find much direct verbal imitation of Virgil. In the introduction we are told that the Hamadryad Chloris is in love with the huntsman Damon. She was herself a clever musician, singer, and dancer, trained by her father Aegon, and in addition to all this was a huntress, like Naïs in the second of Alamanni's *venatoriae*. But Damon refuses to be impressed by beauty or by skill, and Chloris relieves her feelings in a lament in which all the stock themes and motifs appear, but are turned inside out and presented from the feminine point of view.

The constant verbal imitation of Virgil seems a flaw until the reader realizes that in it is contained much of the poem's point. The imitation does not result from any lack of skill or originality on Angelio's part; quite the reverse. In every other line we are purposely reminded of situations in Virgil's *Eclogues,* situations which are here presented in a piquant reverse; without the constant verbal reminiscence, Angelio's treatment of those situations would lose much of their effectiveness.

The second poem, *Glycê* (103 hexameters), combines the huntsman's eclogue with the elegiac situation of the lover (Lycidas) who serenades an unsympathetic sweetheart (Glycê) before her locked door (*paraclausithyron*); the reader can judge of the poem's content from the following:

> Now had the moon revealed itself to view,
> Now was the meadow wet with grateful dew,
> When Lycidas, with languid love foredone,
> His nightly course to Glycê's door had run:

His love, once hid on hill and field,
Before the ruthless door he now revealed.
You now, my friend, whom more I love and more,
Who rule alone within my bosom's core
(Just so the tiny spark can light a flame
That spreads until it covers all the plain),
Receive my verse, and, that an hour may pass,
Read on, and grieve with grieving Lycidas:
"Let my distress invade your nightly rest,
Let dreams reveal my heart with love oppressed.
Your heart shall know how sad my spirit faints,
And fills the world with tearful lover's plaints.
No lioness it was that gave you birth;
No tigress suckled you on Indian earth:
Though hard your heart, and pitiless your mind,
Your soul is human—and your form divine!
Have you no pity for my hopeless care?
How many lovers must your favors share?
As often as you pass, my spirit fails:
It longs to ask your love, but ever quails.
My lovely Glycê, pity love's distress:
Reveal your love, reveal your tenderness.
My death will be your blame for evermore,
A crime abhorred on every sea and shore.
The hunter, as he roves the shaggy hill,
And speeds his questing hounds toward the kill,
Will know my name, and know my wretched yoke,
And read my epitaph incribed on oak.
The bows, the arrows, nets themselves shall grieve,
And woods, and hills, and hounds their grief relieve.
But you despise a lover's every plea,
Reject my gifts, and slight my misery.
My lover's gifts have proved my passion's bane,
Though many maids desired my gifts in vain!
Can this despite be for my hunter's life
Amidst the savage woods, with danger rife?
By day I hunt the boar's ferocious might,
And sleep beneath the open sky by night.
Yet Venus gave Adonis all her charms,
Nor fled his hairy grasp and brawny arms.

Yet never did he sing, in accents true,
Such songs as I can always sing to you,
Such songs as Nymphs and Dryads, through the plain,
Can sing to charm the sweetheart and the swain.
My life the Muses nurtured from the start;
They blessed my efforts, and inspired my heart.
They crowned with ivy-leaves my youthful brow;
They loved me lately, and they love me now.
Now you (Amyntas lately spoke his name)
Love Doryas, and entertain his flame,
Idaean Doryas, whose guileful art
Has oft deceived the virgin's trusting heart.
My plaintive Muse assaults your oaken door:
The door remains as silent as before.
Your heart remains unmoved, and you alone
Ignore the piper's melancholy tone.
Your name I've cut on every beechen tree
And told the tale of Lycid's misery,
That it to every hunter may appear,
That hunts the boar or drives the bounding deer.
What favors, though, did *Leucê* not assure
Would I but sing the praise of *her* allure?
And Leucê's eyes are dark, her hair is light,
Her glance is soft, her breast is snowy white.
And Leucê's not the only eager lass:
Lycotas' daughter longs for Lycidas;
Arctobolus' daughter flaunts her charms:
And both are rich in flocks and farms!
There's Amaryllis, too, and most of all,
Autonoê, who loves the Muses' call,
Who thinks of nothing else, both morn and night,
But Lycidas, and how to mend her plight.
She loves, she longs, she sighs the whole day through,
Esteems my verses, and my singing, too.
And now she boasts, with smug and smiling face,
Disdains your beauty, disregards your grace.
But you (alas!) still trust your native charm,
Nor dream that age can come, or years alarm,
The face grow wrinkled, or the hair turn gray,
The blossom wither at the close of day.

If violets wither and the lilies fade,
Though once they flourished in the garden's shade,
The form that once drew every glance away
Will fade and wither in the selfsame way.
A day will come when you shall grieve to find
Your lovers deaf to pleas, to age unkind.
But why rehearse to idle winds in vain?
Why tell to heedless breezes all my pain?
When all alone she wanders on the hill,
Or gathers fragrant blossoms by the rill,
Or seeks the warmer pleasures of the plain,
I'll press my ardor in a bolder strain.—
Such idle talk is rash, such thoughts are vain;
To manly tasks, turn, Lycidas, again:
'Gainst Hyrcan tigers turn your arrow's flight,
And pit your cunning 'gainst their savage might.
Their claws may tear, their jaws may rend your breast:
Your love with you will die, and give you rest.
How often have you mourned your misery,
And dreamed of death's caress to set you free!
If such your wish, abandon useless strife,
And let the wolves attack your useless life!
Let Glycê still admire her comely smile,
But read my mournful epitaph the while:
     'Here lies the hunter by his wonted hill,
     His woes have ended and his heart is still.'
This read, return to seek another's arms:
Admire your beauty, and adore your charms!"

Two hunting eclogues appear among the bucolics of the Hessian
Peter Lotich the Younger (Lotichius; 1528-1560), one of the best,
if not the very best, of the German Neo-Latin poets. In his eclogues
we may with justice describe him as another Giambattista Amalteo,
in his elegies as another Giacopo Sannazaro.

Lotich was born at Schlüchtern in Hesse in 1528. In 1544 he
entered Marburg University, where he met his lifelong friend,
Johann Hagen (Hagen's biography of the poet is a pleasant piece of
Latin and an invaluable document for the history of classical Humanism in Germany). Next, the two studied under Camerarius
and Melanchthon; Lotich was regarded as a prodigy by both these

men. An idyllic interlude with a Wittenberg girl was cut short by the confusions caused by the battle of Mühlberg (1547).

In 1547 Lotich became an unwilling soldier: anyone who believes that Renaissance Latin poetry is nothing more than the vaporings of pedants or the showpieces of schoolboys should read Lotich's *Elegiae* I, viii—an Ovidian *All Quiet on the Western Front*—or *Elegiae* I, xi, on his return to a ruined home. No one, surely, could question the reality, immediacy, and force of these poems. On the death of his father (1548) Lotich was permitted to return home, much relieved to learn that his uncle had found him a position as tutor to the three sons of Daniel von Stiebar of Würzburg. After visiting half-a-dozen French cities, the group settled down to three years of study at Montpellier.

In Montpellier Lotich received news of the young lady in Wittenberg and a strong hint that she expected him to resume their former relations. With some embarrassment Lotich replied that his conscience was clear in that quarter and that in any case he had become involved with someone else.

A precipitate return to Hesse did not yield the peace and quiet Lotich hoped for. His mother had died shortly before he could reach home, war had broken out once more (if indeed it could be said to have stopped), and his patron was ill. In 1554, accordingly, Lotich left, along with Hagen and others, on what was to be a grand tour of Italy. In 1556, however, Stiebar died, and Lotich's uncle was unable to provide money for further traveling. But in 1557 Lotich was providentially appointed to the staff of the University of Wittenberg, thanks to the good offices of the Kurfürst Otto Heinrich, whom he celebrates in his third eclogue. Lotich remained at Wittenberg until his death in 1560.

Lotich's Latin poems appear in the *Opera omnia* (Leipzig, 1586), to which is prefaced Hagen's excellent biography; but the most convenient edition is that in the *Delitiae poetarum Germanorum*. In these poems Lotich displayed a wide-ranging, easy familiarity, not only with the classical Latin poets but also with Vida, Sannazaro, Flaminio, Giovanni and Giambattista Amalteo, Zanchi, and others among the Italian Neo-Latin poets. Six eclogues appear, of which the fifth (a dirge) has some of the trappings of the huntsman's eclogue but will be described later among epicedia; numbers i and ii are *venaticae* throughout.

The first eclogue, "Sarnis the Hunter" (*Sarnis Venator*; 107 hexameters), begins with a complimentary address to Erasmus

Neustetter (Sturmius). Accompany me now, writes Lotich in his facile Latin, into the glades and shadows; even Apollo sometimes puts aside the lyre for the bow: this is one way of saying that Lotich has for the moment put aside elegiac poetry in order to write a huntsman's eclogue.

It is obvious here that old Lycidas represents Lotich's uncle and that Sarnis represents Lotich himself in the early stages of his Italian journey; as with a number of Italian art-pastorals examined earlier there is no attempt, however, to turn this into a truly contemporary and personal eclogue: the huntsman motif is more important than the personal.

The second eclogue, *Viburnus venator* (126 hexameters), is again a mixture of contemporary and personal matters and huntsman's eclogue: the first half is a lament over the woes of war-torn Hesse in the 1550's. In the second half of the poem, Lycidas (Hagen?) and Acron (a German exile, apparently living near Genoa) appear, and their song consists of amoebaean quatrains in praise of a girl Nisa and of the delights of a hunter's life: this second part, intended to "soothe with song Viburnus' heavy cares," is clearly pure *venatica*. The most notable aspect of the poem is the grim realism of the details in the lament of Viburnus, recalling those in some of the elegies: Lotich had had some experience of wartime atrocities.

Two of the eight eclogues of Jakob de Slupere (Sluperius) of Herzele (1532-1582) are *venaticae*. The second, *Tityrus* (185 hexameters), is preceded by a dedicatory poem in hendecasyllabics giving the date as 1574 and alluding to the religious troubles of the time: De Sluyper hopes that his friend Marius Laureus of Ypres is able to enjoy some measure of peace and quiet despite Protestant attacks from Flanders' neighbors, "the accursed apostates" (*apostatae scelesti*). The third eclogue, *Callirrhoê* (221 hexameters), has no separate dedication, since it really forms part of number ii and is intended to be read continuously with it as a complementary and contrasting poem. Like all of De Sluyper's eclogues, it is over-long, rambling, repetitious in phrasing and choice of detail, and distinctly long-winded, but often showing great technical proficiency in idiom and meter.

iv

From the hunting eclogue we turn to the garden eclogue (*ecloga holitoria*): here, as we should expect, the central situations will prove to be identical with those in the Virgilian bucolic, the *nautica*, the *piscatoria,* and the *venatica,* but the characters will be gardeners, the lover's gifts flowers and even vegetables, and so on; here we shall have occasion to meet seven authors.

The three finest Latin poets of Italy are probably Angelo Poliziano, Giacopo Sannazaro, and Giovanni Pontano of Cerreto in Umbria (ca. 1422-1503). Among Pontano's Latin poems appear six eclogues, of which the first is in reality a series of eight (an introductory eclogue called *Lepidina,* with seven subordinate *pompae* or processions, the whole forming a kind of masque). The poem numbered as the fourth eclogue (*Acon;* 198 hexameters) is a quasi-*holitoria.* Here Petasillus and Saliuncus begin by recalling the story of Acon's love for Napê, her death, and her eventual metamorphosis—the god who effected it is, appropriately, Vertumnus, the Roman god of change who was also god of seasons, a highly suitable deity to appear in a garden eclogue.

In the last section of the poem Petasillus first describes, in a series of formal and rhetorical hexameter couplets, the beauty of the singing voice of Ariadna (i.e., Pontano's wife Adriana) and then quotes Ariadna's love-song to her husband (absent in the Neapolitan army) : she affirms that she will love him so long as the white *virga* is mingled with the blue jonquil (a typical modification, for the garden eclogue, of a pastoral commonplace). There is much that is conventional in this part of the eclogue, as in the two earlier parts, for that matter; but the note of *amor coniugalis* is noticeably and characteristically present.

Battista Fiera of Mantua (1469-1538) we have already met. Of his three eclogues, the second and third are *holitoriae.* The second (*Hortulana;* 142 hexameters) is of some interest: the speakers, Corylê and Pomonis, are two sisters who own a large garden; in the third (*Alcippus;* 72 hexameters) a *hortulanus* named Alcippus attempts to persuade Pasiphile to live with him and be his love— it is less effective than the second.

In Giorgio Anselmo of Parma (born ca. 1470) we find a physician of literary tastes like Battista Fiera. We know little about Anselmo except that he practiced medicine and lectured at the University of Padua, that he served as a soldier at least once in his life, and that he had a son called Camillo.

His collected poems were published at Venice in 1528. Anselmo appears to have had absolutely no relations with his northern contemporaries at Ferrara and Mantua, but he was definitely and demonstrably influenced by the Neapolitans, in particular by Giovanni Pontano.

Of his four pastorals, the second is of the "domestic" sort (to be examined later) and as such can be regarded as evidence of the influence of Pontano; the other three are garden eclogues.

At the beginning of the first poem (*Nenielus*; 149 hexameters) we see the gardener Nenielus attempting to impress a vain young girl named Pytiê. Please accept my gifts of flowers and fruits, he says, and pay attention to what I am saying; and stop looking in that mirror—mirrors should never have been invented. Pytiê replies that such gifts are good enough for someone like Fanissa: let him take them to her; she herself prefers the gifts of the wealthy Pelias and Alcon. Fanissa, replies Nenielus, is downright horrid; and how can you possibly bear to encourage the humpbacked Pelias, the limping Alcon? Pytiê shrugs her shoulders and points out that she has handsome lovers, too—young Itys, for instance. *That* effeminate, grumbles Nenielus; I can outrun, outbox, and outrhyme him any day. Petiê retorts with the name of another lover, the poet Giton. A fine catch, indeed, snaps Nenielus: Brauronia couldn't bear him, and so he has just become engaged to Cochlis, who is less particular.

All this has been expressed as repartee so far; at line 65 Nenielus begins to argue at length; but the girl's mother and brother arrive on the scene at this point and the poem ends abruptly, as so often in eclogue.

This poem is far more worth reading than either of the other two *holitoriae* of Fiera: it has a certain dramatic flavor (especially in the first part), it is varied in expression, lively in manner, contains a certain amount of rudimentary characterization, and provides us, in the story of Sentia (90-146), with a well-written Ovidian sort of short story in verse. Its Latin has a freedom (and difficulty) very similar to that in Pontano's garden eclogue.

The third eclogue (*Glycon*; 126 hexameters) is effective, but much more conventional in pattern. Glycon, a poor *holitor* (kitchen-gardener) stands alone in the early morning in his little garden, near his beehive, and laments (10-121) his ill-success with Peplis.

The fourth poem (*Dercylis*; 50 hexameters) is again conventional in approach: here one of "the garden-Nymphs of Parma" (*Parmesides . . . hortenses Nymphae*), Dercylis, laments the ruin of a flower garden. She describes how at midday, from a clear sky, had come a sudden, torrential downpour of rain, accompanied by wind and, later on, hail. She laments the ruined hopes, the lost work, and describes the grief of the old wife of the gardener, who sees her violets in tatters.

A younger contemporary of Fiera and Anselmo was Elio Giulio Crotti (Aelius Julius Crottus) of Cremona (ca. 1495-1564), a rather minor poet about whom very little is known. He was a close friend of the excellent Neo-Latin poet Niccolò d'Arco (1497-1546), lived at the court of Cesare Gonzaga of Mantua, and then at that of Alfonso d' Este at Ferrara, where he died.

In the one garden eclogue (107 hexameters), Hirtipilê, daughter of the *holitor* Nisus, goes to see what is left of her garden after a sudden storm of wind and rain. She tearfully surveys the ruin, examines one plot after another, and details at great length the plants, flowers, fruits, and vegetables that had been destroyed by the un-expected freak of the weather. The general resemblance to Anselmo's fourth eclogue is obvious, and a detailed comparison of the text of the two poems shows that Crotti had undoubtedly read the *Dercylis* (published thirty years earlier). Crotti's poem is not to be dis-missed, however, as a mere reflection of a reflection. A Renais-sance poet would read another man's poem and then try to do the same thing better; Crotti did not achieve his aim, it is true, but he did manage to do the same thing just about as well.

Among French Neo-Latinists the garden eclogue is rare. The earliest, so far as I know, is the *De laudibus horti* ("The praises of a garden"; 115 hexameters) written by one Gilbertus Nucillanus, a French schoolmaster of the early sixteenth century about whom I know nothing further. In this eclogue Daphnis (clearly the poet himself) and his friend Damon sing in neatly phrased amoebaean verse the praises of the trees, vines, and flowers, that flourish in their respective gardens; the poem is introduced by a cheerful description of the joys of spring and closed by an equally agreeable description of those of autumn. This is a pleasant and attractive bit of verse and one would gladly know more about Nucillanus.

v

The best-known vine-grower's eclogues (*eclogae ampelicae* or *vinitoriae*) are those of John Leech. He had, however, been antici-pated by two Neo-Latin poets, a Frenchman and a German. The first is Claude Roillet or Rouillet of Beaune (ca. 1520?–ca. 1576). His undergraduate career at the University of Paris being inter-rupted by the death of his father, he returned home and resumed his studies under the expert tuition of his brother Nicolas. He did, however, return to Paris in time to take his M.A., finally becoming rector of the University of Paris in 1560.

Rouillet's Latin works are quite extensive—the *Varia poemata* (Paris, 1556) contains four Latin tragedies, three hexameter dialogues, one courtly eclogue, an epithalamium, and a collection of miscellaneous epigrams. There are also an ode on the death of the Duc de Guise (Paris, 1563), a dirge on the death of Charles IX (Paris, 1575), and an elegy on the death of Petrus Gallandius (Paris, 1559). Through his relations with Charles, Cardinal of Lorraine, he must at least have heard of Estienne Forcadel; he certainly knew Joachim du Bellay and Adrien Turnèbe.

There is the occasional pastoral epigram in the *Varia epigrammata* and one vinitory mime among the dialogues, the *Vinearia* (i.e., *vinearia fabula* "a vineyard story"; 248 hexameters). The three dialogues have (e.g., by Alice Hulubei) been given the incorrect collective title of *Vinearia* (i.e., as a neuter plural) and have been described as "poems in praise of the vintage"; but the name (a feminine singular) applies only to one of the three and, as for subject-matter, one is ethical (on Fortune), another is a playlet about Satyrs that is neither pastoral nor vinitory, and the present vinitory dialogue is a shilling shocker, a free and blood-thirsty adaptation of the parable of the laborers in the vineyard.

This mime is classical in idiom but startingly medieval in manner and tone: it reminds the reader forcibly of the sort of mystery play in which Noah's wife appears and announces baldly to her husband, "I am your wife; your children these be." I have included it here partly because any reference to it that I have ever seen has described it incorrectly, partly because it does already introduce incidentally many of the phrases and turns of expression that were to be characteristic of the vinitory eclogue, partly because the mime was closely associated with idyll and pastoral in Theocritus in ancient times and in LeDuchat and Camerarius in the Renaissance.

Of the twenty eclogues of Joachim Camerarius of Bamberg (1500-1574), the fifteenth is a vinitory (*Moeris*; 107 hexameters). It is of no great interest in itself: two *coloni*, Moeris and Corydon, discuss the damage done in their vines by a vicious goat that had escaped from its flock and has been running wild for some time; no one has been able to catch or kill the brute, but the vine-growers hope for the best.

Among the twenty eclogues of John Leech of Montrose and

Aberdeen (ca. 1590–ca. 1630), one section is given over to five vinitory eclogues, of which one is an epistolary, to be examined later.

The first *ampelica* (*vinitoria*) is entitled *Choreae* ("Dances"; 147 hexameters). Here follows a rhyming version of the whole:

The shepherd's care, the fisher's merry toil,
The seaman's labors ere he reach the soil,
I've sung: now may the powers divine
Assist my song beneath the pliant vine.
No more the tender woodland Nymphs can please,
Or Tempê's valleys, fanned by Zephyr's breeze,
No more the hills of Caledon, or Moray's firth,
No more the rural gods of bounteous Earth,
No more the singing of the rustic train,
Or flowers and fruits that flourish in the plain.
From shepherd's pipe and fisher's conch I turn,
And seek the sunny hills that ever burn,
The fields that Bacchus loves to bless with wine,
The swollen clusters and the purple vine.
With me ascend Tmolus, happy still,
With me regard the dance of Nysa's hill;
My song is first: I sing the vine, alone;
Who follows, treads a path now better known.
The time it was, when, happy, through the land,
Pomona blessed the crops on every hand:
Its ripest burden every vineyard yields,
And cheerful songs resound throughout the fields.
Now Lasius at length from toil refrained:
With treading grapes Ampelius was stained.
The two were equal in their years and health,
Their looks, their color, and their humble wealth;
Both sang and answered as the song required,
Both by the fires of Venus were inspired.
These two were ready, at the heat of noon,
To see their sweethearts in the village soon:
Beneath a far-off hill with vineyards gay,
The rural youth had come to dance and play.
Beside the brook and on the village green
The rustic men and maidens all were seen.
Here waited, patient, Lasius' gentle flame,
Here too Ampelius' lovely sweetheart came:

The one was Glycerê, for beauty famed,
The other Apalê her sire had named.
These seen, the two expressed a greeting gay,
And longed to celebrate the festal day.
The dancing throng now makes the welkin ring,
As Lasius and his friend alternate sing:

A.   Embrace me now or let my arms embrace,
For either suits a lover's happy face.
If both I win, I gain immortal bliss:
Embracing win, embraced return a kiss.
      (The dance is fleet, and swift the dancers' feet).

L.   The gentle dove delights to kiss his mate;
And Venus' kiss is Arês' joyous fate;
Come, let me draw you, willing, to my breast;
Come, kiss my lips, with lips together prest.
      (The dance is fleet, and swift the dancers' feet).

A.   Your smiling lips, like Sidon's dye, are red:
Such lips Adonis found in Venus' bed;
Your smiling lips, like Helen's, stir the brain,
But, though they rouse a fire, will chaste remain.
      (The dance is fleet, and swift the dancers' feet).

L.   The flame of love has entered deep my heart,
And when I kiss I feel the love-god's dart;
Full sweet the pain; but, golden Venus gay,
When shall my Apalê embrace me, say!
      (The dance is fleet, and swift the dancers' feet).

A.   The warlike god embraced the Cyprian fair:
He kissed her lips, her throat, her bosom bare;
He found the many loving ways to kiss:
Come, practice Venus' rites to master this.
      (The dance is fleet, and swift the dancers' feet).

L.   Still innocent is Apalê of Paphian joys;
Melaenis vaunts her skill with Cyprian toys;
If Anthia Melaenis' art can learn,
Go, seek her guidance, and a wanton turn!
      (The dance is fleet, and swift the dancers' feet).

A.   Learn not from birds alone; from all things learn;
        For Venus causes all the universe to burn:
        The flocks, the herds, the fish alike confess
        That life is due to Venus' fond caress.
            (The dance is fleet, and swift the dancers' feet).

L.   As willows shrubs, so streams delight the trees;
        As myrtles shore, so hawthorns love the breeze;
        The yew tree craves the chill, the vine the heat:
        I love the hill where she and I can meet.
            (The dance is fleet, and swift the dancers' feet).

A.   Each year let roses spread their perfumes sweet,
        Let violets bloom beneath our dancing feet;
        Let every bloom and blossom scent the air,
        To please my sweetheart and adorn her hair.
            (The dance is fleet, and swift the dancers' feet).

L.   Come, golden Venus, with your wingèd boy,
        Who fill my bosom with a lover's joy,
        On all assembled here your grace bestow,
        And make the swelling clusters richer grow.
            (The dance is fleet, and swift the dancers' feet).

        They ceased, applauded by the village train;
        Their sweethearts then took up the tuneful strain:

G.   To clasp unwedded maids? For shame, for shame!
        Not ours to yield, as in a childish game!
        You Venus and her wingèd son delight;
        Us Dian and the virgin Pallas bright.
            (Join hands in song, and dance your way along).

A.   Virginity's the gods' and Nymphs' delight:
        Hence, Satyrs and the wanton, from our sight!
        These would waylay the Nymphs of Napa's glade,
        Nor spare the outcry of a humble maid.
            (Join hands in song and dance your way along).

G.   I fear the Satyrs, and the Fauns' alarm,
        I fear their coming and I fear their harm;
        I dread the bushes and the whispering leaf,
        I dread the forest as a source of grief.
            (Join hands in song and dance your way along).

A.   As home I trod my homeward way last night,
I heard the outcry of a Nymph's affright;
All suddenly, before my startled eyes,
A Satyr rushes and a maiden flies!
    (Join hands in song, and dance your way along).

G.   This only dread, to fail in conduct staid,
For Venus is a temptress to a maid;
Let wedlock charm, or hope of sons delight,
But fear the tempter's song, the summer night.
    (Join hands in song, and dance your way along).

A.   The scarlet rose each other flower excels;
The oak is monarch in the leafy dells;
One dies if plucked; if felled, the other's base:
One wanton moment spells a maid's disgrace.
    (Join hands in song, and dance your way along).

G.   Amidst the maiden Nymphs Diana shines:
The virgin goddess 'midst her maids reclines;
Amidst the wives, a maiden is a queen,
Amidst the maids a goddess she is seen.
    (Join hands in song, and dance your way along).

A.   As home needs garden, and as garden seeds,
As rivers banks, as river-banks the reeds,
As forests leaves, and leaves the breezes free,
As body soul, so maidens purity.
    (Join hands in song, and dance your way along).

G.   You beauties, keep your heart and body pure,
For maidens' beauty's an enticing lure;
As talk the mind, so charms the maid betray:
As we the dove, so men the fowler play.
    (Join hands in song, and dance your way along).

A.   The wanton miss will earn a wanton's name;
The eager bride will soon regret her fame;
The wanton's odious, and soon disgraced;
The ardent bride's to servitude debased!
    (Join hands in song, and dance your way along).

Thus did they, happy, spend the holiday,
With lively song and dance, and artless play;

When Vesper shed its light on earth below,
Night warned the lovers, and they parted slow.

Leech's second vinitory eclogue, entitled *Comastes, sive Bascaenis* ("The Reveller; or, Bascaenis"; 137 hexameters), is a sort of mime with one character only. This poem clearly written in France like all the vinitories except the fifth) is well written and witty; it is only mildly dramatic, but is certainly highly entertaining.

The third vinitory, *Femina* ("Woman"; 100 hexameters), introduces two argumentative vine-growers, Percus and Ligus. They argue at length about the nature of women, introducing tales of the faithful and faithless; then they turn to amoebaean quatrains (65-96) in which Percus praises women and Ligus damns them—most of the notions introduced are long-familiar, especially those in Ligus' lines. This of itself would not spoil the poem—what does ruin it is that the antithetical quatrains are far too mechanical to be entertaining. The only part of the poem that raises a smile is the poet's own conclusion, in which he describes the amusement of the listening satyrs and fauns and the haughty disapproval of the nymphs and dryads.

The fourth vinitory eclogue (125 hexameters) is entitled *Staphylê*, named after a girl who is courted by two vine-growers named Iolas and Dromus. They quarrel and insult each other in a desultory sort of way from lines 19 to 41. They then put their quarrel on a loftier plane by squabbling in amoebaean quatrains in lines 42 to 57, and then turn to alternate quatrains in praise of Staphylê (58-121), each urging her to live with him and be his love, each praising his own vineyards and garden. The poem is not nearly so good as the first and second vinitories but is more lively than the third.

vi

The new forms of eclogue so far examined have all depended for their point upon new characters—not shepherds, but fishermen, seamen, hunters, gardeners, and vine-growers. There is one more such type—the plowman's eclogue, of which there appears to be only one example extant, the fifth of the twenty eclogues of Joachim Camerarius of Bamberg (1500-1574). In this poem (*Marilê*; 97 hexameters) a plowman named Illus sings the praises of the Muse of pastoral verse, who had been born in Sicily (the reference is, of course, to Theocritus), crossed into Italy (Virgil and the Italian

Neo-Latinists), flown across the Alps and settled in Hesse (Elius Eobanus Hessus and Euricius Cordus). From this Illus passes to the praise of his sweetheart Marilê. The flaw in the poem is that it fails to arouse interest of any sort whatever.

vii

The next two classes of eclogue depend for their novelty not upon a new set of characters as have all the preceding, but upon tone—these are the humorous and the domestic eclogues.

The earliest example of the first sort is to be found in the heavy-handed, heavy-footed humor of the ninth eclogue (untitled; 97 hexameters) of Elius Eobanus Hessus of Bockendorf or Halges-hausen (1488-1540). After some preliminary conversation between two shepherds on the breeding of flocks and herds, the last thirty lines are devoted to amoebaean verses celebrating the uses and merits of wool on the one hand and milk on the other; the humor of these lines is hard to detect and, when detected, to appreciate, but is certainly intended as such, since one of the speakers remarks smugly (lines 91-93) that very few townsmen would understand their witticisms. Quite so.

A far more successful attempt in this line is the adaptation of a Theocritean motif that appears in the second eclogue (*Rivales*; 77 hexameters) of Henri Estienne of Paris (1528/31-1598). The first 68 lines consist of amoebaean hexameter couplets in which Amyntas, a wealthy shepherd, and Menalcas, a poor young goatherd, argue in the presence of Galatea over who should be her favored suitor. The slower-witted, conceited Amyntas is constantly deflated by the younger man, who replies with spirit and never fails to cap a couplet. At this point a wolf appears, whereupon Galatea squeals in fright and girl, heroes, cows, goats, and wolf all take to their heels.

A third examples of the type appears in the second eclogue (untitled; 101 hexameters) of Peter van der Brugge (Petrus Pontanus or Dupont) of Bruges (ca. 1480–ca. 1540). Philtus asks a hunter named Pamphilus why he has abandoned the chase and why he is so gloomy. Pamphilus replies that his story is one that would make the whole world gasp, and, on being offered a present, agrees to tell the tale. Four days ago his sweetheart Phyllis had promised him the ultimate intimacy if he would give her all he had caught in his next day's hunting. He had set out next morning with his flock, left them at the usual pasture with the billy goat tied up, and then entered the woods, only to find that all game animals had mysteriously disappeared. A hard day of searching produced nothing, and Pamphilus, who had had such high hopes of erotic entertainment, had to start back to the pastures. But at the last moment a whole herd of deer appeared from nowhere, and by great good luck Pamphilus was able to shoot two animals. Leaving the carcasses, he started home in great fettle, only to fall headlong into a hunting-pit eight feet deep, almost breaking his hip. Here he spent two days and nights until his father found him and dragged him out. Now, grumbles Pamphilus, the whole countryside knows about it, including all the girls (though Phyllis herself has been sympathetic). The humor of all this is decidedly coarse and crude; the versification is slapdash.

viii

In the one eclogue so far noticed of Giovanni Pontano of Cerreto (1424-1503), the domestic flavor has already been pointed out. It is even more noticeable in his sixth eclogue (*Quinquennius,* "The Five-Year-Old"; 87 hexameters), a poem from which pastoral elements have all but disappeared. Pelvina, a country mother, tries to rock her child back to sleep after he had been awakened by a thunderstorm, but he proves talkative. The little boy is convinced that the shadow in the corner of the bedroom is a bogey man. Pelvina, instead of saying irritably that there is no such thing as a bogey man, calms the child by pretending to chase the visitor away. The poem now develops into the sort of determined catechism that any parent would recognize all too easily. The little boy is at long last ready to go back to sleep, and his mother begins to sing him a lullaby (*naeniola*).

This poem is highly characteristic of the homely, domestic, conjugal side of Pontano's verse, although the ancient pastoral poets would undoubtedly have been astonished at its tone. Even more noticeable is the freedom of style—as observed earlier, Pontano is readier than any other eclogist not only to use Catullan Latin of the most colloquial kind but also to create diminutives and neologisms of every sort.

A poem much more conventionally classical in expression but equally domestic in tone (at least in part) is the second eclogue (*Obstetrix,* "The Mid-Wife"; 141 hexameters) of Giorgio Anselmo of Parma (ca. 1470–after 1528). Here a young woman named Merimna is lying in childbirth (she speaks only twice, at lines 4 and 8, to call on Juno Lucina, the Roman goddess of childbirth), attended by an unnamed midwife. Also on the scene is Gyalis, the husband; there is also an invisible Chorus of Fates.

Here the poem begins with the midwife demanding a basin and hot water from one of the servant girls (several are named through the eclogue, but none speaks) and, after a cry from Merimna, urging another to show a little speed. She urges Merimna to hold her breath and push. The chorus here prophesies (17-25) that Merimna's child will be the healthiest and most beautiful ever seen. The midwife chimes in with the prophecy that the child will be like her mother in beauty and in skill with the needle. The chorus announces that the child's name will be Myricê.

The midwife now hands the new-born baby to the father (line 35) and general rejoicing from father and midwife alternate with gloomy prophecies from the chorus of what will eventually happen to Myricê when she grows up (lines 39-42, 47-54, 60-72, etc.) Phoebus will pursue her as he had pursued Daphne, and she too will be transformed into a tree, one that will never bear fruit (*myricê*, "tamarisk"). The child is put to its mother's breast ("caesia pupa, pete, eia age, caesia pupa, papillas," line 102: this line is very much in the manner of Pontano); the father sings a lullaby and warns off evil spirits and then tells the servants to close the door: mother and baby are now both asleep.

The poem is decidedly unusual. Evidently the utterances of the chorus are supposed not to be heard by midwife or parents, and the point of the poem is the contrast between the father's delight and the chorus' prophecy of the ultimate fate of the child now being born; the contrast extends also to diction, for, while the chorus passages are strictly classical in expression, the words of the midwife and of Gyalis are considerably more colloquial, although not so noticeably so as in Pontano. This eclogue is clearly an experiment, and not a particularly successful one: the story of Apollo's pursuit of Myricê is purest Ovidian genre, and the contrast with the homely realism of the birth scene succeeds only in making the reader uncomfortable.

ix

Further new uses of pastoral appear that depend not on a new set of characters or a new tone, but on a new situation or *mise en scène*—the dream-eclogue and the epistolary.

The only dream-eclogue extant is one by Bartolommeo Facio or Fazio of Spezia (ca. 1400-1457). After studying for six years

(1420-1426) under Guarino at Verona, Fazio first taught the sons of the Doge Francesco Foscari of Venice. After a year (1429-1430) in Florence, Fazio taught school for some time at Genoa (1430-1434). After some years in Lucca as a notary, Fazio then became Francesco Spinola's chancellor in Genoa in 1441 and in 1444 finally joined those Humanists that were receiving such generous patronage from Alfonso I of Naples.

Fazio was no poet; but one eclogue (untitled; 74 hexameters) does survive. In sleep Fazio hears a contest in song between Tityrus (any typical shepherd of pastoral) and a young man he calls Arpinas. This name refers to Giovanni Antonio Campano, the one-time shepherd-boy who rose to become a bishop of the Church and a leading Neo-Latin author. The rest of the poem consists largely of panegyric of the Latin verses of Campano, who did, as a matter of fact, write a great deal of very attractive occasional verse as a young man. But the reader who hopes to find in this poem a significant addition to the extensive literature of dream-poems is fated to be disappointed. Even if we allow for some undoubted confusions in the text, this is a shapeless and pointless little poem which leads nowhere in particular.

x

We earlier met a brief poem by Estienne Forcadel of Beziers (1534-1573) that was properly an invitation addressed to the poet's patron, the first instance of the epistolary eclogue since the death of Dante in 1321.

After Forcadel the first epistolary eclogue we meet is the fifth vinitory (actually it is a garden eclogue, even if it is entitled *ecloga vinitoria quinta*) of John Leech of Montrose and Aberdeen (ca. 1590–ca. 1630), a poem entitled *Orii desiderium* ("Longing for Orius"; 123 hexameters). In bucolic terms the poem invites Bishop George Montgomery to return from England to Scotland for a visit. Young Alcon (i.e., the poet) wonders why it is that Orius has deserted the woods he once loved, to say nothing of Alcon. Is it perhaps because Alcon is beneath the notice of such a one as Orius? Here follows a long passage in which Alcon insists on his skill in growing fruits and flowers and in grafting trees and shrubs. Is it because Alcon is poor? Here follows a lengthy poetic disquisition on the simple life. Rhetoric now begins to get the better of Leech as he reels off the names of the woodland deities that join him in inviting Orius back to Scotland. Surely, he then carries on,

Thames, Severn, and Humber are no more beautiful than the rivers of Caledonia stern and wild! The poet finally calls on the Saxon nymphs and dryads and oreads to release Orius from their loving arms and send him home. It is all far too smooth, far too glib, far too clever.

After Leech the epistolary proper seems to occur for the last time in Niccolò Giannettasio of Naples (1648-1715)—his fourteenth piscatory eclogue (*Cardenides*, "Descendant of Cárdenas; 114 hexameters) is addressed to Carlo de Cárdenas, who had proved a generous friend to the mathematician-poet.

This poem, largely descriptive, is one of great fluency, of great charm of expression, informed throughout with a very real and very obvious affection for De Cárdenas and an equally obvious love for the places and people described: the "golden coast" from Cuma to Amalfi is proverbially one of the most beautiful in Europe.

xi

The final section of this chapter deals with those eclogues which depend for novelty not on new characters or on tone or on a new *mise en scène*, but on a completely new sort of content. The creation of new myths (classical figures in a contemporary landscape) is common in Neo-Latin elegiac poetry, especially among the Neapolitan Latinists. The poet may create some new story about, say, Galatea or Polyphemus or Apollo, placing it in Vomero or Posillipo, or may create a new mythological character (e.g., Sebethis, river-spirit of the Neapolitan stream Sebeto) and may employ the new myth or new figure in an epigram of two lines, an eclogue of a hundred, or an epyllion of two hundred. In eclogues such new myths appear in poems by Giovanni Pontano, Pierfrancesco Giustolo, and Joachim Camerarius; even more common in eclogue is one particular sort of myth—that of metamorphosis.

The eclogues of myth—examples are Giovanni Pontano's fifth (*Corylê*; 165 lines), Pierfrancesco Giustolo's second (*Gengha*; 117 hexameters), and Joachim Camerarius' tenth (*Pan*; 76 hexameters) —require no special comment; but those of metamorphosis do.

The tale of magical transformation in a pastoral setting, the pastoral epyllion or eclogue of metamorphosis, begins with Giacopo Sannazaro of Naples (ca. 1456-1530). His poem "The Willows" (*Salices*; 113 hexameters) tells how the nymph Salix, to avoid being outraged by Pan, prayed to the gods to be saved and was duly transformed into a willow (*salix*). Although there are many reminiscences of Virgil in the poem, there are more—as the reader would expect—of Ovid's *Metamorphoses*. The setting is Neapolitan, naturally, and no doubt Sannazaro's friends in the Neapolitan Academy, as they read the poem, could have recognized the very spot on the banks of the Sebeto where the unhappy Salix was transformed. It is precisely the sort of thing at which Sannazaro excelled—exquisitely finished and polished verse, a tone of "refined" neo-classicism, never-failing tact in the selection of detail, elegantly formal dialogue; of its kind it is very close to perfection.

Very similar to this eclogue is a poem by Daniele Cereto of Brescia (ca. 1460-1528), still another physician-poet, like Battista Fiera of Mantua and Giorgio Anselmo of Parma. Until 1728 (see bibliography), the only literary work of Cereto's that had reached print was the *Salix* (164 hexameters), a poem extremely popular in its day. The plot is almost identical with that in Sannazaro's poem: Salix, one of Diana's nymphs, was espied by Glaucus, the sea-god, as she rested under an oak by the seashore. He violated her and left her to lament through the woods. Here she prayed to the gods for aid; Phoebus replied that she would be transformed into a tree, and lines 129 through 142 describe in detail her inch-by-inch metamorphosis into a weeping willow. It is all very neat and ingenious, but one should be careful to render unto Sannazaro what is Sannazaro's, and to Ovid what is Ovid's. Cereto's *Salix* is not nearly so effective or original a poem as Sannazaro's, yet it appears to have achieved a greater contemporary repute—the history of every literature can provide examples of such undeserved and inexplicable successes.

A rather similar pastoral epyllion or eclogue of metamorphosis appears among the poems of Giovanni Battista Nicolucci, commonly called G. B. Pigna, of Ferrara (1530-1575). In this poem (*Nymphae*; 239 hexameters) a group of satyrs pursues some nymphs of Arcadia, but are frustrated by the transformation of the nymphs into flowers, birds, and trees: here we have not one description of metamorphosis but half a dozen; 239 lines of this sort of thing is too much.

In the Latin poems of Giovanni Battista Amalteo of Oderzo (1525-1573) one eclogue of metamorphosis appears (*Sarnus*; 78 hexameters). It was written for the saintly Cardinal Cernini, later elevated to the papacy as Marcellus II (he died on the twenty-second day of his pontificate, May 5, 1555)—the Cardinal was enjoying a peaceful holiday at the Bay of Naples, and this poem was sent to him there for his entertainment and delectation. We can imagine the Cardinal reading and rereading this poem by the banks of the Sarno itself in an atmosphere of Neapolitan *dolce far niente*. In the history of sixteenth-century vernacular pastoral one of the best-known names is that of Bernardino Rota of Naples (1509-1575), an older contemporary of Giambattista Amalteo and a descendant of an old and wealthy family that had owned estates at Genoa and Naples since the days of Charles of Anjou's conquest of the Kingdom of Naples.

In 1533 Rota completed (but did not publish until 1560) his vernacular Italian *Egloghe pescatorie*, fourteen in number, of which Enrico Carrara rightly remarks that whereas in Sannazaro's Latin poems the smell of the sea can be noticed, these are wholly mechanical. But piscatories were a Neapolitan speciality, and Rota felt constrained to follow in Sannazaro's footsteps. Another Neapolitan specialty was, by now, the sequence of conjugal poems, initiated in Latin by Giovanni Pontano in his *De amore coniugali* and continued in Italian by Bernardo Tasso and Vittoria Colonna. In memory of his wife Porzia, who had died in 1559 at the age of thirty-six, Rota composed a sequence of twenty-six Petrarchistic sonnets, clever, cold, ingenious, over-elegant—a perfect example of polished propriety and methodical imitation.

Precisely the same qualities are to be observed in his Latin poems (published in Naples in 1572)—elegiac poems, meditative lyrics (e.g., on the ruins of Pesto), poems of metamorphosis and myth, with many a cunning reminiscence of Virgil, Ovid, Pontano, and Sannazaro. One of these poems is relevant here—the eclogue called *Carduus* (104 hexameters), addressed in compliment to Domenico Veniero of Venice—a fantastic virtuoso of the sonnet who anticipates almost all the worst extravagances of seventeenth-century Italian poetry. This poem is written in memory of a member of the De Cárdenas family of Acerra already met in Giannettasio's epistolary eclogue mentioned above. This particular De Cárdenas died at Imera in Sicily in 1559 or 1560, and here Rota tells an imaginary tale of "Cardinus" and the tutelary nymphs of Acerra and Imera and of Cardinus' death and metamorphosis into a *carduus* (wild thistle), thereby producing what must be one of the most eccentric epicedia in European literature. The last third of the poem—this part, at least, the reader can take seriously—contains one of those laments, omnipresent in Italian Neo-Latin literature,

over the constant invasions of the country and concludes with a
reference to the sonnet sequence on which Rota was currently
engaged. I add a full translation here, not because of the poem's
excellence but because of its extreme oddity:

Doménico (this pause is not for long)
Renounce the Muses and attend my song.
Your pen is ready and your skill refined,
A true reflection of a learnèd mind;
Yet pause to listen for a moment brief,
While Lycidas displays his song of grief.
My errant flock, feed now where e'er you will,
For constant grief impedes the shepherd still.
Unharmed, the birds may frolic in the plain;
The deer may venture from the woods again.
No net, no arrow is in Lycid's hand:
His weapons useless and neglected stand,
For Cárdenas, my dearest friend, has died,
The shepherds' envy and the hunters' pride.
Can plaintive dirge console the grieving heart?
To tell his story is the better part.
My song through every note of grief shall range:
His fate was woeful, and his death was strange.
Of all the sylvan Dryads most unkind,
What cruelty, Acerra, took your mind?
Why leave alone the gentle youth to die?
Nor greet his passing with a single sigh?
Well could I think the toughest oak on earth
Or hardest rock had brought you to your birth,
Since you have killed, with withering disdain,
The pride, the joy, the glory of the plain.
As naught he counted flock or bow or spear
Beside your love, and held you only dear.
Alas, Acerra, why despise a loving youth?
What madness this? What unconcern for truth?
Your love alone was what he ever sought,
With prayers, appeals, and presents to be bought.
For you he kept his love with ardor due;
You only did he love with service true.
What recompense you gave the youth for this!
Nor winning glances, nor a loving kiss!

Then came the rumour of another maid,
Whose heart was loving, though her glance was staid.
To chaste Diana did you, eager, pray
To send a cruel fate to him that day,
And, as you prayed, new folly struck your mind;
Your sense was clouded and your wit was blind:
"Diana, who delight in maidens chaste,
Whom I have worshiped in the mountain's waste,
If I've preferred your troop to wedded bliss,
And loved the woods more than a lover's kiss,
Take pity now, I pray, in Heaven above,
And punish him who late has changed his love:
Imera is his darling and his life;
Imera is his mistress and his wife."
Scarce had you prayed; Diana heard your plea,
And, wearied as she was with venery,
Implored her brother's aid, who constant burns
And through the firmament for ever turns:
His daily journey through the heavens' reach
Restores the land, the sky, the sea, the beach;
Yet can his beams a sudden fever send,
And bring the strongest to a sorry end.
His shafts can cause a famine in the land,
Or drought, or sudden death on every hand.
His sister heard, Apollo watched his prey,
Who hunted without fear that summer day.
While down the mountain's side he drove the deer
Towards the waiting nets, the fatal spear.
Brave Cárdenas himself was smitten low,
The helpless victim of the Hunter's bow:
The burning fury of the fever's dart
Attacked his veins and raged within his heart.
No mortal can endure that fiery blast:
His spirit left the body, dead at last.
But when Diana saw his mournful fate,
Her hatred melted, and her fires abate:
Nor did she let him perish without fame,
But clad a scarlet blossom with his name,
The spiky thistle, with its blossom red,
That wounds unwary hunters' passing tread.

The weapons of his quiver and his hand
She turned to painful spikes that upright stand.
Enough is told about your woeful fate:
Gaze now upon the earth from Heaven's gate;
In Heaven you tend in peace a different flock
Nor feel the grief of war, the battle's shock.
Thrice blest are those who cannot see or know
The woes that plague us on the earth below.
Now leaps across the Alps the frenzied foe,
And slays the helpless shepherd of the Po;
Now Gauls attack the land with bloodied hands,
Allied in union dread with pagan bands.
By night the humble flock is stol'n away;
The master's mansion's plundered in the day.
A Fury turns Italian minds apart,
And Discord reigns in each Italian heart.
You gods, who love the land of Italy,
Hear now our eager prayer and ardent plea:
That city, Europe's glory, Europe's pride,
The star of Italy, with worth allied,
That city, by the Adriatic's wave,
That city rescue, and her people save!
All men must venerate her ancient name,
Her learnèd senate, and her ample fame.
The foe defeated, may the Ocean's queen
Triumphant over all at last be seen.
While now in grief I court the widowed muse,
To live and die in Venice would I choose.

Enough of song; come, feeding flocks, away:
Another song requires another day.

In the *Epigrammata* (Lyon, 1554) of the jurist Estienne Forca-del of Béziers (1534-1573) appears one brief, untitled poem of thirty-six hexameters which has little of the eclogue in it but which is not unlike the *Salix* of Giacopo Sannazaro. The poem begins with a description of a garden and goes on to tell how Melissa, one of Diana's nymphs, visited it one day. She was seen by the god Zephyr, who pursued her until she prayed to Apollo for the gift of eternal virginity; at the end she was transformed into a bee (*melissa*) that would always fear wind and love gardens. It is a pretty little poem—Forcadel was merely indulging his fancy.

Except for a poem by Jean Regnier (or Reynier) to be noticed later, the eclogue of metamorphosis is rare until we come to a whole series of such poems written by Pierre-Daniel Huet of Rouen (1630-1721), a leading savant in an age of savants; he was the author of technical treatises, much Latin and Greek poetry, and at least one novel (published anonymously), and was a familiar of the salon of Mlle de Scudéry and of the studios of painters.

In addition to several works on theology, philosophy, and classical studies (for example, a history of ancient commerce written at the request of Colbert), Huet published, at the age of seventy, a volume of Latin poems, *Carmina* (Utrecht, 1700)—odes, eclogues, and minor poems—in which he displayed much verve, grace, and warmth. Among these poems appear five eclogues of metamorphosis, of which three were written almost half a century before they were published.

The first eclogue of metamorphosis (*Melissa*; 147 hexameters) is almost identical in plot with the *Melissa* of Estienne Forcadel and contains so many verbal reminiscences as to make it quite clear that Huet had the earlier poem in mind. This eclogue is far longer and much more elaborate than Forcadel's poem: a simple story is provided with an elaborate background of epic machinery.

The second such poem (*Salamandra*; 127 hexameters) begins with a complimentary introduction (1-14) addressed to Cardinal César d'Estrées and then tells how Salamandra, a witness of the rape of Proserpina, had fled in terror to the caves of Mount Etna, beneath which were the blazing forges of the fire-god Vulcan and the Cyclopes. Salamandra is terrified at the advances of the crippled fire-god and attempts to escape. Vulcan is infuriated at the repulse. Do you reject me, he demands, because I am black and crippled and because you are vain of your beauty? Salamandra batters his head and scratches his face furiously, but in the end is left lamenting her maidenhood. She rushes to the top of Etna and is about to hurl herself into the flames of the volcano, when Vulcan transforms her into a salamander to keep her in the power of fire forever. This dexterous poem, with its obvious reminiscences of Ovid, is much superior to *Melissa*; the epic machinery is not so obtrusive and the style is far less florid.

The third eclogue of metamorphosis is the *Vitis* (143 hexameters) written in 1653, as was the *Salamandra*—the two poems are identical in manner and tone, with an appropriate god in each case: in the one the fire-god turns Salamandra into a salamander, in the other the god of wine turns the nymph Vitis into a vine (*vitis*) and her lover Ulmus into the elm (*ulmus*) that inevitably supports the vine in all Greek and Latin poetry.

In the witty introduction (1-14) Huet urges Saumaise, whether he is infuriating the English with his writings (the reference is to the "Defence of Charles I" which called forth John Milton's "Defence of the English People"; both polemics were, of course, in Latin, as they were intended for international circulation), or dealing learnedly with Cleanthes or Roman armor, to listen to his pastoral muse. He goes on to tell how Bacchus had once been gazing down from Parnassus and had caught sight of a lovely oread (mountain nymph), Vitis. Unlike Salamandra, Vitis did not repulse the God's advances but welcomed him to her arms. Later, when bidden by Jupiter to undertake his journey to India, Bacchus made a tearful farewell to Vitis and urged her to be faithful to him. At first Vitis fled to the woods in grief at the separation; on one occasion her laments are overheard by a shepherd named Ulmus. Vitis stands on her dignity for a while but soon allows Ulmus to comfort her— not that she loves the absent Bacchus less but because she loves the present and available Ulmus more:

> She Bacchus loves, and Bacchus loves she true:
> But Ulmus is a likely lad to view.
> The first she loves; the other tempts her mind,
> And so she clips the one that stays behind. (92-93)

All goes well, until, in happy ignorance, Bacchus returns to Vitis' home, whereupon we have a long and Ovidian narrative of the gradual metamorphosis of the two lovers into vine and elm. The most important aspect of this poem is its Ovidian air of elegant farce: the return of Bacchus and his discovery of the two lovers is handled in a way that would have commended itself to the Roman poet.

According to Johann Georg Graevius the next two eclogues are far later work, written perhaps as late as 1700. One is marked by Ovidian farce even more strongly than the eclogue just noticed; the other is a distinct oddity.

We can conclude this chapter by examining a burlesque of this type of pastoral, a versified *nouvelle scandaleuse* written by Jean

Regnier or Reynier (Rainerius) of Lyon (*floruit* 1530), of whom practically nothing seems to be known except that he was a teacher of some sort at Lyon. In his eclogue (*Metamorphosis Mopsi et Nisae*; 421 hexameters) Regnier tells us that the lovely Nisa once lived at Lyon; she was chaste, and modest into the bargain.

Now, goes on Regnier, there was a certain barber named Mopsus living in Lyon, the ugliest man alive, who boasted that he was superior in surgical skill to any man past, present, or future (the verse becomes distinctly mock-heroic here). Nisa developed a sore heel, and this man was called in. When he arrived Nisa was peacefully sleeping in bed, with her hair disarranged (this often happens when a girl is asleep, the poet tells us in a kindly aside), and with her arms, shoulders, and bosom exposed. Mopsus gazed at this vision in delight, "et ruber erigitur saetosa per inguina palus" (70). He took advantage of his situation and the resultant uproar brought the family and servants on the run.

Mopsus, Regnier goes on, hastily saved himself by contending that the girl had an abnormally sensitive skin—she could scarcely bear a touch, and he had barely begun to examine her heel. The servant-girls began to comfort Nisa, urged her to do all that the surgeon required, and left the bedroom with the family.

Mopsus, who had now seen Nisa's muscular brothers, begged her to tell no one what had really happened. She agreed, and if the reader finds this hard to believe, Regnier assures us that it was Fate that made the girl fall in love with the hideous Mopsus—and him an Englishman at that, adds Regnier, maliciously.

Now Nisa had an uncle named Abas, whose opinions carried great weight with the family. At this time he was in dire straits with the Spanish disease (naturally, no Frenchman would call it the French pox) and had had to resort to "the Paeonian art." Whom should he summon but Mopsus? Abas moved into Mopsus' house and undertook a heroic regimen. It so happens, Regnier assures the reader, that the Spanish disease is worse at night than it is during the day; so also is love, so that the outcries of Abas and Mopsus filled the air night after night. Eventually Mopsus managed to cure Abas, who promised to win over Nisa's family in lieu of payment. He eventually succeeded and the ill-omened marriage took place.

The whole tone of the poem now begins to change. Mopsus grew tyrannous, refusing to allow Nisa to visit her family, and on one occasion, when she had disobeyed, kicked her, tore her hair, and blacked her eyes. Nisa fled homeward, but before reaching the house was transformed into a bird. Mopsus fled the haunts of man, eventually losing his reason and thinking that every bird he saw was Nisa. Finally, as he pursued one bird, he found that he could no longer run, but could fly; he, too, had suffered metamorphosis.

The eclogue of metamorphosis is the most flexible of the new forms of pastoral that we have examined in this chapter. It may form an incidental part of an ordinary bucolic of the most Virgilian content, may be idyllic, may be mythological, may be highly Ovidian, or may move as far away from conventional eclogue as any poem possibly could, as in Regnier's. This eclogue starts off as a farcical *novella* in verse, with some of the prurience of fabliau thrown in for good measure; it turns into a tale of intrigue, touches upon melodrama and even tragedy, and ends as Ovidian metamorphosis. It is a curious piece of work, and probably unique in Neo-Latin literature.

IX

NEW USES OF PASTORAL:
RELIGIOUS AND DEVOTIONAL

 very large number of Neo-Latin poets and versifiers employed the eclogue as a medium. Some saluted births, marriages, and deaths in poems that combined the background of pastoral with the content of the conventional genethliacon, epithalamium, and epicedium. Public events received elaborate, even fulsome, treatment in pastoral panegyrics, courtly eclogues, and epinicia. Other pastorals dealt with the most varied of personal interests—self-analyses, expressions of thanks, congratulations on recovery from illness, wishes for *bon voyage*. Another group (and here content frequently overlaps from one type to another) is formed by poems of a didactic or satirical or religious type. Lastly comes semi-dramatic pastoral and pastoral masque, sometimes performed *al fresco* to the accompaniment of music.

i

Some religious topics had been introduced into the cryptic eclogues of Francesco Petrarca (1304-1374), it is true, but the poem that gave the real impetus to the religious eclogue is the eleventh pastoral (lines 136-82) of Giovanni Boccaccio (1313-1374), already discussed. It was pointed out earlier that the New Testament story of the shepherds who watched their flocks by night naturally suggested pastoral treatment of the Nativity story. This led as naturally to similar treatment of later parts of Christ's life, then to the pastoral based on Old Testament narratives, then to the devotional or meditative pastoral, and finally to the sequence of Mary-eclogues. At the same time, it is only natural that Virgil's prophecy of the birth of a marvelous Child and a resultant Golden Age must have influenced the Neo-Latin writers of Nativity eclogues.

The pastoral treatment accorded Christ's birth in Boccaccio's poem is no more than a hint; the first poet to take up that hint appears to have been Francesco Patrizi (Patricius) of Siena (1413-1492).

The only one of his many poems here relevant is his Nativity eclogue, written in 1460 for Pius II, *De natali Christi* (*"The Birth of Christ"*; 150 hexameters); it must have obtained considerable circulation in manuscript, for verbal echoes are frequent in most subsequent eclogues on the Nativity—it was Patrizi, in fact, rather than Boccaccio, who set the pattern for this type of poem.

In the first "scene" (1-80), the shepherds Lycidas and Menalcas (such Greek names are normal in Nativity eclogues) meet unexpectedly. Menalcas has been watching the sky—he expects snow; Lycidas has been searching all night for a lost heifer and is exhausted. Menalcas invites him to warm himself by the fire. Lycidas thanks his new friend heartily and asks him to explain the present state of the sky. Menalcas explains the various positions of the constellations and says that he feels certain that something strange is about to happen—perhaps even the end of the world. Lycidas suddenly notices that his heifer is kneeling and seems to be worshiping—the sheep are doing the same. There is a clap of thunder, and the two men see a winged figure flying down towards them; they are terrified and try to run off. The messenger (*nuntius* is used as a translation of the Greek *angelos*) tells them not to be afraid; he explains that the Almighty has sent His Son to be born on earth, and that the strange behavior of the heavens and of the animals is only prophetic, for the birth of Christ will bring a Golden Age.

In the second scene (81-129), Lycidas urges Menalcas to come and find the miraculous Child promised them. As they walk on, Menalcas promises gifts to this divine Being that had been prophesied by Moses and Alcidamas and the Sibyl, all of whom had said that an Age of Gold would some day bring back Astraea (the goddess of justice) and her sister Peace. At this point Lycidas sees a light in the distance—it is the star which lights up not only the heavenly host but also a stable before which an old man is standing to welcome them.

In the third scene (130-50) the angel reappears and urges the two shepherds to kneel before the Child and Mary; Lycidas and Menalcas sing a hymn of praise to both, and the poem ends with the shepherds entering the stable with Joseph.

This eclogue has some curious faults of meter. Its Greek names at first strike the reader as freakish. To describe the angel by the phrase often used of Mercury by the Latin poets (*Cyllenia proles*) and to provide the Almighty with the attributes of Jupiter seems outlandish (odder things were done in English poetry in the seventeenth century); but the poem is one of obvious sincerity—the prophecy of the Golden Age has the ring of faith, and the brief prayer of Lycidas and Menalcas (136-145) is not mere verse composition, despite its stereotyped phraseology.

A very similar Nativity eclogue is the *De ortu Servatoris* ("The Saviour's Birth"; 131 hexameters) of Andrea Fulvio of Palestrina (*floruit* between 1485 and 1530), written for Pope Leo X. Fulvio was brought up and educated at Rome and spent most of his life there as a scholarly pensioner of the Church.

Fulvio's Nativity eclogue, the "plot" of which is identical with Patrizi's, does more credit to Fulvio's industry than to his poetical talents—Leo X, who could tell poetry when he saw it, probably held no very high opinion of this third-rate piece of work.

The Nativity eclogue of Sébastian Châteillon of Dauphiné (1515-1563) is a little better. Châteillon (the commonly used form Castalio is a Humanistic pen-name) was born of poor parents in the mountains of Dauphiné. His independent spirit turned him to Protestantism and his gentle, reasonable nature drove him from stiff-necked Calvinism to heretical Socinianism. In 1540 he was appointed professor of classics at Geneva on the recommendation of John Calvin, but a quarrel was inevitable—not because of Châteillon's personality but because of Calvin's; Calvin had him not only discharged but exiled from Geneva. Châteillon was welcomed at Basel, where he was appointed professor of Greek; Calvin (with the able and spiteful assistance of Théodore de Bèze) tried to have him discharged from this position also, but was unsuccessful. Châteillon spent the rest of his life at Basel, teaching, studying, writing, and working peacefully in his vegetable garden until he was carried off by plague in 1563. He was a simple, unostentatious, kindly man of great learning.

Châteillon's major works are a version of the entire Bible in Ciceronian Latin, various translations into Latin of vernacular French or German works, and two books that are of lively interest to any modern reader, a defence of heresy in the *De haereticis* and an attack on the death penalty in the *Moses latinus*.

Châteillon's Nativity eclogue is entitled *Sirillus* (89 hexameters). In this, Sirillus describes to Damon the events of the previous night— the appearance of the angel, the songs of the heavenly host, the shepherds' adoration of the Child. The poem closes with a hymn to the power and gentleness of the Saviour; Damon then leaves (82-89) to see the divine Child for himself. The poem is not really very much better than Fulvio's so far as Latin and as poetry are concerned, but it is honest and mercifully free from the pedantries occasioned by Fulvio's scholarly vanity.

Yet another Nativity eclogue is that of João de Mello de Sousa of Torres-Novas in Portugal (ca. 1510-1575). De Sousa was educated at the University of Coimbra, finally receiving a doctor's degree in law and becoming a lecturer in law at the University in 1547. He then passed into the royal service at Lisbon, eventually becoming chancellor of Portugal. His position in Lisbon was similar to that of Pontano in the Kingdom of Naples.

His Nativity poem, "The Shepherds' Eclogue" (*Ecloga pastorum*; 205 hexameters) is the first to use Hebrew names for the shepherds and the first to make them the traditional three in number. The poem consists of introduction (1-29), amoebaean quatrains (30-102), and a concluding section of narrative (103-205); the "plot" is again the same as in Patrizi's poem.

The poets of the next few generations continued to write Nativity eclogues, but made them part of sequences; for the moment I shall confine myself to individual poems and turn to an obscure French writer of the early seventeenth century, Claude de la Place of Paris (*floruit* 1620), probably an instructor in rhetoric at one of the Paris *collèges*. His first Nativity eclogue, "The Shepherds" (*Pastores*; 72 lines) is unusual for its meter, which is elegiac throughout, and its treatment of the theme. So far, all Nativity eclogues have followed the same general pattern, the one set by Francesco Patrizi in the fourteenth century; here, however, we have the words of one shepherd to his companions just after the three have entered the stable. Here is the divine Child (says the shepherd), just as the heavenly messenger foretold—how humble His surroundings! Let us go down on our knees to worship Him, promised to us as He has been for centuries, the Messiah who will bring a new Golden Age; let us give Him our humble gifts and return with more. The poem is skillful enough but is badly spoiled by sentimentality.

The sequel to this poem, published in 1630, is entitled "The Magi" (60 lines); it follows the pattern of the first precisely and is outstanding in no way, good or bad.

The fourth of the nine pastorals composed by Pierre Mambrun of Clermont-Ferrand (1600-1661) is a Nativity eclogue, "Christ's Birth" (*Christus nascens*; 107 hexameters). Mambrun's eclogue (which follows Patrizi's closely) is quite lively, but a far better poem technically is the Nativity eclogue entitled "The Shepherds of Bethlehem" (*Pastores Bethlehemitici*; 156 hexameters) of Peter de Fransz (Francius) of Amsterdam (1645-1704), the third of his six pastorals. It will be noticed that Francius reverts to the custom of giving the shepherds Greek names, here Lycidas and Tityrus:

> Now burned the starry firmament's extent;
> Each shepherd slept within his sheltering tent,
> Save those whose duty 'twas to watch the flocks,
> The frosty valleys, and the freezing rocks,
> When, lo! the sky was split with thunder's roar,
> And clouds of angel-forms appeared before,
> Who sang of joy, who filled the earth with sound,
> And 'mazed the shepherds as they gazed around.
> These did the angel send to view the Child,
> The lowly manger, and the Virgin mild.
> Then Lycidas and Tityrus, the twain,
> With hymns of joy led all the rural train:
> The shepherd-boys acclaim the heavenly Boy,
> Salute their God and King with shouts of joy.
> First Lycidas would raise the tuneful strain;
> Then Tityrus would add his glad refrain:

> Lyc.: How great the mercy of the heavenly Lord,
> How great an honor does he now accord,
> Who sends his angel-ministers to sing
> The joyful praises of the new-born King.

> Ti.: No foolish dream deceives our sleeping eye;
> Ourselves have seen the angel-band on high:

Their holy features shone with pure delight,
The while they sang His birth, this winter's night.

Lyc.: From high Olympus sent, the heavenly Child
Now lives upon the earth in mercy mild;
Now shall the sky and fields alike rejoice
And greet the Golden Age with tuneful voice.

Ti.: In pity at this wretched world's estate,
He saves the world He did Himself create;
His Son He sends to expiate our sin,
To snatch from Erebus and save for Him.

Lyc.: Thus did He promise in the days of old;
The voices of the prophets thus foretold;
The man of sling and lyre and shepherd's crook
Revealed this hope in song by Cedron's brook.

Ti.: Salvation now awaits expectant Earth,
For God is born a man by virgin birth;
A holy Mother bears an Infant blest,
To save the sinful and to aid the rest.

Lyc: From Heaven He comes, to save the race of men,
To you, O little town of Bethlehem;
Now has He left the heavens' lofty dome:
A lowly manger is his earthly home.

Ti.: Thrice happy fields, and town forever blest,
Where now the Infant's at His Mother's breast;
No age will ever see your fame grow cold;
Forever shall the joyous tale be told.

Lyc.: No shrub can match the cypress with its fame:
No city now can equal Bethel's claim;
Nor Tyre nor Babylon shall flaunt their pride;
Nor Salem's mark nor Sidon's shall abide.

Ti.: Now silent, all; the holy stall I see!
Once entered, kneel in prayer on bended knee:
Adore the offspring of a Virgin's womb,
And deck the manger with the rose's bloom.

Lyc.: My ears have heard, my eyes have seen the Boy;
I scarce believe my eyes, my ears for joy!

Yet ears and eyes alike attest my joy:
These eyes have seen, these ears have heard the Boy.

Ti.: True was the promise: here the Infant lies,
And fills the stable with his gentle cries;
The earthly parents smile with holy joy,
As ox and ass adore the tender Boy.

Lyc.: Though blest the man, the Maiden is thrice blest,
As dear to God, preferred above the rest;
We too are blest, this sacred Christmas night,
For God has granted us this holy sight.

Ti.: These, holy Infant, are the gifts we bring,
These rustic honors for a heavenly King;
Accept our homage as our song we raise;
Receive our offerings and our hymns of praise.

Lyc.: Auspicious Boy! The heavens smile on Thee,
And myrrh will flow unbid from every tree;
The balsam flows in Araby the Blest,
Idumê's palms will bear above the rest.

Ti.: The earth unbid will foster every seed,
The flowers unbid will bloom on every mead;
The olives and the grain will grow at will;
The buds will burst on every sunny hill.

Lyc.: The earth is verdant and the woods are green;
The nightingale and swallow can be seen;
The sliding streams and rippling rivers glide;
The fields grow fertile with the waters' tide.

Ti.: The flocks and herds are in the grassy mead,
Nor fear the wolf and lion as they feed;
The shepherd treads a jaunty measure now,
The farmer leaves the labor of the plow.

Lyc.: The Nymphs present their gifts in baskets piled:
Narcissus, amaranth, and crocus wild,
The myrtle, ivy, and the flowering may,
The lilies' garland, and the roses' spray.

Ti.: Three Kings of Orient their riches bear,
And place their dazzling gifts around him there:

      Sabaean odors burn before the King
      As purest gold and smoothest myrrh they bring.

Lyc. : See how the guiding Star refulgent gleams
      And guides the wandering Kings with vivid beams!
      It leads their halting steps toward the stall :
      They come, they kneel, they greet the King of all.

Ti. : I gaze in wonder on the guiding Star :
      Now all the stars are burning brighter far;
      The firmament obeys the heavens' decree,
      And every star is blazing clear to see.

Lyc. : As glows the hyacinth with scarlet hue,
      As shines the cherry or the grape with dew,
      As gleams the wool with Sidon's purple wealth,
      So glows the Infant's cheek with ruddy health.

Ti. : As glows the winter-star from east to west,
      As gleams the morning-star beyond the rest,
      As burns the midday sun with luster clear,
      So brilliant do the Infant's eyes appear.

Lyc. : Come, lovely Boy, advance; our pastures green
      Invite your godlike presence to be seen;
      When you shall tread upon our verdant fields,
      What crops will flourish, and what bounteous yields!

Ti. : Come, lovely Boy, advance; when you are nigh,
      The crop will flourish and the weed will die,
      The serpent vanish, with its poisoned tongue,
      The wolf shall spare the oxen's tender young.

Lyc. : And goodness, mercy, honor, love divine,
      All born with you together at a time,
      Shall ever follow you, the virtues' friend,
      And bring you back to Heaven at the end.

Ti. : And shining Peace, with freshest flowers bedecked,
      Shall save the world that human sin has wrecked;
      All war shall cease on earth at your behest,
      And men enjoy the fruits of peace and rest.

Lyc. : The sheep of Nazareth shall be your care,
      And every flock shall follow docile there;

The sheep of Galilee will heed your voice,
And in the Jordan's waters will rejoice.

Ti.: Those sheep, when fed, you'll lead within the fold,
A chosen flock, selected from of old;
None but the freshest pastures shall they see:
Grass ever green, and waters cool shall be.

Lyc.: As flocks to meadows, silver to the mine,
As grain to fertile fields, and grapes to vine,
As fountains to the grass, as elms to rocks,
So you to every shepherd and his flocks.

Ti.: As heaven makes earth, as stars make heaven bright,
As moon to stars, as sun to Luna's light,
As God to sun and moon and shining star,
So you the Father's pride and glory are.

Lyc.: Yourself a shepherd, hear the shepherds' plea,
Who came to save the world from misery;
To Heaven guide us, who from Heaven came:
We caused your coming and we cause your fame.

Ti.: Yourself a shepherd, hear the shepherd's prayer:
Make us your comrades and companions there;
Each valley, wood, and mountain shall rejoice,
And sing your virtues with eternal voice.

.   .   .   .

Thus sang the shepherds as they turned to see
Their homes beside the lake of Galilee;
Now rose the sun above the eastern hills,
And warmed the chilly fields and frozen rills

ii

Some poets were more ambitious and undertook to write a complete sequence of eclogues on the New Testament story of Christ's life; the earliest example appears in the twelve sacred eclogues (*bucolica sacra*) of Antonio Geraldini of Amelia (1449-1488), who was crowned *poeta laureatus* at the age of twenty-two.

The twelve eclogues, published in Rome in 1485, were written at Saragossa between January 1 and February 14 of 1484. This means that Geraldini must have produced an average of two eclogues a week and twenty-five hexameters a day. His method of composition was not Virgil's or Tennyson's, then; for all that he was still not so high-speed a composer as Mantuan. Yet, despite medievalisms in syntax and diction, the standard of Geraldini's Latinity is high. He displays a thorough familiarity with all the works of Virgil (naturally), with Ovid, Horace, and Lucan, and (less expectedly) Sedulius and Alcimus Avitus. Like most other writers of eclogues on the life of Christ, he introduces many details derived from the popular traditions and fancies of the Middle Ages. Moses is adorned with horns, as in the Vulgate version of Genesis; the Devil is black all over, with glittering green eyes; at the manger the animals kneel before the infant Christ and the ox and ass worship Him; the Magi are Eastern Kings; the story of Judas and the fig tree appears, as does the medieval story that the Apostles contributed one article each to the Creed.

The first poem is entitled "The Birth of Our Saviour" (*De Salvatoris nostri nativitate*; 128 hexameters). Lycidas recalls the stories of the burning bush, Gideon's fleece, the stone in the Book of Daniel, the mission of John the Baptist, and natural portents of the coming birth of Christ. He concludes by suggesting that he and his friends turn to the stable and adore the new-born Child.

The second poem, "The Adoration of the Kings" (*De regum adoratione*; 103 hexameters), introduces three kings called by the classical sounding names of Granicus, Battus, and Micon. The initials of these names are intended to recall the traditional names of the Magi—Gaspar, Balthasar, and Melchior. Strange omens, begins Geraldini (plunging into the narrative in line 1), had brought the three together and impelled them to gather exotic gifts. Then Granicus urged the others to come with him to visit the scene of what could be only a miraculous birth; Battus and Micon agree, and the trio describe in turn their gifts—gold as a symbol of royal power, frankincense standing for the new rites of Christianity, and myrrh to soothe the crucified body of Christ. At the close Micon draws the attention of the others to the Star and suggests returning by a different route.

The third eclogue, "Lament for a Lost Son," (*Questus de filio amisso*; 79 hexameters), has nothing pastoral in diction or content. Joseph and Mary "converse" in set speeches of ten to fifteen lines each as they search for their lost twelve-year-old; it is all very solemn and humorless, especially in the words of Mary (50-51): "As you advise, venerable old man and pleasant husband, to whom my virginity was safely entrusted." This is in reply to his suggestion that they stop and sleep. Instead of resting, however (or is a night supposed to intervene between 56 and 57?), they decide to make one last attempt; they enter a nearby temple and discover Christ disputing with the doctors (61-79). The woodenness and naïveté of the dialogue is more reminiscent of medieval mystery play than of classical pastoral; as for Jesus' reply to his mother's reproaches, it has a painfully priggish tone.

The fourth eclogue is entitled "The Baptism and Temptation of the Saviour" (*De baptismate et temptatione Salvatoris*; 67 hexameters); the only reference to Christ's baptism is in fact in lines 1 and 2, and the only touch of pastoral is the fact that Christ is called Iolas and Satan is called Charon. This is in many ways quite an effective poem, particularly in the temptation episode; but one reference to sheep-folds does not make a pastoral.

The fifth poem, "The Miracles of Christ" (*De Christi miraculis*; 149 hexameters), is at least provided with a pastoral framework. It is a dialogue among three shepherds that represent Geraldini (Lynceus) and two friends in Saragossa (Atys and Parthenius), brought to an end in the conventional manner when Parthenius awards equal prizes to the other two and points out that it is high time to return to the steading. It is a much more coherent piece of work than the first, third, or fourth eclogue.

The sixth eclogue is entitled "The Institution of the Eucharist" (*De institutione sacramenti Eucharistae*; 98 hexameters). This, begins Geraldini, is the age of new rites, rites without bloody sacrifices (1-6): the "shepherd of the great fold" led his flock "to festive banquets and joyous streams" (a decidedly bizarre phrase to describe the Last Supper). Geraldini narrates the rest of the story in the same unfortunate manner; it is one of the least effective of the twelve poems.

The seventh poem, "The Passion of the Saviour" (*De passione Salvatoris*; 125 hexameters), is *called* an eclogue and Christ is throughout called Daphnis; otherwise pastoral elements are wholly lacking. Judas, Barabbas, and Pilate retain their own names, which merely makes the use of the name Daphnis more incongruous.

Rather better is the eighth eclogue, "The Resurrection of the Saviour" (*De resurrectione Salvatoris*; 89 hexameters), which consists of a long monologue (1-64) followed (without intervening narrative) by dialogue. Here Aeglê (i.e., Mary Magdalene) laments the death of Acanthus; Acanthus appears to her in the guise of a gardener and comforts her (65-67), but Aeglê is not deceived by this apparition and bursts into delighted greetings (68-73). Acanthus blesses her and vanishes (74-78), and Aeglê is left to give vent to her feelings of joy and relief (79-89). The pastoral and idyllic atmosphere of the poem is quite carefully maintained and, although most of the poem is simply versified Biblical narrative, there are some good lines here and there.

The ninth eclogue, "The Ascension of the Saviour" (*De ascensione Salvatoris*; 72 hexameters) is unusual in being provided with a chorus of disciples speaking as one, just as Giorgio Anselmo's eclogue, "The Midwife," has a chorus consisting of the Fates. The poem has no pastoral details whatever. There are some effective lines, but the poem as a whole has little to commend it.

The tenth eclogue, entitled "The Token of Christianity" (*Symbolum Christianae religionis*; 78 hexameters), is at least of historical interest. In this poem the author first describes (1-30) how the apostles met on Pentecost; in lines 31 through 78 appear twelve groups of four lines each: in the first line the apostle in question is identified (sometimes quite allusively) and in the other three lines appears his contribution to the Creed.

The eleventh eclogue, "The Last Judgement" (*De ultimo iudicio*; 68 hexameters) is again without pastoral elements. The poem describes with rather gruesome relish the portents preceding the Last Day (10-39), the Day itself, and the gathering of the nations (40-49). The Divine Shepherd appears in a blaze of light along with the heavenly host (50-64); good and evil are weighed in the balance against one another (55-6), and the evil are sent promptly (*sine mora*) to Hell (57-62), the good to eternal happiness (63-68).

In the twelfth and last of the *bucolica sacra*, "The Blessed Life" (*De vita beata*; 99 hexameters), Geraldini returns to pastoral atmosphere. The poem consists of dialogue between Lynceus (Geraldini himself) and Lycus (apparently a real person—presumably some sort of official at Arino, since he is addressed as "guardian of the Hesperides, cultivator of the fields of Arinnum"). Lycus asks Lynceus (addressing him as the "author of a laborious work, offspring of the Geraldine race, born of the ancient Sabines," which leaves no doubt about this shepherd's identity), what reward there is for human toil—if there is none, he would prefer never to have been born. In reply Lynceus hopes that Lycus' toil on earth may be prosperous and that his orchards may bear heavy crops: there is every chance of it, he adds, since "our Hercules" (*Alcides noster:* Ferdinand II the Catholic) has brought back the Golden Age and has rid the land of monsters (i.e., the Moors) ; but the implications of your question are too difficult for me. Nevertheless, insists Lycus, while I plow and while your sheep are peacefully grazing, sing as a solace for my toil: tell me whether the highest good is what we see before our eyes and whether consciousness ceases with the moment of death (26). I am not deceived by Ovid or Aristippus, begins Lynceus; this life is a sphere of struggle (*area militiae*) and its rewards come later. Will there then, asks Lycus, be no wars, no courts, or laws, or ambition, or fear, or poverty, no love, no hate, no greed? No, says Lynceus, and no farm labor, either, and no palaces and no commerce. At this, Lycus pauses for a while in his plowing: as he puts it, it is hard to exercise mind and body at the same time. Will there, he asks eventually, be no more seasons, no rains, no frosts? The world and the universe as we know it, replies Lynceus, will simply cease to exist: there will be a new heaven and new earth, emerging fresh and new, like a snake that has shed its skin; time will cease to exist—amid endless joy, the notion of past, present, and future will become meaningless (95-96). Such will be the Golden Age of the future, concludes Lynceus, provided that our faith is supported by works ("dum manifesta fides operum ratione probetur": 99) : faith without works, says the New Testament (James 2:17, 20, and 26), is dead. Despite occasional pomposities, this is a vivid and effective poem, quite the best of the twelve. An anthology of Neo-Latin pastoral poetry should ideally contain three of Geraldini's eclogues— the best (xii), the worst (iii), and one of average quality (ii or viii).

The next such sequence is a far briefer one, by Cornelius de Schryver of Aelst (1482-1558), who Latinized his name as Scribonius and Grecized it as Grapheus, emerging from the process as Cornelius Scribonius Grapheus.

The first bucolic poem, written shortly before 1536 (numbers ii and iii were written a good deal earlier) is entitled *Panagnê* ("The All-Holy"; 957 hexameters) : in reality it is six eclogues, like the eight that compose Giovanni Pontano's *Lepidina,* which Scribonius may well have read (he had certainly read Vida's *Christiad* and Sannazaro's *De partu Virginis*).

The first part of the poem is introductory, setting the stage. The second part of the poem is what Pontano would have called a *pompa* ("procession") : it is a long description of the crowd that is to attend the wedding of Mary and Joseph. As in Pontano, most are personifications of rivers, mountains, plains, and the like, and the description of each figure that passes by is made to correspond with actual physical appearances. After about fifty examples of this sort of thing (and it takes a long time for the conscientious reader to sort them all out, especially as some are identified allusively), this section of the poem ends with a description of a herald, presumably intended as comic relief, which, to tell the truth, is rather badly needed by now. This buffoon rides on a performing donkey, blows a horn raucously, puffs out his cheeks like a frog, and encourages the donkey to bray and flap his ears: it reads like a description of a carnival clown.

In part three the crowd approaches the house where the marriage is to take place. The young men and girls in the crowd sing marriage songs for the bride and groom; as we should expect, the girls sing for the groom, the men for the bride. The men and girls sing in alternating hexameter stanzas (five lines plus refrain) and then the final stanza is sung by the whole company. Part two of the *Panagnê* is distinctly wearisome; but part three is lively and entertaining.

In part four, the crowd advances on the house, to be met by Nazara, described as the former nurse of the bride, but now her *pronuba* (matron of honor); the guests salute the bride and groom and marvel at the nymphs that attend them—Aretê (virtue), Agapê (love), Elpis (hope), Pistis (faith), Irenê (peace), Homonoea (concord), Chara (joy), Phronesis (prudence), Ischys (strength), Talasis (patience), Apochê (abstinence), and many more, as well as five young men (brothers and cousins of the Nymphs) called Ponus (toil), Symphora (disaster), Thlipsis (tribulation), Staurus (cross), and Pirasmus (temptation). Part four, as the reader will easily guess, tends to the pedantic.

Next, in part five, comes the description of the wedding ceremony, carried out by Pistis, Agapê, and others. In part six the long poem is brought to a close by a cheerful description of rustic dancing and merry-making, much of which sounds distinctly athletic and sweaty.

The second poem of the three, called "The God-Man" (*Theander*; 407 hexameters), consists of a long dialogue among three shepherds—Polymelus, Amnonomeus, and Agraulus; the latter two represent two of the shepherds of Bethlehem. In the introduction Polymelus meets the others and asks what is the reason for the strange but lovely golden radiance diffused over the entire landscape (this takes nearly three pages). Amnonomeus tells Polymelus that the Golden Age has truly returned—lions no longer harm flocks, nor do wolves and bears; griffins now live at peace with horses, fallow deer and rabbits with dogs, and Aepolus has seen a spotted leopard peacefully consorting with his flock. But, says Polymelus, if the Golden Age has truly returned, then surely the child of whom Tityrus (i.e., Virgil) spoke must have been born at last.

Yes, replies Agraulus, He has indeed, and Amnonomeus and I have seen Him lying in a manger surrounded with flowers one moonlit night; Panagnê, smiling, kissed her child as the oxen bowed down and the Nymphs of Napê brought gifts along with Pales, the Satyrs, Dryads, and Oreads, while Pan sang, and shepherds assembled from all sides. Later that night, goes on Agraulus, we were watching our flocks when an angelic voice from Heaven told us that the child, offspring of Panagnê and Panurgus ("All-Creator") was a divine human being (Theander) who would restore the countryside by removing all causes of infertility or blight (paganism), cure the sheep of illnesses (heresies), and drive off wild beasts (hereticteachers like Luther), and restore a Golden Age.

At this point Agraulus and Amnonomeus leave Polymelus, who selects a lamb as a gift and makes his way, guided by the Star, to Bethlehem. He sees the infant Christ, gives Him the lamb as a plaything, promises Him a hoop, and promises to go birds' nesting for Him, ending with a longish prayer. He then returns to his wife Leucogalê, who, he knows, is busy making porridge. The cheerfully domestic tone of Gemütlichkeit in the conclusion is overdone. De Schryver was aiming at the effect achieved by Titian in an early painting (now in the Louvre) called La Vièrge au Lapin, but overshot the mark.

The third poem, Pan (420 hexameters) is contrasted with the second as Il Penseroso is with L'Allegro. In the second eclogue Polymelus had seen a golden world and wonderingly asked the smiling newcomers the reason for it all; here the shepherd Thaumazon sees a world filled with tears, darkness, and evil omens. He asks his friend Algophorus ("Bringer of Painful Tidings") what is the cause, and is told at great length how Pan had met his death as a result of jealousy and betrayal. This narrative is followed by a lament of Nymphs and a prophecy of Pan's eventual resurrection and return to Arcadia.

A third sequence of eclogues on the life of Christ—again not nearly so extensive as Geraldini's—is that by Georg or Gregor Bersman of Annaberg (1538-1611). Bersman appears from contemporary accounts to have been a skillful and versatile teacher, at

Leipzig and Zerbst, and a cheerful, pleasant, and upright man—much more attractive as a man, in fact, than as a poet.

The first poem, "The Birth of Jesus Christ" (*Natalicia Iesu Christi*; 130 hexameters) has little new to offer. Here the shepherds are not Greek youths or Germans with Greek names, but two Hebrew *pastores* named Simeon and Judas; as usual in Christmas eclogues, the time is midnight. The poem is amoebaean and rhetorically balanced throughout except for lines 125-30, a conclusion in the poet's own words. The second eclogue, "On the Saviour's Death and Resurrection" (*De merito mortis ac resurrectione Servatoris Jesu Christi*; 124 hexameters), is in dialogue throughout, the shepherds being Josias and Banaias. In the third sacred eclogue, "The Miracle of the Holy Spirit" (*De miraculo sancti Spiritus*; 120 hexameters) we have a biblical analogue with Virgil's sixth eclogue (the Lucretian song of Silenus). Here Bersman tells how the Hebrew shepherd Josias had sung of the creation of the universe, the history of the Jewish people, the life and ministry of Christ, and the mission of the apostles. It is a dull poem, marred by Bersman's characteristic fault of over-close reminiscence of Virgil.

iii

Pastoral treatment of the story of Christ's birth, life, and death naturally suggested similar treatment of stories and themes derived from the Old Testament; such eclogues are not nearly so common as one might have expected. At the moment we shall deal with only four authors.

We begin with a true curiosity, the third of the six eclogues of Giano Anisio of Naples (ca. 1475-1540), entitled "Wisdom" (*Sapientia*; 61 hexameters). This appears to be an expansion and pastoral reworking of an earlier poem of forty-four hendecasyllabics paraphrasing part of the Song of Solomon: oriental imagery in a classical lyric form sounds decidely strange. In the eclogue, a lover serenades his mistress in language that combines the motifs of Ovidian erotic verse with the characteristic repetitions, parallelisms, and exotic figures of thought and speech of Hebrew poetry; the whole impression of the poem (including its peculiar metrical effects) is one of calculated oddity.

The second eclogue of Pierre Mambrun of Clermont-Ferrand (1600-1661) is far more orthodox. It is entitled "Abel" (*Abelus*; 101 hexameters), and consists for the most part of dialogue between Cain and Abel; but the poem is little more than a jumble, and it is better to pass on to the first two of the six eclogues of Peter de Fransz (Francius) of Amsterdam (1645-1704). The first eclogue, *Moses* (172 hexameters) is an epinicium, a song of victory sung by Moses after leading the Israelites out of bondage. There is nothing of conventional pastoral in this poem, even though a refrain with the characteristically "bucolic" rhythms does appear at irregular intervals. It is an extremely effective poem: the Latin is clear, the rhythms rapid, and there is a quite remarkable sense of urgency, excitement, and triumph communicated. There are many epinicia in Neo-Latin poetry celebrating actual victories; few surpass and most do not equal the standard of excellence that Francius here attains.

In the second eclogue, "David, or, the Prophecy of Christ" (*David, seu eiusdem de Christo vaticinium*; 125 hexameters), the shepherd-king prophesies a Golden Age in the manner of Virgil's *Pollio* (the fourth eclogue). The introduction and conclusion (a total of twenty lines only) are fitted out with the conventional trappings of pastoral, but otherwise there are few bucolic elements. The poet describes how David sat down by the brook Cedron, and, as he felt the power of prophecy stir within him, began to sing. Flow softly, sweet Cedron, he begins, and attend my sacred song: for there shall come a day when a Child shall be born of a virgin; even as I say this the sky grows brighter and I seem to see that Child descend and put on human form in my own city. This is a much more rhetorical poem than the first eclogue, but it is certainly its equal in excellence.

We can afford to neglect the series of eleven *bucolica sacra* written by the prolific Jesuit poet Laurent Lebrun of Nantes (1607-1663)—these are uneven in quality—and examine the huge sequence of biblical eclogues written by Robertus Obryzius or Obrisius (Aubry?) of Hermanville in Artois (ca. 1540–ca. 1584? 1594?), who belonged to the same group of Catholic Netherlandish poets as did Jakob de Sluyper.

Here we have no less than 390 pages of eclogues in which Obryzius covers practically all the Old Testament and the gospels of the New. There are 114 eclogues, all told, arranged in twelve books: Books I-VIII, totaling 86 eclogues, are devoted to the Old Testament, Books IX-XII, totaling 28 poems, to the New; there are about 11,700 hexameters in all of this. Of real pastoral there is very little in the volume. Where it is easy or natural or appropriate, Obryzius presents us with shepherds and flocks, as in his Christmas pastoral

(IX, 42), and usually those shepherds turn out to be Obryzius himself and his friends. The usual frames of eclogue appear—dialogues, Golden Age poems, laments, epithalamia, and so forth; a frequent form of poem is the poet's address to himself: in the poem describing Christ's being found in the temple, Obryzius rounds on himself at the end, reproaching himself for worldliness—it is such priests as he who invite the spread of heresy by failing to set an example:

> Alas, the clouds of heresy grow black,
> And schisms stronger rise as we grow slack!
> A storm of evil doctrine rises from the lea,
> And drives our trembling ship far out to sea.
> The waves of evil tower amid the dark:
> The coming tenth will swamp our laboring bark.
> Ah, Jesu, sleeping, whither are you borne?
> We humbly pray for aid at night and morn:
> Assist the weary and protect from harm;
> To us extend the everlasting arm!

The reader will not be astonished to be told that there are arid stretches in this huge work; but there is almost as much that is readable, and there is even a little that is alive and worthwhile. Yet even the most courageous and enthusiastic student of Neo-Latin literature feels daunted at the prospect of 114 eclogues on a single theme.

iv

The next class of religious pastoral is devotional rather than biblical. Earliest and least interesting here is Mantuan (Giovanni Battista Spagnuoli of Mantua, 1448-1516), of whose ten eclogues two at present concern us. In the seventh, "Pollux" (161 hexameters), two shepherds named Alphus and Galbula tell how a young man named Pollux was warned in a vision by the Virgin Mary of the dangers of the secular world and advised to retire to the safe retreat of Mount Carmel (i.e., the Carmelite Order, of which Mantuan became vicar-general in 1513). The eighth eclogue, "Religion" (224 hexameters), is a sort of appendix to the seventh. It explains that the "nymph" that had appeared to Pollux had been none other than the Virgin herself and follows this explanation with a panegyric of her power and generosity, and also with a long versified list and description of those days which must be kept sacred in her honor, a sort of theme that was congenial to Mantuan. The poem is worth reading by the student of English literature, since it is closely imitated in Spenser's July *Aeglogue*.

A devotional eclogue very similar to Mantuan's seventh appears in the ungainly *Eumorphus* (287 hexameters) of Guillaume Châtelier (Guilelmus Castellus or Castalius) of Tours (1470-1505), of which we need only say that the poem has obvious affinities with the Petrarchan eclogue, both in its language, which is notably medieval, in the cryptic and riddling manner of the first section, and in its praise of *virtus*. A few passages of the last section are rather impressive, but most of the poem is wearisome in the extreme.

Next we come to Euricius Cordus of Simsthausen in Hesse (1486-1535). Of his ten eclogues, one is a religious-devotional—the seventh, "The Good Man" (*Pius*; 141 hexameters). On Shrove Sunday, a shepherd named Pius drives out his flock to pasture; he is unable to attend church, but will pray in the open. The rest of the poem consists of Pius' prayers to Christ and the Virgin Mary. The tone of much of this is exceedingly medieval, and the diction is often reminiscent not so much of classical pastoral as of medieval hymn. And the active animus against the Jews is startling.

A far superior product is the fourth eclogue (untitled; 117 hexameters) of the seventeen written by Helius Eobanus Hessus of Bockendorf or Halgeshausen in Hesse (1488-1540). Its framework is consciously and conscientiously classical: two young shepherds, Tityrus (Justus Jonas, according to Ellinger) and Battus (Peter Eberbach) meet under the shade of a beech tree; they catch sight of an older shepherd called Thrasybulus (Mutianus) and ask him to be the judge of their contest in song.

In five-line stanzas Battus and Tityrus alternate their hymns in praise of the Almighty and the Virgin Mary; Thrasybulus, as well he might, says that both have won and that each should keep his pledge. This is one of Eobanus' most pleasant eclogues; the lines on the Virgin are especially light and attractive, and the hexameters have a lyrical quality rare among German Neo-Latinists. In some Italian Neo-Latin poets the blazing lights and thunderous sounds that surround the Virgin at the moment of the Immaculate Conception remind one of blazing Technicolor and stereophonic sound; Eoban describes the moment (86-89) in words that remind the reader of:

> He came al so stille, where his moder was,
> As rain in Aprille, that fall'th on the gras. . . .

The eighth eclogue (untitled; 100 hexameters) of Peter van der Brugge (Pontanus) of Bruges (ca. 1480–ca. 1540) is marked by his usual tendency to roughness and prosiness of versification on the one hand and coarseness of language and conception on the other. The eclogue consists wholly of dialogue between two vine-growers, Rubus ("Bramble," presumably so called since his thoughts are constantly on the earth) and Cedrus ("Cedar": his thoughts soar heavenwards), on the morning after a disastrous storm. Although there is no doubt where the author's sympathies lie, he may well have irritated some of his contemporaries by assigning all the best lines to the satirical Rubus and all the innocent naïveté to Cedrus; but his own satirical bent made Van der Brugge enjoy annoying the humorless.

All the five eclogues of Denys Faucher of Arles (1487-1562) are relevant here. Faucher entered the Benedictine order in 1508 and eventually became prior of the Abbey of Lérins. He must have been a man of some distinction, for it is clear from his letters and poems that he was on fairly close terms with Cardinal Du Bellay, Cardinal Giacopo Sadoleto, Salomon Maigret (Macrinus), the Cardinal of Lorraine, and the poet Du Bellay, and was at least known to François I and Marguerite de Valois.

His Latin works appear in the annals of the monastery of Lérins, edited by Vincenzio Barrili at Lyon in 1613; among the verses appear five religious eclogues, none of outstanding merit as poetry. It will be quite sufficient to name four ("In Praise of Lérins," 317 hexameters; "Celestial and Divine Love," 290 hexameters; "On the Backsliding of the Monastic Order," 104 hexameters; "The Religious Life," 170 hexameters) and examine one.

The fifth eclogue is entitled "The Desolation of the Monastery of Lerins and the Expulsion of the Monks" (*De desolatione monasterii Lerinensis et de extrusione monachorum*; 112 hexameters). It is a dialogue between two shepherds, Tityrus (representing or at least recalling Virgil, himself once dispossessed) and Candidus (Faucher), carried on in a simple pastoral cipher that is not maintained consistently throughout the poem. Tityrus meets Candidus and asks him why he is so sad. Surely, answers Candidus, you must know what has been happening here over the past two years—our pastures have been taken from us, and now other shepherds wish to drive us out completely. When Tityrus asks the reason for this, Candidus replies that it is the result of an attempt to live in accordance with the rule of Monte Cassino: these rebellious "liberal" shepherds wish, like Medea, to turn old St. Benedict into a sprightly young man. He then (52-93) tells Tityrus a satirical fable of a backsliding Benedictine.

A certain young man, he begins, had been brought up in the good old-fashioned way and had been judged worthy to become a shepherd. He prospered and gained honors that went to his head: instead of simplicity he now practiced every sort of luxury, while diseases became epidemic among his flocks and the attacks of the Wolf became an everyday occurrence. Eventually this shepherd arrived with his extinguished lamp at the gates of Paradise, demanding admittance from St. Peter and depending on the prestige of the name of Benedict. Peter looks dubiously at the man and says that he will have to ask St. Benedict himself; on his arrival the saint says that although the outward trappings are familiar the red face and fair round belly prove that this priest is no Benedictine. Benedict and Peter now open the priest's stomach and discover it to be packed full of the richest foods and choicest wines, whereupon Benedict tells the man (whom he calls Sardanapalus) that only the Cross will bring admittance to Paradise.

Martin Rheder (*floruit* 1578) appears to have been a minor provincial official who yearned to become a Rector of a Gymnasium or lecturer at a university. Since the road to preferment, in education and administration alike, was to demonstrate skill in the use of the universal language, he addressed a Latin eclogue, devotional in character, to the municipal senate of Werningenrode. He probably attained some success as a result of this, for he published the poem in pamphlet form at Wittenberg in 1578—he might well have done this in any case, but would not have been likely to retain the flattering dedication.

The poem, "On the Blessed Life" (*De vita beata*; 106 hexameters) is a dialogue between two rustics named Lynceus and Lycus on the aim of life. Lycus asks his friend what is the goal of human toil and what rewards are to be expected, calling him the "author of a toilsome work." This phrase sounds familiar, and also sounds decidedly odd, since Rheder apparently had not published anything to date; still, the reader goes on. If there is no reward, says Lycus, I would rather never have lived on this malignant earth: this phrase, too, has a familiar ring. Lynceus wishes Lycus joy of his orchard and prosperity now that "our Alcides (i.e., Hercules) has rid the land of monsters," and hopes, too, that his crop of yellow fruits (i.e., oranges: in *Germany*?) will be heavy; but, as for his question, it will be a difficult one to answer. Very well, then, says Lycus, while I plow and your sheep graze, console my toil with your discourse: this, too, sounds suspiciously familiar, and the reader glances quickly through Lynceus' explanation (26-50) of the aim of life (in which he says that he is not deceived by Ovid and Aristippus) to Lycus' words, in which he says that it is hard to exercise mind and body at the same time. At this point the reader is absolutely certain that he has read every line of all this before—and he has, for the first 80-odd lines of this poem are stolen word for word and line for line from the twelfth eclogue of Antonio Geraldini of Amelia (1457-1488), omitting any line that gives away the true authorship (e.g., the fourth, where Lycus, in the original poem, calls Lynceus "offspring of the Geraldine race"). Rheder has left the phrase "author of a toilsome work," which originally referred to the preceding eleven eclogues of Geraldini; he has, with incredible ineptitude, left the references to oranges and to Ferdinand the Catholic's expulsion of the Moors, but has had the sense to tack on a conclusion of his own: Geraldini's Catholic doctrine, with its closing emphasis on salvation through faith *and* works, would not have been welcomed by the Calvinist senate of Werningrode.

Devotional eclogues of the ordinary type do not reappear until the mid-seventeenth century, with Pierre Mambrun of Clermont-Ferrand (1600-1661). His third eclogue, entitled "Phasithea" (61 hexameters) proves, like the last of his eclogues examined, to have an allegorical cast. It is cryptic, but probably owes nothing to Petrarch, being typical, rather, of the seventeenth-century baroque "metaphysical" approach. The poem can be read as simple pastoral, and once the point of the bucolic masquerade is seen, there are no difficulties whatever, which is not true of Pre-Humanist pastoral. Phasithea is a beautiful woman (her name means "the sight, appearance, vision of God"), but she is in a sense cruel, for she permits her lovers to gaze on her face only after the most unremitting toil. Calling himself Daphnis, the poet, like a bucolic lover, longs to gaze on her beauty.

The most remarkable aspect of this extremely skillful poem is the precision and tact with which the pastoral conventions and situations are maintained: the whole eclogue can be read in complete innocence as art-pastoral, and there is not a single word or phrase that could not appear in a classical poem.

A sequence of devotional eclogues was written by a Dutch Jesuit, Willem de Beka or van der Beeck (Guilelmus Becanus) of

Antwerp (*floruit* 1645-1655), who appears to have been attached to the Vatican *curia* under Alexander VII. Becanus' poems (reprinted half-a-dozen times between 1655 and 1728) include nine eclogues and two books of elegiac poems. The eclogues are entitled *Idyllia sacra* and some contain more pastoral elements than others; we need only name some (number i, "Joseph," 86 hexameters; iii, "Isodorus," 79; iv, "David," 87; v, "Moses Exposed," 67; vi, "Mycon," 78; vii, "Thyrsis and Daphnis," 76; ix, "Moses Found," 67) and examine one.

In the second poem, "Thestylis" (109 hexameters), Becanus begins by praising the poetic gifts of François de Montmorency (a Jesuit friend) and urging him to continue to rival Horace and Pindar; his own verse, he says, aspires no higher than simple pastoral—yet the "Maiden of the Grudian Woods" does not despise rustic praise (the reference is to the building, by Leopold Wilhelm, Archduke of Austria, of a new church to the Virgin Mary at Louvain). He goes on to prove this by telling the story of Thestylis, a country girl who lived near Louvain. Thestylis had found an old, forgotten church in the woods and wept to see how dilapidated and tumble-down it had become—she lamented that she had not been born of a wealthy father; otherwise she might have rebuilt the church in magnificent style. She brings fruits and garlands to the statue of the Madonna and Child in the church; she prays, and begs that these simple gifts may be accepted: they are not so grand as those that Phyllis or Aeglê or Iolas or Zacharides might have brought, but they are all she has.

Her constant service of the altar led to neglect of her home and flock and made her parents suspect the existence of a secret lover. When they charged her with a guilty secret, Thestylis prayed that she might die in the service of the Virgin; the Virgin herself heard the prayer and answered it, telling the dying shepherdess that when the last day came they would see each other face to face. May such an assurance be mine, concludes the poet.

Of Pierre Écoulant (*floruit* 1730) little is known save that he was a Jesuit; he almost certainly taught at the Collège Louis le Grand in Paris. His one eclogue (untitled; 64 hexameters), published at Paris in 1730, appears in a bound collection of pamphlets in the Bibliothèque Nationale entitled *Recueil de poésies latines et françoises faites au sujet de la canonisation des saints Stanislaus Kostka et Louis Gonsague de la compagnie de Jésus:* the actual canonization had taken place in Rome in 1726. The poem represents a dialogue between Stanislaus Kostka of Rostkow and Luigi Gonzaga of Mantua in youth, at the time of their entering the Jesuit order; in actual fact they could never have met, since Kostka (1550-1568) died in the year of Gonzaga's birth (1568-1591). In structure the poem is extremely formal: lines 1 through 60 consist of twenty three-line stanzas; 61 through 64 are two concluding couplets. Gonzaga and Kostka congratulate each other on their decision to abandon the world, rejoice in the freedom from mundane cares that faces them, look back with affection on their parents and other relatives, praise the power and mercy of Christ, and resolve to keep Him always before their eyes. The poem is clever and competent, but the reader grows tired of the future saints' raptures long before he has reached the end. Except for the amoebaean form, there is nothing pastoral in the poem, not even in its diction.

v

I shall conclude this chapter by examining a form of pastoral of which we have already seen an example in Becanus' second *Idyllium sacrum*—the Mary-eclogue. Three poets only appear here, though many more must surely have written eclogues of this type now lost or uncatalogued in European libraries.

Of the half-dozen leading French Jesuit poets of the seventeenth century, one of the best was certainly René Rapin (Renatus Rapinus) of Tours (1621-1687). His life was spent in teaching at the Jesuit Collège de Clairmont in Paris (founded in 1563; it was later reorganized as the Collège Louis le Grand), where he did as much as any to encourage original composition modeled on Cicero and Virgil. His most famous and influential work is the *Réflexions sur l'Art Poétique d'Aristote* (1674); of more interest to the student of Neo-Latin literature is his excellent didactic poem on gardens (translated into English verse by John Evelyn) in four books (*Hortorum libri iv*). Of his three Latin pastorals the first two are Mary-eclogues.

The first poem, "David, or, The Shepherd-Poet" (*David, seu pastor vates*; 122 hexameters), begins with a narrative of David's killing of the lion and the bear (the subject of Becanus' fourth eclogue); it then describes how David rested after his exploit in a nearby cave and dreamt of a glorious Virgin who would some day be born to the Jewish people.

The second poem, "The Sacrificers" (*Sacrificuli*; 86 hexameters), is not nearly so good. It is a dialogue between the shepherds Amasias and Adonias as they prepare a rite to purify the Virgin from all traces of original sin. The poem as a whole is stiff, self-conscious, and disappointing; certainly it lacks the liveliness of the first eclogue.

Niccolò Giannettasio of Naples (1648-1715) we have already met as a skillful and almost unbelievably prolific Latin poet. Three of his fourteen piscatory eclogues fall under the present category. The second poem, "Parthenis" (this woman's name is formed from the Greek word *parthénos*, "virgin"; 86 hexameters), is reminiscent of the erotic sounding poems addressed to the Virgin by some English poets of the seventeenth century. Here the fisherman Iolas wanders to the shore of the Bay of Naples and stops by the home of his beloved Parthenis, near Mergillina, to sing her praises and pray for her love. His song contains most of the stock motifs of the typical fisherman's song. Iolas asks why Parthenis hides her face from her faithful lover, calls the rocks and waves to bear witnesses to the purity and faithfulness of his love, reminds her that rocks and caves have for long re-echoed with the name of Parthenis, wonders whether she spurns his love because he is only a poverty-stricken fisherman, and reminds her that her own Son had chosen fishermen as companions (this is an unhappy inspiration on the poet's part), offers flowers from Capo di Massa as well as the usual fisherman's gifts; the gifts are poor, he admits, but who could possibly bring gifts worthy of so glorious a being? He reminds her that in his heart he salutes her every morning, noon, and night, and that he gazes raptly every day on her portrait. The whole poem, for all its eloquence, must make the modern reader squirm with discomfort. We know that in his own devotions Giannettasio was deeply devoted to the cult of the Virgin, so much so that he adopted "Partenio" as a second name; but this does not prevent the poem from being little more than a freakish aberration.

The eighth eclogue, "The Birthday" (*Genethliaca*; 84 hexameters) is equally a piscatory, but here the Virgin is herself, not a fisherman's sweetheart. In this poem two fishermen, Zephyraeus and Artemidorus, come with others, on the anniversary of the Virgin's birth (September 8), to the church of the Blessed Virgin Mary at Posillipo. After a trim introduction, Zephyraeus sings (9-43) five six-line stanzas in praise of the Virgin; Artemidorus then sings (48-82) a parallel group of five six-line stanzas. Neither the formality of the structure nor the heaping up of piscatory mannerisms can prevent this from being an excellent poem; the cheerfulness and musical rhythm of the hexameters are so admirable that the reader is willing to accept conventional features that he could not stomach in the *Parthenis*.

The twelfth eclogue, "Moeris" (*77* hexameters), is rather less successful. Phrasidamus meets Moeris by the shore of the Bay of Naples and asks what young lady is to receive the magnificent roses and black corals he is carrying, warning him that love is like a raging lion. The last part of Moeris' reply resolves itself into a sort of hymn, with just enough liturgical repetition to suggest the point. Phrasidamus congratulates Moeris on his good fortune and, on expressing the wish that the same might some day befall him, is invited to accompany Moeris to the Virgin's church to pray for her favor.

The last author whose work I shall mention here is Tommaso Ravasini of Parma (1665-1715), a little-known Humanist whose religious poems, entitled *Amores Parthenii* ("Parthenius' Love-Poems"), consist of eclogues, elegiacs, and lyrics. The use of such a title is curious, but characteristic of the seventeenth century; in any case it is not nearly so odd as his "The Art of Loving Mary," modeled on Ovid's *Ars amatoria*. Among the lyrics appears an Alcaic ode in dialogue: questioned by Lycon about the roses he is carrying, Daphnis says he is taking them to the altar of Parthenis. The situation (and even the kind of flower) is the same as in Niccolò Giannettasio's twelfth eclogue (the pen-name "Parthenius" is also an allusion to Giannettasio; but it is probable, and characteristic of the period, that the title *Amores Parthenii* also alludes to the *Erotica* compiled by the original Parthenius for Cornelius Gallus).

Besides this not very successful experiment in lyric dialogue, there is a sequence of Mary-eclogues; a later twelfth eclogue is religious in tone but does not properly form part of the sequence.

In the first poem, "The Happiness of the Virgin's Servant" (*Parthenici clientis felicitas*; 99 hexameters), the speakers are a vine-grower named Meliseus and a gardener named Syncerus: these names intentionally recall Giovanni Pontano and Giacopo Sannazaro. Here Meliseus exclaims at the fertility of Syncerus' garden; Syncerus explains that his happiness and prosperity stem from his service of Parthenis (no doubt the reference is to the *De partu virginis*). The Latinity of the poem is excellent, its meter is irreproachable, and a discreet balance is held between the conventions of pastoral and the Catholic content; in this it is far superior to Giannettasio's second eclogue.

The second eclogue is cumbrously entitled "A Contest in Love

for the Virgin" (*Erga Deiparam amoris certamen*; 78 hexameters).
Those who dislike rhetoric on principle will find the amoebaean praise
of the Virgin tiring; those who regard rhetoric as language en-
hanced by devices of style and object only to its abuse will find much
to praise and little to blame in Ravasini's blend of the simple and
the sophisticated.   A version follows:

> Where all is green and fresh by Parma's town,
> And rivers from the hills come tumbling down,
> There Alcon met with Lysias one day—
> Both young, both skilled to sing the tuneful lay.
> "I burn for Parthenis!" young Lysias cried;
> "With love my heart is full!" his friend replied.
> While thus they spoke, they mingled tears and sighs
> And raised their faces to the sunny skies,
> Prepared to praise the Maid with voices strong,
> And prayed for favor with alternate song.

A.:   Sweet in the vineyard's path to make my way,
> And watch the clusters ripen day by day;
> But sweeter far to sing this sacred lay.

L.:   The garden-flowers are all my heart's delight;
> Their fragrant scents refresh the summer night;
> But sweeter far to love with all my might.

A.:   Who longs to rid his heavy heart of care,
> Enjoy tranquillity and quiet rare,
> Then let him love the Virgin, kind and fair.

L.:   Who longs to spend his days in grief and strain,
> To have a heart replete with woeful pain,
> Should her reject, and sad vexation gain.

A.:   No garden longs for autumn's cooling streams,
> When parched by summer's heat and searing beams,
> As longs my heart to see my dearest dreams.

L.:   No vineyard, after biting cold and rain,
> So longs to feel the sunny warmth again,
> As I do long her tender love to gain.

A.:   More dear to me, more lovely, as you stand,
> More glorious is there none within the land;
> Your aid is given to all with heart and hand.

L.: No common love with yours can ev'n compare;
As you no being on the earth is fair;
As you no beauty in the sky is rare.

A.: What beauties nature holds, what loveliness,
Must yield to praise of your own tenderness.

L.: Not Iris, with her colors rich and rare,
Nor yet Aurora's beauty can compare.

A.: If I compare you with the stars of night,
I fail: your beauty far outshines their sight.

L.: If I compare you with Apollo's beams,
I fail: from you a greater brightness streams.

A.: A fool he is, and with a heart of stone,
Who would not love you true and you alone.

L.: A fool he is, who could be loved by you,
But turns aside and hides him from your view.

A.: But happy he, who from his early years
Devotes to you his love and hopes and fears.

L.: Unhappy he, who wastes the spring of life,
Who spurns your love, whose heart with sin is rife.

A.: Who has not loved your face, and loved it well,
What love can be, that man can never tell.

L.: Who has not learned how love for you can grow,
What love can be, that man will never know.

A.: Would that with such a love at last I die,
And leave this earth to be enthroned on high.

L.: Or live or die, so that you hear my plea:
May life or death befall along with thee.

A.: While yet the breath remains within my frame,
Then always may I love thy holy name.

L.: Let never other love this love expel;
Let this control my life till passing knell.

A.: If I do not prefer your love to all,
Then may the driving rain and hailstone fall;

May seed committed rot and turn to mold,
And gardens perish with the freezing cold.

L.: When I forget your love for mortal maid,
Reject your favor, or refuse your aid,
Then autumn's flowers and summer's heat shall fail,
The springtime's breezes, and the winter's hail.

· · · · · · · · · ·

These vows and others did they utter there,
And felt a holy love suffuse the air;
The river-spirit heard, and raised his head,
Nor in his rapid course accustomed sped.

The third eclogue, "The Virgin's Aid" (*Virginis auxilium*; 135 hexameters), is in two parts. Two vine-growers, Menalcas and Damoetas, meet by the river Parma after a violent hailstorm. Menalcas, with great relief, remarks that the storm has done no damage to his vineyard and that he owes this mercy to the Blessed Virgin.

The fourth eclogue (104 hexameters) is untitled but is preceded in the 1696 edition by a note that reads, "The Mother of God is adumbrated as Virgin by the flower of the cedar, and as Mother by the fruit"; the reference here is to *Ecclesiasticus* (Chapter 24): "I have been exalted as the cedar on Lebanon," and "My blossoms are the fruits of honor." Alcimus and Jonathan, two rustics, foregather at the foot of Mount Lebanon and alternate their praises of the Virgin, comparing her with the cedar. Their songs are a mass of rhetoric whose distinctly baroque elaboration reminds the reader of the incredibly complicated carvings on many pulpits in seventeenth-century churches, or of the capitals of pillars in many baroque buildings; a less reverent reader might be reminded of Dr. Johnson's remark about the dog that walked on his hind legs—the wonder is not that he does it well, but that he does it at all. The poem undoubtedly has many infuriating faults; but they are faults committed by an excellent craftsman, and certainly the poem does maintain the pastoral atmosphere far, far better than many of the ordinary sort of devotional eclogue.

The fifth eclogue, "Anemonê" (*Anemon flos*; 94 hexameters), is an elaborate series of comparisons made by the gardeners Mopsus, Lygdon, and Moeris, of Christ to the anemone (cf. Song of Solomon, Chapters 2 and 5) as the fourth had compared the Virgin to the cedar of Lebanon. The sixth eclogue (untitled; 128 hexameters) is another flower-poem, with the same speakers; it is a sequel to the fifth, and the dialogue is supposed to have taken place on the following day. These, incidentally, are the sort of poem that would be called "allegorical" by Ellinger, who gives the same name to Petrarch's eclogues; but this poem is in no way cryptic. To put it at its crudest, these poems make sense even without interpretation— most of Petrarch's do not; they must be read as cryptic verse or not at all. And these poems display a skill in words, a shape, and a structure that Petrarch's lack.

The seventh eclogue (untitled; 156 hexameters) contrasts sacred and profane love. A dialogue throughout, between the vine-growers Daphnis and Meliboeus, it is one of the best of Ravasini's eclogues— it is lively, witty, and well written.

The eighth eclogue (untitled; 84 hexameters) recalls, in its elaborations, the fourth. Corydon and Amyntas, on the banks of the Parma river, vie with each other in praising Christ and the Virgin in a most studied (perhaps "labored" would be a better word) series of alternating amoebaean groups: seven lines are answered by seven, four by four, three by three (three times over), two by two (eight times over), one by one, and two by two. A small extract will give the reader a sufficient notion of the whole:

Corydon: I was to finish; but the heavenly Child
          Demanded further song, with bidding mild.

Amyntas: I was to finish; but the Virgin maid
          Demanded further praise of her be said.

Corydon: Enough to say that Jesu is my joy.

Amyntas: Enough to praise the mother of the Boy.

Corydon: More would I sing; but to my sacred song
          Nought but the name of Jesu can belong.

Amyntas: More would I sing; but all that I can name
          Is Mary's beauty, love, and holy fame. (69-78)

The above is typical of the entire eclogue, which obviously suffers from the worst defects of amoebaean verse; for all its technical virtuosity it is not comparable for one moment with the fourth.

In the ninth eclogue (untitled; 88 hexameters), when Manasylus asks Iolas why it is that he can remain so happy amid all the troubles of the Austrian invasion, the older man replies that it is because of

a glorious dream that he had had the night before. Just before
dawn, when he had sunk into a heavy second sleep, the beloved
Parthenis appeared to him in a vision; in his dream, Iolas wished
to kneel, to pray, and to stretch out his hands to the Virgin, but as
he reached out she disappeared gradually into nothingness, and he
awoke. In reply to a question from Manasylus, Iolas says that
she looked gentle, tranquil, and kind, just as he had so often seen her
in the portrait in the city (this might refer to any one of a number
of paintings of the Virgin by Coreggio still to be seen in Parma's
cathedral and art-gallery) : no words could describe her. This is
not one of Ravasini's best poems, but it is certainly one of the better
eclogues.

The tenth eclogue (untitled; 64 hexameters) is a rhapsodical
monologue in praise of the Virgin, on the anniversary of her birth
(for the subject, compare Giannettasio's eighth eclogue). On closer
inspection this poem proves to be a fairly close translation of Giacopo
Sannazaro's third Italian eclogue in the *Arcadia,* in which a shepherd Galizio sings in praise of the rustic goddess Pales on the day
of her festival, the Palilia. Since Ravasini's tenth is in that case
not an original poem, we may pass it over; but the reader may wish
to compare a few lines of Sannazaro's Italian with the corresponding
Latin of Ravasini:

> Sovra una verde riva
> Di chiare e lucid' onde
> In un bel bosco di fioretti adorno
> Vidi di bianca oliva
> Ornato e d'altre fronde
> Un pastor, che'n su l'alba a pie d'un orno
> Cantava il terzo giorno
> Del mese innanzi aprile;
> A cui li vaghi uccelli
> Di sopra gli arboscelli
> Con voce rispondean dolce e gentile:
> Ed ei rivolto al sole,
> Dicea queste parole. . . .

This appears in Ravasini as:

> Fontis ad herbosam nemora inter frondea ripam
> constiterat cana frontem praecinctus oliva

pastor; eum patulae sub tegmine vidimus orni
octavum mensis, qui Octobrem praevenit, alto
concelebrare diem sub prima crepuscula cantu.
ille ut erat roseum solis conversus ad ortum,
arborea volucrum coetu plaudente sub umbra
non responsuris narrabat talia ventis. . . .

This brings to an end our examination of the Neo-Latin religious
pastoral, only one of the many new uses to which the eclogue was
put in the Renaissance and Baroque eras; the others will be treated
in the next three chapters.

X

NEW USES OF PASTORAL:

COMMEMORATIVE

n this chapter I shall examine three types of eclogue
—that written to celebrate either a birthday or a
birth (eclogue written as genethliacon), the wedding eclogue (epithalamium), and the dirge (epicedium), commonly called "elegy" in English,
although, as earlier mentioned, this word has a
different meaning when applied to Greek or Latin
poetry.   Genethliaca in the form of eclogues are rare in Neo-Latin
literature, but epithalamia and epicedia appear in great numbers.
Identification of persons is occasionally difficult; in the following
chapters, to the end of the book, it can be assumed that the identifi-
cations are those given in the editions cited in the bibliography or are
obvious to any reader of the Latin texts.   Where persons cannot be
identified, I have said so.

i

We have already met Giambattista Pigna (Nicolucci) of Ferrara
(1530-1575).   The tenth of his nonsatirical *Satyrae* is a genethliacon eclogue called "Salvius" (530 hexameters).   This is an exceedingly elaborate piece of work written to celebrate the birthday of
Cardinal Giovanni Salviati, nephew of Pope Leo X.   There are

obvious reminiscences everywhere of Catullus' *Marriage of Peleus and Thetis,* but it is not nearly so well done as in Giovanni Pontano's earlier *Lepidina.* The poem shows a great deal of technical skill; but 530 lines of birthday congratulations are too much for the modern reader.

The fourth of the purely bucolic eclogues of John Leech of Montrose and Aberdeen (ca. 1590–ca. 1630) is a genethliacon written to celebrate the birthday of the future Charles I, now ten years old. The poem is an excellent example of its kind; a full translation follows, both as an illustration of the genre and as a melancholy footnote to the later events of 1645-1649:

Thus far, my gentle Muse has fled the light,
But now must turn to sing of themes less trite;
No more the shepherd's pipe shall tell the tale
Of sweetest Syrinx dancing in the vale,
Or trill the joys of resting by the trees
While Amaryllis wanders in the breeze
And grazing flocks move slowly o'er the lea
Through lowly shrubs and under every tree.

What blaze now strikes, with unaccustomed light,
The dazzled heavens, startled with affright?
See how the flashing splendor northward streams
And dazes ev'n Boötês with its beams
What presage now, what fate this light portends,
Let *her* reveal, whose art the world defends:
Bring forth, in radiance clothed, your form divine,
O Themis, and assist this song of mine.
With voice prophetic now she sings the name
Of him that shall succeed the father's fame:
That father's wisdom mild and counsel sage
Has now restored for us the Golden Age:
Astraea's self to earth from Heaven descends,
And blesses all she sees, as warfare ends;
Peace now appears, her brows with laurel tied,
And Pallas brings her arts and crafts beside.
These promise to the Prince a happy life,
A further Golden Age, exempt from strife,
For whom the speeding chargers of the Sun
Their tenth celestial course have joyous run.

Recall your father's spirit, noble youth;
Fulfil our hopes; like him respect the truth.
With precious gems Britannia decks her hair,
Rejoicing loud she dons her raiment rare;
To celebrate this day of History's page,
Juverna's self forgets her wrinkled age.
Accept these gifts with favor, gracious boy,
That happy shepherds bring with tuneful joy:
Amidst the clinging ivy rises fair
The noble laurel for your golden hair,
The olive and the myrtle join their leaves
And crown the heaping pile of Ceres' sheaves.
The humble violet and lordly rose contend
To do you honor, and their perfumes blend;
The hyacinth and fair narcissus, too,
Unite to send their fairest blooms to you;
Acanthus and the lily now compete
To spread a fragrant carpet for your feet.
Now lovely Chloris, decked with garlands bright,
Prepares to give to you your royal right;
Now Pales and the Satyr-bands appear,
Sylvanus, and the Pan with pointed ear;
Now, too, Silenus and his lord draw nigh,
And bring you tribute from an eastern sky;
Nor shall the Nymphs and Fauns forget this day:
From hill and spring and wood they make their way.
Whatever harm exists from ancient times
Must now retreat and pass to other climes:
No longer shall the dragon's jaw dismay,
No longer shall the serpent's poison slay.

But when your rising youth shall shade your cheek
And when maturer age shall learning seek,
Then shall the orchards bloom unbidden here,
And grain shall ripen, with its tasseled ear;
From mournful cypress shall the honey fall,
And peace shall flourish in the hearts of all.
Then Pan shall pipe his music without end;
Apollo shall from Helicon descend:

The god shall take your hand and lead you forth,
The pride, the boast, the glory of the North!
Then shall Decorum sage, Persuasion fair,
The Graces, dancing from their sylvan lair,
The Muses, coming from their mountain-spring,
Shall all instruction and their favor bring.

But when, to manhood grown, and king's estate,
You learn to rule, and strictly meditate,
Then keep Juverna's land from quarrels free,
And rule this happy breed in amity,
From Thames to Tay, from Tay to rushing Dee,
From Shetland to the Channel's fretful sea.
Nay, more, the Gallic rivers and Moselle
Shall long to join your kingdom's rule as well.
No more need merchant sail the roaring main,
No more we hear the pauper's mournful strain,
No more will Englishmen be forced from home,
No more will hapless exiles wretched roam;
No ruin shall destroy the farmer's stores;
Ev'n toil shall disappear within these shores.
Unbidden, earth shall fragrant harvests bring
And perfumed herbs, to celebrate the King.
Unlabored harvests shall the fields adorn,
And clustered grapes shall blush on every thorn.
Untended, woolly flocks shall homeward speed,
And lowing herds secure from lions feed.
No more the stag shall flee the savage hound,
No more the wolf shall drag the hind to ground.
All fear shall vanish; then, from care set free,
All men shall live in peace and liberty.
May kindly fate prolong my life's extent
Till I may sing your full accomplishment;
Then should I strike the very stars with pride,
With Homer coupled and with Virgil tied!
Grow, then, in favor, and fulfil your fate,
Recall your father, and regard the state;
For, see, all nature lays its age aside,
Renews its vigor and augments its pride.

No more the sun, eclipsed, in darkness stands,
But sheds its brightest glory on our lands;
No more the moon, affrighted, hides her face,
But shows her silver light to every race,
While every star, through countless ages whirled,
Can promise only joy to all the world!

The second of the three eclogues of Antonio Figueira Durão of Lisbon (ca. 1617-1642) is a genethliacon (*Balthazar*; 48 hexameters—less than one-tenth the length of Pigna's eclogue on Salviati), celebrating the birth of Prince Philip of Austria, later Philip V of Portugal and Spain. It is a good piece of formal courtly verse, but scarcely outstanding; it is extremely formal, it is extremely decorous, and it is all rather dull.

The only other genethliacon to be mentioned is one by Gerrit Jordens (Gerardus Jordensius) of Deventer (1731-1803), entitled "Menalcas" (98 hexameters); this was written on the occasion of the birth of a son to Jordens' close friend, Jakob de Rhoer. Durão's poem on Prince Philip contains nothing pastoral save the solitary phrase "shaggy shepherds"; here the pastoral atmosphere is carefully maintained throughout—as verse the poem is certainly the best of Jordens' three eclogues; it is rather prettified here and there, but is a pleasant poem for all that.

ii

The earliest use of pastoral as a medium for the marriage poem (epithalamium) appears among a group of minor poets of the Venetian and Ferrarese territories during the early fourteenth century. The first such poem appears to have been written by one Antonio da Camplo of (?) Padua (*floruit* 1433) for the marriage of the daughter of a local physician named Cermisone. The poem has been printed, but I have not had the opportunity of reading it. Five years later Tobia del Borgo of Verona (*floruit* 1438) wrote a similar pastoral for the wedding of the remarkable bluestocking Ginevra Nogarola (1419–ca. 1465); and Leonardo Lusco of (?) Ferrara performed the same duty for Ginevra's even more learned sister Isotta (1418-1466); both poems limp rather badly, but their style is more similar to that of the classical Humanists than that of the Pre-Humanists.

Far more significant is the one eclogue of Count Niccolò d'Arco

(Nicolaus Archius; 1479-1546). Some of his Latin poems were published in three books under the title of *Numeri* ("Numbers," i.e., "Rhythms") at Mantua in 1546; they became popular in the eighteenth century—new editions appeared in Padua in 1718 and 1739 and again (with the addition of a fourth book) in Verona in 1762. Nearly all his amatory verse still remains in manuscript. The collection displays Niccolò d'Arco as a kindly man of retiring nature, with an excellent style that owes much to the poems of Marcantonio Flaminio; Tiraboschi with reason considers him one of the best Neo-Latin poets of the sixteenth century.

The third book of the *Numeri* contains one eclogue, entitled "Galatea" (31 elegiac lines). The poem is a pastoral prothalamium honoring the betrothal (1545) of Galatea (Catherine, daughter of Ferdinand, brother of Charles V) to Faunus (Francesco Gonzaga, first Duke of Mantua); the "Lycidas" of the poem is, presumably, Niccolò d'Arco himself. At the time of the betrothal Duke Francesco was only twelve; Mantua and its territories were being ruled (extremely well) by his uncle, Cardinal Ercole Gonzaga, and by Margherita, widow of Federigo Gonzaga II.

Lycidas urges Galatea to come to Faunus, now that peace has returned to northern Italy, promising a Golden Age of prosperity; he goes on to describe the warmth of the greeting that she will receive and the beauty of the masses of flowers that will decorate her apartment. Lycidas passes to a rhapsodical description of Galatea's beauty and then to a more restrained catalogue of the manly virtues of Faunus; he prophesies the happiness of their married life and the popularity they will enjoy. In actual fact the marriage lasted only four months: Francesco died early in 1550 at the age of seventeen, and a year later Catherine was briskly married off to Sigismund Augustus of Poland.

Much more matter of fact is the long (258 hexameters), untitled epithalamium written by Joachim Camerarius of Bamberg (1500-1574); it is the eighteenth of Camerarius' bucolics and although called an eclogue has few pastoral details. This poem, written for the marriage of the poet's friend Erich Volkmar, relates how the young man made his way in early spring from Hesse to Meissen in order to claim his bride Lucretia. Here (as in the *Obstetrix* of Giorgio Anselmo and the ninth eclogue of Antonio Geraldini) a chorus appears: a group of young women describes the bride's beauty, praises the institution of marriage, and prophesies healthy children. Beginning with line 147 a group of young men praises the groom and his family: they laud to the skies his oratorical ability and his knowledge of civil and canon law, and then, in extremely outspoken language indeed, promise Volkmar the delights of a virgin bride. The poem closes with further praise of the institution of marriage. It is not nearly so dull as the reader might think.

We return to the pastoral atmosphere in an untitled eclogue-epithalamium of 93 hexameters by Matthaeus Argyllander (of Wittenberg?; born ca. 1500?), of whom all that is known is that he was a contemporary of Camerarius and that he wrote excellent Latin— the present poem, written for the wedding of Argyllander's own sister, is an unpretentious work that would deserve a place in any anthology of Neo-Latin pastoral.

Argyllander is known only by name; but the next poet that we meet is one of the most famous men of the sixteenth century—Jean Dorat (Auratus) of Limoges (ca. 1502-1588), certainly the best French Hellenist of his day. Of him Mark Pattison remarks that he represents "the moment in French literature when Greek learning was in alliance with public taste and polite letters."

His first five eclogues form a sequence of poems in celebration of the marriage (1570) of Charles IX of France and Elizabeth of Austria. Of these poems the first is introductory, setting the stage; the remainder are courtly panegyrics of a special and, to us, not especially attractive kind—their point depends on a number of anagrams on the names of the royal pair. The anagrams are certainly clever; but they are learned trifling of a sort that has long been out of fashion in any sort of verse, Neo-Latin or vernacular.

In 1571 appeared another pastoral epithalamium celebrating the same marriage, a poem written by Légier Duchesne (ca. 1520-1588), who Latinized his name as Leodegarius à Quercu. Like Dorat, Duchesne became a professor at the Collège Royal, where he made himself notorious for the virulence of his attacks on Calvinists. After the death of Coligny and Petrus Ramus he addressed several astoundingly violent poems to Charles IX in which he urged the extermination of every Huguenot in France; his later defense of the massacre of St. Bartholomew's Eve is even less attractive.

The present eclogue (untitled; 165 hexameters) begins with a conversation between two shepherds, by name Euthymus and Synesius, who conclude from omens lately observed that a new Golden Age is about to burst upon a waiting earth. At line 47

Euthymus is startled by cannon explosions; at this point Galatea, newly returned from Paris, assures her two friends that these explosions are those of guns saluting King Charles and his bride. Her description of the triumphal arches, flower-strewn streets, and the like is followed by one of the "nymph" Elizabeth, her husband (given the pastoral name of Codrus), and of the attendant servants.

Turning once more to Italy we find that the tenth and eleventh poems in the *Sylvae* of Giambattista ("Cinzio" or "Cinthio") Giraldi of Ferrara (1504-1573) are pastoral epithalamia. Giraldi began his career as professor of medicine and philosophy at the Ferrarese Studio; in 1541 he succeeded Calcagnini as professor of Latin and Greek literature; after a quarrel with the ducal family of d'Este he taught literature at Mondovi, Turin, and Pavia. But he is best known for his hundred novellas (*Ecatommiti*), the finest of all imitations of the *Decameron*.

The tenth poem of the *Sylvae* (Ferrara, 1537) celebrates the wedding of Bartolommeo Prospero (one of the secretaries of Duke Ercole) to a lady called Beatrice. Here a shepherd called Lycon systematically catalogues the charms of Phyllis and the virtues of her betrothed, Nisus. The poem is a pastoral reworking of an elegiac epithalamium written a few months earlier for another Ferrarese wedding—no doubt Giraldi was busy and felt that he must kill two birds with one stone.

The eleventh poem of the *Sylvae* is again a pastoral epithalamium, this time in honor of the marriage of Francesco Guarini of Ferrara to a lady called Ursina Machiavelli; in this poem Pan praises the groom (Alcon), and the assembled nymphs praise his lady (Alcippê), in phrases not much different from those of the earlier poem. But one reason that this poem shows greater evidence of care than its predecessor is that Ursina's sister Fulvia was Giraldi's wife.

The remainder of the poets to be considered here are, with the exception of the last, all Germans. First we meet Georg Sabinus (Schuler) of Brandenburg (1508-1560), regarded by Germans of his own day and by the twentieth-century critic Georg Ellinger as by far the most important Neo-Latin poet of the Wittenberg group. The best discussion of his life and love-lyrics appears in Adalbert Schroeter's *Beiträge zur Geschichte der neulateinischen Poesie Deutschlands und Hollands* (Berlin, 1909), pages 129-52.

Of Sabinus' two eclogues the second (untitled; 192 hexameters) is a pastoral epithalamium for the marriage of Albert, Marquis of Brandenburg, and Anna Maria, daughter of Erich, Duke of Brunswick. In this lengthy specimen of court-poetry, the speakers are Palaemon and Faustus. It is not very enthralling reading for us today, since, like Camerarius' eighteenth eclogue, it contains a great deal of genealogical detail on the Brandenburg and Brunswick families that can be of interest to only a few readers of the twentieth century. But the last part of the poem is worth reading at least once, with its vivid references to knightly combats and its one attempt at homely humor. If one were to begin reading Sabinus with this poem, however, one would never guess how much far better verse does appear in the collected edition of the poems (Leipsic, 1581).

Of Johann Seidelius practically nothing is known, except that he was born in Ohlau, probably about 1510. In 1554 he published at Wittenberg a pamphlet containing an untitled pastoral epithalamium of 218 hexameters celebrating the wedding of Lucas Conon to Dorothea Arnold. There is less contrivance here than in many other epithalamia, and more of an attempt at realism in portraying the rustics. Seidel has more affinities with such poets as Mantuan, Eoban, or Cordus than with Georg Sabinus, Johann Stigel, or Peter Lotich.

The Latin poems of Johann Schosser of Emleben (1534-1585), published in Leipsic in either 1560 or 1561, have an appendix containing epithalamia on his marriage written by Johann Bocer, Lactantius Johannes Codicius, Michael Haslob, Tobias Hubner, David Chytraeus, Johann Bockel, Johannes Posselius, and Wenceslaus Ecker, plus a few letters of congratulation from Georg Sabinus, Philip Melanchthon, and Justus Menius. Of the epithalamia only one is pastoral—that by Wenceslaus Ecker of Pilsen (born ca. 1520?), an untitled poem of 134 hexameters. Of Ecker himself little is known, although his name certainly appears in distinguished company.

Despite some over-prettified passages, the occasional few lines that follow Virgil too closely, and some excessive learning, this poem is one of the best of Neo-Latin pastoral epithalamia. It is lively, amusing, and well written and, despite the incrustations of literary convention, displays a warmth of feeling for the man whose wedding it was intended to celebrate; its one real oddity is that it has remarkably little to say about the bride.

In Joachim Camerarius' eighteenth eclogue and Georg Sabinus' fourth we met the sort of pastoral epithalamium in which genealogical detail is emphasized; at least one pastoral epithalamium occurs in which the panegyric of the bride and groom (as in the prose wedding orations of Francesco Filelfo) becomes a most elaborate exercise in genealogy. The poem in question is the sixth eclogue (untitled; 647 hexameters) of Peter Lotich the Younger of Schlüchtern (1528-1560), which celebrates the wedding of Johann Wilhelm, Duke of Saxony, to the Hessian princess Dorothea. At first sight the reader may well be appalled at all the elaboration; but, if he once summons up the hardihood to plunge into this poem, he may find much to attract him, for Lotich's skill as a Latin poet is sufficient to overcome even such massive disadvantages as the form of the poem imposes on him.

Sebastian Scheffer of Aldenburg (born ca. 1530?) is another German Neo-Latin poet of whom very little is known; he was a student of Georg Fabricius and a friend of Camerarius (who was greatly his senior), and certainly spent many years at the University of Leipzic. His extensive collection of Latin poetry was published at Frankfort in 1572.

His one eclogue (untitled; 306 hexameters) was written for the wedding of Wolfgang Eilenbeck, an official at the court of Augustus, Elector of Saxony, and Ursula Lindemann (a widow); it is only half the length of Peter Lotich's sixth eclogue but seems twice as long— it contains some of the flattest, prosiest, heaviest lines imaginable.

The Neo-Latin pastoral epithalamium appears to have died an ignoble death at this point, but it was resurrected once more in late seventeenth-century France for a royal wedding. Louis XIV and the members of his immediate family were subjected to a veritable flood of Latin poetry between 1650 and 1690. The commonest form of poem addressed to the Roi Soleil is the formal Alcaic or Sapphic ode, in which references to Apollo are as common as the sun-motif in the decorations at Versailles. The theme of the new Golden Age, naturally, is recurrent in scores of poems addressed to the King, poems that took the form of odes, panegyrics, epinicia, requests for favors, *gratulationes,* laments, epigrams, and so on. Almost as many Latin poems were addressed to the great-grandson of the Roi Soleil, Louis XV; but I know of only three Latin poems addressed to Louis XVI (in 1775, 1782, and 1785), and one to

Louis XVIII (in 1822) ; many, however, were written on Napoleon, one of them an eclogue to be discussed in a later chapter.

Amidst all this profusion we find a pastoral epithalamium written by Julien Fleury of Paris (ca. 1650-1725). Fleury's life was wholly without incident: after a conventional education he taught in various minor positions until he was appointed professor of rhetoric at the Collège de Navarre and also Canon of the Cathedral of Chartres. He was associated with Pierre-Daniel Huet in editing the series of Latin texts produced *in usum Delphini* (the Apuleius is his, and it is one of the best editions in the whole series). He wrote one eclogue (untitled; 212 hexameters) celebrating the marriage (1680) of the Grand Dauphin to Maria Anna Christina Victoria of Bavaria, the Princess Palatine; as far as I know, this is Fleury's only published verse, and certainly it is a very competent piece of courtly poetry, worth reproducing in a full translation to conclude our consideration of pastoral epithalamium:

Damon: Since on the grass our flocks together feed,
        While rougher goats prefer the river's reed,
        Come, rest beneath the pleasant, leafy shade
        That lofty beeches and the elms have made.

Tityrus: This very spot invites the swain to sing,
        For Nature has accomplished all the spring:
        The violets and hyacinths arise
        And flourish now beneath the sunny skies.
        Begin you first, and either sing the praise
        Of her, to Spain removed in recent days,
        Or one that loves his sweetheart without end;
        Begin: the willing lad your flock will tend.
        Myself shall join your song in due refrain;
        Then shall you raise your tuneful voice again.

Damon: Such themes, 'tis true, attract my rustic lay,
        But greater themes befit this happy day:
        The shout of "Daphnis!" rings throughout the land,
        The name of Daphnis sounds on every hand.

Tityrus: I, too, have sought, with kindly rustic strain,
        To sing of Daphnis and his lovely flame.
        We now can join in praising wedlock true,
        And Thyrsis can decide between the two.

See, now he comes in view near yonder tree
And leads his goats to pasture on the lea.
Shall we contend in song with pledges set?
This yearling from the fold shall be my bet.

Damon: Two thriving lambs have I, but lately grown;
Now, Thyrsis, choose, and choose the best alone.

Thyrsis: My age has bid the Muse a long farewell,
My pipes no more with wanton music swell,
But hang forgotten by my cottage door:
But yours are songs that I should love to hear:
Your pipes are tuneful and your voices clear.
Meanwhile my flock can satisfy their need;
Start, Damon, and let Tityrus succeed.

Damon: Set laurel, festive Muses, by the road:
A lovely bride on Daphnis is bestowed.
This glory of the lands has all his love:
Weave floral garlands and your favor prove.

Tityrus: Now light the torches, Muses, for the train;
Escort the maiden to the fertile plain;
The eager groom awaits his shapely bride,
The rustics' songs resound by Danube's tide.

Damon: All Pindus loves Apollo's tuneful son
Whose rustic song the Muses' prize has won;
None can withstand the father's martial fire:
What beauty can deserve such groom, such sire?

Tityrus: So Amaryllis, with her tuneful strain,
Charms every rustic through the Noric plain;
Her modesty enhances all her charms:
What sire, what groom's deserving of her arms?

Damon: So long as Daphnis loves the shepherds' lay,
No warlike bugle shall that song outweigh.

Tityrus: So long as Amaryllis loves to sing,
Minerva's skill must be a lesser thing.

Damon: Both come of kingly race, and both are kind,
And both to hear the Muses are inclined:
Each one is worthy, and of equal mind.

Tityrus: As vines deserve the elm tree's solid aid,
As faithful doves by loving mates are stayed,
So she deserves the man, the man the maid.

Damon: Now leave your father's house, resplendent maid,
Now leave, and let the love of homeland fade;
Let silken veils conceal your maiden charms,
And know that Daphnis now awaits your arms.

Tityrus: Now, Daphnis, leave your royal home in state;
Now welcome her who comes to share your fate;
Fair Amaryllis makes her joyous way,
To be saluted by yourself today.

Damon: See where she comes, surrounded by her train,
See how the torches sparkle through the plain,
How flutes resound along the river's brim,
And hills re-echo with the joyous hymn.

Tityrus: From caves excited come the Naiad bands;
Ev'n Father Rhine arises from the sands,
Where late in sad defeat he grieving fled
And hid from mortal sight his gory head,
When great Apollo ravaged all his lands
And made him cringe before his conquering hands.
Now has he gained at last a glad release,
Since Amaryllis's heart is pledged to peace:
Her wedlock ends the battle's fearsome roar,
And Rhine will love her name for evermore.

Damon: Go, lovely maid: attain that blessed land,
And greet Apollo with a loving hand,
Lest dreadful sounds of arms affright our men,
And rivers flow with brothers' blood again.
The sword forgotten, bugles laid aside,
Let Gallic groom receive the German bride:
Let valleys ring as shepherds dance along,
And let the fields resound with rustic song.
Amidst rejoicings of the Gallic race,
Be met by Daphnis with a fond embrace,
Let every day be filled with pleasure bright,
Let tranquil rest receive you every night.

Both late recalled to Heaven by God's decrees,
Your sons for long shall rule our destinies.

Tityrus: No word she speaks; but blushing ever fair,
She drops her glance, and ponders Heaven's prayer.
Our hopes she answers, for with gracious tread
She now advances to the river's bed:
See how the Graces all attend her side
And Cupids flutter near the destined bride;
Fair Hymen, too, with flowers above his head,
Leads all the joyful throng with stately tread.
Now gleams the Gallic shore with cheerful flame
As shouts of welcome rise, and rise again.
Now dawns a Golden Age of peaceful joy,
For flocks no longer need the shepherd-boy;
No hawk attacks the dove with cruel claw;
No wolf attacks the fold with raging maw;
But crowds of rustics sing, on every hand,
"Let Hymen Hymenaeus rule the land."

Damon: The fleecy sheep can wander in the hills,
The grazing herd can grace the river's rills;
If Venus fail to raise their number high,
The flock will dwindle and the herd will die.
(Let Hymen Hymenaeus rule the land).

Tityrus: Crops fill the fields and blooms the garden-space;
But from the skies if showers refuse their grace,
Earth's bosom's bare, and ev'n the richest field
Will lack the blooms and lose the harvest's yield.
(Let Hymen Hymenaeus rule the land).

Damon: The birds delight the ear and please the view
The sea is filled with fish of every hue;
If Venus fail to make the pairs agree,
No birds will fly, no fish swim in the sea.
(Let Hymen Hymenaeus rule the land).

Tityrus: The woods resound with shepherds' songs of glee;
The maids in frolic dance upon the lea:
If Venus' ardors leave our native shore,
No songs shall ring, no dances flourish more.
(Let Hymen Hymenaeus rule the land).

Damon :   Love warms the lovers with affection's might;
           But if they fail to join in Hymen's rite,
           Fair Venus cannot aid their ardor's flame,
           Or grant the honor of an honest fame.
              (Let Hymen Hymenaeus rule the land).

Tityrus :   Love can restore the signs of war's disgrace,
           And bless with progeny our fertile race;
           If Hymen fail to join us with his tie,
           No lawful children please the parents' eye.
              (Let Hymen Hymenaeus rule the land).

Damon :   See, now the joyful maid approaches plain;
           The hills and rivers past, she sees our train.
           Delay not, Daphnis; go, salute and greet
           The bride that you have ever longed to meet.
           See how her eyes with fond affection glow,
           The lips like cherries and the breast like snow;
           Lo, how her cheek with mantled blushes fires
           To see the object of her chaste desires.
              (Let Hymen Hymenaeus rule the land).

Tityrus :   Fair Amaryllis, see your groom advance;
           See how he welcomes you with tender glance.
           Remove the modest veil with gesture glad,
           And fix your chaste regard upon the lad:
           Observe the youthful features of the Heir,
           The modest bearing, and the kingly air,
           The mind rejoicing in the Muses' lyre,
           His mother's beauty and his father's fire.
              (Let Hymen Hymenaeus rule the land).

Damon :   Let youths now celebrate the coming rite,
           As Vesper heralds the approach of night;
           See how the torches burn with brighter flare,
           A happy omen for a happy pair.
              (Let Hymen Hymenaeus grace the land).

Tityrus :   The bride accompanies the youthful god,
           Nor stumbled on the threshold as she trod;
           All favor Heaven grants the pure of heart,
           The bride has come; let nuptial music start.
              (Let Hymen Hymenaeus grace the land).

Damon: He reckons every shining star that glows,
        Who every joy that now awaits you knows.

Tityrus: He reckons every fragrant flower that grows,
          Who every joy that now awaits you knows.

Damon: Soon shall a son reward the happy pair,
        Whose features shall the look of either share;
        Each parent shall the infant mind refine,
        And urge Iolas to the Muses' shrine.

Tityrus: Pierian nymphs, attend that infant's bed,
          And rouse immortal longings in his head:
          Let song remain his first and greatest love,
          And may he charm the Powers that rule above.

Damon: The lily shall adorn his every day,
        The violet, narcissus, and the bay;
        The very bees shall bring their fragrant store
        To give him all the eloquence of yore.

Tityrus: Begin, Iolas, as you gaze about,
          Your parents' countenance to single out;
          And when Apollo rests from war's alarms
          Rejoice when cradled in his mighty arms.

Damon: Where Lilies tame the Lion's raging eyes,
        This tell to me: then take the lamb as prize.

Tityrus: Where Eagles quail before Apollo's flame,
          This tell to me: then take my pledges twain.

Thyrsis: When I can rest and hear such songs as these
          Once more I love the light and pleasant breeze.
          So slight a difference in your singing lies
          That both have won, or both deserved the prize.
          Among my flock, now feeding on the plain,
          These two are best: I gladly give the twain.
          These take, as both deserving of the best;
          These take, then singing lead your flock to rest.
          Now let the hills rejoice in Daphnis' fame
          And woods re-echo Amaryllis' name.

iii

The third section of this chapter deals with the use of pastoral as epicedium (dirge), a common practice, of which the Latin example best known to English-speaking readers is John Milton's "Damon's Epitaph" (*Epitaphium Damonis*), a pastoral dirge on the death of Charles Diodati.

Among Italians the first to put the pastoral epicedium to contemporary use was Giovanni Pontano of Cerreto (1424-1503), in his second and third eclogues. In the second poem, "Meliseus" (248 hexameters), Pontano records his own grief at the death of his wife Adriana Sassone, calling her, as always, Ariadna and himself Meliseus. Here two shepherds, Ciceriscus and Faburnus, meet and speak of Meliseus' sorrow. It is a sincere and eloquent poem—as one would expect of Pontano—and it is notable throughout for its characteristically warm tone of domestic affection; but it is marred by a certain eccentricity in diction and content, to say nothing of repetitiousness. The curious name "Ciceriscus" sets a tone of oddity which is maintained throughout most of the eclogue and causes no little discomfort to the reader. For all that, this poem appears to have been the most famous of its type in Italy; imitations and reminiscences are very numerous indeed, and not in pastoral poems alone. A partial version follows:

Cic.: Here Meliseus sang his song of grief
And carved these words beneath the hazel leaf:
"Your death, your death I saw, my dearest wife;
Yet did not die as you withdrew from life."

Fab.: Poor Meliseus, has this second dart
Now taken Ariadna from your heart?
A daughter's life fled wailing on the breeze,
And left you weeping by the willow trees.

Cic.: Her name re-echoed through the sounding plain
As Meliseus sang his sad refrain:
"I follow, Ariadna, follow soon,
I follow, Ariadna, through the gloom."
And as he sang, below a wooded hill,
He cast aside the pipe, that murmured still,
"I follow, Ariadna, follow soon,
I follow, Ariadna, through the gloom."

Fab.: Has he now cast that shepherd's reed from view
That charmed the water-nymphs and Muses, too?
Has neither Corydon nor Thyrsis sought
To find the pipe amid the grassy rot?

Cic.: The nymph Patulcis found it by the hill
And keeps it as a gift for Daphnis still
(For Daphnis, who shall sing the poet's praise
When he has reached the limit of his days).
She touched the silent reed with tender hand,
Then sighed, and with her voice filled all the land:
"Beside her husband Ariadna sowed,
Beside her husband still she toiled and hoed;
She stored the harvest at her husband's side,
The stalks she gathered in a round and tied;
Beside her husband, winnowed golden grain,
As both rejoiced to sing their songs again.
At night she laid her weary limbs to rest,
Beside her husband, to his bosom pressed.
Now torn from family, home, and husband's care
Her soul has vanished through the yielding air;
Now Proserpine has carried her below
And Meliseus lives in silent woe.
Let field and garden mourn her early death,
Let home and neighbors grieve with every breath;
Let even drooping crops in fields lament
The lost reward of labor fruitless spent.
The very meadows and the willow-bed
Lament her loss, nor count the tears they shed.
In sadness, woods and valleys sound her name;
The rocks re-echo with the sad refrain.
The lofty mountains "Ariadna!" cry,
The streams and rivers mourn her, gliding by.
Let owls assemble in a mourning throng,
Let nightingales repeat their woeful song,
Let every bird from every tree complain,
Let every leaf join in the sad refrain.
With practiced hand she plied the spinner's art,
And as she span she sang with merry heart.

In shining mounds, the fashioned threads were laid
In wicker baskets she herself had made.
The weaver's art then followed spinner's skill;
Domestic labors kept her busy still:
For child and husband clothing must be made,
And she herself in mantles be arrayed,
To take to market fruit and early rose,
To take to altar every flower that grows.
But even as she span the gathered wool
And filled the ever-waiting basket full,
The spinner-Fates released the purple thread
And cast a grievous shadow on her head.
Could neither merry heart nor labor save
And keep her body from the woeful grave?
Once fed by Ariadna's loving hand,
The mourning doves in deep dejection stand;
Once, as she wove, they fluttered to and fro,
And kissed her fingers as she let them go.
The swallow from its lofty nest would dart
When Ariadna's merry song would start:
The busy spinning wheel, revolving, whirred,
As Ariadna watched the darting bird.
Now let the swallow grieve and murmur low;
Now let the kinglet sing its equal woe:
Let shepherds gather in the country lane,
Let every flock and herd with grief complain,
Let caves re-echo with their tearful groan,
Let even mountains and the shadows moan.
Shut goats and sheep within the fold again,
You maiden daughters of the rustic plain,
And, while your mothers weep before the bier,
Seek every tender flower that blossoms here;
Recall the husband's grief, the son's regrets,
The while you weave a wreath of violets.
When you yourselves have called aloud her name,
Inscribe these lines to swell her growing fame:
'In place of spindle, wheel, and busy loom
We bring these blossoms to the silent tomb,
And lay them down amid the verdant shade
That waving laurel and the cypress made.

In place of skillful work in warp and weft,
These tears we bring to you of life bereft;
These bowls of milk and honey here we lay,
And bid a long farewell this grievous day. . . .'" (1-101)

The third eclogue, "Maeon" (*77* hexameters), written on the
death of a Neapolitan physician named Paolo Artaldi, is a curiosity
among epicedia. Here two shepherds, Syncerius (Sannazaro) and
Zephyraeus (no doubt some other member of the Neapolitan Academy), meet and express their grief over Maeon's death, lamenting
that the only reward for his labors and discoveries is oblivion. They
bid his spirit farewell and resolve to enjoy life while it is still possible to do so; the remainder of the poem (*33-77*) consists of a
cheerful amoebaean interchange of couplets, quatrains, triplets, and
the like (arranged 2, 2, 2; 4, 4; 6, 6; 5, 5; 3, 3, 3). The two singers
celebrate the voluptuous kisses of Phyllis and the more modest
caresses of Lychnis, the grace of Acilla and the tuneful voice of
Philaenis, the pleasures of summer days and those of winter eve-
nings, and so on. It may not be everyone's notion of an epicedium,
but it is undeniably a very fine piece of Latin poetry.

The first of the six eclogues of Giano Anisio of Naples (ca.
1475–ca. 1540) is a pastoral dirge of 133 hexameters, entitled
"Meliseus," mourning the death of Giovanni Pontano (1503). The
shepherd Mycon repeats to Aegilus the lament (its recurrent refrain has a curiously jaunty rhythm) supposedly uttered by that
excellent Neo-Latin poet Giovanni Cotta of Vangadizza (1479-
1510). There is nothing original in the poem.

Baldassare Castiglione (1478-1529), born of a famous and
ancient family at Casanatico near Mantua, is known to everyone as
the author of "The Courtier"; but he was also a fluent and readable
Latin poet of great elegance whose talents were recognized and rewarded by so good a judge as the Medicean Pope, Leo X.

In Latin poetry Castiglione's work has strong affinities, in its
formal aspects at least, with that of Bembo, Cotta, and Navagero—
grace and elegance abound, but there is little depth of feeling, except
in the poem we are now about to examine, a pastoral dirge of 155
hexameters called "Alcon." Since this poem is excellent in any case,
and since it almost certainly exerted a strong influence on John
Milton's *Epitaphium Damonis*, it is worth giving a full version:

Now snatched from glowing life while still a boy,
Young Alcon, in his life the maidens' joy,
Whom fauns and dryads always loved to hear,
To whom Apollo lent a willing ear—
Him every shepherd wept throughout the plain,
But in his grief Iolas led the train:
The stars, the Fates, the gods he chided sore;
Not Philomel for fledglings sorrows more,
Nor gentle dove, whose careless mate has died,
The victim of a rustic bowman's pride.
No more he rested in the beech's shade,
Nor heard the music that the river made;
But still lamented with a piteous groan,
And filled the lofty forest with his moan.
No day was free from lamentation's cry,
From early dawn to evening's flaming sky.
No more was it Iolas' heart's delight
To drive the cattle forth at morning light,
Or lead the flock toward the river's brink
And watch their merry frolic as they drink;
But ever, in the woods or by the shore,
Indulged his grief for Alcon ever more;
Forgetful that the darkness was at hand,
He thus lamented to the rocks and sand:

"My Alcon, darling of the Muses' heart,
And of my loving soul the greatest part,
What god, what fate has torn you from my **breast,**
And why must death come early to the best?
No farmer harvests wheat before its time,
Or grapes that hang unripened on the vine;
Yet cruel death has plunged your life in night
And torn your tender years from mortal sight.
With you have perished all the country's charms;
All joy and pleasure vanish from our farms.
From all the mourning forest fall the leaves,
Denying pleasant shade to him who grieves;
The meadows lose their beauty, grasses die,
The springs are languid, and the rivers dry;
The fields deny their promised yield of wheat,
The harvest withers in oppressive heat.

Unkempt the flock, unkempt the shepherd, too;
Unguarded stables lie exposed to view:
No longer skulking in the fearful wood,
The hungry wolf attacks, and tears his food.
All nature grieves, and sounds a sad refrain:
The woods, the springs, the brooks, the hills, the plain.
Your death is mourned by every woodland sprite:
The nymphs of Napê mourn throughout the night;
The shepherds see the tears of Pan revealed,
And satyrs weep in every rustic field.
But neither tears nor grief the Fates can move,
And vengeful Death is deaf to all our love.
When torn by plows the grasses rise again,
And clothe with verdant turf the fertile plain.
So, too, the Sun, that blazed so bright at noon,
Must set, to be succeeded by the Moon;
But, when refreshed by slumbers of the night,
He'll rise and view the earth with morning light.
For us, when touched by Lethê's chilly wave,
And locked within the confines of the grave,
For us no path appears; all hope must fade;
Eternal sleep involves us in its shade:
In vain our tears, in vain our mournful pleas;
Our prayers are ravished by the mocking breeze.
No more shall I, as throngs mill to and fro,
See Alcon win the contest of the bow,
Or hurl the skillful spear, or win the race,
Or best his fellows in the wrestling-space.
No more shall I at Alcon's side recline,
To rest from labor in the summer time;
No more his tuneful pipe shall charm the throng
Or praise Lycoris in a tuneful song;
No more shall Galatea's words acclaim
My voice and Alcon's as we strive for fame.
Together did we live, from mothers' breast,
Together did we share what each possessed,
Together bore the cold and summer heat,
Together shared our toil with friendship sweet.
What joy remains, when Alcon is no more,
Who died when I was on a distant shore?

A hostile fate removed me from my friend:
I could not touch him as he neared the end,
Nor close his eyelids at his death's approach,
Nor kiss his lips, nor hear his last reproach.
Far better fared Leucippus at his death,
For Alcon bade farewell with dying breath,
And gazed upon Leucippus as he fled,
And kissed him ere he joined the woeful dead.
Leucippus, you approached that humble bier,
And paid the tribute of an honest tear,
Then, mourning over, and the rites complete,
Accompanied his bier with dragging feet,
Yet soon refused your friendless life to save,
And followed Alcon to an early grave;
And now you tread with joy the Elysian shore,
And now shall live with Alcon evermore.
Some other shepherd, at the river's edge,
Had wept for both together, by the sedge,
Had prayed for both, for both had sung lament,
With accents joyless, and with clothing rent;
No tears I shed within that somber room,
No rites I offered to the common tomb,
For ignorant of death and fate's decree
I still could dream of happiness to be.
"Soon shall I see (I said) my native land;
Soon Alcon shall I see, and grasp his hand.
The frowning mountains and the rocky hills
He'll leave, to see my fields and purling rills.
My pastures shall he see, my rivers bright,
And feast his eyes on every lovely sight.
I'll rush to meet him as he comes in view,
Then greet him warmly, and be greeted, too.
Thus reunited shall we both rejoice
To see the other's face, to hear his voice,
And tell of hardship past and grief endured,
And hear the other's tale, of joy assured.
Then shall we two renew our former life
As peaceful rustics, free from noise and strife.
These favored fields are loved by every god;
The seed is fertile in the springy sod;

Here Ceres grants her choicest gifts to all,
And thriving flocks and herds fill every stall.
Within these hills the graceful nymphs delight
To hunt the beasts and lead the dance by night.
Here Tiber's stream in rapid current flows,
Past many an ancient temple as it goes.
Here are the woods, the springs, the rustic charms,
Where Corydon once sought Alexis' arms.
Then come, my youthful friend, to this estate:
You streams and woods and meadows all await;
The nymphs weave garlands for your handsome brow,
And wait with joy for your arrival now.
The fertile earth sends up her blossoms rare,
Though none of these can boast a bloom so fair."
This hoped I, witless of my wretched state,
All ignorant of Alcon's bitter fate.
Now that my hopes have vanished into air,
Now that his death has left me filled with care,
Now may his spirit fly to view my grief,
And see these tears that flow without relief.
An empty tomb I'll raise beside the stream
To quell my sorrow and recall my dream;
There shall I kneel throughout the summer day,
There, too, compose my grieving heart to pray.
Come, shepherds, join me by the empty tomb,
And duly scatter every fragrant bloom:
The blushing hyacinth, the roses red,
The white narcissus from its flowering bed;
Let ivy drape its leaves on every side,
And laurel spread its grateful shade beside.
Bring cassia, and eastern frankincense,
Whose odors overwhelm the fainting sense:
Young Alcon loved us all, and well we might
Accord such honors every day and night.
Meanwhile, let sylvan nymphs come into view
To scatter amaranth with honors due,
And mark this epitaph upon the stone,
Since even hills for Alcon can but moan:
> *Since fate removed him from our grieving sight,*
> *All sweet is bitter, day is turned to night.*

This poem was written in memory of a young Mantuan named Falcone who had been a constant companion of Castiglione at Urbino; his death occurred in 1505. Iolas, naturally, is Castiglione himself; Galatea can represent only Elisabetta Gonzaga, and the name Lycoris presumably stands for that of one of the ladies of the court. Leucippus represents Girolamo Castiglione, the poet's brother, who died in 1506, while Baldassare was in England.

Of the three eclogues published in the *Carmina minora* of Marco Girolamo Vida of Cremona (1485-1566), the third is a pastoral dirge, in large part, at least. In this poem ("Nicê"; 96 hexameters) a woman called Nicê (in Greek the word means "victory") has been lamenting the recent death of her lover Davalus; Damon (representing the secular world?) attempts to recall her from her excessive transports of sorrow, but with little success. Vittoria Colonna (ca. 1492-1547) is clearly the widow referred to (she is called "Nicê" in poems by Niccolò d'Arco and Marcantonio Flaminio) and Davalus is Hernando (Ferrante) d'Avalos, Marquess of Pescara, who died in 1525. Despite obvious imitation of Moschus' *Lament for Bion*, this poem is quite the best of the three eclogues of the *Carmina minora*.

We cannot be complimentary about another pastoral written by Vida, published separately at Rome in 1513 or 1514, under the title "Quercus." This poem is a bucolic lament in no less than 539 hexameters over the death (February 21, 1513) of Pope Julius II, the hero of Vida's unfinished epic, the *Juliad*. It is too long, it is too rhetorical, and it borrows far, far too heavily from Virgil.

Two epicedia appear among the sugary courtly eclogues of Julius Caesar Scaliger (his true name may have been Bordone) of La Rocca on Lago di Garda (1484-1558), who claimed to belong to the famous Della Scala family of Verona and indeed not only to be a lineal descendant of Can Grande della Scala but also a relative of both Matthias Corvinus of Hungary and the Emperor Maximilian. His own highly colored account of his early years has often been doubted, and with good reason. Whatever may be the truth about his early military and scholarly career, no one can doubt that after he settled in France (at Agen) in 1525 he did achieve an eminence in letters absolutely unparalleled by any other man of his time. His philosophical writings and his treatises on grammar, literary criticism, and the natural sciences gave him a tremendous international reputation: the doctrines of the *Poeticê* held sway in France until e Romantic period. Yet his violent animosities and his eternal assumption of omniscience eventually injured his reputation; succeeding generations refused to be dazzled by a man more brilliant han reliable and rightly awarded the palm to his far greater son (one of fifteen children), Joseph Justus Scaliger.

Among Scaliger's writings appear a prodigious number of Latin poems, many of them poor, and most of them of practically no interest oday, except as a historical exhibit. The most readable are his Catullan lyrics, written in hendecasyllabics, many of which are extremely witty, and his series of seven pastorals, entitled *Nymphae indigenae* and written at the castle of Basens at Agen. Most of hese eclogues are courtly and amatory and present a lively picture of the social life of the French-Italian group of aristocrats at Agen; two of the poems, however, are pastoral epicedia—the second and he sixth.

In the sixth eclogue, "The Nymph of Napê" (*Napaea*; 98 hexameters), a shepherd named Aelinus (Benedetto Scaligero or Bordone, he poet's father) laments the death of his wife (Berenice Lodroni). The worst faults of the poem, as in most of these eclogues, is the tendency for sentences to sprawl on at excessive length; had another Neo-Latin poet written this pastoral Scaliger would have had much to say in his *Poeticê* (had he deigned to notice it) about *duritia, inscitia,* and the like. The virtue of the poem is the close maintenance of pastoral atmosphere and of specific pastoral detail: there is not the painful contrast between form and content that we find in many German Neo-Latin bucolic poems. Its chief curiosity is the fact the Benedetto actually died before his wife.

The second eclogue, "The Mountain-Nymph" (*Oreas*; 70 hexameters) again deals with the Scaliger family. The poem is rather uninteresting, on the whole, and is marred by technical flaws that Scaliger could easily have avoided.

Three pastoral dirges appear on the death (1548) of the eminent poet and prince of the Church, Pietro Bembo, all anonymous and all undistinguished; we can afford to ignore these, turning instead to Basilio (originally called Pietro) Zanchi of Bergamo (1501-1558), a poet of very considerable abilities. Zanchi was educated at Bergamo by Giovita Rapicio, gained the favor of Pope Leo X at Rome by his extreme fluency and facility in Latin verse, and joined the *Canonici regulares Laterenses* in 1524. He then traveled extensively through Italy and continued to do so even after Paul IV ordered all monks to return to their monasteries in 1558; for his disobedience Zanchi was promptly committed to the Castel Sant' Angelo, where he died the same year.

Among his poems (Rome, 1550), all of which had a remarkable vogue in sixteenth-century Germany, the major work is the allegorical "Garden of Wisdom" (*De horto Sophiae*), two books of hexameters on the doctrines and principles of Christianity. Of his four eclogues, the third, "Phyllis" (90 hexameters), is a pretty but unimportant art-pastoral. The first, "Meliseus" (132 hexameters), is a pastoral dirge on the death (1503) of Giovanni Pontano of Naples. At dawn Amilcon brings out his flock, and while they feed he laments his friend's death: he calls on Nature and the nymphs to grieve, and himself regrets that Meliseus' music and verses will never again be heard. There is naturally much local reference to Mergillina, Sebeto, Posillipo, and the like throughout the poem. The second eclogue, "Damon" (105 hexameters), is rather heavier. Lycidas asks the cause of Thyrsis' gloom and his friend bursts forth (19-105) into a long lament on the death (1529) of Damon (Baldassare Castiglione). An additional fifth eclogue (which I have never seen) laments the death (1529) of Andrea Navagero. These three pastoral epicedia show Zanchi's literary affiliation—with the Veneto-Lombardic poets, the Roman Academy, and the Neapolitan Academy. The fourth eclogue, "Licmon" (184 hexameters), is again a pastoral epicedium on the death of a fellow poet, this time Giovanni Cotta (died 1520). This eclogue is notable for the passage (147-163) in which Zanchi congratulates Cotta on having died before he could witness the horrors attendant on the sack of Rome (1527).

There are dirge eclogues by Luigi Pasquale of Rome (*floruit* 1550), Francesco Vinta of Volterra (*floruit* 1560), Giambattista ("Cinzio") Giraldi of Ferrara (1504-1573), and Pompeio Arnolfino of Lucca (*floruit* 1570), but none of these melancholy poems makes much of an impression on the reader.

Two of the four eclogues of Pietro Angelio of Barga (1517-1596) are pastoral epicedia. The third poem deals with the death of Caterina Cibo-Malaspina; the eclogue—it is entitled "Evageê" (97 hexameters)—is extremely elaborate. Caterina Cibo, Duchess of Camerino, was much admired by sixteenth-century writers for her singular knowledge of Greek and Latin; some of her vernacular poems are still extant. This poem is well written and adroit; its chief drawback is its tone of sugary sweetness.

A good deal preferable to the third is the fourth eclogue—"Varchius" (120 hexameters), a lament by the Etruscan nymph Daphnê at the grave of Varchius (the Neo-Latin poet Benedetto Varchi, 1503-1565). It is quite as dexterous as the third and repeats a good many of the stock ideas already used there, but avoids the saccharine manner that had marred the earlier poem—the eighteenth century would have called this the more "manly" poem, as indeed it is.

Of the six eclogues of Marco Publio Fontana of Bergamo (1548-1609), the sixth is a burlesque of the pastoral epicedium—a lament, already examined, for a pet goat. The second poem, "Daphnis" (192 hexameters), is a straightforward yet elaborate epicedium on the death (ca. 1574) of the Latin poet Giovanni Antonio Taigeto (Taygetus, i.e., Taglietti) of Brescia (often confused with the other Neo-Latinist Giovanni Angelio Taigeto of Brescia), whose brilliant *ecloga nautica* describing the battle of Lepanto will be examined in a later chapter.

Of the four eclogues of Giovanni Battista Arcucci of Naples (*floruit* 1560-1570), the first two are pastoral epicedia. The first poem (untitled; 88 hexameters), addressed to Archbishop Mario Caraffa of Naples, is an eloquent lament on the death of the poet's sister. The poem naturally introduces many stock effects, but does avoid excessive elaboration and in addition is unusual in presenting a picture of the death scene.

The second poem (also untitled; 74 hexameters) is a dialogue between Amyntas (the poet) and another shepherd, named Lycidas. The poem is of the highly stylized variety: after a brief introduction, the two shepherds sing a series of fourteen quatrains (lines 14-69) that are not only amoebaean but notably antithetical as well. Amyntas praises the poetic abilities of his one-time instructor (whom he calls Uranius) and laments his death; Lycidas praises the beauty and charm of Phyllis (probably Ippolita Gonzaga) and regrets her early death. Uranius is described as a Neo-Latin poet who had written didactic poems on astronomy and the culture of oranges; this sounds rather like Pontano, but he had died a quarter of a century before Arcucci was born.

Among the extensive poems (Paris, 1642) of Maffeo Barberini (later Pope Urban VIII) of Florence (1568-1644), two eclogues appear, of which one is a pastoral epicedium. This poem ("Iulus";

100 hexameters) was written after the death of the famous general Alessandro Farnese (1545-1592), great-grandson and namesake of Pope Paul III, after 1580 Duke of Parma and from 1578 to 1581 governor-general of the Low Countries for Philip of Spain. The poem is a monologue uttered by "Iulus'" sister Galatea as she wandered near Mantua on the banks of the Mincio. She laments her own loss, asks herself why such a man should have been struck down at so early an age, calls on nymphs and Nature to mourn forever, and promises eternal faithfulness to her brother's memory. There is nothing, in other words, that is unusual about the contents of the poem; its expression is graceful, elegant, smooth, and rather cold and over-correct. In the whole poem there is nothing, either in its virtues or its vices, to distinguish it from the work of a dozen other Neo-Latin poets one might name.

We can pass over the astoundingly dull *Ecloga pastoralis* (299 hexameters) of Andrea Catullo (*floruit* 1650), in which is deplored the death of Andrea Mangelli, and at least mention a poem by Agostino Favoriti of Lucca (1624-1682), secretary to the college of Cardinals at Rome. It is odd that a poem on so close a friend as Sidronius Hosschius should be so coldly formal ("Aegon," 127 hexameters).

The last Italian Neo-Latinist to be noticed here is Niccolò Giannettasio of Naples (1648-1715), two of whose piscatory eclogues are epicedia. The ninth, "Dorylas" (104 hexameters), is a lament on the death of the poet's most promising pupil, Oronzio Montalvo; Dorylas is Giannettasio, Iolas is Montalvo, and Anthus is Niccolò Cesareo, another student at Naples. In this poem—a typical piscatory eclogue in every way—the fisherman Dorylas laments the death of Iolas and is duly comforted by young Anthus. The scene is, as usual, the beach, the usual loving references to the Bay of Naples and its famous beauty-spots appear in every other line, and allusions to every sort of fisherman's paraphernalia are even more frequent than they are in Sannazaro.

The fifth poem, entitled "Thyrsis" (101 hexameters), is arranged as dialogue, not as two set speeches. Corydon (Alfonso Filomarino) suggests to Mopsus (a young friend of Alfonso, name uncertain), that they rest at the mouth of a seaside cave and urges him to sing, complimenting him on his skill in music and poetry and insisting that his abilities surpass those of his rival Iolas as a swan surpasses a grebe in beauty and sweetness of voice. Mopsus replies with a lament (20-47) on the death of Thyrsis (Alfonso's brother Ascanio, Count of Torre Annunziata and nephew of Cardinal Ascanio Filomarino).

The use of the eclogue as epicedium was almost as common in Germany as in Italy; but the quality of the verse is, in general, rather low, and it will be sufficient merely to indicate rather summarily the poets and the persons commemorated.

The sixth eclogue of Elius Eobanus of Bockendorf or Halgeshausen in Hesse (1488-1540) is entitled "Iolas' Epitaph" (*Epitaphium Iolae*; 122 hexameters). Here Daphnis, on being questioned by Meleterus about his downcast appearance, laments the recent death (1509) of Iolas (Wilhelm II, Margrave of Hesse); Meleterus encourages Daphnis by reminding him that the successor to Iolas is the excellent young man Eurynomus (Philip of Hesse)— thieves will soon fly the country, wolves will be checked, and the young of the flocks will be safe.

Johann Fabricius of Metz (1527-1566), Swiss by descent but Alsatian by birth, was educated first in Switzerland and later at the University of Marburg, where he came in contact with Peter Lotich the Younger. On his return to Switzerland he married a twenty-year-old girl with whom he seems to have enjoyed the happiest of marriages, which, however, lasted little more than a year, for the young woman soon died in childbirth. Her death is mourned with obvious sincerity in an eclogue called "Orion" (104 hexameters). After an introduction of half-a-dozen lines we have a monologue uttered by Orion (Fabricius) over the death of Threnê: every field blooms, flowers spring in every meadow, and birds sing merrily —he alone is dejected. Fabricius' technical skill does not even approach Lotich's, but the merits of this poem are great, for all that.

The fifth of the eclogues of Peter Lotich the Younger of Schlüchtern (1528-1560) is a pastoral epicedium entitled "Daphnis" (161 hexameters); it is a dialogue between a huntsman called Celadon and a fowler named Myrtilus, in which is lamented the recent death of an Alsatian friend and fellow poet who had evidently spent part of his life in Italy and had met his death by drowning in a river. We know that Hilarius Cantiuncula (Hilaire Chansonette) on completing his studies in Italy, was drowned in the Rhine and that this poem was dedicated by Lotich to Baron Saurau, who was a distant relative of "Daphnis."

Georg Bersman of Annaberg (1536-1611) we have already met

as the author of three unremarkable religious pastorals. He was a prolific poet, and one part of his work seems to the modern reader a trifle lugubrious: he published two considerable collections of epicedia on the deaths of the great and the learned. The third poem of Book II is an eclogue called "Alcon" (129 hexameters) on the death (1574) of Joachim Camerarius; it is a pastoral re-working of *Epicedia,* II, iii. This poem is certainly far from outstanding and certainly borrows with an over-eager hand from Virgil; but it has more interest than the religious pastorals.

We come now to the name of Bernardus Praetorius of Hesse (*floruit* 1580-1600), whose *Ecloga funebris* commemorates the death (in 1592) of a later Wilhelm, Margrave of Hesse. This is one of Neo-Latin literature's most remarkable documents: Virgil's eclogues vary in length between 63 and 111 lines (the average is 83); this overpowering dirge extends to 5,500 hexameters, a work of epic dimensions, covering 158 pages of small print in the *Delitiae poetarum Germanorum.* Vida's pastoral lament for Julius II (539 hexameters) and Lotich's pastoral epithalamium (647 hexameters) seem moderate by comparison.

The pastoral epicedia of the French Neo-Latinists not only deal —at least in the sixteenth century—with more interesting persons but are usually far better written than those of the German authors just considered. The earliest author here is Simon Nanquier of Paris (born ca. 1460), whose family name appears to have been Lecoq or Du Coq. He was probably a Benedictine monk, attached either to the abbey of St. Faron or to the convent of Cerfoir. Two major poems are extant, and both can be read with interest—an elegiac poem on human life (*De miseria hominis*) dedicated to Robert Gaguin and Publio Fausto Andrelini, and an eclogue (untitled; 179 hexameters) on the death (1498) of Charles VIII of France. The two poems were published together under the title "The Deceptive Course of Time" (*De lubrico temporis curriculo*).

The eclogue, although decorated with false quantities, syntactical errors (more politely termed medievalisms), and unrhythmical lines, and although written in a rough manner almost totally devoid of art, is at least interesting from its tone. Much of it is decidedly satirical in manner, and one does not have to read far before realizing that, eclogue or no eclogue, the poem derives its diction and themes and *sententiae* not from Virgil but from Juvenal, with occasional echoes of Lucan.

The pastoral epicedium does not appear to recur in France until exactly sixty years later (1558), in the first eclogue, "A Memorial for Mellin St.-Gelais" (*Tumulus Mellini Sangelasii*; 354 hexameters in the unpublished first version) of Jean Dorat of Limoges (ca. 1502-1588). Nanquier's poem was more than inclined to be shambling and shapeless; Dorat's, though simple in outline, is a consciously elegant work. A comparatively brief introduction is followed by a huge series of quatrains, each with a recurrent refrain, uttered by the shepherds Carylus (Lancelot de Carle) and Dorylas (Dorat). The poem often becomes tiresomely rhetorical and repetitive: the poet *must* find a balancing quatrain for Dorylas each time, and genius does not always burn. But the eclogue is fluent and readable, if occasionally rather obscure. By far the most valuable parts of the poem, for the modern reader, are those digressive passages in which the poet describes how St.-Gelais had originally presented him to the king and comments on the relations between St.-Gelais, Ronsard, and Dorat on the one hand and Henri II, his sister Marguerite, Charles of Lorraine, and Odet de Coligny on the other. In 1586 Dorat issued a revised and much abbreviated version of the poem from which much of this material, all of interest and even importance for the literary historian, had been cut. Even so, the revised version runs to 198 hexameters.

Of Gervais Sepin of Saumur (*floruit* 1550) we know little that is precise. We know the names of his parents, of one brother and one sister (there were others), and of the teacher (Robert Carré) who grounded him thoroughly in Virgil and Cicero. As a young man Sepin entered the services of François du Bellay de Lire and his wife Louise de Clermont (a relative of Diane de Poitiers), as tutor to their only son, the delicate Henri. Sepin accompanied the family on their removal to Paris, and was fascinated by what he saw there; his opportunities for observation were almost unlimited, since Louise was a close friend and confidante of the Queen (Catherine de Médicis). Dependent or not, Sepin not only found ample opportunities for gallantries with minor ladies of the court but also scraped acquaintance, and more than acquaintance, with Jean Salmon (called Macrinus or Maigret, the French Horace, protégé of Cardinal Jean du Bellay), who doubtless lent his good offices to the publication of Sepin's Latin poems (*Erotopaegnion libri tres,* Paris, 1553).

The seven eclogues were later in date. The first six were written before Henri's premature death, as didactic poems in pastoral form, intended for the instruction of the poet's youthful pupil; the seventh poem, "Alexis" (367 hexameters), was written in memory of Henri, who died at the age of thirteen on May 7, 1555. This eclogue, which runs from page 818 to 829 of Volume III, part ii, of the *Delitiae poetarum Gallorum,* is not only long but elaborate as well. In Mopsus' lament for his youthful ward Alexis, we have the usual reproaches addressed to Heaven, the doubts about the possibilities of a future life, recollections of happier days, panegyric of the boy's virtues and intelligence, promises of an annual rite at the grave, and the like, the whole decorated with classical allusions, mythological digressions, elaborate similes and metaphors, artful anaphoras, apostrophes, rhetorical questions, and all the paraphernalia of the most erudite form of poetic rhetoric. But beneath the crust of artifice can be discerned a real affection for a clever, delicate pupil: "la vie et le rêve se mélangent dans une mélancolique harmonie" (Alice Hulubei).

The next French author we meet is Antoine Fumée, Sieur de Blandé (1511-ca. 1575). Fumée, born of a well-known family of Touraine, became, as early as 1536, an active member of the Paris *parlement,* eventually becoming *maître de requêtes* (an office his father had held under François I) and an adviser of the King of France. As a suspected crypto-Protestant he was later forced to retire from Paris to Orléans in 1562; but in 1563 he was attached to the Breton *parlement* and became its president in 1572. The accession of Henri III (1574) he celebrated by a brief but lively flurry of literary activity—a history of the Creation in French, a panegyric (also in French) on the occasion of Henri's return from Poland, and three courtly eclogues in Latin ("Daphnis," "Amaryllis," and "Livia"); but Fumée's responsibilities as courtier, adviser, and lawyer prevented him from devoting any further time to literature. This is no great loss, for, although he is a correct and often a dexterous versifier, the general effect is one of mediocrity.

The eclogue "Livia" (141 hexameters) was published as a pamphlet, at Lyon and certainly late in 1574 or early in 1575. Here Fumée commemorates the death in childbirth of Marie de Clèves (the King's mistress), as did Desportes, Passerat, Pasquier, and Ronsard. This is the best of the three pastoral poems—straightforward in expression, smooth in rhythm, restrained in manner; it is quite clear, incidentally, that Fumée had read Dorat's poem on Mellin de St.-Gelais with care.

Here a shepherd named Iolas lies dreaming by a spring. A vision of his sweetheart Livia appears to him, pale and sad of face. He tries to embrace her, but the shade swiftly disappears, crying, "Livia is dead, and handsome Iolas grieves!" As Iolas gazes about him in fright, he catches sight of a funeral cortège of birds (this is borrowed from Dorat). Below them, suspended by cords hung from the birds' necks, floats a coffin in which is placed the body of Livia. Other birds draw along a carriage in which is placed the statue of a young woman reclining on a dark-purple bed, around which are grouped doves and their young: at this point Iolas realizes the truth—that Livia had not survived the pain of childbirth and was indeed actually dead. He bursts into self-reproach and then into lament for the dead girl and praise of her beauty. Finally, Iolas awakes and goes in search of his flocks. One curiosity about the poem (one of the very few dream-eclogues in Neo-Latin literature) is that Henri III seems in fact to have had a warning dream at Lyon, when returning from Provence to Paris—Ronsard and Passerat both allude to it.

We now come to François Tillier of Tours (ca. 1515–ca. 1580), who was an advocate in his native city and is today known only from a rare work entitled *Philogamê, ou ami des noces* (Paris, 1578), a collection of translations of erotic and salacious passages taken from classical and Renaissance Latin verse, and a single eclogue (untitled; 110 hexameters) lamenting the death (1574) of Henri III's predecessor, Charles IX. It is a dialogue between the rustics Gallus and Damon, in which lines 79 to 106 are quatrains. Fumée's poem is unusual in being a sort of phantasmagoria; but Tillier's is wholly conventional—one shepherd pours forth laments, wishing that he had never been born to see this day, and another asks in astonishment what has caused his grief; the first shepherd gives only a partial answer and is gradually drawn, in an interchange of couplets, to say flatly that King Charles is dead (line 41). The two then exchange laments for the next thirty lines or so, after which Gallus suggests alternate songs, with forfeits. This last is an unhappy touch, for it recalls one of the stock situations of pastoral lovers about to praise their respective sweethearts.

Tillier's epicedium on the death of Charles IX and Fumée's on that of Henri III's mistress Marie de Clèves are followed by another on the death (1589) of Henri III himself—the overblown, pedestrian, long-winded, unimaginative, and wholly unpoetic "Alcon" of François Petremot of Paris (ca. 1528–ca. 1600), *maître de requêtes* to Henri III. What little we know of Petremot is derived from a hasty note scribbled on the title page of the unique manuscript of the poem (it has never been published) in the Bibliothèque Nationale. The event it describes is well known—the last Valois king was stabbed to death by Jacques Clément. Much of the poem is taken up with an epic narrative of the victories of Daphnis (Charles IX), the election of Damoetas (Henri III) to the throne of Poland, his return (1574) to France on his brother's death, and his allegedly glorious reign. All this leads up to a narrative of the assassination of Damoetas by a man in priest's clothes (the assassin's name is indicated at line 484 when the adjective *inclemens* is used, and again at 522, where *inclementia* appears).

Far better is the untitled eclogue (97 hexameters) produced by Pierre de Vallongnes (*floruit* 1650-1660), a Jesuit instructor at the Collège de Clairmont, of whom I have been able to learn literally nothing. His poem is a lament for the death of a three-year-old child named François Foucquet or Fouquet, conceivably a son of Nicolas Fouquet (1615-1680); if this supposition is correct, then the "Alcimedon" of the poem may well refer, as in other French Neo-Latin verse, to Louis XIV. Certainly the print of the pamphlet in which this eclogue was published (no place and no date are given) suggests the 1650's, and the elaborate care with which the poem is written suggests a highly-placed family as the addressee. It is a very attractive eclogue; there is much conventional detail, but, as Vallongnes' sympathy does not seem assumed, the modern reader can examine the poem with more than antiquarian interest. Moreover, the intimations of immortality and the religious romanticism of lines 10 to 29 are likely to impress him as distinctly unusual in so formal a genre as pastoral.

A contemporary of Vallongnes was Pierre Halley or Hallé of Bayeux (1611-1689), a well-known jurist, orator, and poet of the mid-seventeenth century. Halley studied at Caen and not only gained the chair of rhetoric there at the age of twenty-four but became the rector of the University in 1640. In 1646, thanks primarily to his own abilities but also to the good offices of Pierre Séguier, the French chancellor, he was appointed Regius professor of Greek and Latin at Paris and in 1654 became professor of law.

In Book IV of his poems (Paris, 1655) appears a pastoral epicedium ("Lycidas"; 136 hexameters), on the death of "Capreolus," i.e., the Carthusian Jacques du Chevreuil or Chevreul, Regius professor of philosophy and principal of the Collège d'Harcourt. Among the rustic characters of the poem Aegon represents the writer, Lycidas du Chevreuil, Amyntas Pierre Padet, and Thyrsis Antoine Halley. The eclogue is followed by four brief epitaphs on du Chevreuil in elegiac verse of which the first is typical:

> No leisure was my lot: for all my life
> Was toil and worry, study, care, and strife;
> Ev'n at my final hour still forced to stand,
> At last I rest, through death's relenting hand.

On this quatrain a marginal note says, "The disease from which he died prevented him from lying down": presumably this refers to something like bronchial asthma.

We have already examined the two religious eclogues of the Jesuit René Rapin of Tours (1621-1687). The third eclogue is an epicedium of 95 hexameters, entitled "Alphonsus." It is very readable; but there is nothing unusual or even interesting about it. Two shepherds, Illus and Almon, lament the premature death of a young man who had evidently been one of Rapin's most promising pupils.

The next poet—again a Jesuit—to whom we turn is Robert d'Esneval (born perhaps ca. 1660), of whom I have been able to learn only the fact that he was a professor of rhetoric at the Collège de Clairmont in 1701, in which year he published, as a four-page pamphlet, an untitled pastoral lament of 79 hexameters on the death of Louis XIV's brother, Philippe, Duke of Orléans, called Timander in the poem. The eclogue is certainly competent in structure and expression but introduces nothing beyond the stock themes. A few lines, in their allusive references to contemporary events, provide the reader with entertaining puzzles.

Finally we meet Jacques Charles Aubry (born 1689), who at the age of twelve years and eight months produced an untitled bucolic dirge of a little over 100 hexameters on the same subject as Robert d'Esneval's poem. It is preceded by an insufferably pompous dedicatory letter addressed to young Charles's instructor in Latin, Guillaume de Segaud, S.J. The precocious schoolboy calls himself *parvulus . . . humanista* and adopts the tone of a leading

Italian fifteenth- or sixteenth-century Humanist; the preface to his 1702 volume of Latin epigrams is even more priggish. In Master Aubry's poem, Alexis, Corydon, and Daphnis lament the death of Philippe, describe the siege of St. Omer, and praise the noble duke (who was in fact sadly mediocre and immoral to boot). There is no attempt at pastoral fiction: Louis XIV is not, say, Alcimedon or Hercules Gallicus, but Lodoïcus; Philippe is simply Philippus, Borbonius, or Borbonis; St. Omer is Audomarus; Mt. Cassel is Casselicus Mons; the French are Francigenae or Liliaca gens; and so on. Aubry is not, of course, describing anything he has seen; he is not even reproducing contemporary accounts: he is snipping out bits and pieces from the *Aeneid* and other poems and pasting all together. This poem, from start to finish, is the worst sort of Neo-Latin posing, and the fault is entirely that of this wretched boy's instructors.

Among Dutch Neo-Latinists the pastoral epicedium appears a few times, beginning with Jakob de Sluyper (Sluperius) of Herzele (1532-1582), whose eighth eclogue, "Menalcas" (397 hexameters) records the death (1574) of Franciscus Richardotus, bishop of Artois; even for de Sluyper, the poem is long-winded and flat.

Much more interesting and far more readable is the "Daphnis" (102 hexameters) of Janus Dousa the Younger (Jan van der Does) of Noortwyck, near Leyden (1571-1597), eldest son of the lord of Noortwyck. After elementary schooling at Noortwyck, Dousa studied from the age of twelve at Leyden, his most famous teacher being Justus Lipsius. Dousa had all Aubry's precocity without his priggishness. He was an expert in Latin, Greek, Hebrew, law, ancient history, and mathematics, and practiced Latin verse composition from childhood. At eighteen he was appointed private tutor to the children of Louise de Coligny, widow of Willem I. Two years later, in 1591, he was made librarian at Leyden. In 1594 he visited England with his two brothers, and, on his return in 1596, joined Philippe Duplessis-Mornay in a trip to Poland, but was forced to return through illness and died suddenly at his home at the age of twenty-six. He was a *Wunderkind,* but a pleasant one; the great Scaliger said of him, "Le pauvre Jean était si bon, si simple!"

Among the poems (the most complete edition is that of G. Rabus, 1704) appears a single pastoral epicedium: it is a dirge, no doubt much revised before publication, on the death of Sir Philip Sidney at the battle of Zütphen (1586). The song of Lycidas, as he stands by the river Thames, describes the conventional situations and introduces the stock motifs; nevertheless this work is typical of the work of the *poetae Belgici* at their very best: it is not too long, it is not excessively panegyrical, it is not maudlin. It is, admittedly, expressed with all the self-conscious virtuosity of the Neo-Latin littérateur, but for all that is as sincere and honest a tribute as any Englishman might have written.

The "Thyrsis" (129 hexameters) of Daniel Heinsius of Ghent (1590-1655), on the greatest scholar of the age, the younger Scaliger, Joseph Justus (1540-1609), should be read in conjunction with Heinsius' funeral oration on Scaliger and that of Domenicus Baudius (1561-1613). English versions of both appear in G. W. Robinson's *The Autobiography of Joseph Scaliger* (Harvard, 1927). Heinsius was deeply attached to Scaliger, and the poem is correspondingly effective, despite the excessive use of an elaborate rhetoric of the sort we have already had occasion to observe in the elder Heinsius' Latin poetry.

A younger contemporary of Heinsius, called *ornatissimus* and *praestantissimus* by the great scholar of Leyden, was the Frisian Leo Aetsema of Franeker (*floruit* 1610-1620), whose epicedium (untitled; 58 hexameters) on a prince of Brunswick we may pass over as illustrating all too well Mark Pattison's description of later Neo-Latin and vernacular pastoral as "the dilapidated debris of Arcadianism." We shall also ignore the eighth eclogue (untitled; 112 hexameters) of the Jesuit Willem Beke (*floruit* 1655-1665), already met as a writer of religious idylls; the poem, which commemorates the death of Natale Rondinini, secretary of briefs to princes under Pope Alexander VII and brother of Cardinal Paolo Rondinini, is in fact not an *ecloga* but an hexameter epicedion pure and simple—there is not a single pastoral allusion or expression in any of its 112 lines.

The last Dutch Neo-Latinist to be mentioned here is Peter Fransz (Francius) of Amsterdam (1645-1704), the sixth and last of whose eclogues ("Lycoris"; 146 hexameters) is a pastoral epicedium on the death of the poet's sweetheart, a monologue in the poet's own words, with the twelve-times-repeated refrain, "extinctam Siculae lugete Lycorida Musae." The poem is extremely elaborate and highly rhetorical, in the manner of Heinsius: antithesis and **anaphora** are done to death.

In English Neo-Latin poetry the first appearance of the pastoral epicedium seems to be in the first and fourth eclogues of Giles Fletcher of Watford in Hertfordshire (ca. 1549-1611). He was educated at Eton and Cambridge, where he became a fellow of King's in 1568; he was made Deputy Orator of the University in 1577 and granted the degree of LL.D. in 1581. He served as a diplomat in Scotland, Russia (where he was shockingly ill-treated), and Germany but after 1589 devoted the remainder of his life to service of the court and the law in a large variety of positions; he must have been a very honest man or a very quarrelsome one, for the record of his ups and downs is spectacular. His writings—few of which are of general interest today—were numerous, their titles filling two columns in the *Dictionary of National Biography.*

Like much English Neo-Latin verse of the period, the two eclogues referred to above have an extremely old-fashioned ring by comparison with the more sophisticated contemporary Latin verse being produced on the Continent and in Scotland. The first pastoral, written while Fletcher was still an undergraduate at Cambridge, is on the death (1659) of the notorious Edmund Bonner; it is less an epicedium than an aggressive defense of Protestantism; the fourth poem, "Adonis," is similarly an early work, in which Lycidas (Roger Ascham's friend Walter Haddon, himself a good Latin poet) laments the death of Adonis (Haddon's son, Clare).

Two pastoral epicedia were written by William Gager of London (1555-1622), one of England's best-known Neo-Latin writers, leader of a group of University wits at Christ Church. Both lament the death of Sir Philip Sidney. In these poems, as Leicester Bradner points out, we find a real grief, a real reaction to national shock at the death of a brilliantly promising man; we also find, in contrast with the younger Dousa's poem, much awkwardness of expression and many technical faults of versification.

We can pass over the wholly conventional and unimaginative pastoral dirge, "Meliboeus," on Sir Francis Walsingham's death (1590), written by Thomas Watson of London (1557-1592), author of the eighteen art-pastorals called *Amyntas* and *Amyntae gaudia.* We can omit likewise the various pastoral epicedia (anonymous) published at Broadgates Hall, Oxford, on the death of

Henry, Prince of Wales, in 1612 (these I have not read, but Leicester Bradner speaks highly of them), and turn to the Neo-Latin pastoral dirge most likely to interest English-speaking readers, the "Lament for Damon" (*Epitaphium Damonis*; 219 hexameters) of John Milton (1608-1674), a poem on which A. S. P. Woodhouse remarks that "*Lycidas* and the *Epitaphium Damonis* are the crowning achievements of Milton's early verse . . ."; but Woodhouse vastly overestimates the originality of Milton's treatment of the themes of pagan lament and Christian consolation.

Of John Milton's Latin poems, all except one belong to the period before 1639. Some were written as early as 1626, but, in accordance with Neo-Latin practice, had certainly been extensively revised and polished before final publication. In 1645 Milton called them "vain trophies of my frivolity" ("nequitiae . . . vana trophaea meae") ; but it is noteworthy that he so described them in the volume in which he also took good care to publish them. A complete English version of the pastoral lament for Damon (Charles Diodati, who died in 1638) appears in any edition of William Cowper's poetical works.

Turning to the Scottish Neo-Latinists, we first meet David Hume of Godscroft, near Dunbar (ca. 1560–ca. 1630), controversialist, poet, and historian. Hume was educated at St. Andrews, and, after some travel in France and Switzerland, became secretary to his cousin Archibald Douglas, eighth Earl of Angus. His Latin verses, many of which appear in the *Delitiae poetarum Scotorum,* were published in London in 1605, but most were written a great deal earlier than this date; later editions appeared in Paris in 1632 and 1639.

Hume's verse (which earned the praise of so discerning a critic as George Buchanan) is fresh, vigorous and lively, showing a wide and deep acquaintance not only with the classical Latin poets (Ovid above all) but also with contemporary French Neo-Latinists. Least successful among his poems are the four eclogues; he seems, as Leicester Bradner rightly points out, to be chiefly interested in the mechanisms and machinery of this genre, and this, I would suggest, is largely owing to the influence of French courtly Neo-Latin eclogue —at his most elaborate and artificial Hume reminds the reader all too strongly of Jean Dorat.

The first eclogue, "Philomel" (*Philomela*; 77 hexameters), is in part a pastoral lament over the death (1603) of Amaryllis (Elizabeth I). As usual, all Nature mourns; but this well-worn theme soon gives way to the equally threadbare motifs of panegyric. At the coming of Daphnis (King James) the whole world blooms with roses and eagerly looks forward to a new Golden Age of peace and prosperity; jealousy and fear now vanish, Pan and Pales return to the hills and the plains, and Saturn's *aurea saecula* reappear. The poem is of historical interest only.

Five eclogues, as we have already seen, appear in the works of John Barclay of Pont à Mousson (1582-1621), author of the *Argenis* and *Satyricon*. Of these poems one ("Daphnis"; 114 hexameters) is a pastoral epicedium of some interest, although it has little real distinction as verse. Here Tityrus and Corydon lament the murder of Daphnis, under whose rule a Golden Age has dawned on earth. All this evidently refers to the assassination, in 1610, of Henri IV and the succession of Louis XIII under the regency of Marie de Médicis.

The second piscatory eclogue ("Dorylas"; 115 hexameters) of John Leech (Leochaeus) of Montrose and Aberdeen (ca. 1590–ca. 1630) is a dirge uttered by the fisherman Lycabas on the death of the poet's father, Andrew Leech. The arrangement of lines in Lycabas' song is extremely formal; after six introductory lines ("Where were ye, Nymphs?" *o ubi vos, Nymphae?*) and refrain, the poem proceeds by a gradual expansion: two couplets (each with refrain) are followed by two triplets or triads (again each with refrain), and refrains continue to follow each of the successive pairs of four, five, six, and then seven lines.

The last poem to be mentioned in this chapter is one by Antonio Figueira Durão of Lisbon (ca. 1620–ca. 1645), already met before now. Of his three eclogues the third, "Viennus" (77 hexameters), is a pastoral dirge for the poet's father. It presents nothing new, being constructed on the usual pattern of lament, panegyric, and consolation distributed as dialogue between Durianus (the poet) and his friend Andrianus (unknown). Durão is a skilled versifier, but few readers, surely, will be able to find this poem anything but depressing, even if they do not come upon it after fifty other poems of a precisely similar type.

XI

NEW USES OF PASTORAL:
PUBLIC

n the third, or "public," class of the new uses of pastoral appear panegyrics of public men, victory poems (epinicia), courtly eclogues, and poems that deal with contemporary events.

i

In the last chapter we saw the tone of panegyric recur constantly in pastoral genethliaca, epithalamia, and epicedia; pastorals intended as panegyrics pure and simple are common during the Renaissance and later. Perhaps the earliest Humanist to employ Neo-Latin pastoral thus was Basinio de'Basini of Vezzano near Parma (1424-1457), whose eclogue on the accession (1447) of Pope Nicholas V is better forgotten.

Four of the ten pastorals of Matteo Maria Boiardo of Scandiano (1441-1494) are panegyrical. In the first eclogue (*Syringa*; 100 hexameters) appear the god Pan and a rustic named Poeman, who presumably represents the poet. Pan says that he has deserted Arcadia, the bucolic paradise, where there is now nothing but disturbance and even war and has sought out the peaceful streams of northern Italy: at this Pan bursts into a panegyric of the labors of the Hercules of myth and of the achievements of the new Hercules

(Duke Ercole d'Este) who excels even the merits of his remote ancestor (the Estes claimed descent from Charlemagne).

In the fourth eclogue (*Vasilicomantia*; 100 hexameters) Boiardo pretends to relate an ancient prophecy of a Golden Age fated to begin in northern Italy 1440 years after Christ's birth (cf. lines 18-21). It was in 1441 that Borso d'Este (d. 1471) succeeded to the rule of Ferrara. The poem is relatively conventional, introducing in the usual manner the usual themes of peace, prosperity, and miraculous fertility of the soil.

The framework of the sixth eclogue (*Herodia*; 100 hexameters) has a familiar setting. The poet tells how at dawn he had been wandering near the foot of a hill near Ferrara and had heard the shepherd Bargus singing the story of Italy from its earliest times; he sang of primitive Italy, of the arrival of Aeneas, and of the early kings and heroes of Rome, until at length he came to describe the Este family, especially, of course, Duke Ercole.

In the ninth pastoral (*Hercules*; 100 hexameters) the two speakers are the shepherds Tityrus and Corydon; in this poem there is much more of the pastoral proper than in the first and sixth.

The last of the ten poems (*Orpheus*; 100 hexameters) narrates the story of Hercules' loss of Hylas and tells how Orpheus tried to comfort the hero in song. The song itself (34-72) proves to be a prophecy of the future Golden Age in Italy under the beneficent rule of a namesake and descendant of Hercules himself. The remainder of the poem is straightforward panegyric, celebrating the military exploits of Duke Ercole in Calabria, Sicily, and elsewhere. Like all of Boiardo's bucolic panegyrics, this poem is well written but rather dull; the constant references to the modern Hercules pall, even on the most sympathetic reader.

A far better poem than these is an eclogue called "Damon" in ninety-nine hexameters by the Venetian Andrea Navagero (1483-1529), which is in part a panegyric of Pope Julius II.

The poem can be dated with ease. On Easter Sunday, 1512, a bloody battle was fought at Ravenna between the Holy League (the Papal Corps and the Spaniards) and the French army of Louis XII, led by Gaston de Foix and allied with Alfonso d'Este of Ferrara. De Foix was killed outright at the moment of victory, a victory gained largely through the accuracy of the French artillery. The papal captains surrendered; even the papal legate, Fabrizio Colonna, was taken prisoner. Two months later, the situation was reversed,

with the French in full flight and the desperate Duke of Ferrara
begging for mercy from the savage old man who occupied the
throne of St. Peter. This is clearly the campaign described in
Navagero's prologue as an introduction to the theme of panegyric,
the entire poem being treated in terms of pastoral convention. It is
wholly typical of its class, and I accordingly append a translation in
full; incidentally, the shepherds Damon and Aegon represent Castiglione and Pontano:

> Arise, you nymphs, from Ocean's deepest waves
> To hear my song, and leave your glassy caves;
> Come, make my music worthy of my theme,
> While thus I sing by Adriatic's stream:
> Not all the flowers of all the summer days
> Suffice as garlands for the one I praise.
>
> What sorrow spread throughout Italian plains,
> What mourning filled the land with plaintive strains,
> When from the icy Alps the foeman tore
> And plundered all the wealthy Roman shore!
> Reluctant grew the grass within the glade;
> Reluctant fell at night the grateful shade;
> For, see! the flocks are driven from their stalls;
> The foeman burns the barns and shepherds' halls!
> The goat-foot fauns, the hornèd satyrs fled;
> Each lovely nymph in terror hid her head.
> Now had the fury filled the land entire:
> All Italy endured the foeman's ire.
> See where in troops the ruffian soldiers roam:
> They ravage city, forest, farm, and home!
> No spot so sheltered in the smiling plain,
> No crag so lofty in the mountain-chain,
> No hill so void of pasture, none so cold,
> No ground so unreceptive to the fold,
> But that the roving bands drove off the flocks,
> Protesting dumbly, from familiar rocks.
> Advancing slow, these heard the billows' roar,
> And gazed affrighted at the unknown shore:
> In place of clover, shrub, and verdure green,
> In place of willow and the sedges' sheen,

They drank the brackish waters of the lea,
And dreaded murmurs of the angry sea.
Had not our champion foiled that foreign band,
And driv'n the foeman from our native strand,
Then not a shepherd had been left to see
Destruction rife on every ruined lea;
Then had we wandered to a foreign shore
And begged for shelter at a stranger's door.
This man restored us every field and glade:
"Now graze (he said) the oxen in the shade;
Now let the shepherd sing a merry tune;
Now let the hills with music echo soon!"

As to Apollo and to Pan, the swains
Each year shall pray to you throughout the plains.
All now is joy, in place of bitter woe:
The rocks, the stones, the valleys—all shall know
The shepherds' joy, the shepherds' songs of praise,
The hymns of thankfulness we all shall raise.
Whatever oak shall flourish in the plains
We'll deck with presents from the grateful swains;
We'll carve your name upon that sturdy tree,
That every rustic ever mindful be:
When forth or back he leads the lowing flocks
The farmer shall recall the battle-shocks
And know that peace by *you* has been restored,
That blessings on this land by *you* are poured!
Should you accept our worship with a nod,
Our prayers shall rise to you as to a god:
Myself, I'll raise a double altar fair,
And place the votive laurel garlands there,
There, too, perform the solemn yearly rite
That seeks your peerless merits to requite,
While blossoms on the springing meadow blow
And birds make all the world resound below.
There shall the rustics all, from morn till night,
Contend with heavy spear or dagger light,
Or send the winged arrow into space,
Or struggle in the contest of the race;
There shall the brawny wrestlers grapple long
To gain the prize and earn acclaim in song;

There, too, shall Damon sing the artful lays
He learned at Naples in his younger days.
So once, the captive of the Syrian swain,
Dionê floated to this earth again;
The stars rejected and the heavens declined,
She sought Adonis and with him reclined.
With you, Adonis, did she tread the rocks,
And milk, with milk-white hand, the wanton flocks,
And, while embracing you, did not refuse
The byre, the stall, the stable, or the mews!
There Mars, neglected, wasted in his baffled ire;
Here did the lad enjoy Dionê's fire:
Here, lying in the shade, he sang her charms;
Here, laying pipe aside, he sought her arms.
To him the goddess gave her warm embrace,
And shed a sweet enchantment from her face.
So, Damon, were you blessed, so fortunate,
Whose youth was favored by a kindly fate;
So could you rest beside Sebeto's rill
And learn the songs of aging Aegon still.

Had fate permitted me such joyous days,
What plaudits, mighty Father, could I raise!
What little skill Apollo grants to me
Shall be devoted still to praise of thee;
Nor should I wish for more poetic art
Than needful to applaud your hand and heart:
When I attempt in verse *your* mighty name
To none am I inferior in fame!
With me should Damon's self in verse contend
Ev'n Damon would be vanquished in the end!
Meanwhile, receive the tribute of a rustic song,
And guard the Peace for which you strove so long.

In Marcantonio Flaminio of Serravalle (1498-1550) we come
to one of the best-known literati of the sixteenth century. His early
education was supervised with great care by his almost equally well-
known father, Giovanni Antonio Flaminio; he proved not only precocious but a child prodigy and was accordingly introduced at the
age of sixteen into the circle of Humanists who throve on the generous but discriminating patronage of Pope Leo X. It was not only

in Rome that Flaminio made his name: he became the honored guest of scholars, clerics, and princes at Naples, Urbino, Bologna, Genoa, Padua, Verona, Viterbo, and elsewhere. For fifteen years he was secretary to Bishop Matteo Giberti at Verona, and, for a brief time, of Cardinal Reginald Pole.

Besides two books of lyric *lusus pastorales* ("pastoral toys" or pastoral vignettes), in which Flaminio followed and perfected a form introduced by Bembo and Navagero, there appears one full-scale eclogue. The statement, occasionally met, that "Flaminio wrote five books of eclogues" appears to be the result of a misunderstanding of a sentence in Tiraboschi's history of Italian literature. Flaminio's one eclogue, entitled "Thyrsis" (73 hexameters), is in part a panegyric of Baldassare Castiglione of Casanatico (1478-1529), whose guest Flaminio had been in 1515. The poem is more properly a panegyrical "bread-and-butter" note, in which Thyrsis represents the poet himself and Menalcas another young man of Serravalle named Tito Cesano. It is a youthful tour de force, the work of an astoundingly precocious adolescent; at the same time it should be emphasized that the poem has none of the excruciating affectations that mar the verse of the unfortunate Charles Aubry, and that, although it is easy to recognize whole phrases lifted bodily from Virgil and Navagero, the eclogue is not a poetical jigsaw puzzle.

A more typical pastoral panegyric appears in the Latin poems of Basilio Zanchi of Bergamo (1501-1558), an untitled idyll of a hundred lines in praise of the Golden Age of Pope Leo X. Equally conventional is another and later panegyric (untitled; 69 hexameters) that prophesies a new Golden Age at the accession of Charles V (1519).

Three of the poems of Girolamo Amalteo of Oderzo (1507-1574) belong here. His fifth, entitled "Iolas" (105 hexameters), is addressed to Michele della Torre, bishop of Ceneda; the seventh ("The Comet"; 69 hexameters) praises Cardinal Commendone; the fourth ("Amalthea"; 107 hexameters) praises the same man. All are remarkably fulsome; but then all of Girolamo's poems are far too lush.

The fifth poem, "Silis" (89 hexameters), of Girolamo's much younger brother, Giambattista Amalteo of Oderzo (1525-1573) is, in part, a restrained panegyric of Federico Savorgnan of Venice and description of the Golden Age of peace and plenty he is instituting in Venice: the theme is well worn if not downright threadbare by Amalteo's time, yet, as he handles it, it seems, if not fresh, at least sincere.

Two poems of Giovanni Battista Pigna (Nicolucci) of Ferrara (1530-1577) belong here. The fourth of the *Satyrae* is a poem of 72 hexameters entitled "The Prophetess" (*Fatua*). Here the goddess of prophecy sings the praises of Florence in general and of the Medici family in particular. Much of this is obviously catalogue, but the poem is worth examining in order to observe the skill with which Pigna can say the same thing over and over again without verbal repetition.

With Pigna's "Prophetess" we may compare the single eclogue (untitled; 120 hexameters) of Roberto Tizio of Burgo (*floruit* 1620), which celebrates the accession (1609) of Cosimo II, Grand Duke of Tuscany (1590-1620). Here the sailors of a ship headed for Palermo learn of the accession of Cosimo and sing his well-merited praises, prophesying a new Golden Age. It is a good enough poem, although riddled with poetic clichés. It seems so very much better than it really is because Cosimo, his wife Maria Maddalena, his brother Francesco, and his sisters Eleonora and Caterina had such uniformly engaging characters—their court was a brilliant one, and as we read Tizio's poem we can forget that at this period Tuscany was steadily sinking into a position of less and less importance in the affairs of Europe.

We earlier met a pastoral epicedium written by Maffeo Barberini of Florence (1568-1644), the later Pope Urban VIII, on the famous general Alessandro II Farnese (1545-1592); a still earlier eclogue on the same man, "Alexander" (92 hexameters) we can now pass over with a bare mention: it is a conventional hexameter panegyric, containing no pastoral details whatever. We can omit discussion, too, of the second eclogue of Agostino Favoriti of Lucca (1624-1682), a lengthy panegyric, written years after his accession (1655), of Pope Alexander VII, entitled "Nicander" (225 hexameters).

The last Italian author we shall meet here is another cleric of the curia—Ignazio Cianci (*floruit* 1750), a rather minor career-priest who belonged to a tedious literary group called "the Arcadians" (*Arcades* or *Arcadici*). These were a group of twenty-five, of whom three were Jesuit poets and seven were professors of Greek, Latin, or Italian. In 1757 they issued a forty-seven page volume of twenty-five poems on the recovery from illness of Pope Benedict XIV—elegies, epigrams, lyrics, and the like. One of these poems

is an eclogue (untitled; 111 hexameters) in which the two speakers
are Dasmon (the author) and an older shepherd named Meliboeus.
Most readers would probably approach this poem, on learning the
nature of its topic, with some misgivings; and yet it has more wit
and liveliness than would be expected.

Six German Neo-Latinists produced their due share of pastoral
panegyrics; since these poems are minor, it will be sufficient to give
only a summary account of them.

Of the ten eclogues of Euricius Cordus (Heinrich Solde) of
Simsthausen in Hesse, one is a pastoral panegyric (untitled; 162
hexameters). Most of the poem is straightforward panegyric of
the looks, strength, and generosity of Philip of Hesse, "the Hessian
Lion," expressed in amoebaean quatrains, with a final prophecy of
the new Golden Age that will soon set in.

Among the seventeen eclogues of Elius Eobanus (Koch) of
Bockendorf or Halgeshausen in Hesse (1488-1540), four are bucolic panegyrics. The sixteenth, written in 1526, is a panegyric
(untitled; 177 hexameters) of the city of Nuremberg. The encomium (pastoral or not) of a city was a recognized genre of Neo-
Latin poetry; the first eclogue (untitled; 158 hexameters) is a
double panegyric of Thuringia and Hesse. The sixth, "Iolas' Epitaph" (*Epitaphium Iolae*; 122 hexameters) sings the praises of
Wilhelm and Philip of Hesse very much as Cordus' first had done,
and the thirteenth (untitled; 125 hexameters) praises Philip alone.
In this last, Eoban praises in particular the military exploits of
Philip in Denmark and Germany.

Practically nothing is known of the German Humanist who
called himself Johannes Antonius Modestus (born about 1505 or
1510). Like other poets attached to the court of François I, he
tried his hand at pastoral poetry at least once. His one known
eclogue, "The Fauns" (*Fauni*; 83 hexameters) is extant in manuscript at the Bibliothèque Nationale; this is no doubt the original
presentation copy, for it is elaborately illuminated throughout and
written with the greatest care on parchment of a very fine quality.
In the introduction (lines 1-25) we are told that Corydon and Tityrus once met by the banks of the river Seine, and, as they wandered
about, caught sight of two fauns resting under an oak. The two
shepherds were about to flee in terror when one of the fauns called
them back to listen to the song they were preparing to sing. From

lines 26 to 77 we have the alternating songs of the two fauns, arranged as alternating quatrains, and a brief conclusion follows in lines 78 through 83. It is an eloquent panegyric; it is also a pretty and elegant little poem, and the stylized picture of the fauns and listening shepherds grouped in the shade of the old oak tree is a pleasant one.

Among the Latin poems of one of Georg Sabinus' students, Felix Fiedler (died 1553), appears one eclogue, "Philotas" (116 hexameters). So little is known of Fiedler that it is quite impossible to interpret the references in the poem. Much easier and far more worth reading is the third eclogue (*Nicer*; 94 hexameters) of Peter Lotich the Younger of Schlüchtern (1528-1560), a panegyric of the Kurfürst Otto Heinrich, to whom Lotich owed his appointment at the University of Heidelberg. The *Nicer* is by all odds the best written of the German pastoral panegyrics; Lotich is, after all, the only German Neo-Latin bucolic poet who can compare with the best of the Italians.

The earliest pastoral panegyric among the French Neo-Latinists is the first eclogue (*De laudibus Lerinae insulae*; 317 hexameters) of Denys Faucher of Arles (1487-1562), written shortly after 1522; more rewarding than Faucher's poem are the two pastoral panegyrics of Antoine Fumée, Seigneur de Blande (1511-1576), the "Amaryllis" (97 hexameters) and the "Daphnis" (190 hexameters), which were probably written in the same year (1574) as the "Livia," already examined. The "Amaryllis" is written as the monologue of a lover who reproaches his lady for her disdain, praises her beauty, charm, wit, and brilliance, protests his own undying devotion, and ends by imagining her apotheosis. It is written, in other words, wholly as an art-pastoral, and a skillful one, too; but it is clear that Amaryllis is the Queen-Regent Catherine de Médicis. Fumée is very far from being France's best Neo-Latin poet; but this poem is a joy to read after Faucher's inept encomium.

Even so, most readers would probably find "Amaryllis" excessively flowery and would turn with greater interest—despite its length—to "Daphnis," a panegyric of Catherine's son Henri III of France, composed at the time of his expected return from Poland. It is elaborate and artificial, it must be admitted; yet the reader detects a restrained but honest enthusiasm that makes the poem readable for other than purely historical reasons—it is not true of this eclogue, as Wade-Gery once said of Hesiod's *Theogony*, that it raises no emotion higher than the urge to do research.

After Fumée we come to Claude Roillet or Rouillet of Beaune (ca. 1520–ca. 1576). His published verses contain one true eclogue (untitled; 355 hexameters) in praise of Cardinal Charles of Lorraine on his return (1556) to France after a highly successful diplomatic mission to the volcanic Pope Paul IV. The poem is a long and elaborately composed dialogue among the three shepherds Thyrsis, Lycidas, and Menalcas. The poem is frequently obscure to the present-day reader but would have presented no difficulty to a contemporary, for its allusiveness is not the Petrarchan one of ostentatiously cryptic symbolism.

We can omit all reference to Guillaume Le Blanc of Albi (1561–1601) and turn to Henri Bougier, of whom I know only that he was connected with the Collège de Navarre and that in 1681 he published as a pamphlet an eclogue entitled "Daphnis Safe" (*Daphnis salvus*; 473 hexameters) that resolves itself into a long and elaborate panegyric of Louis XIV, his Queen (Marie Thérèse), the Grand Dauphin Louis, and the Dauphine (Maria Anna Christina Victoria of Bavaria). The poem displays great knowledge of Latin idiom, great metrical skill, great ability to vary expression; but it becomes wearisome, not only from its excessive length but also from its tone of fustian exaggeration: it frequently degenerates into elegant silliness. In form the poem is a *soterium*, a prayer of thankfulness for the Grand Dauphin's recovery from illness, but, like Cianci's poem on Benedict XIV, is more panegyric than anything else. The epithalamium of Julien Fleury on the wedding (1680) of Louis and Maria, discussed earlier, is far more interesting and effective than this tiresome piece of work; so also is the next piece of work to be discussed.

Pierre Pestel was an extremely prolific Latin poet of the late 1600's, as a glance at the general catalogue of the Bibliothèque Nationale will show; but I have been able to learn of him only that he was *professor in Cardinalitio,* i.e., professor (of rhetoric) in the Collège Cardinal le Moine. One of his poems is an eclogue entitled "The Triumph of Astraea" (82 hexameters), extant in a manuscript bound with a large number of printed pamphlets in the Bibliothèque Nationale. Most of the poems in this collection are odes in praise of Louis XIV or elegiac and lyric poems on the betrothal (1696) of the Grand Dauphin's son, Louis, duc de Bourgogne, to Marie Adelaide of Savoy. Pestel's poem is not an epithalamium, but a panegyric of the young Dauphin, composed at the actual time of the betrothal (the marriage did not take place until 1697). Let those who are greedy of fame, begins the poet, celebrate the labors of the mighty Hercules (i.e., Louis XIV) ; I myself, all unwarlike as I am, will sing of the joys of peace. Astraea, goddess of justice (he goes on), had seen the hideous destruction caused by Bellona (war) and had hidden herself in terrified exile among the Alps (i.e., in Savoy) as had even the god Phoebus himself. But now that the French have laid down arms, she has returned to the haunts of men. Now dawns a new Golden Age: Astraea has returned, and with her the arts of peace.

After a lacuna caused by the trimming of the bottom edge of the first sheet of the manuscript, we find Astraea addressing the young duke. I bring a new Age of Saturn, she announces, and I announce your betrothal to the princess of Savoy. All vestiges of original sin will begin to disappear in this new Golden Age, and hoary Faith will once more raise his head; the Horn of Plenty will pour its goodness over the earth. The Lion will now consort peacefully with the Cock, the Eagle will become gentle, and even Lilies and Roses will grow intertwined in France and Britain.

Astraea now (in very Virgilian language indeed) exhorts the duke to advance proudly into the future that lies before him, promising him success and power, and praising the merits that deserve them. There are lines or phrases here and there that are modeled too closely on Virgil; but this is quite an impressive poem for all that.

Finally, among French Neo-Latinists, we come to the name of Michel Hébert of Caen (1672-1711). Hébert entered the Jesuit order in 1689; he then taught belles lettres for six years and rhetoric for one, eventually becoming the associate of Père de la Chaise and Père Tellier, who were successive confessors of Louis XIV. Among his literary remains are an amusing burlesque-didactic poem, "The Art of Jest" (*Ars iocandi*; Paris, 1698), four more or less allegorical poems in which the four seasons represent the stages of human life (Caen, 1704), and one untitled eclogue (Paris, [1701?]) of 65 hexameters, extant in a pamphlet collection (at the Bibliothèque Nationale) of Latin poems addressed to Philip V of Spain (Philippe d'Anjou, grandson of Louis XIV). The stock themes are tricked out with the stock decorations that pastoral poetry had been building up for two thousand years; nevertheless, the poem is a restrained panegyric of much grace and an excellent one with which to close this section of the present chapter.

ii

A special class of pastoral panegyric is the one (epinicium) that celebrates a victory. All through the Renaissance we find Neo-Latin poets urging this or that king to undertake a campaign against the Turks. More often than not, the king in question was more interested in slaughtering his immediate neighbors than in freeing the Holy Land; but with Don John of Austria's naval victory at the battle of Lepanto (1571) Neo-Latinists by the score burst into excited verse—a large anthology of odes, elegies, epigrams, and epyllia composed by poets of half-a-dozen nationalities could easily be compiled.

In pastoral, however, we find fewer Lepanto-poems than one would have expected. The first one we shall turn to is by Giovanni Antonio Taglietti (Taygetus) of Brescia (*floruit* 1560), a minor figure about whom it is difficult to learn much. His briefer poems— erotic and occasional—are successful enough; but his attempts at heroic verse can be turgid. His Lepanto-poem, naturally, is composed as an *ecloga nautica* ("Idmon," 412 hexameters). In this poem a Cretan seaman named Eurydamas, who has so far heard of this battle only at second hand, asks for details. Idmon complies, and 342 hexameters of narrative follow, after which (411-12) Eurydamas suggests that they return thanks to God for Don John's famous victory. Clearly the poem is a heroic epyllion with introduction and conclusion tacked on to justify the name *ecloga*.

The major episode within the battle-passage is the hand-to-hand engagement between Don John and Halys (Ali Pasha): John eventually decapitates the Turkish leader, after deeds of incredible valor, and plants the gory trophy on a spear. The *aristeia* of John is followed by others of Colonna and Doria, until the Turkish fleet is destroyed, its leaders killed or put to flight, and the Christian captives released. There is a tremendous amount of "literary" writing in all this, but there are also scores of small details and incidents which were likely learned, at first or second hand, from eyewitnesses of the battle.

Earlier, we have occasionally referred in passing to the youngest and least important of the three Amalteo brothers—Cornelio Amalteo of Oderzo (1530-1603). His forty-two poems are in three groups—longer and more ambitious hexameter poems, a number of elegiac and lyric poems, and a collection of *epigrammata*. His second poem, "Proteus" (91 hexameters), is extremely closely modeled on Giambattista's fifth ("Silis," already discussed). At early morning, we read, the old sea-god Proteus rises from the waters of the Adriatic, accompanied by sea-nymphs, who demand a song. Like Virgil's Silenus, he begins with a tale of the creation of the world and then goes on to give a long string of allusive and often epigrammatic descriptions of mythological characters, finally turning to describe, as far greater than anything that has so far been achieved by mortals, the battle of Lepanto (50-85); in this Cornelio shows that, while he cannot for a moment compare with Giambattista, he can occasionally write at least as well as Girolamo. This passage lacks the mass of specific detail provided in almost overwhelming abundance by Taglietti and is extremely exclamatory, but it is spontaneous and enthusiastic.

The first and fourth piscatory eclogues of Niccolò Giannettasio of Naples (1648-1715) are epinicia. The first, entitled "Tityrus" (107 hexameters), celebrates the Emperor Leopold I's alleged victory over the Turks in 1683: in fact, when the Turks made their determined effort to overrun all of southeastern Europe, Leopold, who would far rather have been a prince of the Church than Holy Roman Emperor, fled from Vienna as fast as his legs could carry him; nevertheless the Turks' two-month siege of Vienna was frustrated by John III Sobieski of Poland.

The fourth piscatory eclogue, "Caesar" (94 hexameters), refers to the same victory of 1683. It begins as a prophecy of the new Golden Age that will spread throughout Europe now that the "Scythians" have been driven back; naturally, a reminiscence of Virgil's fourth eclogue is everywhere.

Finally we should notice an epinicium (untitled; 425 hexameters) in the form of an eclogue written by Stefano Laonice (*floruit* 1800), an Italian whose only other published work, I believe, is a discussion of the economic condition of the Papal States (Rome, 1795). The present poem was addressed, immediately after the battle of Marengo (1800), to the Consul, Napoleon Bonaparte. In a prose preface the author remarks that others no doubt will praise Napoleon's prudence and courage; but he himself, as a recipient of the Consul's bounty, prefers to load him with praise as he sets out in charge of new Republican armies and to prophesy new and even greater victories. He adds that Napoleon's achievements deserve epic treatment; yet (with an allusion to Virgil's fourth eclogue, addressed to the consul Asinius Pollio) "pastoral woods have ever been worthy of a Consul," and so his slender Muse now dares to address Napoleon himself.

The conclusion of the poem confidently prophesies a Golden Age under Napoleon, draws a picture of all the races of Europe bringing tribute to the Consul, prophesies the confusion of Napoleon's enemies and the welcome Napoleon will receive on his return to Paris, and again foretells a Golden Age. The poem is far, far too long and elaborate, but some of the quatrains of the shepherds are neat, epigrammatic, and worth reading once.

iii

A third "public" form of pastoral we can term the courtly eclogue. It is naturally panegyrical in tone, dealing as it does with kings and queens, dukes and duchesses, lords and ladies. Most examples are of precious little interest today, except for one sequence to be examined first.

Among French courtly eclogues the earliest and most important are five of the seven poems in the series of pastorals called *Nymphae indigenae* ("The Nymphs of This Place"), written by Julius Caesar Scaliger of La Rocca on Lake Garda near Verona (1484-1558) at the castle of Agen on the Garonne, sometime after 1541, while he was still physician to Antonio della Rovere, the bishop of Agen.

The first poem, entitled "The Dryads" (89 hexameters) is a courtly poem of farewell (*propempticon*) on the departure of the *novellista* Matteo Bandello from Agen for Italy, in which the Dryad Ias represents Violante Borromeo of Florence and Augê stands for Camilla Scarampa (both of whom were now living at Agen). Ias sings of Bandello's coming departure and marvels that he shows no fear of the sea. Augê now sings a love-song in which she tries to tempt Bandello back to Agen: she has every sort of pastoral gift ready for him, but fears that he will spurn them. The poem closes with the two ladies exchanging airy compliments on each other's verses.

The third poem of the series is entitled "The Nereid" (*Nereis*; 52 hexameters in quatrains throughout). Here a shepherd named Ocnus (probably Bandello) tries to urge his love on the shepherdess Talarisca (Lucrezia Gonzaga, daughter of Piero Gonzaga) and is amiably and wittily repulsed. It is a cheerful and engaging poem and was no doubt vastly applauded by the group of Italian expatriates at Agen.

The fourth poem is called "The Naiad" (*Nais*; 103 hexameters), and in this the Mantuan Naiad Andis represents Ippolita Torelli of Mantua and the youth Hersillus her husband, Baldassare Castiglione of Casantico. The Naiad laments that for all her gifts and attentions Hersillus had despised her love. This is not to be taken literally; it only means that Castiglione had been absent on some diplomatic mission or post and had not yet returned to his anxious wife.

Ippolita died in 1520 and Castiglione in 1529, while Scaliger's poem cannot have been written earlier than about 1545; the only reason for its inclusion in this collection, presumably, is that the poet wished to compliment Lucrezia Gonzaga, Castiglione being himself a Gonzaga on his mother's side.

The fifth eclogue of the series is "The City Girl" (*Politis*; 64 hexameters), in which Alcon, the country boy, is Scaliger and Macarê, the girl from the city, is Cornelia, daughter of Girolamo Torriani, professor of medicine at Padua and Ferrara. The poem begins with the girl's breaking from Alcon's embrace and running away, to turn and bespatter him with abuse and then rush off home. The second half of the poem is Alcon's lament over the cruelty of city girls in general and of Macarê in particular; he concludes with a heartfelt curse on Venus. Despite the over-rhetorical manner (characteristic of Scaliger's eclogues) this is a lively and entertaining poem, especially in the passage (6-23) that quotes Macarê's elegant Billingsgate.

The seventh and last poem is entitled "The Hamadryad" (*Hamadryas*; only 37 hexameters), and this time the Dryad in question represents Constanza Rangone, lamenting the "absence" of her husband, Cesare Fregoso (called Teuthus in the poem). Fregoso, a general of François I, was assassinated in Italy in 1541, and this poem, written some time later, is a mass of *double-entendre* decidedly distasteful to a twentieth-century reader, no matter what it may have seemed in 1545.

Thirty years later (1574) we come on an elaborate courtly eclogue addressed to Henri III on the occasion of his return from Poland to France. Antoine Fumée had hoped that the Nymph Adria (Venice) would not delay Henri's return to Paris. In a poem by Bernardino Tomitano of Padua (ca. 1516-1576) we find a description of Henri's reception in the Italian city—this poem is the highly mythological "Thetis" (231 hexameters).

In this eclogue Tomitano describes how the sea-nymph Adria rose at dawn to salute the victorious youth Henricus and to prophesy for him a brilliant reign full of happiness which would bring peace and prosperity to true orthodox believers and utter disaster to Huguenots. At the conclusion she imagines the welcome Henri will receive in France, pictures his triumphant progress towards Paris, prophesies a new Golden Age, and closes by calling down every conceivable blessing on Henri III of France and IV of Poland. The adulation of Henri in this eclogue is no more exaggerated than that in scores of other Latin and vernacular poems produced in 1574; how many of these effusions were actually read by the royal hero we shall never know, but it is certain that the poets and poetasters of 1574 read each other's work with the greatest assiduity.

Earlier I mentioned the first five of the eight eclogues of Jean Dorat of Limoges (ca. 1502-1588); these were a series of pastoral poems inspired by the wedding (1570) of Charles IX of France to Elizabeth of Austria, and their chief feature was the use of various anagrams—lucky omens in verse constructed with great ingenuity from the royal couple's names. The next two of Dorat's eclogues are dedicated to Charles's sister, Marguerite de Valois, and are also "anagrammatic" pastorals, of the courtly type. The eighth eclogue (an epicedium) has also been noted.

The sixth poem is entitled "The Laurel" (*Laurea*; 187 hexameters) and is described by the author as an "anagrammatismus." It is composed throughout as a dialogue between the rustics Mycon (Jacques Amyot, the translator of Plutarch, from 1560 Grand Almoner to Charles IX) and Aurillus (i.e., Auratus, d'Aurat, Dorat). What madness, asks Mycon in astonishment, has made you leave your retirement, Aurillus (in 1567 Dorat had retired to a country house near the Abbey of St. Jean de Latran), and return to court? No madness, replies Aurillus, but misfortune (Dorat's house at Limoges had been damaged by soldiers in the second war of religion in 1568; Charles IX eventually made good the poet's losses). Phoebus is the one whose aid I seek, goes on Aurillus; it was he who caused my loss (this seems an oddly blunt statement in a request-poem) but he can repair it—his anger is not implacable, as the wise woman Manto told me on casting her magic lots. In reply to Mycon's curious queries, Aurillus continues: Manto took twelve wooden slips, marked them with letters and then put them in an urn that she shook violently; when the slips flew out onto the ground they spelt *Laurea regis amata* ("Laurel, the King's darling"; the letters rearranged spell *Margareta Valesia*, Marguerite de Valois). She told me, goes on Aurillus, that Phoebus loves the laurel and that if I were to approach him bearing a laurel branch and repeating the verses of Manto I should gain all I might desire. Mycon (naturally) wishes to hear Manto's verses, and Aurillus agrees to sing them if Mycon will sing the refrain. From line 91 to line 165 we have a series of fifteen quatrains, after each of which Mycon sings *Laurea regis amata, o, Laurea regis amata*; the poem then concludes (181-187) with Aurillus' heartfelt thanks.

If the above eclogue belongs to 1568, its sequel can scarcely be much later. The seventh eclogue, entitled "The Laureate" (*Laureus*; 239 hexameters), is no doubt intended to express Dorat's thanks for favors received. The poem is a monologue uttered by Aureolus (Dorat) in which he recounts a conversation he had held, in a dream, with Petreolus (Francesco Petrarca). Reminiscence of Petrarch's third and twelfth eclogues, in which Laura is called a laurel over and over again, is natural; reference to Petrarch's laurel crown, received at Rome, is also frequent. The allegory in which the poem is expressed is not Petrarchan cryptic symbolism, yet Alice Hulubei's comment on this pastoral is just: "Outre le thème du laurier, Dorat est redevable à messer Francesco de la conception même de ses deux églogues à Marguerite, affligées d'une allegorie obscure [this at least is overstated] et trop subtile. Il est par consequent bien plus près de l'esprit du moyen âge qui règne dans le 'Bucolicum carmen' [i.e., of Petrarch] que de la claire idylle de Theocrite, simple et littérale, ou même de l'églogue virgilienne allégorique." Dorat also owes to Petrarch the especially vainglorious and blunt type of claim to immortality that mars a passage in the *Africa* referred to in Chapter Two above.

We can conclude our examination of the court eclogue by noticing the work of half-a-dozen North Britons, of whom five belong to the Golden Age of Scottish Neo-Latin poetry and one is best described (in Leicester Bradner's words) as "a late straggler." We have already met David Hume of Godscroft (ca. 1560–ca. 1630) as the author of a pastoral that includes lament for the death of Elizabeth I (Amaryllis) and panegyric of her successor, James

VI and I (Daphnis). His three other eclogues are courtly. The second poem (untitled; 88 hexameters) is a sequel to the first and is clearly intended to be read continuously with it, since it begins, "This (i.e., the first poem) did Philomela sing . . . and then with his shepherd's pipe Alphesiboeus next began. . . ." This shepherd describes, with a wealth of flattering adjectives, how Amaryllis now looks down from Heaven and rejoices in the thought of her successor.

This poem is followed by the equally flowery "Moeris" (224 hexameters), written throughout as dialogue between Lycidas and Moeris. Encouraged by Lycidas, Moeris delivers himself of a lengthy song in praise of King James, beginning by prophesying a new Golden Age and at the close reaching such heights of adulation as not even Ben Jonson achieved.

The fourth eclogue, "Meliboeus, or, The Union" (*Meliboeus, sive Unio*; 88 hexameters) is earlier than the third. It is in dialogue throughout, in responsive quatrains. Meliboeus and Menalcas alternate their praises of James, Anne of Denmark, Prince Henry, the rivers of Scotland, those of England, the beauty of Phyllis (Scotland) and Amaryllis (England), prophesy a new Golden Age of peace now that the two kingdoms are united, and finally call upon the youth of each nation to support the Union. It is capable and fluent, but like all of Hume's eclogues, not really outstanding by Italian standards.

Three poems by Henry Anderson (*floruit* 1615; nothing seems to be known of him) are printed in the *Delitiae poetarum Scotorum*, all pastoral, all courtly in nature, and all rather second-rate. The first poem, entitled "The Complaint of the Muses" (*Musarum querimonia*; 341 hexameters), is a plea to Daphnis (James, of course) not to forget the North Country. The date of this poem (in which precious little of the pastoral appears) is clearly 1617, when James paid a ceremonial visit to Perth. The second poem, "Amaryllis Complaining" (*Amaryllis expostulans*; 111 hexameters), represents the city of Perth (Amaryllis) longing for the return of Daphnis; the third poem, "Amaryllis Rejoicing" (*Amaryllis exsultans*; 161 hexameters), is a natural sequel to the second.

The last of the five pastorals of John Barclay of Pont à Mousson (1580-1621) is a courtly eclogue entitled "Corydon" (55 hexameters); here James is called not Daphnis but Phoebus, in the French manner. This poem is, without a doubt, the least interesting of

Barclay's pastorals, just as ceremonial and court eclogue is on the whole the least interesting of all new forms of Neo-Latin pastoral. The poem does contain some deft lines, but on the whole its chief virtue is its brevity.

I shall only mention the "Royal Eclogue" (*Ecloga regalis*) of A. Abernethy (*floruit* 1620), which I have not seen, and turn to the one eclogue of the courtly type written by John Leech (Leochaeus) of Montrose and Aberdeen (ca. 1590–ca. 1630). This is the second of his bucolic eclogues (i.e., of the five purely pastoral eclogues, as opposed to his piscatory, nautical, and vinitory eclogues). This poem is called "The Return of Daphnis" (*Daphnis redux*; 148 hexameters) and, as the reader will expect, deals yet again with the return of James VI and I to Scotland and his state visit to Perth. Of the courtly eclogues we have examined this is undoubtedly the best; the amoebaean quatrains are as neat as any that appear anywhere in Renaissance Latin literature.

There is one eclogue among the poems of James Kennedy the Younger of Aberdeen (*floruit* 1660), and it is of the ceremonial and courtly type. Kennedy, who was later knighted, was Sheriff Clerk of Aberdeen, but very little is known of the events of his life. His Latin poems include an epic called "The British Aeneas" (*Aeneas Britannicus*) of which only 212 lines are extant, although a summary gives an outline of the whole work: it tells the life of Charles II in exile, the restoration, and the King's marriage to Catherine of Braganza; also extant is an epithalamium (non-pastoral) on the wedding and an eclogue called "Crown and Miter, or, The Return of Daphnis and the Druids" (ΔΙΑΔΗΜΑ ΚΑΙ ΜΙΤΡΑ, *seu, Daphnidis et Druidum Reditus*; 80 hexameters) published in Aberdeen in 1662 and dedicated to James Sharpe, Primate of Scotland. "Daphnis" refers to Charles II; the "Druids" are the Episcopalian Bishops. Sharpe had originally been a Resolutioner and hence allied with the Covenanters, but in the days of Charles he abandoned the cause he had been chosen to defend in the days of Cromwell. He it was who was responsible for the re-establishment of Erastian Episcopacy in Scotland in 1661, here celebrated. Sharpe was "vain, vindictive, perfidious, at once haughty and servile, rapacious and cruel" (Laing).

In the present poem Kennedy reveals himself as strongly pro-royalist; probably the city of Aberdeen hoped for favors from Sharpe, a graduate of King's College (1637). If this is correct, then Aberdeen was at odds with the rest of Scotland, which bitterly resented that "return of the Druids," which Dryden also saluted:

> At length the Muses stand restored again
> To that great charge which Nature did ordain,
> And their lov'd Druids seem reviv'd by fate . . . .

iv

The last type of eclogue to be examined in this chapter is that which deals with contemporary matters or public events; the earliest example is an anonymous poem preserved in wretched textual condition in a manuscript in Florence. It is similar in tone and manner to the eclogues of Giovanni Quatrario of Sulmona (1336-1402), dealing as it does with the troubles of the Angevin dynasty of Naples.

Giovanna I had eventually been succeeded by Charles III, King of Naples from 1382 to 1386, who was in turn succeeded by his son Ladislaus (1386-1414) and his worthless daughter, Giovanna II (1414-1435). In 1420 Giovanna appointed Alfonso V of Aragon her heir: the Angevin dynasty had long ago lost Sicily and was in imminent danger of losing all southern Italy, whereas Aragon had taken the lead among the Spanish principalities as an expansive European power under Ferdinand I (1412-1416) and his son Alfonso. Unfortunately, Giovanna changed her mind and on her death (1435) bequeathed the kingdom of Naples to René of Anjou, whereupon Alfonso advanced north from Sicily and, with the assistance of Filippo Maria Visconti, Duke of Milan, wrested the kingdom from René in the War of Angevin Succession (1435-1442): in 1443 the victor was formally recognized by "the great inopportunist," Pope Eugenius IV, as Alfonso V and I the Magnanimous, King of Aragon, Naples, and Sicily.

Alfonso proved to be a Humanist king of the first rank, a genuine Maecenas whose rule was hailed as a new Golden Age by many a Neo-Latin poet; his court became a center of literary studies that equaled, if it did not surpass, the courts of northern Italy in its passion for learning and splendor.

In the eclogue in question, the wealthy shepherd Daphnis sends off Tityrus to summon Mopsus. It is clear from hints later in the poem that Daphnis represents some generous prince or governor, that Tityrus is his chancellor, and that Mopsus is a rustic singer who is to be rewarded by patronage if he can charm Daphnis' weary leisure with music. But when Mopsus arrives on the scene he is full of laments: the age in which he lives is not propitious to the arts; eventually he is persuaded to narrate the course of a quarrel he had recently heard among shepherds, and it requires no great penetration to see in Megophis (Greek for "great viper"—a viper was the symbol of Milan) Filippo Maria Visconti, in Polyphemus (always associated with Sicily) Alfonso, and in Ginnarus René d'Anjou. The expression of this poem is full of medievalisms, the content is strongly reminiscent of Quatrario's work, and the cast of characters reminds one of early pre-Humanist pastoral of the days of Dante and Giovanni del Virgilio.

If this anonymous eclogue more properly belongs to late medieval literature, the next to be examined is undoubtedly Neo-Latin —it is the tenth eclogue, "Bembus" (204 hexameters), of Giovanni Battista Spagnuoli ("Mantuan") of Mantua (1448-1516). This poem employs a form that had had a long history in classical and medieval verse—the debate. The alleged shepherds represent the two great divisions of the Carmelite Order (of which Mantuan became Vicar-General in 1513): the Discalced, or highly orthodox, Carmelites and the Conventuals, who followed a much mitigated rule. The speakers discuss the various abuses that had crept into the Order and had caused the schism in 1459, and the "umpire" advises a return to the good old ways. The content of the poem no doubt had considerable interest for contemporary readers, but the matter of the correct color of a priest's habit holds few charms for us today—at least as a subject for poetry.

Our next author is in fact a Portuguese; but his whole adult career and literary output belongs to Italy, and it is easiest to deal with him here. Enrique Cayado of Lisbon (ca. 1465–ca. 1508) had originally been sent, apparently with a grant from the King of Portugal, to study law in Italy, but Cayado's interests were all in literature; what drew him was not jurisprudence but the fame of Angelo Poliziano (1454-1494) as a teacher and poet. After studies at Florence, Rovigo, and Ferrara, Cayado appears to have accepted the inevitable by completing his degree in law at the University of Padua. Of his later years practically nothing is known. Lilio Giraldi says he was "a pleasant-spoken fellow, rather fat" ("obesulus corpore, sermone facetus").

His poems appeared at Bologna in 1496, with the title *Aeglogae et Sylvae et Epigrammata* ("Eclogues, Miscellaneous Poems, and

Epigrams"), and an enlarged edition appeared at the same place in 1501. The eclogues are nine in number, and some had been "performed" publicly in Bologna in the manner of masques. Gröber (*Grundriss der romanischen Philologie*) says of them that they are "the first epoch-making work in Portuguese Latin poetry"; to the student of Neo-Latin pastoral "it is perhaps enough to say that they are interesting both in themselves and because of what they tell of the author's teachers, patrons, and friends" (Mustard).

Of the nine, five deal with public affairs. The first poem (untitled; 117 hexameters) is addressed to Diogo de Sousa, Ambassador (to the Roman curia) of John II of Portugal, and is dated from Florence, July, 1495. The background of the poem is the suffering caused to the people of Tuscany by the French invasion of Italy by Charles VIII in 1494-1495; its treatment may be judged from the following version of the whole:

> My Muse shall tell of shepherds brought to harm
> Of bitter conflict, and of war's alarm.
> My friend, support and aid my first emprise,
> And give to me the favor of your eyes.
> Now do I sing the fields, in rustic strains,
> And hymn the woods and streams and level plains:
> I hope for praise amid bucolic lawns,
> Amid the peaceful folds and homes of fauns;
> But soon shall I pursue a higher aim—
> To sing of princes and to laud their fame:
> Then, like Maecenas, may you aid my pen,
> Extend your favor, and assist again.
>
> While gentle sheep yet through the meadows grazed,
> While lively goats from lofty uplands gazed,
> The good Philemon, at the noon-day hour,
> Retired within a shady cavern's bower,
> Where Faustulus, from Florence late returned,
> Thus clamored, while his heart with anger burned:

> F.:   This latest age is filled with constant strife,
> And shepherds lead a sad and wretched life.
> What hope remains for us amidst our woe?
> The dead alone can peace and quiet know!
> Their bones now rest within the silent tomb,
> Nor ever feel the dread of coming doom.

But danger still besets us living swains,
And bleak disaster marches through the plains.

P.: How can this be? May gods avert your fear;
Tell now your troubles to my waiting ear.
If fields by scorching heat are parched and dry,
Think then that rain will drench them by and by.
Your grief's excessive: every age must change,
And from the lowest to the highest range.
Think how the world by Phaëthon was burned,
How every living thing to ash was turned;
Yet all the world recovered: breezes blow,
The seed now sprouts, and pleasant rivers flow.
Next came, in turn, old Pyrrha's age of flood:
The human race then drowned in seas of mud,
And Nereus then by Jove's divine decree
Abandoned ocean—for a lofty tree!
'Neath lowering clouds the seething floods destroyed
The herds, the crops, the fruits, till all was void.
Then cattle swam with wolves, a portent dire:
Such marvels well befit a Grecian lyre.
Yet soon the earth revived: soon other flocks,
Soon other shepherds filled the dripping rocks.
Tell, then, these troubles now, that cannot last:
A joy 'twill be to view them when they're past.

F.: These marvels had I never heard, old friend;
More would I hear, had we but time to spend.
But Gauls attack the Tuscan walls and gates:
The city seems abandoned by the Fates.
About it every form of death abounds,
From every gate a horrid crash resounds.
Scarce welcome day succeeded peaceful night
And heav'n had sprinkled fields with dewdrops bright,
When from their stalls I drove my herds and flocks
To graze upon the fields below the rocks.
Ten cattle drove I to the Arno's rill,
And left my wife and boy to tend them still.
Then endive, mushrooms, rosemary, and rue,
Three kids, fresh onions, new-made cheeses, too,

I took to market, with a tempting hare
Caught in the brambles by Lycisca there.
And these I took, laid in a rustic cart,
To sell for profit in the city's mart;
A scythe I meant to buy, to reap the hay,
And to Amyntas all my debt repay.
Fool that I was! My journey led to naught.

P.:   With danger was your anxious journey fraught?

F.:   Join in my grief: a brigand, by the gate,
Full-armored, hateful, cruel, lay in wait,
Attacked me with his sword, and swore to kill,
If I but breathed a word—I tremble still.
I held my tongue, a prey to countless fears;
The soldier recked but little of my tears
No wolf more savage than that brutal sort;
No fiend so much delights in cruel sport.
May lightning daze his mind, his members maim,
May fire consume his limbs and burn his brain!
But to my tale: within the city fled,
I told my loss and showed my bloody head.
I sought the city's help, the praetor's aid:
No law, no praetor rules with judgment staid.
There all is ruled by Mars with force of arms,
And all are terrified by war's alarms,
Full sure that Florence soon will bite the dust,
And lie the victim of a foeman's lust.
If such a doom the gods now hold in store,
The blazing torch will fire the palace door,
The fields will perish, scythes be turned to spears,
The plowman's face be drenched with bloody tears.
We shepherds, too, who wind and sun sustain
And icy hail and drenching storms of rain,
But other times recline within the shade,
To watch the cattle or to kiss the maid,
We, too, shall be the cruel foeman's prey
And see him drive our bleating flocks away.
Soon shall we lose our cattle, one by one,
And lose our life with all the wealth we've won.

P. :   Cease, cease, good Faustulus, to moan and sigh;
        And wipe the gathering tears from either eye.
        This woe, I prophesy, will soon be past,
        And Florence shall be rid of Gaul at last.
        No witch Medea's here, no Atreus grim;
        Thyestes finds no banquet laid for him;
        No husband here was slaughtered by a wife,
        No son has blotted out his mother's life.
        To Jove and every god is Florence dear.
        Whose temples rise from earth to heaven's clear,
        Whose priests observe decorum night and day—
        They work and meditate and constant pray.
        Your fervent prayer will gain its end at last,
        And soon the time of torment will be past.
        But night approaches fast: recall your herd—
        I pray it be augmented soon a third!

The sixth poem (again untitled; 118 hexameters) is addressed to Antonio Bentivoglio, apostolic protonotary; it is written in honor of the four sons of Giovanni II Bentivoglio of Bologna. The eclogue refers in particular to the retreat (1495) of Charles VIII of France from Naples and tells the good news of the battle of Fornovo (also described in Mantuan's *Trophaeum Gonzagae*).

The seventh eclogue (untitled; 164 hexameters) is written in honor of the three sons of João Teixeira, Chancellor of John II of Portugal—Tristão (Thyrsis), Luiz (Lygdamus), and Alvaro (Alphesiboeus)—and was addressed to Alvaro from Ferrara in 1500.

In the eighth eclogue (untitled; 121 hexameters written at Rovigo in 1500), Contarenus and Barbadicus represent Zaccaria Contarini, the Venetian governor of the Polesine, and Agostino Barbarigo, Doge of Venice.

The last poem (again untitled; 124 hexameters, addressed from Ferrara, 1500) consists wholly of alternating quatrains sung by two shepherds, Alexis and Polyphemus. Polyphemus sets forth, very neatly and epigrammatically, the praises of Duke Ercole of Ferrara under the inevitable name of Alcides (i.e., Hercules): the achievements narrated in Polyphemus' successive stanzas are in fact the Labors of Hercules, but they are described in such a way as to be applicable to Ercole d'Este as well. Alexis sings the praises of the god Apollo—his killing the Python, his building of the walls of Troy, his defeat of Marsyas, and so on; in each case an achievement of Hercules is contrasted with one of Apollo, always to the credit of Hercules. At the end the shepherds agree—although no umpire is present—to award the palm to Hercules.

Two of the six eclogues of Sannazaro's friend, Giano Anisio of Naples (ca. 1475–ca. 1540), belong here. The second poem, entitled "Murenus" (107 hexameters), must have been written just after Fernandez Gonzalo or Gonzalvo (Hernando Consalvo) of Corduba's defeat of the French army of Louis XII at the Garigliano (Liris) River near Naples on December 29, 1503. The speakers in the dialogue are Murenus (a fisherman), Quercius and Hircanus (two shepherds), and an unnamed messenger.

The fourth eclogue, entitled "The Goatherd" (*Aepolus*; 81 hexameters), celebrates the return of Giacopo Sannazaro from exile, the interlocutors being Syncerus (Sannazaro himself) and Aepolus (Anisio, presumably). The fourth eclogue holds a good deal less interest than the second: its manner is rather vague, its tone is lachrymose, and it lacks life, for all its neatness of form.

Two (numbers 3 and 6) of the eight eclogues of Paolo Belmisseri of Pontremoli (ca. 1480–ca. 1547) belong here; each is worth reading for the sake of the content and dramatis personae, at least, but their neatness of style is owing rather to industrious imitation of Virgil, Calpurnius, Nemesianus, Mantuan, Andrelini, and Sannazaro than to any great poetic talent on Belmisseri's part.

As verse, the fourth poem of Lelio Capilupi of Mantua (ca. 1500-1563) can be ignored, since it is only another of his perversely ingenious Virgilian centos (*centones ex Vergilio*); its theme, however, is of some importance in Neo-Latin literature, being one ever recurrent from earliest to latest times—under the mask of pastoral song it is an appeal to the Christian kings of Europe to drive the Turks from the Holy Land rather than to waste their resources in the Franco-Spanish war that had broken out on the death of the Duke of Orléans in 1552. The fifth poem, also an eclogue, addressed to the Cardinal-elect Rainutio Farnese, is a similar plea for peace in Europe.

We can pass from this jigsaw poetry and examine instead the fourth eclogue of Marco Publio Fontana of Bergamo (1548-1609), a poem first published in 1578. Entitled "Phyllis" (133 hexameters), it is addressed to Cesare Ducchi of Brescia, a lawyer, historian, and excellent minor poet. Matthew Prior's "Love Disarmed" is virtually a translation of Ducchi's *Epitaphium Amoris*, thus illustrating Dr. Johnson's remark that "I have traced him [Prior] among the Latin [i.e., Neo-Latin] epigrammatists and have been informed that he poached for prey among obscure authors," in which, however, he did no more than Alexander Pope, who "sought for images and sentiments from modern writers of Latin poetry" (Greswell, 1805).

It is plain that "Phyllis" represents the city of Brescia itself, which had recently been visited with an epidemic. The flowery tone of the introduction is maintained throughout the poem and, although Fontana is always a clear and vigorous poet, this eclogue can scarcely be claimed as one of his best. It is, in fact, the skillful verse of an expert craftsman who has allowed learning and dexterity to get the better of tact and discretion.

Of the fourteen piscatory eclogues of Niccolò Giannettasio of Naples (1648-1715), two can be dealt with at this point. The sixth poem, entitled "Glaucus" (87 hexameters), is dedicated to Marcantonio Giustiniano, Doge of Venice, and celebrates the occasion when the Venetian fleet set out in 1684 to attack the Turks and win another Lepanto. Giannettassio's first eclogue had been a victory poem (epinicium) celebrating the relief of Vienna by the Emperor Leopold (actually by King John III Sobieski) in 1683; in the following year, at the urging of Pope Innocent XI, Venice joined the Holy League. She had already fought five wars against Turkey and, now that the Turks' attempt to overrun all southern and central Europe had misfired, was ready for a sixth. Francesco Morosini did in fact recover Morea (Greece) in the campaign of 1684-1685, but the province was lost again in 1716. The present poem was written practically at the moment Morosini's expedition set out.

As usual, the poem is simple in arrangement—an address to Giustiniano (1-11) is followed by an introduction in which the poet sets the stage (12-24), Glaucus' song (25-85), and a brief, almost brusque conclusion (86-87). Giannettasio urges the Doge of Venice to receive graciously his prophecy of victory and promises to sing a loftier strain when actual victory is announced. He then goes on to tell how the Baian fisherman Milcon caught sight of the old sea-god Glaucus singing on the shore.

Glaucus tells first how he had recently seen a mighty armada sail forth with all the sea-gods and Nereids and dolphins of the Adriatic escorting it joyously. The Nereids swam around the ships, while Triton blew his horn in anticipation of a Venetian triumph. Glaucus imagines the Turks hearing the sound and retreating in fear to the Dardanelles and prophesies that they will be driven back to the Black Sea itself and beyond; a new Golden Age, he is certain, will soon dawn for the Greek people. Even now flocks and herds are wandering more freely through the valleys; shepherds once more recline at their ease beneath poplars and sing their pastoral lays. This is not one of the most outstanding of Giannettasio's piscatories, but it is agreeable to read and is far more restrained in manner than the eclogue of Fontana mentioned above.

Among Germans I shall deal at this point with five poets, four of whom we have already met: Euricius Cordus, Elius Eobanus Hessus, Joachim Camerarius, Georg Sabinus, and Johann Stigel.

Of the eclogues of Euricius Cordus (Heinrich Solde) of Simsthausen in Hesse (1486-1535) two are relevant. The sixth poem (untitled; 215 hexameters) is a dialogue between two shepherds named Sylvius and Polyphemus in which the latter bitterly assails the tithe system and the greed and luxury of some priests. Sylvius does his best to point out that one evil priest should not damn all, but Polyphemus will not listen. When this poem was written, Cordus was still a Catholic and a supporter of Erasmus' point of view, not Luther's; it is Sylvius, then, not Polyphemus, who represents the author. The poem itself is a vigorous piece of work and well worth reading; its date is probably about 1524, in which year there were no less than 30,000 German peasants in arms, refusing to pay tithes.

The ninth eclogue (again untitled; 150 hexameters) combines realistic details from the hard life of real German peasants with the conventional details derived from the long tradition of pastoral writing. In this poem Aepolus asks the aged Lollus why at his age he must continue to work so hard as a woodcutter. Lollus recalls bitterly that he had once been comfortable but had become involved in a wretched litigation with the wealthy Lycidas; over the years he had lost everything and had had to take a thorny piece of land almost impossible to clear. To add to his troubles his wife Foenilia continued all this time to be more fertile than any mouse (et fecunda super murem Foenilia coniunx": 66). Lollus grieves over the loss of his original farms, which had resulted in the first instance from the greed of a new city-official called Philarchus (the references to this man make it reasonably clear that he is an actual person), and lines 84 to 108 are a virulent attack on this official's life and character. Aepolus advises the old man to do as Tityrus did in Roman days—take his case to the imperial court (in this case, to Philip, Margrave of Hesse), but Lollus laments that this is a barbarous age—only money will bring what a man wants, and he has none. It is a pity that we cannot yet interpret the many contemporary references which are scattered throughout the poem—an understanding of these would lead to a far more lively appreciation of what seems to me a work of quite considerable importance.

One of the eclogues of Elius Eobanus (Koch) of Bockendorf or Halgeshausen in Hesse (1488-1540) will be examined here—the seventeenth, entitled "Erfurt; or, The Collapse of the University and the State" (*Erphurdia; de collapso Scholae et Reipublicae statu*; 255 hexameters). In this poem the speakers are the nymph Erysiptolis ("protectress of the city") and the river-god Hieras (a stream still called Gera runs past Erfurt). The nymph asks Hieras the reason for his sadness. You know the reason, he replies, for you love a certain city as much as I do. The Muses (he continues) have fled from our city, driven out by a hostile race (Luther's anti-humanist clergy, that is); freedom of speech has disappeared. After a panegyric of the city of Erfurt and its university, Hieras turns finally to a lament over poetry, fated to disappear amid the din of religious contention and civil discord. As verse the poem is not much better or worse than any other of Eoban's bucolics; its real interest lies in its tone and content—it vibrates with wrath, and it offers an insight into university life carried on under difficulties: the Reformation for long had a disastrous effect on the German universities; Erfurt never recovered from the damage done it by the Reformation.

We can now examine two of the twenty eclogues of Joachim Camerarius (Liebhard) of Bamberg (1500-1574). The first poem, entitled "Thyrsis" (48 hexameters), has as its background the Peasants' Revolt of 1524-1526 and is clearly one of the earliest of Camerarius' bucolic poems, written long before the publication date of 1568. Behind all the Greek names and beneath the layer of pastoral artifice and contrivance we can see clearly a picture of the misery of a real German peasant: the complaint of Thyrsis was to be heard everywhere in the Germany of the sixteenth century and is little different from that of the aged Lollus in Cordus' ninth eclogue. The once terrified but now triumphant dukes, electors, margraves, and knights were once more firmly in the saddle at the close of a revolt in which 130,000 peasants died, and after which widows and orphans were everywhere: the princelings were enjoying a protracted revenge. In this poem Thyrsis bewails the oppression now being suffered by small farmers in general and himself in particular.

The twentieth eclogue, entitled "Corydon" (68 hexameters), is much calmer in tone than the first poem and may well have been written twenty or thirty years later: the violent reaction to the Peasants' Revolt had ceased, but the lot of the peasant was still hard. The poem ends with a prayer (39-68) for peace—Lycidas hopes that religion, law, learning, the Muses, and agriculture may all flourish and that war and civil discord may never more tear Germany apart. The prayer is quite obviously Camerarius' own, for it expresses concisely and fervently the aims of all the efforts of that ardent reformer's strenuous life.

Two more eclogues on contemporary themes are by Georg Sabinus of Brandenburg (1508-1560) and Johann Stigel of Gotha (1515-1562); both poems deal with the same events. In Sabinus' pastoral (untitled; 120 hexameters) a German named Lycidas meets an Italian called Aegon and asks him what has driven him so far from home; Aegon replies it was "fierce monsters" that had driven him from the wealth he had once enjoyed. In reply to Lycidas' further questioning, Aegon tells him that far away where the Sequana (Saône) twists and turns there is a royal garden where grow golden lilies (those of France, that is) guarded by a cock (*gallus,* i.e., *Gallus,* François I), a bird as powerful as Jove's eagle (the Emperor Charles V). Near the banks of the Po, however, there is a serpent (Francesco Sforza, Duke of Milan), guardian of the Insubrian land. The cock conceived a deadly hatred for the serpent (the capture of Milan was one of the first aims of François' invasion of Italy), flew over the Alps, and devastated the whole valley of the Po. But at length, continues the shepherd, there appeared from the Vindelican Alps the queen of birds, the eagle, *Iovi quae tela ministrat* (70). This eagle (here, the troops of Charles V) then attacked Gallus by the waters of the Ticino; they tore at each other with beak and claw until Gallus was at last defeated (the battle of Pavia, February 24, 1525, at which François was captured). The eagle then carried Gallus off and set him down in the land of Hercules (the reference is to François' imprisonment in a tower in Madrid); yet Gallus escaped (François was released under the terms of the Treaty of Madrid, January 14, 1526), goes on Aegon, and returned to Italy more savage than ever, assisted now by the Bear (*Ursus*: a bear, it is true, was the badge of the Swiss mercenary forces of the day; but the reference here appears to be to Henry VIII: Lautrec invaded Italy with an army of 30,000 men subsidized by England; the army was officially called "the army of the Kings of England and France," although it actually contained no English troops). Now that these two monsters have joined forces, says Aegon, I have come here with my three goats, the survivors of my hundred flocks. The poem is not difficult to understand today and would, of course, have been crystal clear to any contemporary anywhere in Europe. And it should be added that this eclogue is rather more than a mildly entertaining puzzle; it is well written and readable.

Johann Stigel of Gotha (1515-1562) studied classics at Wittenberg from 1531 and then turned to law, which, at Melanchthon's urging, he combined with medicine, science, and astronomy. He eventually became a professor at Wittenberg but was forced to retreat to Weimar at the outbreak of the Schmalkalden War, finally settling in Jena at the Gymnasium founded there by Melanchthon. His one eclogue (*Iolas*; 183 hexameters) deals in an almost identical manner with the subject treated by Sabinus in the above poem.

Three Dutch poets now appear: Peter van der Brugge (Pontanus) of Bruges, Jakob de Sluyper of Herzele, and Petrus Stratenius of Goësa. Of the ten eclogues of Pontanus (ca. 1480–ca. 1540), the seventh (untitled; 100 hexameters) deals with war and peace in a dialogue between Virbius, a soldier newly returned to his home in France, and a shepherd named Phorcus. As a work of art it is, like all Pontanus' eclogues, negligible; Pontanus himself, self-revealed, is always far more interesting than his often crude verse. The poem *calls* itself an eclogue, is written in the conventional hexameters, and contains the odd line modeled on Virgil (seldom with happy results); but there is nothing pastoral in the manner: the tone is satirical and the diction is reminiscent of Terence at the beginning and of Horace and Juvenal elsewhere.

The theme of war and peace reappears in the ninth eclogue (untitled; 100 hexameters), a dialogue between Dolphus and Battus. Dolphus laments that all he has gained in the last dozen years has now been lost as a result of war and especially through the depredations of undisciplined soldiers. He reflects bitterly that the Christian kings of the Golden Age of Europe did not waste the wealth of their own subjects in making war on other Christians; in those golden days the "sons of Mahomet" did not dare to touch the soil of Europe—Christ alone ruled. But now Christian blood is shed by Christians everywhere (75)—Christ alone grieves. It is as well that Pontanus did not live to see the alliance struck between François I and Suleiman the Magnificent ten years after the battle of Pavia.

Of the eight eclogues of Jakob de Slupere or de Sluyper (Sluperius) of Herzele (1532-1582) two refer to contemporary matters. The sixth poem, entitled "Aegon" (386 hexameters), was addressed to a friend from Boesinghe near Ypres in June 1563, some time after the death (1559) of Henri II of France ("Aegon"), and like many of the Sluyper's eclogues is full of references to the misfortunes of Catholics in the Low Countries and to John Calvin and his "sweet poison."

The seventh eclogue, called "Daphnis" (356 hexameters, addressed from Boesinghe, June 1563), has all the faults of the sixth: here (line 103) the main speaker, as in many of Sluperius' eclogues, announces that he will tell his tale as briefly as possible (*quanta potero brevitate*) but the promise is soon forgotten; and Sluperius is not content to write a poem almost four times its proper length but must precede it by an introductory poem of thirty-six elegiac lines. But there are longer pastorals in Neo-Latin literature: we have already mentioned Bernardus Praetorius' mammoth pastoral epicedium (1592) on William, Margrave of Hesse, that extends to more than 5,500 hexameters.

Of the five eclogues of Petrus Stratenius of Goësa (1616-1640) we shall notice one at this point—the first (untitled; 70 hexameters), the brevity of which provides a welcome change after Sluperius' *Langatmigkeit*. The poem refers to the French civil war of 1628-1642, during the reign of Louis XIII, the fourth since his accession as a boy in 1610. Here the shepherd Calydon laments (with a recurrent refrain) the fate of France, now overrun by a brutal soldiery. But this is no foreign enemy: the arms are those of Frenchmen, the rage is that of Frenchmen whom no fear of God restrains. All piety, all honesty, all honor is gone. Mars and Bellona rule; no heed is paid to Pan (as in other pastorals, Christ) or Pales (the Virgin Mary, as commonly in Neo-Latin pastoral since the days of Francesco Petrarca). Calydon goes on to pray to fauns, dryads, and satyrs that they protect his flock and hasten the return of golden peace. Yet, he concludes, peace may not be so very far distant: God bids us hope and so does the venerable father that possesses the walls of Rome (Maffeo Barberini, Pope Urban VIII; reigned 1623-1644). This is a capable poem in which the pastoral manner is clearly but unobtrusively maintained, as is, too, a careful balance between the obscurity that can often result from pastoral cipher and the even less attractive incongruity that can arise from undisguised, naked references to contemporary men and events.

Finally, we shall notice briefly the work of eight French Neo-Latinists, representing a tradition that runs from 1538 to 1739.

We have already seen how Georg Sabinus and Johann Stigel turned history into a sort of pastoral beast-fable in their poems on the battle of Pavia; they had been anticipated by Gilbert Ducher (Ducherius) or Vulton of Aigueperse in Auvergne (ca. 1495–ca. 1538), a fairly prolific poet of whom I have been able to learn very little. He published editions of Caesar and Martial and a two-book collection of original poems (*Epigrammata*; Lyon, 1538) that provides interesting sidelights on the literary history of sixteenth-century France, containing as it does poems addressed to Giacopo Sadoleto, Erasmus, Philip Melanchthon, Clement Marot, and many others. His best-known piece of verse is the following epigram on Pope Julius II:

> "Death to the French!" the Papal tyrant roared
> As smoke from every humble cottage poured.
> His sword he brandished at the thought of blood,
> Hurled Peter's Keys into the Tiber-flood,
> And cried, "If Peter's Keys are useless now
> The Sword of Paul shall guard my holy vow!"

A late poem (but written before 1536) is his one eclogue, "The Dolphin" (*Delphinus*, which in Latin can also mean "Dauphin"; 128 hexameters), of which Alice Hulubei writes, "à défaut d'un style propre, Ducher, qui est trop sous le charme des hexamètres virgiliens, se rabat sur l'exposition, qu'il réalise avec mesure, clarté, et mouvement," and again "on ne lit pas sans plaisir." Here the shepherd Moeris tells Meliboeus how his native land had always been blessed with magnificent rivers whose waters were full of every sort of fish. And in the Rhône, near the *arces Turnonis* (Lyon), was a dolphin which he had hoped would be the finest in the world and would rule all waters from the Loire to Naples. But a certain Austrian shepherd came from Spain and egged on a Spanish subordinate to catch the dolphin with a poisoned hook and poisoned water. Meliboeus exclaims that this must be the reason for the various dire portents observed at Marseille; but night, he says, is falling and it is time to return home for fear of wolves. This all refers to the death of François de Valois, eldest son of François I. He died, presumably of pleurisy, as a result of drinking too much cold water after a violent game of tennis. Suspicion fell upon Count Sebastiano Montecucoli of Ferrara (an amateur student of poisons), who was believed to be an agent of Charles V's two generals, Antonio de Leyva and Ferdinando Gonzaga. The wretched Ferrarese was publicly torn apart by horses, in the presence of the King, the court, and its ladies, on October 7, 1536.

Yet another French Neo-Latinist whose poems are connected with the court of François I is Jacques Gohory or Gohorri, nicknamed *le Solitaire,* of Paris (ca. 1500-1576), naturalist, Latin historian, and vernacular poet. In the Bibliothèque Nationale is a beautifully written manuscript (dated 1543) of an eclogue written by Gohory, called "Francis" (*Franciscus*; 137 hexameters). It is on eight sheets of parchment, in a magnificent Italic hand; the edges are gilded, as is the initial letter of the first line of the Latin text; *folia* 1 recto to 2 verso contain astronomical diagrams explaining references in the text.

The poem is not simple. After Sabinus, Stigelius, and Ducher it is easy to recognize the Cock (François), the Eagle (Charles V), the Lion (Henry VIII), and the Viper (Italy, with particular reference to Milan); but to pastoral cipher and beast-fable Gohory has added astronomy and astrology, which prompts Alice Hulubei to describe the poem justly as "obscure comme un rébus, à l'imagination extravagante, un bizarre assemblage de provenances variées, que rachètent quelques traits descriptifs assez heureux." She wonders, too, what impelled Gohory to call this curiosity of literature an eclogue in the first place and suggests that his only reason was the presence of a recurrent refrain. But Gohory clearly must have known Ducher's pastoral beast-fable and accordingly have considered his poem an eclogue of the same sort, excelling by ill-imitating.

The eclogue that deals with contemporary events does not re-appear in France for almost a century, when we come to Abraham Ravaud (1600-1646), who was professor of rhetoric at Paris and *poeta regius* in the reign of Louis XIII. His vernacular writings appear under the pseudonym Abraham Rémy; the Latin form of the name appears as Remius or Remmius. His two books of Latin *Poemata* (Paris, 1645) are largely occasional, with a sprinkling of religious poems in the second book.

The fifteenth poem of Book II is Remmius' only eclogue (un-titled; 147 hexameters), which deals with an event that interrupted the civil war of 1628-1642, the attack by Flemish troops in the pay of Spain on Picardy in 1637, their capture of Corbie, and their eventual defeat. This poem, largely taken up with panegyric of Louis XIII, is a remarkably exclamatory piece of verse—it often sounds more like a versified declamation than a bucolic, as the reader will see from the following version:

Menalcas: Alas, too near our wretched province lies
To hostile lands! Whenever wars arise,
We first become the prey of every foe!
Through Picardy the hostile banners go!
Why must we ever fear a dreadful fate,
What anguish must we rustics now await?
Now have we fled our own, our native lands,
And left our homes in fear of savage bands.

Thyrsis: Now all is lost, no hope of life remains,
Now speeds the cruel horseman through the plains!
Our fields in ruins lie, our farms are bare:
Here, ruined, lies a tower, a cottage there!
The flocks and herds are driven from the field,
The troopers burn the harvest's golden yield.
They desecrate the altar's holy fane
And fill each house with terror—or with flame!
What sights I saw before me as I fled:
The cities, towns, the very plains now bled!
Now fully ripened, golden waving grain
Had blessed our labors through the fertile plain.
This harvest did the vengeful horseman fire:
Forthwith the raging flames to heaven aspire!

Menalcas :   Some hurl the blazing torch within the cottage-door;
             Each city hears in turn the blazes' roar.
             The holocaust continues without end,
             And stars grow pale to see the flames ascend!
             Now flies the shrieking missile through the air.
             And clouds of acrid smoke now billow there!
             Meanwhile the rustics flee in craven fear,
             The prey of blazing flame or dripping spear.
             The mother wails her sorrow to the sky,
             The greybeard leaves his corner but to die.
             The starving child laments his orphaned state,
             The ruined virgin mourns her wretched fate.
             All these the savage horseman tramples down,
             As rapine spreads through every Picard town!
             Blood fills the busy city, smiling farm,
             And not a living thing is safe from harm!

Thyrsis :   This fate was prophesied by omens dread:
             The whining hounds, the owls, the restive dead!

Menalcas :   Alas for Picardy, now flame and ash,
             The helpless victim of a tyrant's lash!
             How blest are they who know not such a fate,
             Who spend unknowing years in blissful state.

Thyrsis :   The valley of the Somme, once my delight,
             The home of graceful swans and meadows bright,
             No more shall be my everlasting home:
             By Flemings vanquished must I grieving roam!

Menalcas :   Each wooded hill, each peak, each craggy rock
             Has gazed with horror on the battle-shock;
             These hills, once covered by the gracious vine,
             No more I'll see, but ever must repine.

Thyrsis :   Who now shall lead the sheep to river's edge,
             Who now shall feed them by the waving sedge,
             Who clip their wool, who keep them safe from harm,
             If God make not an end to war's alarm?

Menalcas :   The gods delight in peace: but where is peace?
             Where hid? Who'll give me sweet release?

Who'll help me cross the seas to India's shore,
Who'll save me from the cruel battle's roar?

Thyrsis: The plains of Araby that Sheba won,
The hills first gilded by the rising sun:
There Peace still lives: here Mars erects his throne;
There Quiet dwells: here Furies build their home.

Menalcas: Go now, and drive your hopeful furrows straight,
And till your land, and sow your seed till late,
That Flemish soldiers may enjoy your gain,
And leave the weed to flourish in the plain!

Thyrsis: Go now, and herd your flock beside the grove,
And with your cattle by the river rove,
That Flemish thieves may steal your day's reward,
And kill you by starvation or the sword!

Menalcas: My country, dear to Heaven's just decrees!
One day the sword shall come to such as these!
The day shall come when, to our home restored,
We shall rebuild each shattered brick and board!

Thyrsis: When shall we go, released from fear of death?
When shall we rest beneath the zephyrs' breath?
When turn to dancing and the tuneful lay?
When shall the echoes ring by night and day?

Menalcas: But now comes Lycidas: his glance serene
Belies his turmoil and his passion keen!

Lycidas: O blessed day, when eager plaudits ring,
To grace the triumphs of a mighty King!
Let Grief and Anguish hide their mourning face!
Let naught but gladness fill the Gallic race!
You rustics, battered by a brutal foe,
May now in joy and gladness homeward go:
Our LEWIS drove their bands in headlong flight,
And enters Paris on the morrow's light!

Thyrsis: Each Gallic heart now swells with stern delight
To hear this joyous tale of Gallic might!
But tell whence came for us this gleaming Star
To pierce the shadows, blazing from afar!

Lycidas: What foolish darkness clothed your fearful mind?
            What folly made you woeful, made you blind?
            Know that while LEWIS lives we live secure!
            His mighty arm provides a fortress sure!
            Now see the Flemish horsemen turned to flight,
            And those whose squadrons flaunted late their might!
            Their martial leader now, whose every frown,
            Brought death and ruin on some peaceful town,
            Defended though he was by wall and tower,
            No sooner saw than fled the Royal power!
            Rise, then, and go rejoicing to your farms:
            Your river-god awaits, with loving arms.
            All fear removed, he gazes on those banks,
            No more besieged by serried foeman-ranks.
            The nymphs, arisen from the river-bed,
            Now link their arms, their fairest measures tread:
            The god surveys the scene, and smiles anew,
            And plans what honors to the King are due.
            You rustics now may greet the joyful day
            In Picardy, nor tarry on the way.
            Build there an altar by the river's brim
            To honor LEWIS and to rev'rence him.
            Now has his Gallic sword repelled our foes;
            For Fate is just and can recall our woes:
            Once swelled the Spanish King with fiery pride:
            Now, driven by the French, is forced to hide!
            Now stands our sword above the Pyrenees!
            Our ships display their might on all the seas!
            The Alps no longer bar our martial might,
            And Padua herself must mourn her plight!
            Ausonia admits our proud advance;
            Italian ruin shall our power enhance!
            Imbrued with Spanish blood, the river Po
            Now bears its corpses to the sea below!
            And Germany, for triumphs widely famed,
            Now licks her wounds and owns her spirit tamed:
            The Main, the Elbe, the Rhine, the Danube's flow
            No longer save her from the Gallic foe.
            Once safe, the German cities suppliant stand.
            And beg for mercy with an outstretched hand.

> Reduced to beggary, the German brood
> Now live in caves, and scratch to find their food!
> Now go, my friends; return to Picard skies,
> And honor LEWIS with a victor's prize!

Menalcas: You shall we follow, Lycidas, to sing the praise
Of Royal LEWIS in these happy days!
Soon shall we meditate a joyful song,
And pray that LEWIS live to guard us long!
Him shall I sing, him shall I duly praise,
Him shall I celebrate in sounding phrase,
When first arrives the day's first dawning light,
When first appear the shadows of the night!

Thyrsis: I, too, his name shall celebrate for long,
And sing his virtues in my rustic song,
When winter's early frosts shall first appear,
When spring shall clothe the earth with vernal cheer!

After a passing reference to Jean d'Hérouville (born ca. 1670), Nicolas Piat (b. 1680?) and Chrétien Le Roy (1711-1780), one name only remains to be mentioned, that of the Jesuit Thomas Masson, of whom I know only that he was a slightly younger contemporary of Le Roy who wrote an eclogue (untitled; 50 hexameters) on Louis XV's recovery from illness at Metz and published it as a pamphlet at Paris in 1744. It is brief, neat, typical of its age, and a suitable conclusion for the present chapter:

> Let France again rejoice both day and night:
> Let youthful Jest and merry Dance unite!
> If tears be shed, let these be tears of joy:
> At last no fears alarm, no cares annoy;
> Now rises LEWIS from his fevered pain:
> *Sing, Muses, till the welkin ring again!*
> But late he drove the foe in headlong flight
> (The glory of his race, amid the fight),
> But, stayed by illness, faltered in the race,
> And (greatly loath) abandoned late the chase.
> As tempests overwhelm the lordly wood,
> As floods can tear the oak from where it stood,
> So did the sudden fever's deadly power
> Strike LEWIS down in triumph's very hour.

But calm your fear, and all your grief restrain:
Sing, Muses, till the welkin ring again!
None in the Gallic land but felt the blow
When spread report that death had laid him low;
None in the Gallic land restrained his grief,
As prayers besieged the gods for his relief.
But cease your tears, let gladness fill the plain:
Sing, Muses, till the welkin ring again!
The mothers clasped their children to their breast,
And weeping sore, would rock them to their rest.
Despairing shepherds ceased to sound their song,
And broke the pipes that they had loved so long.
The darkest woods of France joined the lament,
As up to Heaven their leafy sighs they sent.
Now let the mother rouse the sleeping child,
Let shepherds sing, and joy inform the wild.
Our present joy's as great as former pain:
Sing, Muses, till the welkin ring again!
The mother, daughter, child to Heaven prayed
That once again the Reaper would be stayed;
Not vain the prayers that France to Heaven sent,
Not vain the glance that present Heaven bent;
The healing god descended to the plain:
Sing, Muses, till the welkin ring again!
Come, France, supported by the rustling breeze,
Come like the wind that stirs the rushing seas;
Once evil-tongued and filled with rumor dread
Now bring the truth, and merriment, instead.
As Echo once redoubled all your tale
Let Echo now rejoice in every vale!
As shepherds once lamented by the hill,
Now let them wander happy, happier still.
Let every grove re-echo with your praise,
Let joy be your reward through all your days.
So take the trumpet, sing with might and main:
Sing, Muses, till the welkin ring again!

XII

NEW USES OF PASTORAL:

PRIVATE

n this final chapter six subdivisions of pastoral appear—eclogues dealing with all sorts of personal matters from vigorous vituperation of an enemy to mild-eyed discussion of literary topics; dramatic eclogues in which the influence of Terence and Plautus is strong or in which the earliest form of masque is anticipated; eclogues that show a strong influence of Ovid's *Heroides* (verse letters of deserted heroines of myth to their absent lovers); satirical eclogues; eclogues of debate that continue a medieval tradition of long standing; and, finally, eclogues of a didactic or moralizing nature.

i

In some of these classes no more than two or three examples are extant; but in the first (general personal matters) nearly fifty authors are represented. The earliest writer here is Leonardo Dati of Florence (1408-1472), of whose career little is known but who was secretary to two cardinals and no less than four successive popes.

Of his two eclogues the second (*Miriltas*; 100 hexameters) recalls the seventh of Calpurnius: the shepherd Miriltas returns wide-eyed to the country and describes to his friend Vigorus in breathless tones the splendors of Florence, where a week of festivities had just taken place in honor of the city's patron saint, St. John the Baptist. Its subject and the fact that Dati was an eyewitness of all he describes gives a certain amount of life and interest to the poem; but the style is rough, and hardly superior to that of the poets of the late fourteenth century.

The first eclogue (*Chirlus*; 100 hexameters) is better. It is a highly personal invective directed against some enemy of the poet whom the shepherd Chirlus (clearly Dati himself) calls Vespa ("Wasp") and accuses of spreading lies of every sort and of poisoning the mind of a patron to whom the poet gives the name of Damnis. The other speaker in the poem, the shepherd Bindus, joins in the vituperation readily. It is possible that "Vespa" is none other than Leon Battista Alberti (1404-1472), who competed against Dati with a play in 1441 and who appears to have been on distinctly touchy terms with the poet.

The six eclogues of Fosco Paracleto of Corneto (died about 1487), dealing almost wholly with the poet's relations with Pope Pius II, display little skill and contain less of interest; we can pass these over and turn to a major collection of Neo-Latin pastoral poems, those of Publio Fausto Andrelini of Forlì (ca. 1462-1518), one of those Italians most active in bringing the new learning to France, an intimate of Erasmus and protégé of the king and queen of France. As an eclogist he is always readable, although his work never became so influential or famous as that of Mantuan and certainly never reached Sannazaro's level of excellence. Andrelini studied at Bologna and at Rome, where he was granted a laurel crown for his elegiac sequence, "Livia." While at Rome he met Ludovico Gonzaga, bishop of Mantua, who became his generous patron from 1484 to 1488. In 1488 he proceeded to France, bearing a letter of introduction (still extant) to the bishop's niece, Chiara Gonzaga, and her husband, Gilbert de Montpensier, Comte-Dauphin of Auvergne. In 1489 he was admitted to lecture publicly at the University of Paris, where he remained for the rest of his life except for brief sojourns at Toulouse and Poitiers. His position at Paris was at first difficult because of the jealousy of Girolamo Balbo, but soon improved, partly through the efforts of Robert Gaguin, until in later life he could claim that four chancellors of France had been his patrons.

The first eclogue (untitled, as are all the others; 86 hexameters) is in dialogue throughout, like all Andrelini's pastorals; it was written just before the poet's departure for France. Here Faustulus (Andrelini) announces to the shepherd Lydus (a Florentine acquaintance) his intention of abandoning "the Ausonian farms," and rehearses, for Lydus' admiration, the complimentary address he has prepared for his new patrons. Allusions to Andrelini's earlier life abound, as in practically all the poems: in lines 33-43, for instance, he refers to his unrewarding years as a secretary of the *curia* at Rome, a topic to which he reverts in the second poem (87 hexameters), written after his arrival at Paris, after gaining the favorable notice of Guillaume de Rochefort, chancellor of France.

In the third eclogue (131 hexameters) the two speakers are Mopsus (Andrelini) and Lycidas (a French Humanist, unidentifiable). Mopsus comes upon his fellow shepherd Lycidas who is sitting alone and disconsolate while others celebrate. Lycidas informs the newcomer that he is in mourning for an old friend, Menalcas. When Lycidas' lament is over Mopsus tells him that other men have troubles, too; he himself had been achieving success in France and had ingratiated himself with "the Palatine Apollo" when a foreign shepherd arrived from Italy (this cannot be Balbo, for he arrived at Paris before Andrelini did) and began to stir up enmity. He was all too successful, adds Mopsus; but if ever I complete my present work (a reference to Andrelini's *De vera religione*, never in fact finished) envy will be crushed.

The fourth poem (136 hexameters) is a singing-match between two shepherds before a third, as in Virgil's third eclogue and Calpurnius' sixth. They try to sing each other down, their subject being the glories of the reign of Charles VIII. The date of the poem is suggested by a reference in line 120 to the re-union of Brittany and France resulting from the marriage (December 1491) of Anne of Brittany and Charles.

The fifth eclogue (93 hexameters) is modeled on Calpurnius' fifth and is well described by Mustard as a "kind of Georgic in bucolic form," in which Amyntas (6-52) sings of the life of the farmer and Corydon (53-90) describes the care of the vine.

The sixth poem (74 hexameters) seems to have been written at about the same time as the first. Here the elderly shepherd Gallus (Ludovico Gonzaga?) discovers young Francus (Andrelini) brushing and preening a pet deer which he proposes to present to his new mistress (Chiara Gonzaga). Gallus upbraids the young man for ingratitude; Francus replies with praise of the Gonzagas in general and of Chiara in particular. It is a pleasant enough poem and certainly is far more attractive than the whines and threats of the third.

The seventh eclogue (82 hexameters) reflects some serious setback in Andrelini's career. Stripped of pastoral convention, the monologue of the shepherd Harmon (Andrelini) boils down to this, that he had at first achieved some success in the face of difficulties and then suddenly found himself without his patron's support at the crucial moment; he is now desperate and regrets abandoning Italy, but he hesitates to return there because he knows that he will make himself a target for the malicious if he does. He bitterly reflects that he has refused the substance for the shadow; from now on he should avoid courts and princes as the devil avoids holy water. In the eighth eclogue (65 hexameters) the topic is continued; one such eclogue is enough, two is too much, and the reader becomes impatient when he discovers that the ninth poem (63 hexameters) is yet another complaint on the identical theme.

Andrelini's crisis has passed by the time we reach the tenth eclogue (135 hexameters written in 1496). Iolas has now appeared before the king and sung of the conquest of Naples; for this he has been granted a royal pension and can hope for greater rewards in the future: Andrelini was in fact made a canon of Bayeux in 1505.

The eleventh eclogue (139 hexameters) was composed much earlier than then tenth, in the spring of either 1491 or 1493. The poem, dedicated to Robert Gaguin, refers in the pastoral manner to Girolamo Balbo's departure from Paris and teems with invective: the poem ends with charges of homosexuality and prophecies of doom. Balbo in fact became a respectable and successful professor of law at the University of Vienna.

The last eclogue (302 hexameters addressed to Louis XII) was not included in the first editions of the *Bucolica*; it was written about 1498 and was first printed in 1512. Corydon preens himself on his assured success and comparative wealth; it is three times as long as it should be.

We have already seen that five of the eclogues of Enrique Cayado of Lisbon (ca. 1460–ca. 1518) dealt with matters of contemporary and public interest; the rest are private and personal.

The second poem (113 hexameters) is addressed from Florence (November, 1495) to a friend and patron at the Portuguese court, Rodrigo de Pina; it describes Cayado's arrival at Florence and goes on to relate how he succeeded in catching a violent chill after swimming in a pond near the city. The tale is told with a good deal of mock-serious elevation and much quiet humor.

The third eclogue (104 hexameters, addressed from Bologna, February, 1496, to Jorge, illegitimate son of King João of Portugal) is largely panegyric of one of Cayado's friends, the young Portuguese poet Diogo Pacheco.

The fourth eclogue (112 hexameters) is a monologue by the poet; it was, as Mustard points out, written with great care, since it was addressed to Cayado's professor at Bologna, Filippo Beroaldo the Elder (1453-1505). The covering letter is dated from Bologna, April 1496. But the poem turns out to be merely a long string of highly conventional praises of country life in which reminiscences of Virgil, Horace, Ovid, Seneca, and Poliziano are frequent.

The fifth eclogue (162 hexameters) is of much greater interest, at least to the English-speaking reader, for the two shepherds of the dialogue are Robert Langton (Lantonus), archdeacon of Dorset and nephew of Thomas Langton (archbishop-elect of Canterbury), at this time living in Bologna, and a younger Englishman called William Harrington (Harynthon) : there is no attempt to portray the actual characters of the two men; they are simply introduced into this poem out of compliment. At one point the poem introduces a panegyric of the beauty of England, its climate, its peacefulness and security from attack, its power, and the loyalty of the English people to their "great-hearted leader" (Henry VII, the first Tudor).

We can pass over the unimportant fourth eclogue (*Aepolus*; 81 hexameters) of Giano Anisio of Naples (ca. 1475–ca. 1547) and the equally unimportant first of Paolo Belmisseri of Pontremoli (ca. 1480–ca. 1547), turning instead to the first eclogue (*Daphnis*; 86 hexameters) of Marco Girolamo Vida of Cremona (1485-1566), in which the point that will strike most readers is the contrast between the floods of tears shed by the lachrymose shepherds Amyntas and Lycidas and the trivial *raison d 'être* of the poem. As one reads, one has the impression that Daphnis is dying or has died under the most tragic circumstances possible; but a very brief examination of the background of the poem shows that Vida is lamenting, in the most exaggerated manner, the temporary absence from Rome of the ecclesiastic Matteo Giberti, who was to spend some time at Florence on the staff of Cardinal Giovanni de' Medici.

Various eclogues of this type appear among the poems of Giulio Camillo or Delminio of Friuli (ca. 1485–ca. 1545), G. B. Giraldi of Ferrara (1504-1573), G. B. Amalteo of Oderzo (1525-1573), Pietro Mirteo (born ca. 1530?), and Marco Publio Fontana of Bergamo (1548-1607); but none needs comment.

The tenth and thirteenth of the piscatory eclogues of Niccolò Giannettasio of Naples (1648-1715) are personal. The tenth ("Chrysis"; 116 hexameters) is a memorial poem; in our examination of epicedia we have frequently seen lamenting shepherds promise to build an altar and carry out an annual rite in memory of a dead friend. Here we see such an anniversary memorial being carried out by two East Indian fishermen at the mouth of the Ganges. Ladon represents Giannettasio himself, Polydorus is Giovanni Bernardo, and Chrysis is a Jesuit-friend named Saveri or Saverio. Giannettasio, himself a Jesuit, was at the time of writing seriously considering abandoning his career as professor of mathematics at the Jesuit college in Naples in order to go to India as a missionary. This eclogue is the work of an exceedingly skilled writer who knows all the tricks of the trade but is sometimes, as we have seen before, inclined to overdo them; he has learned all the lessons that Giacopo Sannazaro could teach him but has added rather too much of his own.

The thirteenth piscatory eclogue (untitled; 117 hexameters) is dedicated to Cardinal Giacopo Cantelmo, archbishop of Naples; it refers to an occasion when the archbishop had made an expedition by sea to Massa (Massalubrense) on the peninsula of Sorrento in order to visit a shrine there (Santa Agata sui due Golfi?) and had walked about the district in company with the poet. Lycabas represents the poet and Mopsus is perhaps some actual friend; the archbishop is referred to only as *heros* and *princeps*:

> Young Lycabas, one pleasant summer day,
> Outstretched beside the Rock of Pallas lay;
> The breath of Zephyr stirred poetic fire
> The while he sought to tune the sounding lyre.
> But soon came Mopsus, from the gleaming strand,
> The wealthy Mopsus, from the yellow sand:

M.:   Why, Lycabas, why waste the time of day?
          Ev'n now the ships approach across the bay!
          If ever you must sing with tuneful voice,
          This hero offers now a theme of choice,
          This princely one, in purple garments bright,
          Whose heart is open and secure his might:
          For Proteus now foretells his coming soon,
          To fill our wishes and to grant a boon!

L.:   I too have heard the god's prophetic song
          As late I steered my fisher's boat along:
          The sea was glassy and the waves were still,
          The moon was rising over yonder hill.
          But have you seen the ships approaching fair?
          Then shall I run to greet and join him there!
          Beyond the stars in song I'll raise his fame,
          Nor will he spurn my humble Muses's name!

M.:   Late was I sailing in the ocean's stream
          To net the chromis and to fish for bream;
          Three vessels saw I, speeding ever near,
          To bear the princely one, to bring him here.
          About the ship there swam a lovely crowd
          Of Nymphs, rejoicing as they sang aloud.
          Amidst them leaped the dolphins' merry crew;
          The Tritons blew their horns and praised him, too.
          The sea resounded with the tuneful song,
          And rocks re-echoed as they sped along.
          Now tune your pipe into a joyful strain,
          And let these shores with music ring again.

          Thus urged, thus moved by Mopsus' eager plea,
          The other sang, beside the glassy sea:

L.:   Speed through the waters, cleave the gentle wave,
          Come, Nymphs, to join me in the shady cave.

          Come where the Sun at dewy eve must hide
          And send his light to grace the eastern tide;
          Each day he rises fresh and rises new,
          And stains the heaven with his scarlet hue.

          Speed through the waters, cleave the gentle wave,
          Come, Nymphs, to join me in the shady cave.

Now speeds the princely guest towards the shore:
The cliffs re-echo with the cannon's roar;
The very heavens gleam with flashes bright,
And all the seas reflect the joyous light.

Speed through the waters, cleave the gentle wave,
Come, Nymphs, to join me in the shady cave.

Not Chiron's self admired Achilles more,
Nor Dictê loved the god whom Rhea bore,
Than now rejoices Massa in her noble guest:
Such joy now steals throughout her loving breast.

Speed through the waters, cleave the gentle wave,
Come, Nymphs, to join me in the shady cave.

Parthenopê, as in a golden dream
Regards us from beloved Sebeto's stream,
Parthenopê, whom loving fate has blest
With such a guardian as Sorrento's guest.

Speed through the waters, cleave the gentle wave,
Come, Nymphs, to join me in the shady cave.

All golden-haired, the gracious Nymphs advance,
To join the Sirens in a graceful dance;
The Naiads come in crowds to view our sands,
And greet the princely visitor with waving hands.

Speed through the waters, cleave the gentle wave,
Come, Nymphs, to join me in the shady cave.

For such a prince the Zephyrs always blow,
For such a prince the sun will ever glow,
For such a prince the level seas rejoice,
For such a prince the Nereids raise their voice.

Speed through the waters, cleave the gentle wave,
Come, Nymphs, to join me in the shady cave.

The mossy gifts of ocean's sandy floor
Bring now in baskets to the sandy shore:
Bring urchins from the kindly ocean's store,
And bring him rarest oysters by the score.

Speed through the waters, cleave the gentle wave,
Come, Nymphs, to join me in the shady cave.

Such gifts will prove his manly heart's delight:
He seeks not glowing gold nor silver bright;
He passes by the gems that others seek:
Through virtue modest and through merit meek.

Speed through the waters, cleave the gentle wave,
Come, Nymphs, to join me in the shady cave.

Such gifts he'll not despise in haughty pride;
Nor sole nor grayling will he cast aside;
Then fill with these your fragrant baskets high,
And bring the choicest of the sea's supply.

Speed through the waters, cleave the gentle wave,
Come, Nymphs, to join me in the shady cave.

Let Sirens now with loving heart rejoice,
And greet the longed-for prince with merry voice,
As now his vessel skims the sparkling bay,
And all but ended is its joyful way.

Speed through the waters, cleave the gentle wave,
Come, Nymphs, to join me in the shady cave.

Within the cave let every Goddess wait,
Then greet the princely visitor in state;
Then Nymphs shall dance and sing his praises due:
He will deserve those songs, and dances, too.

Speed through the waters, cleave the gentle wave,
Come, Nymphs, to join me in the shady cave.

Let Nymphs who dwell in Capri's rocky height
Descend to ocean's wave to greet his might,
Surround the vessel as they swim around,
While conches raise the echoes with their sound.

Now cease your swift career amid the wave,
Now leave the ocean for the mossy cave.

See, now he comes from Neptune's azure realm,
As Nymphs surround the ship from prow to helm,

As dolphins leap amid the ocean's spray,
To testify the honor of this day.

Now cease your swift career amid the wave,
Now leave the ocean for the mossy cave.

He now approaches close Sorrento's shore,
As cliffs reveal their outlines ever more;
The shoals receive the gliding vessel's keel:
A kindly warmth all nature seems to feel.

Now cease your swift career amid the wave,
Now leave the ocean for the mossy cave.

From lofty stern he steps and, on the strand,
Now greets the waiting throng, and treads the sand;
Spread myrtles, Nymphs, and scatter roses rare,
Let Arab perfumes scent the evening air.

Now cease your swift career amid the wave,
Now leave the ocean for the mossy cave.

This hasty song from Massa's shore I send,
A humble tribute from a humble friend:
Grant but your favor to my modest Muse,
And Phoebus greater power will not refuse.

Four Germans wrote eclogues on personal matters. The second (untitled; 175 hexameters) of Euricius Cordus (Heinrich Solde) of Simsthausen in Hesse (1486-1535) is similar in subject to one of Mantuan's and another of Belmisseri's, being a defense of modern Latin poets, a lament over the meager rewards of poetry, and a hopeful prophecy of better times to come. The poem has technical flaws, but it is lively, dramatic, and in parts distinctly amusing.

The eleventh eclogue (untitled; 199 hexameters) of Elius Eobanus (Koch) of Bockendorf or Halgeshausen in Hesse (1488-1546) is downright vituperative. Here Corydon represents Eoban Koch himself, and the arrogant Philondas is the Italian Neo-Latin poet Riccardo Sbruglio of Udine (so Ellinger). After a few tentative insults, there follows a slanging-match in stanzas of two, three, or four lines apiece. Corydon finally bids Philondas a mocking farewell, and his sneering words bring this far from attractive piece to a close. The twelfth eclogue of Eoban (untitled; 135

hexameters) is spoiled by much self-conscious vanity of a sort that reminds the reader all too forcibly of certain passages in Petrarch.

Two of the twenty eclogues of Joachim Camerarius (Liebhard) of Bamberg (1500-1574) can be considered here. The sixth poem, entitled "Carpolimaeus" (164 lines), has as its two speakers Carpolimaeus (the poet himself) and Palicus (almost certainly Philip Melanchthon). In the lament of Palicus we see reflected Melanchthon's own worries over the difficulties of the day: the disasters resulting from the Peasants' Revolt, his own troubles in re-establishing or establishing schools and universities, the threat of renewed warfare, personal trials—all this is described in pastoral terms, a picture of the Golden Age in reverse.

In the twelfth eclogue, "Battus" (91 hexameters), a lament by Battus is followed by consolation, encouragement, and exhortation from his fellow shepherd Menalcas. Battus describes the dryness of the soil, the poverty of the crops, and the shortage of food in all Germany and on his farm in particular; Menalcas replies that any farmer must learn to co-operate with the inevitable and urges him to pluck up his courage in the hope that next year will be better. The probability is that Battus is again Melanchthon.

The last German Neo-Latin pastoral to be mentioned here is the fourth eclogue ("Lycidas"; 86 hexameters) of Peter Lotich the Younger of Schlüchtern (1528-1560), a difficult poem which, as Ellinger rightly points out, is strongly Italian in manner. Lycidas, we are told, lamented the cruelty of Ocyroê, at length hurling himself to the ground in a frenzy of grief. Eventually he rose to his feet and began his long journey home; but, although he reached the river Rhine, his friends and family never saw him again, for he remained wandering forever. The very oddity of this poem suggests that "Lycidas" refers to some real person; the probability is that, like the fifth eclogue, this poem refers to some German friend met at Padua during Lotich's visit to Italy. It may be that some German student had, as a result of some bitter disappointment (not necessarily in love), been forced to return to Germany but had been ashamed to return to his own home.

Of Dutch authors represented here, all are already familiar. We can begin with the first eclogue (untitled; 100 hexameters) of Peter van der Brugge (Pontanus) of Bruges (ca. 1480–ca. 1540). The theme is the well-worn complaint that poets go unappreciated and unrewarded in thick-witted Flanders. The poem was not published until 1513, but no doubt was written about 1505 (the date when the poet left the Netherlands for Paris) and no doubt it reflects his actual feelings at the time. As with all of Peter van der Brugge's eclogues, the personality of the author and the vigor of the contents triumph over the inelegance of the verse.

Besides the seven eclogues that appear in the Antwerp (1575) edition of the Latin poems of Jakob de Sluyper of Herzele (1532-1582), there is an extra poem, "Iolas" (45 hexameters), published in the *Delitiae poetarum Belgicorum*. This unusually brief (for Sluperius) eclogue was written later than the others, at the time when religious troubles—"the Protestant pest," *Geusia pestis*—had forced the author, already exiled from Ypres, to abandon Boesinghe (1566). In a monologue he laments that his flock will be abandoned and that the shepherds and shepherdesses of his poems will no longer wander about the pleasant fields of Boesinghe. Sluperius introduces most of the characters of his other eclogues—Eucharis from the fifth, Daphnis from the seventh, Aegon from the sixth, Damastor from the fourth, Amyntas from the first, and so on. It it a pity that all his eclogues are not so brief and to the point as this one.

In the fourth eclogue ("Damoetas"; 129 hexameters) of Peter de Fransz (Francius) of Amsterdam (1645-1704), Iolas (Francius himself) laments the departure of Damoetas: the poem was written when Jan van Broekhuyzen (Janus Broukhusius) left Amsterdam. Like all Francius' poems, it is unusually skillful and professional; yet it is not nearly so attractive (despite its being written to a close personal friend) as other eclogues of Francius met earlier: this time the rhetorician gets the better of the poet too often. Broukhusius served in America with Admiral Ruyter in 1674, and the present eclogue belongs to that year.

The fourth eclogue of Broukhusius himself, entitled "Celadon, or Home Thoughts from Abroad" (*Celadon, sive Desiderium patriae*; 60 hexameters) may well describe the poet's own feelings in 1674. Here Celadon sits at the stern of his ship, looking back in the direction of Holland, and recalls the friends he may never see again, imagines the life he will soon be leading amid naked savages, prays to the nymphs of the sea for a swift journey, and promises to bring them gifts of sugarcane and a bird of brilliant plumage. It is possible, however, that this is rather an *ecloga nautica,* describing a Dutch seaman's feelings on a voyage to the East Indies, for the *picta avis* is less likely to be a West Indian parrot than a bird of paradise.

Both the eclogues of Caspar van Kinschot of The Hague (1622-1649) belong here. Kinschot, who was descended from a noble family that had produced eminent jurisconsults since the beginning of the 1500's, studied law at Utrecht and Leyden and then traveled fairly widely. He returned to Holland in 1646 and was shortly appointed a member of the Dutch commission that took part in drawing up the terms of the Peace of Westphalia. His early death cut short what would probably have been a decidedly distinguished career in law, politics, and polite letters. Kinschot's poems have all the grace and precision that we associate with the best Dutch Neo-Latin poets, and his abilities deserve the praise given them by Nicolaus Heinsius.

Among Kinschot's poems appear two excellent eclogues. The first, "Thyrsis" (135 hexameters), was written when Heinsius left for England (1641). This poem, like others of its type, is filled with every sort of artificiality, yet is undeniably attractive. The shepherd Iolas, after a sleepless night, makes his way into the well-known fields by the river, but can find no pleasure in his usual tasks; instead, while his flock wanders uncared for, he sings a reproachful lament over the departure of his friend Thyrsis.

The second eclogue, "Iolas" (141 hexameters), is addressed to Adriaan, a relative of Jakob van der Walle (or Vandewalle) of Courtrai, probably one of his six brothers. The poet invites his friend to come to the country to hear the song of the shepherd Iolas; the song proves to be, as in scores of art-pastorals, a love-song in which the shepherd urges his lady to look more kindly upon him. But it is clear that Iolas is the poet himself and that Amaryllis actually does represent a young lady of The Hague whom he wished to marry. In all probability, then, Amaryllis is Marie Brouxaux, for whose marriage to Caspar van Kinschot Hugo Grotius wrote an excellent Latin epithalamium.

Among French Neo-Latin poets the number of eclogues dealing with personal matters is quite large, but many of the poems are minor, particularly those of the eighteenth century. Even their historical importance is of little account, and I shall content myself with giving only the most summary report of the history of this type of eclogue in France from 1539 to 1786.

The first author we meet here is Philibert Girinet of St. Just en Chevalet (a friend of Gilbert Ducher and Jean Regnier) whose dates may be ca. 1490–ca. 1550. Beyond the fact that he was treasurer of the church of St. Étienne at Lyon, we know practically nothing of his life. In his one extant eclogue, first published in 1546 (untitled; 253 hexameters), Girinet describes the election of Pierre Gautier to the ancient and honorable post of "King" of the basoche celebrations at Lyon in 1539: he has become *princeps pragmaticorum Lugdunensium* (*roi des basochiens Lyonnais*). The poem is of some interest to students of French literature but need only be mentioned here.

One eclogue appears among the extensive collection of Latin poems published by Jean-Edouard du Monin of Gy in Burgundy (ca. 1557-1586), surely one of the most bizarre personalities of the sixteenth century. He accumulated a vast, ill-digested store of learning in the course of his studies of Latin, Greek, Hebrew, mathematics, theology, and literature, and his poems are as fantastically *précieux* as might have been expected. He manifests a vast admiration for himself.

His one eclogue (untitled; 161 hexameters) is addressed to his patron, Cardinal du Perron; Maenalius is the Cardinal, Meliboeus the poet, and Tityrus is the poet's friend François Jordein. This poem, unlike those in the author's vernacular *Phoenix* (1585), is easy to understand, but, as Mme Hulubei cuttingly remarks, "its limpidity is deceptive," covering no more than a banal simplicity as bland as warm milk and as insipid as unsalted porridge. Much fulsome praise of Du Perron brings this poem (obviously a glorified begging-letter) to an undistinguished close.

We can refer in passing to a number of poems by Scévole de Ste. Marthe of Loudon (1536-1623), Pierre Labbé of Clermont-Ferrand (1594–ca. 1680), Pierre Mambrun of Clermont-Ferrand (1600-1661), Simon Cordier (*floruit* 1680), and Jean Commire of Amboise (1625-1702), turning now to Jean-Baptiste de Santeul or Santeuil (Santolius) of Paris (1630-1697), who has been called "le plus célèbre des poètes latins modernes." Santeul, a member of an old merchant family, studied at the Collège de Ste.-Barbe, and at the age of twenty entered the regular canons of St. Victor; he accepted the rank of sub-deacon but refused to rise higher. His whole life was devoted to study and to the cultivation of Latin poetry. His verse was exceedingly well known in his own day; he was described by a contemporary as Paris' favorite poet, and Paris in fact granted him a pension for life, as did the king. La Bruyère, who knew him well, contrasts one aspect of his character (*facile, doux, complaisant*) with the other (*tout à coup violent, colère, fougueux*), describes him again as *simple, ingénu, crédule, un enfant à cheveux gris,* and finally bursts out with *quelle verve, quelle élévation, quelles images, quelle latinité!*

His complete Latin poems appear in a volume of 362 pages (Paris, 1695). The first eclogue is an attractive bit of writing, but there is nothing specifically pastoral about it (untitled; 86 hexameters).

The second eclogue, "Damon and Aegon" (95 hexameters), is a pastoral *gratiarum actio,* expressing the poet's thanks for the generosity of the Abbé de Daquin (the Aegon of the poem). We are first shown a picture of the shepherd Damon sunk in dejection while his flocks wander untended. This picture is as traditional as can be, and can be paralleled from a score of art-pastorals by Italians and others; here Santeul manages it all with much grace and elegance. The poet then proceeds to tell us that Damon's song had recently been rejected in favor of one by Amyntas (conceivably René Rapin). Time was, goes on Santeul (16-31), when the whole world listened to Damon alone: here follows a great list of those who did, each neatly and sometimes epigrammatically described in a word or phrase. How literally all this is to be taken I am not sure; but the hurt feelings seem real, and it is likely that this eclogue does actually refer to a literary reverse suffered by Santeul. If it were possible to date the poem interpretation would be easier.

The "personal" eclogues that continue to appear at Paris in pamphlet form (e.g., one by Charles Fabiot Aunillon, 1684-1760, nicknamed *le petit curé de la comédie* from his fondness for actresses) grow less and less interesting as time goes on. There is some life, however, in an eclogue called "Codrus" (115 hexameters), probably written (in 1700?) by Father Pipon of the Collège du Cardinal le Moine, describing a secession of its instructors to Ivry—it contains much personal, satirical, and topical matter difficult to decipher at this late date. An anonymous eclogue of the same year entitled "Umbricius" (164 hexameters) is similar and refers several times to the "Codrus" by name. Here the shepherd Menalcas asks Umbricius why he is abandoning Paris for a shepherd's life, and Umbricius, like his original in Juvenal's third satire, replies with a vicious tirade against everything that Paris and the University stood for.

Another anonymous eclogue (117 hexameters), written by an instructor at the Collège du Cardinal le Moine in 1732, describes in pastoral terms the celebration of the Feast of St. Andrew. Yet another anonymous pastoral is the "Ste.-Barbe Eclogue" (135 hexameters) of 1786, describing festivities on the feast of St. Barbara; there is much that is satirical and topical here, and the constant references to places and scenes (the mud of the Paris streets, the beggars, street-corners in the Latin Quarter) lend a certain liveliness to the poem.

Four Scottish poets can be mentioned here, the most famous being George Buchanan of Stirlingshire (1506-1582), called by Joseph Justus Scaliger the greatest poet of his age.

One of the most interesting of his satirical poems is the first of the *Elegies,* written while Buchanan was a regent at Ste.-Barbe. It is the perennial cry of the tired teacher: Buchanan describes in detail the difficulties of getting a good night's sleep amid the din of Paris, the dull routine of classwork, the annoyance of parents when a teacher fails to make a silk purse out of a sow's ear, poverty, and the realization that old age would offer no escape.

The time was to come, however, when Buchanan would long to return to Paris. His first eclogue, entitled "Longing for Paris" (*Desiderium Lutetiae*; 92 hexameters), was written during his ill-fated stay in Portugal—it may, indeed, have been written in prison. Like a good many of the poems noted in this chapter, it is composed throughout as an art-pastoral, but it is clearly personal. The speaker, Daphnis, begins with a passionate outburst: lovely Amaryllis, it is now seven long years since I last saw you! Yet seven long winters, he goes on, have not removed your image from my heart— morning, noon, and night I think of you (1-20). Often I gaze out over the waters that separate us, even envying the wind and the waves that are free to travel to France (21-43). I have been faithful, too: those pretty Portuguese girls, Lycisca and Melaenis, have done their utmost to attract me, and their mothers have hinted at generous dowries (44-83). But, concludes Daphnis, sooner will dogs love wolves, or a bull bears, or rabbits a fox, or a doe lionesses, than Lycisca or Melaenis will change my mind: Amaryllis was my first love and will be my last.

This is an eclogue of the most personal kind, and, of all those so far met in the present chapter, it is the one most charged with genuine feeling; it should be observed at the same time that it is full to the brim of stock phrases, stock turns of expression, stock figures. Every line of the poem is expressed in the most traditional, even artificial manner, yet the eclogue is a highly successful one. "It would be hard," writes Leicester Bradner, making the same point, "to find a better example of the power of a poet to use a highly conventional form . . . to express successfully an extremely personal emotion." The same comment, *mutatis mutandis,* could be made of Milton's *Epitaphium Damonis.*

The second eclogue of Buchanan is entitled "Longing for Tastaeus" (*Desiderium Ptolomaei Luxii Tastaei*; 105 hexameters). This was written earlier than the first poem, while Buchanan was teaching at the Collège de Guyenne in Bordeaux. Here the shepherd Agrius laments the temporary absence of Tastaeus in Poitou; it is a well-written piece of work but rather overdone.

Two of the eclogues of John Barclay of Pont à Mousson (1582-1621) next claim some attention. The first of these is entitled "Corydon's Complaint to Phoebus" (*Planctus Corydonis ad Phoebum*; 102 hexameters): Corydon is the poet and Phoebus is James VI and I. In its own way, this is as effective and certainly as interesting a poem as Buchanan's *Desiderium Lutetiae*; its skill would certainly have impressed King James, and its tone of brusque demand no doubt gave him a certain sardonic amusement.

The second eclogue, "Corydon's Gratitude" (*Corydonis Carmen eucharisticon*; 76 hexameters), is the sequel to the first, and, although it may have been composed some time subsequently, it is clearly intended to be read continuously with the first. The "Complaint" had ended with Corydon's prostrating himself before the figure of Phoebus; the "gratitude" begins with the god's stretching out his hand and raising the suppliant from the dust. The rest of the poem (10-76) consists of Corydon's thanks.

In the bibliography of his *Musae Anglicanae,* Leicester Bradner mentions an eclogue by William (?) Hart (1605) called "Caledon"; this I have not seen, nor have I read the series of ten eclogues (most of which deal with the author's own troubles) written by Andrew Aidie of Aberdeen and published at Danzig in 1610. I shall refer instead to six of the twenty eclogues of John Leech (Leochaeus) of Montrose (ca. 1590–ca. 1630), three of them (numbers i, iii, and v) piscatory eclogues (unbearably dull), three of them bucolic pastorals.

The three relevant poems among Leech's bucolic pastorals are worth examining. The first bucolic, entitled "Aita" (123 hexameters) is a pleasant bit of work, introducing us to three friends of Leech—William Alexander (Master of Requests to James VI and I), John Scot of Scotstarvet (a well-known lawyer and connoisseur of Neo-Latin poetry who encouraged the production of the *Delitiae poetarum Scotorum*), and William Drummond of Hawthornden. At the beginning of the poem Leech refers to them as Amyntas, Damon, and Alexis and then identifies them (allusively) in the last half-dozen lines of the eclogue.

Leech announces that he has abandoned city life for the delights of the country. He goes on to promise rustic entertainment for the three friends from the meadows of Menultrie, the hills of Tarvet, and the hawthorn thickets he knows so well. This is an excellent and lively poem and comes as a considerable relief after the three piscatories just mentioned.

The third bucolic, "The Enchantress" (*Pharmaceutria*; 109 hexameters), derives its title from Virgil's eighth eclogue; but Leech has given his poem this traditional title merely because it contains a magic song of binding—no enchantress actually appears. Lycidas bitterly remarks that poetry reaps no reward and that Thyrsis had ignored his poems (this may refer to John Scot of Scotstarvet, who had advised Leech to seek honest employment as well as poetic fame).

The fifth of the bucolic pastorals, entitled "The Bard" (*Vates*; 166 hexameters), is as pleasant a poem as the first; it is a pastoral version of a form of poem (usually written in elegiac couplets) that had been a favorite for generations—a review of the poet's predecessors or contemporaries in poetry, Latin or vernacular. Here it comes as a disappointment that most of the names so allusively introduced cannot be identified; but in Themistor, the Scot in Rome, it is easy to recognize John Barclay.

ii

We have now examined the pastorals that deal with purely personal affairs; they are very numerous, but the other categories here (except for the satirical poems) are not nearly so well represented at any period.

All pastorals are "dramatic" in the sense that they usually contain dialogue and have a certain amount of action; but there are some so clearly influenced by dramatic language or technique that we can justifiably make a separate classification. As early as Petrarch there is the occasional passage in a bucolic which is obviously reminiscent of Terence's elegant but colloquial language; there is the occasional passage, too, where a rustic "enters" and, before approaching the other characters, makes an aside to the reader like any actor to an audience. This sort of thing is not very common, but it is frequent enough to make it worth mentioning.

Again, one poem by Claude Roillet (Rouillet) we found to be a real pastoral mime, a rustic blood-and-thunder playlet based on the parable of the unjust laborers in the vineyard. Full-blown pastoral plays too, did exist in Latin (e.g., those by Donato Mazzoli of Rome and Carolo Oddi of Perugia), usually in praise of the Virgin, with such characters as Daphnis, Amyntas, Damoetas, and Alcon. But even apart from this, the dramatic pastoral proper could also exist, halfway between pastoral mime on the one hand and fully developed pastoral play on the other. It was a natural development, for more than one Neo-Latin eclogue had been presented in public, and at least two vernacular eclogues were presented to the accompaniment of music, one at Versailles in 1702, the other in Toulouse, perhaps a little later. And, long before that, at least some of Cayado's eclogues (to say nothing of Virgil's) were performed in Bologna; in a letter of 1496 Cayado speaks as though this were not at all unusual.

It is not then astonishing to find that the "Lepidina" of Giovanni Pontano of Cerreto (ca. 1424-1503) is a sort of pastoral masque, forming one of the most elaborate and remarkable of all the hundreds of Neo-Latin pastorals in existence. Its eight hundred lines and more consist of an introductory and more or less conventional eclogue (practically complete in itself) followed by seven separate scenes or *pompae* ("processions"), of which the original speakers of the introductory poem are the spectators and on which they comment from time to time; the structure is that of a play within a play and must surely be one of the very earliest European instances of that useful device. It would not be at all astonishing if the *Lepidina* had been publicly performed *al fresco,* as one vernacular *egloga rusticale* certainly was in 1508.

At this point we might examine the whole work in some detail. In the heat of a summer noon, Macron urges his wife Lepidina to rest, now that they have reached the shore of the Bay of Naples. As they rest, they describe at length the happiness of their marriage (it is perhaps not too fanciful to see in this rustic pair the youthful Pontano and his wife Adriana Sassone), and Lepidina hopes that the forthcoming marriage of Parthenopê (Naples) and Sebethus (the stream Sebeto) will prove as idyllic as their own.

It is at this point that the *pompa prima* begins, a twenty-four-line poem of twelve hexameter distichs sung by men and women of the procession as they arrive from the country; if this was ever actually presented, the two groups no doubt formed antiphonal choirs. The formal balance of the distichs is naturally accompanied by a corresponding balance in their content:

Women: Desert the fold: let myrtle bind your brow;
        Come with us, boy; the city draws you now.

Men: Now yield, Parthenopê, with gentle heart;
        Now learn what love and wedlock can impart.

Women: Learn now to give a husband's fond caress,
        The joy of love, the joy of happiness.

Men: To his embrace submit with ready grace:
        A husband never loves a sullen face.

Women: Though dark her eyes, her hair is black as jet;
        Though sweet her touch, her glance is sweeter yet.

Men: His ruddy cheek the glow of health reveals;
        His slender frame the strength of two conceals;

Women: A blossom rare awaits the eager boy;
        A ripened fruit awaits the lover's joy.

Men: That blossom shall he pluck with ready hand,
        To gain the fairest flower in any land.

Women: The stream that issues from the rock's crevasse
        At last becomes in time a foaming mass.

Men: A single tear a single glance will move:
           A single tear becomes a tide of love.

Women: A single flame a single spark will raise:
           A single flame becomes a roaring blaze.

Men: Just so the spark of love will burst in flame,
           And, coursing hot, will rage in every vein.

The next *pompa* is mute: that is, the procession of nereids is merely described by Macron and Lepidina in a poem of eighty-nine lines. In the actual performance, the scene had no doubt been a brilliant and fantastic one. As each nereid was in turn described, a girl representing her—no doubt accompanied by a swarm of attendant male and female sea-sprites—would dance across the space serving as a stage.

Triton follows the last of the nereids, and his song, praising Parthenope, forms the third *pompa*. He displays the nereids' gifts and promises the love and loyalty of all the Tritons, upon whom he then calls to raise the marriage-cry of *Hymen, o Hymenaee, Hymen ades, o Hymenaee* (line 34).

The fourth *pompa* now approaches—a procession of *Nymphae urbanae et suburbanae*. Again the *pompa*—which, no doubt, could have been made as spectacular as the stage manager's resources could arrange—is mute, as Macron and Lepidina describe and praise the nymphs who parade past, representing the various districts of Naples and its surroundings.

At the beginning of the fifth *pompa*, Macron points to an approaching figure, which proves to be that of the nymph Planuris, whom Lepidina invites to name the members of yet another procession, which can be seen approaching from the distance. Planuris first describes the strange hairy and hornèd sprites of cave and forest, stream and lake that mop and mow about the head of the procession, and then identifies the heroes of myth who appear in the rest of the *pompa*; these heroes are not those of classical mythology but of a mythology of the Humanist's beloved Naples.

In the sixth *pompa* a nymph, calling herself Patulcis, makes her appearance, lamenting that while every other nymph has her lover, she has none, and bewailing the fact that the young man she loves is under the spell of the nymph Nisa.

In the seventh *pompa*—the climax of the whole work—it is

Antiniana who leads the epithalamium of Parthenopê and Sebethus, with a chorus of young men and women. After a final invocation of Hymenaeus, Antiniana and her attendants leave the stage and the long eclogue ends as it had begun, with Macron and Lepidina alone, deciding what wedding gifts they will give Parthenopê and Sebethus.

Thus ends an eclogue, or series of eclogues, completely characteristic of Giovanni Pontano. His fluent Latin, his neologisms, his free use of the later Latin vocabulary, his sensuous admiration of the physical beauty of women, coupled with the domestic *Gemütlichkeit* that he shares with such a Neo-Latin poet as Girolamo Fracastoro, his entirely natural and unselfconscious use of the international language are all illustrated here. The invariable exuberance of his Latin verse and his occasional lack of care in versification are in striking contrast with the invariable elegance and occasional languidness of his younger contemporary Sannazaro.

The next poet we meet here is Francesco Barlettani (Barlectanus) of Volterra (perhaps 1470-1525) of whom little is known except that he belonged to Pope Leo X's Golden Age of patronage. His one eclogue (untitled; 470 hexameters) is a dramatized pastoral novelette in hexameters, preceded by an elegiac poem of dedication addressed to Cardinal Giovanni de'Medici (i.e., the later Pope Leo X: this at least dates the poem before 1513) at some time well after the death of his father, Lorenzo the Magnificent (1492), in which the poet quite bluntly says that he is suffering hard times and hopes that the son will be as generous as the father had been. The eclogue is as long as a little play. Its language is strongly influenced by Terence and Plautus (the exclamations *pol, hem,* and so on appear frequently), there are changes of scene, entrances and exits, asides to the audience, and the like throughout the poem. As a stylized medium for private theatricals, this pastoral playlet no doubt could have been presented with no little success before Giovanni de'Medici. Despite all its conventionality and formality, it is a very lively, entertaining, and attractive piece indeed, and it is astonishing that more Neo-Latinists did not follow Barlettani's example or go beyond it.

The only similar poem I know is an eclogue (untitled; 499 hexameters) composed by an otherwise unknown writer called Nicolas Yvelin, who was "procurator of the Norman nation" at the Collège du Plessis in 1587, the date of his poem's publication. Yvelin quite clearly intended the pastoral to be taken as a playlet, for he heads it *"Dramatis personae*: Damon, Lycoris, Lycidas,

Meliboeus, Pan, Moeris." The playlet introduces quite a number of pastoral themes and techniques—the shepherds' quarrel, amoebaean couplets, amoebaean quatrains, the pastoral love story (novelette, rather), the marriage song, the refrain, and so on; at one point we are even reminded of Pontano when Moeris praises Lycoris' skill in spinning. As in Barlettani's poem we have Terentian Latin, entrances and exits, the lover and his helpers, and a helpful deity, who in this poem appears *in propria persona*.

iii

There seem to be only a couple of extant examples of the third class of eclogue studied in this chapter. Ovid had written a series of poems called *Heroides,* "The Heroines," in which deserted or lonely women write to their absent husbands or lovers; their tone is usually elaborately rhetorical, and Virgil would no doubt have been startled at Dido's plea to Aeneas as Ovid wrote it.

The Neo-Latin poets knew the *Heroides* well; Elius Eobanus (Koch) wrote a whole series of Christian *Heroides* in which the writers are female saints. Joachim Camerarius (Liebhard) of Bamberg (1500-1574) wrote one eclogue that is a combination of pastoral romance and heroine-epistle: this is the eleventh (*Oenonê*; 121 hexameters) of his twenty eclogues. The fifth of Ovid's *Heroides* is supposed to be a letter written by the nymph Oenonê of Mount Ida after Paris, the one-time shepherd, had been recognized as Prince of Troy and had abandoned her to resume his rightful place in Troy.

Camerarius adapts the story and the situation to Virgilian pastoral. A longish introduction (1-34) tells us that by now the Trojan ships were sailing to Greece in quest of Helen and that Paris was all forgetful of the life he had once led on Ida (here Camerarius introduces rustic and idyllic details with a lavish hand); this is followed (35-112) by Oenonê's lament, in which there is naturally much reminiscence of Ovid but no direct copying or deliberate cento. Oenonê ends by wishing Paris a happy voyage and hoping that on his return he will abandon Helen and come back to *her*. Certainly this is a very readable poem, as in fact are most of Camerarius' pastorals.

A more obvious example of the *Herois*-eclogue appears in a manuscript of the Bibliothèque Nationale, dated 1676. Here a shepherdess named Elygias (who represents the town of Nivers) writes to her lover Tityrus (a French nobleman of Nivers with whom the anonymous author of the poem was in some way connected and who was now obviously occupied in a grand tour of Italy). Elygias, with a wealth of pastoral detail, recalls their former happiness in the countryside around Nivers, urges him to return, fears that some Italian shepherdess may cause him to forget her, and again urges him to return. It is a brief (45 hexameters) and not very clever poem, but it is worth mentioning as an example of a type.

iv

The fourth class of eclogue is much better represented: satirical eclogues are common from the early sixteenth century to the late eighteenth, beginning with four of the ten eclogues of Mantuan (Giambattista Spagnuoli of Mantua; 1448-1516).

The fourth poem, entitled "Alphus, or, The Nature of Women" (*Alphus, sive de natura mulierum*; 252 hexameters), is a rather long-winded eclogue in the tradition of medieval satire on women. It is lively enough in parts, but often degenerates into noisy blustering and name-calling; it has always, however, been one of the best known of Mantuan's bucolics. The reader will get an adequate notion of this long denunciation of the much abused sex from a version of 110-134, in which appears a famous string of adjectives:

> The female sex is servile, proud, and crude:
> No measure modifies its manners rude.
> No notion has it of the Golden Mean:
> Now sunk in sloth, now rushing is it seen.
> A woman's either freezing winter drear
> Or blazing summer's dryness, hot and sere.
> No middle course she follows in her life;
> She either loves, or stirs eternal strife.
> If grave she turns, she plays the pedant's part;
> If merry, then there's naught within her heart.
> She weeps, she laughs, she rages, fears, or dares,
> And inconsistent shows her changing wares.
> She's restless, fickle, talking, vain, a cheat;
> She's vengeful, vicious, wrathful, indiscreet;
> She's evil, greedy, whining, jealous, sly;
> She's hasty, headlong, rash, a living lie;

She's lazy, showy, superstitious, vain;
She's sluttish, stupid, petulant, a bane;
She's priggish, prudish, snappish as a tod;
She's riggish, whorish, shrewish as a bawd;
She's feckless, fearful, fawning, forward, fell,
A hissing, hateful harpy hot from Hell.

The fifth poem, called "Candidus, or, The Behavior of Patrons to Poets" (*Candidus, sive de consuetudine divitum erga poetas*; 190 hexameters), deals with a topic already thoroughly canvassed by Theocritus, Juvenal, Martial, and Petrarch, one that was to be handled many more times by many more Neo-Latin poets in half-a-dozen mediums. English readers know the theme best from Alexander Barclay's fourth *Egloge* and Edmund Spenser's *October Aeglogue,* of which the first paraphrases, the second closely follows, Mantuan's poem.

The sixth poem, "Cornix" (255 hexameters), is a dialogue between Cornix (the name means "crow") and Fulica ("coot"), the subject being the same as in the satirical debate of Barlettani's pastoral playlet—town life versus country life; Barclay's fifth *Egloge* is again no more than a paraphrase of this poem.

The ninth eclogue, entitled "Falco, or, The Ways of the Roman Curia" (*Falco, sive de moribus Romanae curiae*; 232 hexameters), belongs to the later group of Mantuan's eclogues. It is a satire on the methods of the central government of the Roman Church and probably reflects Mantuan's own experience when he had gone to Rome on some business connected with the Carmelite order. Elsewhere Mantuan says, "Our temples, priests, altars, rites, and prayers are all for sale; so is Heaven and even God himself," and, again, "These shepherds hate their flocks; their only interest is to shear the sheep." Such poems as this eclogue were eagerly read by English and German Protestants and became the model for many an attack on Popish prelates. The clearest imitation is Spenser's *September Aeglogue,* but it is probable also that Milton (who knew Italian Neo-Latin poetry well and had demonstrably read many of Mantuan's poems) had the *Falco* in mind, in writing, "the hungry sheep look up and are not fed."

The first eclogue (*Fuscula*; 113 hexameters) of Pierfrancesco Giustolo of Spoleto (ca. 1450–ca. 1529) is the next to appear among satirical bucolics. Here we have a monologue uttered by a rustic

named Faustulus (Giustolo himself)—he is living at the noisy
capital, but hopes soon to return to the country home of Colotius
(Angelo Colocci, a nobleman of Spoleto) and to his sweetheart,
Fuscula.   Faustulus prays to Pan to help him escape from the
throngs of bandits that infest the crowded streets of Rome and
return to the hill (i.e., the Rocca) of Spoleto: better a *sordidula
vita* there than riches at Rome.   Faustulus complains of having to
make way for arrogant servants in the streets, of being spattered
with smelly mud, and of being disturbed by noise of quarrels and
of construction work.   He contrasts all this with home—but only
briefly, for in a moment he is interrupted by the street-cries of
vendors of nuts and fish; this reminds him that noise goes on in
Roman streets until midnight:

> Their screeching voices still assail the ear
> Who vend their fish, their soap, their oil, their beer;
> And, would you sleep in cellar or in dome,
> No sleep is possible in noisy Rome.

Much of the expression of this poem is derivative; but anyone
who has visited modern Rome will sympathize with Giustolo's complaints about the din in Roman streets late at night and early in
the morning—it has grown worse since the sixteenth century.

Two of the eclogues of Paolo Belmisseri of Pontremoli (ca.
1480–ca. 1547) are satirical.   The fourth (untitled; 139 hexameters) again deals with town life (praised by Politicus) and country
life (praised by Philogaeus).   The poem is perhaps less a satire
than a set rhetorical debate (*agon, rhesis*); but it is lively and
vigorous, and for once Belmisseri's expression matches the liveliness of the content.

Belmisseri's fifth eclogue (untitled; 135 hexameters) is a satire
on women in the manner of Mantuan's fourth: sometimes the lines
are comical, sometimes epigrammatic, sometimes merely ill-humored.

The first part of the fourth eclogue (untitled; 195 hexameters)
of Euricius Cordus (Heinrich Solde) of Simsthausen in Hesse
(1486-1535) is satirical.   The tone of personal rancor is strong
and the satirical gibes at the shepherd Theon quiver with spite;
clearly he was a real man whom Cordus disliked intensely.

Even more bitter is the religious satire of the one extant eclogue
(*Romulus*; 171 hexameters) of Eucharius Synesius (born ca.

1485/90?), about whom I have been able to learn nothing. Here
we have the lament of the shepherd Romulus (i.e., Pope Leo X)
as he lay beside the river Tiber. He laments his loss of prestige
among all the shepherds he knows and describes how a new shepherd
named Catharus has usurped his position; there is no doubt who is
intended, for Martin Luther used Aretius Catharus ("Virtuous
Pure") as a pen-name at least once. Romulus considers suicide,
but yawns and falls asleep before he can decide on the method. A
parody of the well-worn refrain-device appears at irregular intervals
in Romulus' lament: "me lugete meae miserum, lugete, Camenae."

The satirical element has appeared frequently, although incidentally, in many of the eclogues already discussed of Peter van der
Brugge (Pontanus) of Bruges (ca. 1480–ca. 1540); four of the
ten poems are wholly satirical in content—their expression is as
rough-and-ready, their tone as lively, their diction at times as
medieval as ever.

The fourth poem (untitled; 100 hexameters) is yet another
satire on women. Two ancients, Crispus and Canus, shake their
heads over the folly of young men and express themselves sourly on
the perennial topic: they complain that things are not as they once
were, that immorality is on the increase, and that it is entirely the
fault of women; all this leads up to a tirade against women in lines
83 to 99 that is clearly modeled on Mantuan's.

The fifth poem (untitled; 100 hexameters) had an equally traditional topic—the stinginess of patrons towards the hard-working
poet: Orpheus and Amphion themselves, growls the poet, would have
the devil's own time extracting a crooked farthing from Charles of
Flanders.

The sixth poem (untitled; 100 hexameters) is on the quarrel
between youth (represented by Amyntas) and age (Pinus); the last
of Pontanus' ten eclogues (untitled; 100 hexameters) repeats the
traditional libels on married life—Pontanus was happily married, but
had a cheerfully sardonic nature that made the topic congenial.

I have not seen Jacob Bryant's burlesque pastoral (like Barlettani's and Yvelin's poems, a playlet) on the Gin Act of 1736, a
poem "in a class by itself. . . . As a piece of gay exuberant fun it
has few equals in Latin verse" (Leicester Bradner). The poem is
discussed at length by Professor Bradner in his *Musae Anglicanae*
and the reader is referred to the passage on pages 286-89, where
the final comment is "nor is this pastoral without its connections

with the 'Newgate pastoral,' *The Beggar's Opera*." I must also refer the reader to *Musae Anglicanae* for discussions of the satirical eclogue of William King (*floruit* 1719-1763), Principal of St. Mary's Hall and leader of the Jacobite party at Oxford. In his third eclogue (*Scamnum*, "The Bench"), King assails the corruption of eighteenth-century British government; Prince Charles Edward, by contrast, is praised to the skies under the name of Iulus, and the poem ends with a prayer for the return of the Stuarts. I suppose that the last thing one expects in studying Neo-Latin pastoral is to discover Bonnie Prince Charlie lurking behind a rustic disguise.

The last satirical pastoral to be noticed here is the elegiac "Tityrus Fasting, or, The Self-Tormenting Clergyman" (*Tityrus jejunans, sive Ecclesiastes heautontimorumenos*; 100 lines) of Arthur Johnston of Caskieben in Aberdeenshire (1577-1641). In form it is a soliloquy by a clergyman whose income, no doubt as a result of the political events of the times, has fallen low; he informs his flock querulously of the short commons to which he has been reduced: "It is a wonderful grouping, for an ecclesiastical [rather, satirical and political] purpose, into one anthology [*sic*], of the varied imagery of pastoral life and occupations" (Geddes). Pastoral convention, it is true, is everywhere in the poem, but there are remarkably few really classical allusions and a correspondingly large number—naturally—of contemporary references to the Churches of England and Scotland.

This vigorous poem is typical of Johnston, most Ovidian and most finished of all Scottish Neo-Latin poets—even Leech was no match for him. Many of Johnston's poems have lost their appeal today, but most Aberdonians and many others, too, would still be delighted with his long description of salmon-fishing. He describes with relish net-fishing at the mouth of the Dee in Aberdeenshire as well as the far more exciting sport of fishing for salmon in such places as the rapids at Bridge of Feugh near Banchory.

v

The fifth class of eclogue recalls a good many met in earlier chapters—the eclogue of debate. Of the three that I have postponed to this chapter, one is eccentric and the other two are dull. The first is the "Autarches" (199 hexameters) of Claude du Verdier of Vauprivas (1566-1649), a minor, waspish, vain critic of philosophy and literature: Mme. Hulubei well refers to him as *ce petit Boileau de la fin du siècle*. In this poem Autarches ("Self-Sufficient") defends the shepherd's life, but his friend Aepolus ("Goatherd") is all for abandoning it to become a soldier, especially now that Mopsus has done so well for himself since leaving the meadows and hills of Arcady. There is the occasional good line here and there —some amusing ones, too; but the versification is odd and occasionally outlandish.

The other two poems here are far more competent technically but are lifeless. Jean Jacques Boissard of Besançon (1528-1602) has an eclogue in the *Delitiae poetarum Gallorum* in which Philo, a vine-dresser, and Janus, a shepherd, debate the merits of their respective ways of life. The jurist Nicolaus Cisner of Mosbach (1529-1583) has another in the *Delitiae poetarum Germanorum* (1612) called "The Praise of May and Spring" (*De Maii et Veris laudibus*; 304 hexameters) in which two shepherds debate the merits of spring and autumn; the reader loses interest after fifty lines, especially as Strozzi had done the whole thing much better a century earlier in Ferrara.

vi

We come now to the final section of the final chapter in the history of Neo-Latin pastoral, where we meet a number of didactic, ethical, moralizing, or pedagogical eclogues written by Italian, German, and French Neo-Latinists. These vary widely in quality from the pleasant elegance of Girolamo Fracastoro to the German good sense of Joachim Camerarius to the un-Gallic dullness of Gervais Sepin.

The first poet here is a major figure of Italian science and Neo-Latin literature alike—Girolamo Fracastoro of Verona (1478-1553), polymath, polygraph, and founder of modern pathology. Fracastoro studied philosophy and medicine under Pomponazzi and Achillini at Padua (where he met and was friendly with Copernicus). After some years of teaching at Padua and Forlì he retired to Incaffi, near Verona, to devote the rest of his life to writing and the study of philosophy, medicine, and astronomy. He is well described in the *Enciclopedia Italiana* as "un gran signore della più varia cultura cinquecentesca."

Of Fracastoro's poems the most famous is the *Syphilis* (three books of hexameters, addressed to Cardinal Pietro Bembo). At the moment we are concerned only with his single eclogue "Alcon" (180 hexameters) in which the poet combines the manner and diction of Nemesianus' eclogues with the content of the same Roman poet's didactic work on the training of hunting dogs. A partial version follows:

Old Alcon, as Italian hunters say,
Once rested from the burning heat of day;
Where lofty pines to heaven's arch ascend,
He bade the youth Acastus to attend:

"My aging limbs, my failing powers forbid
That I should scale the heights where game is hid.
No longer can I hunt with bow and spear:
Then mark my counsel, with attentive ear.

Now is it fitting that *you* scour the plain
And let me see my youth renewed again.
The summer's heat and winter's cold endure,
To set the crafty net and cunning lure;
To you my bow and spear I now assign
(Now shall be yours what other-while was mine).
But, lest you rashly trust your hunting skill,
Trust more the dogs to find and track the kill:
No stag's too fleet to fear their fleet pursuit,
No bear's too strong, no lion's too astute.
Then mark my counsel, and recall it, too,
When game is started with a loud halloo.
First must you to their strain and stock give heed
Nor choose the hunter from the lap-dog breed;
Choose those with noble instinct well ingrained,
To toil accustomed, and to hunting trained.
This ponder well, nor let your caution tire:
A different dog a different whelp will sire.
If you aspire to hunt the fiercest game,
And risk your spirit to enlarge your fame,
Seek dogs bred from the rugged Spartan kind,
Or strong Molossians that are hard to find,
Or choose the British or the Libyan hounds,
Those from the Celtic and the Afric bounds:
But should you hunt the timid deer, or hare,
Set lean and speedy dogs to find the lair.

And should you seek the deepest woods remote,
Avoid the heavy dog with shaggy coat.
The Persian or the Saxon dog is best,
To find the game, and win in any test.
For every purpose seek the smoothest coat,
The lofty carriage, and the burly throat,
The lively eye, the broad and ample jaw,
The sharpest hearing, and the widest maw.
Let legs be strong and widely set apart,
Let chest be broad (a sign of fearless heart).
No need to add that muscles must be strong:
The hunting-dog must run both fast and long.
In early spring, then, couple dam and sire,
When love arouses quick the ardent fire.
But long restrain the willing pair from love,
Nor let the female with her master rove:
Restraint will guarantee a stronger brood,
Of courage virile and of vigor rude.
No sooner has the litter come to breast
Than keep the finest and discard the rest.
Put all the litter close to fire, and then
The dam will save the finest for her den.
Now, as the whelps increase in power and size,
First train them on the hill, to gain a prize.
Then let them fast pursue the lively hare
Across the plain, and sight the quarry there.
Then, too, teach due obedience to your call.
The master's voice must long be known to all.
Soon will their thews increase as on they rove:
Soon will you trust them to the deepest grove.
Soon will they range the lofty mountains there,
Soon will they risk the savage panther's lair.
Scorn you the timid hare, the fearful deer?
Then seek the boar, the lion with your spear.
Spare now their food and exercise each limb,
Yet keep them locked within the kennel dim:
Release the leashes when the need arise;
Then every hunter the more eager flies.
Now shall I tell, when illness strikes, the cure,
That you yourself may save the litter sure.

At times a hidden fever steals their rest—
To keep their bodies cool is far the best;
With oil of rose then mix the purple wine,
And daily—thrice—administer in time.
Soon shall the hateful fever pass away:
The pack will rise to meet the coming day.
But if the dogs grow languid and recline,
Mix lapith-juice and butyrus with wine. . . . (1-90)

. . . .

But, see, the present hour of fleeting time
Reminds that day by now is past its prime:
Now Coridallus waits without the glade,
And darkness slowly 'gins to spread its shade. (177-80)

The seventh eclogue (untitled; 71 hexameters) of Paolo Belmisseri of Pontremoli (ca. 1480–ca. 1547) is an undistinguished piece of prosy moralizing in which Philetaenus attempts to encourage the gloomy Dacrychus; the poem does arouse some faint interest in its references to German campaigns around Bologna.

Three of the twenty eclogues of Joachim Camerarius (Liebhard) of Bamberg (1500-1574) definitely belong here. The ninth poem ("Daphnis"; 82 hexameters) is moralizing and pedagogical, its subject being similar to that of Mantuan's second bucolic—the unhappy results of love and especially of illicit love. The choice of theme is probably not to be regarded as mere traditionalism; the German Humanists had a strong moralizing tendency, and this poem was undoubtedly meant to instruct as well as to delight. The plot is similar to that of many a derivative art-pastoral but the reader is clearly expected to take the moral of Daphnis' troubles to heart.

The thirteenth eclogue ("Daphnis"; 120 hexameters), despite the title and despite the fact that *dirus Amor* appears, is not a sequel to the ninth; it is an art-pastoral employing a "new" myth and introducing the didactic element casually and almost incidentally at its conclusion.

The fourteenth poem ("Illus"; 79 hexameters) is a domestic eclogue of advice, in which Camerarius, in addressing his own son, shows a pleasant ability to combine a pedagogical or moralizing aim with the idealized background of the Never-Never Land of pastoral. His string of precepts (not so long as George Washingtons' fifty-seven rules of behavior—more like Jefferson's half dozen) is intentionally composed in an old-fashioned, simple, almost naïve manner.

Of the seven eclogues of Gervais Sepin of Saumur (*floruit* 1553) we have noted the last, a pastoral epicedium on the death of the author's delicate pupil, Henri du Bellay. The first six eclogues appear to have been written for the boy's education, and form a connected cycle or sequence of didactic poems in which the doctrines of the aged Menalcas are expounded at tremendous length—the series runs to 2,566 hexameters, an average of 427 lines a poem. In no other set of pastorals in the whole range of Neo-Latin literature has the eclogue become so exclusively a medium for the presentation of ideas that are completely non-pastoral. It would serve no useful purpose to give the reader a running analysis of all six poems —I know of only three persons who have read them in their entirety in the past century, and there seems little reason why they should be fully introduced to a larger public.

We have now followed the uneven course of Neo-Latin pastoral from Dante Alighieri in 1320 to Stefano Laonice in 1800 and have seen it develop from Pre-Humanist pastoral of the fourteenth century into the humanistic art-pastoral and then into the special forms and special uses that flourished from 1400 to 1800. Hardly a generation passed during all this time that could not display half-a-dozen examples of a genre that flourished with astonishing vitality —other forms of Neo-Latin poetry might languish or even die out, but never pastoral. In this period we can count a large number of worthless poems (as in any literature in any language), an even greater number of merely mediocre ones, and an unexpectedly large number of excellent ones: an anthology of the best would make a sizable volume. The death-blow came with Joseph Schneider's collection of religious pastorals (1878); but the rot had already set in over a century earlier, and I may close this study with a reference to John Hubbock's "Thames" (*Thamesis*; 89 hexameters), written in 1735 to celebrate the wedding of Princess Anne. This poem is typical of several dozen pastorals that appeared in England between 1700 and 1850 celebrating royal marriages and welcoming royal personages on visits to Oxford or Cambridge. The sight of Daphnis and Amaryllis, Amyntas and Neaera, Palaemon and Phyllis prettily linking hands to warble an amoebaean welcome to portly Hanoverian princes on the banks of Isis or Cam is a melancholy one: such poems are indeed the tattered remnants of Arcadianism.

BIBLIOGRAPHY

I GENERAL WORKS

Alberti, Rafael. *Églogas y fabulas castellanas*. Buenos Aires, 1944.

Albini, G. *L'egloga di Giovanni del Virgilio ad Albertino Mussato*. Bologna, 1925.

Allen, D. C. "Latin Literature," *Modern Language Quarterly*, II (1941), 403-20.

Allgemeine Deutsche Biographie, 1875-1921 (56 volumes).

Altamura, Antonio. *Giacopo Sannazaro*. Naples, 1934.

Arnaldi, Francesco. *Poeti latini del Quattrocento*. Milan, 1964.

Avena, Antonio. *Il Bucolicum Carmen e i suoi commenti inediti*, Padua, 1906 (*Padova in onore di Francesco Petrarca*, Volume I).

Baiocchi, F. *Sulle poesie latine di Francesco Maria Molza*. Pisa, 1904.

Bayo, M. J. *Virgilio y la pastoral española del Rinaciemento* (1480-1530). Madrid, 1959.

Benfenati, I. "Le egloghe del dolore nel Bucolicum carmen del Petrarca," *Convivium*, nuova serie (1948), 671-78.

Berry, Lloyd E. "Three Poems by Giles Fletcher the Elder," *Notes and Queries* (N.S.), VI (1959), 132-34.

Bertoni, G. "Umanisti Portoghesi a Ferrara," *Giornale storico della letteratura italiana*, CXIV (1939), 46-49.

Bolgar, R. R. *The Classical Heritage and Its Beneficiaries*. Cambridge, 1955.

Bolisani, E. *L'esaltazione di Albertino Mussato nella poesia di Giovanni di Virgilo*. Padua, 1961.

Bottiglioni, G. *La lirica latina in Firenze nella seconda metà del secolo xv°*. Pisa, 1913.

Bradner, Leicester. *Musae Anglicanae.* New York, 1940.

————. "Latin Drama of the Renaissance," *Studies in the Renaissance,* IV (1957), 31-70.

Brunet, I. C. *Manuel du libraire.* Paris, 1820-1834 (7 volumes).

Buchanan, David. *De scriptoribus Scotis.* Edinburgh, 1837.

Budik, P. A. *Leben und Wirken der vorzüglichsten Dichter des xv.-xvi. Jahrhunderts.* Vienna, 1828.

Campaux, A. *De ecloga piscatoria.* Paris, 1894.

Carrara, Enrico. *La poesia pastorale.* Milan, [1907?].

————. "I commenti antichi e la cronologia delle egloghe petrarches-che," *Giorn. stor.,* XXVIII (1896), 123-53.

————. "Cecco di Mileto e il Boccaccio," *Giorn. stor.,* XLIII (1905), 444-51.

————. "La bucolica di Fausto Andrelini," *Giorn. stor.,* LXXVI (1920), 20-81.

Carrington, F. *The Shepherds' Pipe.* New York, 1903.

Clarke, M. L. *Classical Education in Britain,* 1500-1900. Cambridge, 1958.

Cosenza, Mario. *Bio-bibliographical index of Italian humanists* (micro-film), Renaissance Society of America. New York, 1954.

Cosmo, U., and P. Gerosa. *Da Dante al Pontano.* Torino, 1927.

Costa, E. *Un poeta pontremolese* (i.e., Belmisseri). Parma, 1887.

Dictionary of National Biography, 1908-1909 (22 volumes).

Dictionnaire des lettres françaises (Le seizieme siècle). Paris, 1951.

Dictionnaire des lettres françaises (Le dix-septieme siècle). Paris, 1954.

Dictionnaire universelle de biographie, n.d. (45 volumes).

Eckstein, F. A. *Nomenclator philologorum.* Leipzig, 1871.

Ellinger, Georg. *Geschichte der neulateinischen Literatur Deutschlands in sechzehnten Jahrhundert.* Berlin, 1929-1933 (I, II, III i: all published).

Enciclopedia Italiana, 1939-1948 (36 volumes).

Frati, F. "Un'egloga rusticale del 1508," *Giorn. stor.,* XX (1892), 186-204.

Fucilla, Joseph. "Petrarch and the Modern Vogue of the Figure Ady-nata," *Zeitschrift für romanischen Philologie,* LVI (1936), 671-78.

Garin, E. *Prosatori latini del Quattrocento.* Milan, 1952.

Gerhardt, M. I. *Essai d'analyse littéraire de la pastorale.* Paris, 1950.

Graesse, I. G. T. *Trésor de livres rares et précieux.* Paris, 1859-1869 (8 volumes; Milan reprint, 1950).

Gragg, Florence. *Latin Writings of the Italian Humanists.* New York, 1927.

Grant, W. Leonard, "Early Neo-Latin Pastoral," *Phoenix,* IX (1955), 19-26.

———. "Later Neo-Latin Pastoral, Part I," *Studies in Philology,* LIII (1956), 429-51.

———. "Later Neo-Latin Pastoral, Part II," *Studies in Philology,* LIV (1957), 481-97.

———. "New Forms of Neo-Latin Pastoral," *Studies in the Renaissance,* IV (1957), 71-100.

———. "Neo-Latin *Lusus Pastoralis* in Italy," *Medievalia et Humanistica,* XI (1957), 94-98.

———. "Two Eclogues of Giano Anisio," *Philological Quarterly,* XXXIII (1954), 10-18.

———. "An Eclogue of Giovanni Pontano," *Philological Quarterly,* XXXVI (1957), 76-84.

———. "An Eclogue of Giovanni Quatrario," *Studies in the Renaissance,* V (1958), 9-14.

———. "A Forgotten Latin Eclogue," *Renaissance News,* IX (1956), 249-51.

———. "Neo-Latin Verse-Translations of the Bible," *Harvard Theological Review,* LII (1959), 205-11.

———. "An Eclogue of Francesco Filelfo?" *Manuscripta,* III (1959), 171-72.

———. "Neo-Latin Materials at St. Louis," *Manuscripta,* IV (1960), 3-18.

———. "An Anonymous Neo-Latin Eclogue," *Renaissance News,* XIII (1960), 9-11.

———. "A Classical Theme in Neo-Latin," LATOMUS (*Revue d'études latines belge*), IX (1957), 690-706.

———. "A Neo-Latin 'Heraldic' Eclogue," *Manuscripta,* IV (1960), 149-63.

———. "Neo-Latin Biblical Pastorals," *Studies in Philology,* LVIII (1961), 25-43.

———. "Neo-Latin Devotional Pastorals," *Studies in Philology,* LVIII (1961), 597-615.

———. "A New Naldi Manuscript," *Renaissance News,* X (1958), 249-51.

———. "Naldo Naldi and codex Urbinas Latinus 1198," *Manuscripta,* VI (1962), 67-75.

———. "The Major Poems of Naldo Naldi," *Manuscripta,* VI (1962), 131-54.

———. "The Minor Poems of Naldo Naldi," *Manuscripta,* VII (1963), 3-17.

———. "The Minor Poems of Naldo Naldi (concluded)," *Manuscripta,* VII (1963), 90-102.

———. "The Life of Naldo Naldi of Florence," *Studies in Philology,* LX (1963), 606-17.

————. "Neo-Latin Studies," *Renaissance News,* XVI (1963), 102-6.
————. "The Shorter Latin Poems of George Buchanan," *Classical Journal,* XL (1945), 331-48.
Greg, W. W. *Pastoral Poetry and Pastoral Drama.* London, 1906.
Greswell, W. P. *Memoirs of Angelo Poliziano* [and others]. 2nd ed. Manchester and London, 1805.
Hall, H. M. *Idylls of Fishermen.* New York, 1912.
Hamblin, F. R. *The Development of Allegory in the Classical Pastoral.* New York, 1928.
Harrison, T. P. *The Pastoral Elegy.* Austin, Texas, 1939.
————. "The Latin Pastorals of Milton and Castiglione," *Publications of the Modern Language Association,* L (1935), 480-93.
Hauvette, H. *Boccace.* Paris, 1914.
————. *Un exil florentin à la cour de France au xvi*ᵉ *siècle.* Paris, 1903 (on Luigi Alamanni).
Hedberg, Betty Nye. "The Mediaeval Tradition of Bucolic." Unpublished Ph.D. dissertation, Bryn Mawr College, Bryn Mawr, Pennsylvania.
————. "The *Bucolics* and the Mediaeval Poetical Debate," *Transactions of the American Philological Association,* LXXV (1944), 47-67.
Highet, Gilbert. *The Classical Tradition.* Oxford, 1949 (corrected reprint, 1951).
Hortis, A. de'. *Studi sulle opere latine del Boccaccio.* Trieste, 1879.
Hulubei, Alice. *L'églogue en France au xvi*ᵉ *siècle.* Paris, 1939.
————. *Répertoire des églogues en France au xvi*ᵉ *siècle.* Paris, 1940.
Jöcher, C. G. *Allgemeines Gelehrtenlexicon.* Leipzig, 1750-1819 (4 volumes).
Kinsley, James (ed.). *Scottish Poetry.* London, 1955 (chapter three, by J. W. L. Adams, is an excellent survey of Scottish Neo-Latin poetry).
Krauss, Werner. "Ueber die Stellung der Bukolik in der aesthetischen Theorie des Humanismus," *Archiv für Studien,* CLXXIV (1938), 180-98.
Lefranc, A. *Histoire du Collège de France.* Paris, 1893.
Levrault, Léon. *Le genre pastorale.* Paris, 1914.
Liruti, A. *Notizie delle vite ed opere scritte da' letterati di Friuli.* Venice, 1762 (2 volumes).
Macrì-Leone, F. *La bucolica latina della letteratura italiana del secolo xiv*⁰. Torino, 1889 (Volume I: all published).
Malagola, C. *Antonio Codro detto Urceo.* Bologna, 1878.
Manacorda, G. *Della poesia in Germania durante il Rinascimento.* Rome, 1907.
————. *Piero Angelio de Barga.* Pisa, 1904.

Martines, Lauro. *The Social World of the Florentine Humanists.* Princeton, New Jersey, 1963.

Messini, D. A. "Il Cantalicio," *Giorn. stor.,* CXV (1940), 15-38.

Müller, Lucian. *Geschichte der klassischen Philologie in den Niederlanden.* Leipzig, 1879.

Murarasu, D. *La poésie néo-latine et la renaissance des lettres classiques en France.* Paris, 1928.

Osgood, C. G. *Boccaccio on Poetry.* Princeton, New Jersey, 1930.

Pasqualigo, F. *Egloghe di Giovanni del Virgilio e di Dante Alighieri.* Lonigo, 1887.

Percopo, E. *Vita di Giovanni Pontano.* Naples, 1938.

Pökel, W. *Philologisches Schriftsteller-Lexicon.* Leipzig, 1882.

Rossi, V. *Il Quattrocento.* 5th ed. Milan, 1948.

Sainati, A. *La lirica latina nel rinascimento.* Pisa, 1919.

Sandys, Sir J. E. *A History of Classical Scholarship.* Cambridge, 1908. Vol. II.

Sapegno, N. *Il Trecento.* 5th ed. Milan, 1948.

Saulnier, V. L. "Le tombeau du Dauphin," *Bibliothèque d'Humanisme et de Renaissance,* VI (1945), 50-57.

Schroeter, A. *Beiträge zur Geschichte der neulateinischen Poesie Deutschlands und Hollands.* Berlin, 1909.

Scolari, F. *I versi latini di Giovanni del Virgilio.* Venice, 1845.

Senatore, G. "Giovanni Pontano, poeta della famiglia," *Archivio storico per le provincie napoletane* (nuova serie), XXV (1939), 15-24.

Sicard, A. *Les études classiques avant la révolution.* Paris, 1887.

Sperduti, Alice. *Petrarch on Poetry.* Cornell University Abstracts of Theses, 1947, 15-18.

Staton, W. F., Jr. "The Influence of Thomas Watson on Elizabethan Ovidian Poetry," *Studies in the Renaissance,* VI (1959), 243-50.

Tiraboschi, G. *Storia della letteratura italiana.* Modena, 1787-1794 (16 volumes).

Toffanin, G. *Il Cinquecento.* 4th ed. Milan, 1950.

———. *Storia dell'umanesimo.* Bologna, 1950 (3 volumes).

Van Tieghem, Paul. "La littérature latine de la Renaissance," *Bibliothèque d'Humanisme et de Renaissance,* IV (1944), 177-418.

Voigt, G. *Die Wiederbelebung des classischen Altherthums.* Berlin, 1880-1881 (2 volumes).

Vollaro, G. *Giano Anisio.* Naples, 1914.

Woodhouse, A. S. P. "Milton's Pastoral Monodies," in *Studies in Honour of Gilbert Norwood.* Ed. Mary E. White. Toronto, 1952.

Wotke, Karl. *Lilius Gregorius Giraldus: De poetis nostrorum temporum.* Berlin, 1894.

Zabłocki, Stefan. *De Gregorio Samboritano bucolicorum carminum auctore quaestiones.* Warsaw, 1962

Zarden (i.e., Erika Lipsker). *Der Mythos von goldenen Zeitalter in den Schäferdichtung Italiens, Spaniens, usw.* Berlin, 1933.

Zumbini, R. "Le egloghe del Boccaccio," *Giorn. stor.,* XXVII (1896), 94-152.

II ANTHOLOGIES OF LATIN TEXTS

Boehme, J. G. *Poetarum Polonorum Carmina Pastoralia.* 2nd. ed. Altenburg, 1779.

Bottari, Giovanni (also attributed to Tommaso Buonaventuri). *Carmina illustrium poetarum Italorum.* Florence, 1719-1726 (11 volumes).

Carmina quinque Hetruscorum poetarum. Florence, 1526.

Costa, E. *Antologia della lirica latina in Italia nei secoli xv e xvi.* Città di Castello, 1888.

Exequiae P. Sidnaei. London, 1587.

G., A. F. G. *Delitiae poetarum Germanorum.* Frankfort, 1612 (6 volumes in 12).

Geddes, Sir W. D., and W. K. Leask. *Musa Latina Aberdonensis.* Aberdeen, 1892-1910 (3 volumes).

Gherus, Ranutius (Jan Gruter). *Delitiae poetarum Belgicorum.* Frankfort, 1614 (4 volumes).

——. *Delitiae poetarum Gallorum.* Frankfort, 1609 (3 volumes).

——. *Delitiae poetarum Italorum.* Frankfort, 1608 (2 volumes in 4).

Johnston, Arthur (library catalogues speak of Johnston as the editor; but J.'s prefatory letter to this anthology twice speaks of Sir John Scot of Scotstarvet as selecting the poems; cf. also Geddes and Leask, Vol. III, pp. 283-84). *Delitiae poetarum Scotorum.* Amsterdam, 1637.

Lertius, J. B. *Selecta patrum societatis Jesu carmina.* Genoa, 1747.

Musae Anglicanae, London, 1692; 2nd ed. (1699) by J. Addison, reissued in 1714 and 1721; 5th ed. (1741) by Vincent Bourne, reissued in 1761 in two volumes, with a spurious third in 1717.

Olivet, Pierre. *Recentiores poetae Latini et Graeci selecti quinque.* Leyden, 1743.

Oporinus, Johannes. *Bucolicorum autores . . . farrago eclogarum.* Basel, 1546 (the actual selection of poems was made by Erasmus' one-time secretary, Gilbert Cousin of Noseroy, 1506-1572.

Paoli, U. E., *Prose e poesie di scrittori italiani.* 6th ed. Florence, 1942.

Poemata selecta Italorum. Oxford, 1808.

Popham, E. *Selecta poemata Anglorum Latina.* 2nd ed. Bath, 1774-1776 (3 volumes).

Reis (Reyes), Antonio dos. *Corpus illustrium poetarum Lusitanorum.* Lisbon, 1745-1748 (8 volumes).

Rostgaard, F. *Delitiae quorundam poetarum Danorum.* Leyden, 1693 (3 volumes).

Selecta carmina orationesque clarissimorum in Universitate Parisiensi professorum. Paris, 1727.

Septem illustrium virorum poemata. 2nd ed. Amsterdam, 1627.

III INDIVIDUAL AUTHORS

In the following section titles are abbreviated; this is only a working bibliography of texts actually used—it does not necessarily cite the first edition or all editions of a given work, nor does it give its page references in, say, *Carmina illustrium poetarum Italorum* (*CIPI*), if read elsewhere. In each case I have indicated the library from which the text would be most easily available.

Aagaard, Christian. *Del. poet. Dan.,* I, 542-45. Harvard.

Aetsema, Leo. *Poemata.* Franeker, 1617. Harvard.

Alamanni, Luigi. *CIPI,* I, 447-55. Harvard.

Alighieri, Dante. *CIPI,* I, 115-19; Albini, G., *Dantis eclogae,* Florence, 1903; Wicksteed, P. H., and E. G. Gardner, *Dante and Giovanni del Virgilio,* Westminster, 1902. Harvard.

Allegretti, Giaccobbe. *See* Coluccio Salutati. *Epistolario.* Ed. Novati. Index. Harvard.

Amaltei, gli. *Trium fratrum Amaltheorum carmina.* Venice, 1627. See pp. 325-488 of the 1728 edition of Sannazaro (q.v.). *Versi editi ed inediti di Girolamo, Gian Battista, e Cornelio, fratelli Amaltei.* Treviso, 1817. Bodleian.

Amalteo, Cornelio, *CIPI,* I, 179-81. Harvard.

Amalteo, G. B., *CIPI,* I, 148-60. Harvard.

Amalteo, Girolamo, *CIPI,* I, 140-47. Harvard.

Ammonius. *See* Rena, della.

Anderson, Henry, *Del. poet. Scot.,* I, 24-40. New York Public.

Andrelini, Publio Fausto, Oporinus, 281-332; *The Eclogues of Faustus Andrelinus and Joannes Arnolletus.* Ed. W. P. Mustard. Baltimore, 1918. Harvard.

Angelio, Pietro, *CIPI,* I, 213-14; *Poemata omnia,* Rome, 1585 (2 volumes in 1); *Poemata omnia,* Florence, 1618 (edited by Roberto Tizio). Harvard.

Angeriano, Girolamo, *Erotopaegnion,* Florence, 1512; *Del. poet. Ital.,* I, 174-230. Harvard.

Anglicus, Michael. *Varia opuscula.* Paris, 1507. Bibliothèque Nationale.

Anisio, Giano, *Varia poemata et satyrae,* Naples, 1531-32; Oporinus, 409-32. Bodleian.

Anon. *Codrus,* n.p., n.d. (the MS catalogue of Neo-Latin works in the Salle de Réserve of the Bibliothèque Nationale attributes this to "Le

Révérend Père LeJay," i.e., Gabriel-François LeJay, professor in the Lycée Louis le Grand and a prolific Latin tragedian).

———. *Ecloga* (the Angevin eclogue), MS Laurent., 12, plut. 90, inf. Biblioteca Lorenz., Florence.

———. *Incerti auctoris tres eclogae,* Oporinus, 460-72. Bodleian.

———. *Incerti auctoris piscatoria,* Oporinus, 469-72. Bodleian.

———. *In Petri Bembi mortem eclogae tres incerti auctoris,* in Volume III of the 1567 edition of Bembo's *Opera omnia,* Basel, 174-86; published separately: Venice, 1548. Bodleian.

———. *Iolas piscatoria,* Oporinus, 465-69. Bodleian.

———. *Musa Nivernensis,* Paris MS nouv. acqu. franç. 6282 (dated 1676). Bibliothèque Nationale.

———. *Pax ecloga,* Paris MS nouv. acqu. franç. 6282. Bibliothèque Nationale.

———. *Pharmaceutria,* Oporinus, 460-65. Bodleian.

———. "The Ste.-Barbe Eclogue," in *Carmina recitata cum Sanctae Barbarae sodalitium Patronae suae solemne Festum celebraret,* Paris, 1786. Bibliothèque Nationale.

———. *Umbricius* [Paris], n.d. Bibliothèque Nationale.

———. *Ecloga Lycidas,* Vat. MS Barb. lat. 1820. Pius XII Memorial.

———. *Ecloga Alcaeus,* same MS.

———. *Ecloga Alcon,* same MS.

———. *Ecloga Iolas,* Vat. MS Barb. lat. 2163. Pius XII Memorial.

———. *Ecloga Lycidus* [*sic*], MS Vat. lat. 3908. Pius XII Memorial.

———. *Eclogae sex,* MS Vat. lat. 5245. Pius XII Memorial.

———. *Fragmentum eclogae,* Vat. MS Ferraj. 679. Pius XII Memorial.

Anonymus Venetus. *See* Monoia. *Della Vita e delle opere di Albertino Mussato.* Rome, 1884. Bibliothèque Nationale.

Anselmo, Giorgio. *Epigrammaton libri septem.* Venice, 1528. Harvard.

Arco, Niccolò d'. *Numerorum libri iv.* Verona, 1762. Harvard.

Arcucci, Giambattista. *Odarum libri ii.* Naples, 1568. Harvard.

Argyllander, Matthaeus. *See* Oporinus, 792-96. Bodleian.

Arnolfino, Pompilio, *CIPI,* I, 362-65. Harvard.

Arnolletus, Joannes. *See* under Andrelini; Oporinus, 263-80. Bodleian.

Aubry, Charles. *Ecloga seu pastorale colloquium.* Paris, 1701. Bibliothèque Nationale.

Aunillon, P. C. F. *Ecloga.* Paris, [1701]. Bibliothèque Nationale.

Barberini, Maffeo. *Poemata.* Paris, 1642; *CIPI,* II, 57-63. Harvard.

Barclay, John, *Poematum libri ii,* London, 1652; Cologne, 1626 (Harvard); Oxford, 1636 (Harvard); *Del. poet. Scot.,* I, 93-103, 113-15. New York Public.

Baerle, Melchoir van, *Del. poet. Belg.,* I, 23-40. Harvard.

Barlettani, Francesco, *CIPI,* II, 87-101. Harvard.

Barola, Paolo, *Eclogae duae,* Vat. MS Ferraj. 520. Pius XII Memorial.

Barsi, Vincenzo, *CIPI,* XI, 253-60; Pensa, *Teatro degli Huomini . . . della famiglia Carmelitana,* Mantua, 1618. Harvard.

Basini, Basinio de', *Opera praestantiora,* Rimini, 1794 (ed. Ireneo Affo); *Le poesie liriche di Basinio,* Torino, 1925 (ed. F. Ferri); *Trium poetarum . . . opuscula,* Paris, 1539 (ed. C. Preudhomme). Bodleian.

Beka, Willem de. *Gulielmi Becani Idyllia.* Antwerp, 1667 (but the imprimatur is dated 1655). Harvard.

Bellay, Joachim du, *Del. poet. Gall.,* I, 413-5. Harvard.

Bellirius, Franciscus, *Eclogarum libri ii ad Actium Syncerum,* MS Vat. lat. 2833. Pius XII Memorial.

Belmisseri, Paolo. *Opera poetica.* Paris, 1534. Harvard.

Berni, Francesco, *CIPI,* II, 149-51; *Carmina quinque etc.,* 117-20. Harvard.

Bersman, Georg (Gregor). *Poemata.* Cologne, 1576; *Del. poet. Germ.,* I, 424-35. Harvard.

Beverini, B. *Carminum libri vii.* Lucca, 1674. Harvard.

Boccaccio, Giovanni, Oporinus, 598-699 (Bodleian); Massèra, A. F. *Opere latini minori del Boccaccio.* Bari, 1928. Harvard.

Bodecheer, Jan. *Poemata.* Leyden, 1637. Harvard.

Boiardo, Matteo Maria. *Le poesie volgari e latine di M. M. Boiardo.* Bologna, 1894. Ed. A. Solerti. Bodleian.

Bonis, Giovanni de. *See* Enrico Carrara in *Archivio storico lombardico,* XXV (1898). Harvard.

Borghi, Tobia. *See* R. Sabbadini in *Giorn. ligustico,* 1891; Sabbadini, *Epistolario di Guarino,* III, 354-55. Harvard.

Bougier, Henri. *Daphnis salvus.* Paris, 1681. Bibliothèque Nationale.

Broekhuyzen, Jan. *Jani Broukhusii Poemata omnia.* Amsterdam, 1711. Harvard.

Brugge, Peter van der. *Petri de Ponte Caeci Brugensis decem Aeglogae hechatostice [sic].* [Paris, 1513]. Harvard.

Buchanan, George, *Poemata,* Edinburgh, 1615 (the first complete edition); *Opera omnia,* Edinburgh, 1714-1715 (ed. Thomas Ruddiman; 2 volumes). Bibliothèque Nationale.

Camerarius, Joachim. *Libellus continens eclogas xx et alia quaedam poematia.* Leipzig, 1568. Harvard.

Camillo, Giulio, *CIPI,* III, 108-113. Harvard.

Camplo, Antonio, in *Libellus de ornamentis Paduae,* ed. Segarizzi, in *Rerum Italicarum Scriptores,* Lapi, p. 39. Harvard.

Cantalicio. *See* Valentini.

Capilupi, gli. *Carmina Capiluporum.* Rome, 1590. Bodleian.

Carrara, G. M., in G. Giraldi, "Il Bucolicum carmen di G. M. Carrara," *Giorn. stor.,* CXXXI (1954), 548-74. Harvard.

Casanova, Marcantonio, *Ecloga,* MS Vat. lat. 2833. Pius XII Memorial.

Castiglione, Baldassare, *Poem. sel.* Ital., 30-35 (Bodleian) ; *Del. poet. Ital.,* I, 716-20. Harvard.

Cayado, Enrique. *The Eclogues of H. Cayado.* Baltimore, 1931. Ed. W. P. Mustard. Harvard.

Cecco di Mileto. *See* Rossi.

Cereto, Daniele, in the 1728 edition of Sannazaro (q.v.), pp. 307-12. Harvard.

Châteillon, Sébastien, Oporinus, 796-99. Bodleian.

Châtelier, Guillaume. *Elegiae, una cum sibyllino carmine, egloga, epigrammatibus, ac plerisque aliis versibus.* Poitiers, [1506]. Harvard.

Chester. *See* Wake.

Chigi, Fabio. *Musae juveniles.* Rome, 1645. Harvard.

Chytraeus, Nathan, *Del. poet. Germ.,* II, 334-37. Harvard.

Cianci, Ignazio, in *Pro restituta valetudine Benedicto XIV Arcadum carmina.* Rome, 1757. Harvard.

Cisner, Nicolaus, *Del. poet. Germ.,* II, 446-55. Harvard.

Commire, Jean. *Carminum libri iii.* Paris, 1678. Bibliothèque Nationale.

Condrata, Bartholomaeus, *Ecloga unica,* Vat. MS Urb. lat. 368. Pius XII Memorial.

Cordier, Simon, *Ecloga,* n.p., n.d. Bibliothèque Nationale.

Cordus, Euricius, Oporinus, 343-408. Bodleian.

Corsi, Pietro, *Ecloga quae Erasmus inscribitur,* n.p. [ca. 1513]. Bibliothèque Nationale.

Cotta, J. S., *Ecloga prima ad Franciscum Sfortiam,* Paris MS anc. fonds lat. 8382 (the second eclogue and any others Cotta may have written seem to have been lost). Bibliothèque Nationale.

Croce, Luigi Annibale della, Oporinus, 747-50. Bodleian.

Crotti, Elio Giulio. *Aelii Julii Crotti Opuscula.* Ferrara, 1564. Bodleian.

Dati, Leonardo, *Miriltas:* cf. F. Flamini in *Giorn. stor.* XVI (1890) ; *Chirlus,* ed. L. Cisorio, Pontedera, 1893. Bibliothèque Nationale.

Decembrio, Candido, *Ecloga,* Cod. Ambros. D.112, inf., and see Borsa in *Arch. stor. lomb.* XX (1893). Harvard.

Denalio, Francesco. *Poemata.* Bologna, 1563. Harvard.

Does, Jan van der, *Del. poet. Belg.,* II, 177-79. Harvard.

Dorat, Jean. *Poematia.* Paris, 1586; *Del. poet. Gall.,* I, 377-83. Harvard.

Ducher, Gilbert, Oporinus, 750-55. Bodleian.

Durão, Antonio Figueira, *CIPL,* V, 430-39. Harvard.

Ecker, Wenceslaus, in Schosser's *Poemata* (q.v.).

Écoulant, Pierre. *Idyllium amoebaeum.* Paris, 1750. Bibliothèque Nationale.

Eidyllia [anonymi varii] (Broadgates Hall, Oxford), Oxford, 1612. Bodleian.

Eobanus, Elius, Oporinus, 510-98. Bodleian.

Erasmus, Desiderius, Oporinus, 473-77 (Bodleian); C. Reedijk, *The Poems of Erasmus,* Rotterdam, 1956. Harvard.

Esneval, Robert d'. *Pastores San-Clovianorum.* [Paris, 1701]. Bibliothèque Nationale.

Estienne, Henri, *Del. poet. Gall.,* III, 837-45 and 856. Harvard.

Everaerts (Secundus), Jan, Oporinus, 503-9 (Bodleian); *Del. poet. Belg.,* IV, 329-34. Harvard.

Everaerts (Grudius), Niklaas, *Del. poet. Belg.,* II, 650-65. Harvard.

Eynde, Jakob van, *Del. poet. Belg.,* II, 391-97. Harvard.

Fabricius, Johannes (Montanus), *Del. poet. Germ.,* III, 101-4. Harvard.

Faucher, Denys, in *Chronologia sanctorum virorum Sacrae Insulae Lerinensis.* Lyon, 1613. Bibliothèque Nationale.

Favoriti, Agostino, *CIPI,* IV, 208-17 (Harvard); *Septem,* 43-54. Harvard.

Fazio, Bartolommeo, in *Anecdota litteraria.* Rome, 1774. Volume III. (Ed. Giovanni Cristoforo Amaduzio). Bodleian.

Fiedler, Felix, *Del. poet. Germ.,* III, 133-37. Harvard.

Fiera, Battista, Oporinus, 333-43. Bodleian.

Filelfo, Mario, *Bucolicorum libri iii,* Paris MS anc. fonds lat. 8368 (dated 1473). Bibliothèque Nationale.

Flaminio, Marcantonio, *Carminum libri iv,* Florence, 1552 (Bodleian); F. M. Mancurtius, *Flaminiorum Carmina,* Prato, 1831. Bodleian.

Fletcher, Giles (I), in William Dillingham, *Poemata varii argumenti,* London, 1678. Bodleian.

Fletcher, Phineas. *Sylva poetica.* Cambridge, 1633. Bodleian.

Fleury, Julien. *In nuptias Ludovici Delphini,* n.p., n.d. Bibliothèque Nationale.

Fontana, Marco Publio. *Poemata omnia.* Bergamo, 1752. Harvard.

Fonzio, Bartolommeo. *Opera.* Frankfort, 1621. Bodleian.

Forcadel, Étienne. *Stephani Forcatuli Epigrammata.* [Lyon], 1554. Bibliothèque Nationale.

Fracastoro, Girolamo, *Opera omnia,* n.p., 1621 (Bodleian); *CIPI,* V, 70-75 (Harvard); *Del. poet. Ital.,* I, 1083-88. Harvard.

Fransz, Peter de. *Petri Francii Poemata.* 2nd ed. Amsterdam, 1697. Harvard.

Fürstenberg, Ferdinand von, in *Septem,* 175-78. Harvard.

Fulvio, Andrea, *CIPI,* V, 152-231 (Harvard); *Aegloga de ortu Salvatoris* [Rome?, 1517?]. Harvard.

Fumée de Blandé, Antoine, *Daphnis,* Lyon, 1574; *Livia* [Lyon, ca. 1574]; *Amaryllis,* [Lyon, ca. 1574]. Bibliothèque Nationale.

Gager, William, in *Exequiae P. Sidnaei.* Bodleian.

Gambara, Lorenzo. *Poemata omnia*. Rome, 1576 (Bodleian); *CIPI*, V, 254-56. Harvard.

Gaurico, Pomponio, Oporinus, 699-709. Bodleian.

Geraldini, Antonio, Oporinus, 220-65 (Bodleian); *The Eclogues of Antonio Geraldini*, Baltimore, 1924 (ed. W. P. Mustard) (Harvard); *Ecloga de familia Geraldini*, MS Vat. lat. 6940. Pius XII Memorial.

Giannettasio, Niccolò. *Opera poetica*. Naples, 1715 (3 volumes), Harvard; *CIPI*, V, 294-336. Harvard.

Giraldi, Giambattista, Oporinus, 487-503 (Bodleian); *Poemata*, Ferrara, 1537 (Bodleian); 1537; *Poematia*, Basel, 1544. Bodleian.

Girinet, Philibert, Oporinus, 738-47. Bodleian.

Giustolo, Pierfrancesco. *Justuli Spoletani Opera*. Rome, 1510. Harvard.

Gohory, Jacques, *Franciscus ecloga*, Paris MS anc. fonds lat. 8398 (not 8389 as listed in Mme. Hulubei's *Répertoire*). Bibliothèque Nationale.

Goineo, Giambattista, Oporinus, 790-92. Bodleian.

Grotius, Hugo. *Hugonis Grotii Poemata omnia*. 5th ed. Amsterdam, 1670. Harvard.

Grudius, see Everaerts.

Guarino, Battista. *Carmina*. Modena, 1496. Bibliothèque Nationale.

Gundelius, Philippus. *Aeglogae duae*. Vienna, 1518. Bibliothèque Nationale.

Hallé, Pierre. *Petri Hallaei Orationes et poemata*. Paris, 1655. Bibliothèque Nationale.

Hawkins, William. *Eclogae tres Virgilianae*. London, 1631. Bodleian.

Hébert, Michel, *Ecloga*, n.p., n.d. (the MS catalogue of Neo-Latin works in the BN Salle de Réserve calls the author of *Hispanus auctor*; but Hébert is certainly the writer in question).

Heinsius, Daniel. *Poemata*. 2nd ed. Leyden, 1621. Harvard; *Del. poet. Belg.*, II, 1026-29; 1097-1101. Harvard.

Hérouville, Jean d'. *Ecloga*. [Paris, 1719]. Bibliothèque Nationale.

Hubbock, John, in *Epithalamia Oxoniensia*. Oxford, 1735. Harvard.

Huet, Pierre-Daniel. *Poemata*. 4th ed. Utrecht, 1700. Bibliothèque Nationale; *Salamandra*, n.p., n.d.; *Melissa*, Paris, 1712. Bibliothèque Nationale.

Hume, David. *Poemata omnia*. Paris, 1639 (British Museum); *Daphnamaryllis*, London, 1605 (British Museum); *Del. poet. Scot.*, I, 418-30. New York Public.

Johnston, Arthur, *Poemata omnia*, Middleburgh, 1642 (Bodleian); *Parerga*, Aberdeen, 1632 (King's College, Aberdeen); Geddes and Leask, II, 219-22. Harvard.

Jordens, Gerrit. *Gellia; accedunt . . . eclogae*. Leyden, 1763. Harvard.

Kennedy, James, *Diadema kai Mitra, seu Daphnidis et Druyadum* [*sic*] *reditus,* Aberdeen, 1662 (King's College, Aberdeen); Geddes and Leask, III, 170-73. Harvard.

King, William. *Scamnum ecloga.* London, 1740. British Museum.

Kinschot, Caspar van. *Poemata.* The Hague, 1685. Harvard.

Labbé, Pierre, *Aristus ecloga,* Lyon, 1640 (Bibliothèque Nationale); *Lugduni et Massiliae de Aristo amabilis pugna* [Lyon], 1640. Bibliothèque Nationale.

Lambert, J. M. *Ecloga.* Paris, 1741. Bibliothèque Nationale.

Laonice, Stefano, *Carmen pastorale ad Bonampartem,* Paris, Year IX. Bibliothèque National.

Latewar, Richard, in *Exequiae P. Sidnaei.* Bodleian.

LeBlanc, Guillaume. *Poemata.* Paris, 1589. Bibliothèque Nationale.

Lebrun, Laurent. *Virgilius Christianus.* Paris, 1661. Bibliothèque Nationale.

LeDuchat, Louis-François. *Praeludiorum libri iii.* Paris, 1554. Bibliothèque Nationale.

Leech, John. *Johannis Leochaei Musae priores.* London, 1620. Harvard.

Lenicaerus, Albertus. *Ecloga allegorica.* Wittenberg, 1555. Harvard.

Lerou, Philippe, *Idyllium,* n.p., 1722. Bibliothèque Nationale.

LeRoy, Chrétien. *In pacis reditum ecloga.* [Paris], 1739. Bibliothèque Nationale.

Lotich, Peter II, *Del. poet. Germ.,* III, 1440-75 (Harvard); *Poemata omnia,* Amsterdam, 1754 (2 volumes). Harvard.

Lusco, Leonardo, in Maffei, *Verona Illustrata* (1825), III, 189. Harvard.

Maccius, Sebastianus, *Ecloga piscatoria,* Vat. MS Urb. lat. 730. Pius XII Memorial.

Major, Johannes, *Del. poet. Germ.,* IV, 177-81, 220-22. Harvard.

Mambrun, Pierre, *Eclogae et De cultura animi libri iv,* La Flèche, 1661 (Bibliothèque Nationale); *Umbra,* n.p., n.d. Bibliothèque Nationale.

Mantuan. *See* Spagnuoli.

Mario, Antonio, *CIPI,* VI, 245-47. Harvard.

Masson, Thomas. *In Ludovicum XV ecloga.* [Paris], 1744. Bibliothèque Nationale.

Masures, Louis des. *Carmina.* Lyon, 1557. Harvard.

Mileto. *See* Rossi.

Milton, John. *Epitaphium Damonis.* London, [1640]. British Museum.

Mirteo, Pietro, *CIPI,* VI, 404-6. Harvard.

Mod, Franz, *Del. poet. Belg.,* III, 597-630. Harvard.

Modestus, Johannes Antonius, *Aecloga de Francisci laudibus,* Paris MS anc. fonds lat. 8399. Bibliothèque Nationale.

Moisant de Brieux, Jacques. *Poemata.* Paris, 1663. Bibliothèque Nationale.

Monceaux, François de. *Bucolica sacra.* Paris, 1587. Bibliothèque Nationale.

Monin, Jean-Edouard de. *Miscellaneorum poeticorum adversaria.* Paris, 1578. Bibliothèque Nationale.

Morhof, Daniel Georg. *Opera poetica.* Lübeck, 1697. Harvard.

Naldi, Naldo, *CIPI,* VI, 456-61 (Harvard) ; Paris MS anc. fonds lat. 8389 (dated 1475) ; Paris MS nouv. acqu. lat. 476; Siena, Biblioteca Comunale degli Intronati, MS lat. J. IX, 13; Eton College MS No. 157.

Nanquier, Simon. *De lubrico temporis curriculo.* Paris, 1560. Bibliothèque Nationale.

Navagero, Andrea, Oporinus, 433-38 (Bodleian) ; *Andreae Naugerii Opera omnia,* Padua, 1708. Bodleian.

Nicolucci, Giambattista. *Johannis Baptistae Pignae Carminum libri iv.* Venice, 1553. Bodleian.

Norris, John, *Musae Anglicanae,* I, 162-65. Bodleian.

Novellinus, Balthasar, *Ad Falconem Aureliacum Ecloga,* Paris, MS anc. fonds lat. 8371. Bibliothèque Nationale.

Nucillanus, Gilbertus, Oporinus, 733-38. Bodleian.

Obrysius, Robertus. *Eidyllia sacra libris xii comprehensa.* Douai, 1587. Bibliothèque Nationale.

Palladius, Blosius, *Ecloga,* Vat. MS Cappon. 75. Pius XII Memorial.

Partenio, Bernardino. *Carminum libri iii.* Venice, 1579. Bibliothèque Nationale.

Pasquale, Luigi, *CIPI,* VII, 141-44. Harvard.

Patrizi, Francesco, *CIPI,* VII, 145-49. Harvard.

Persius, Baptista, Oporinus, 772-76. Bodleian.

Pestel, Pierre, *Triumphus Astraeae* (MS bound with a collection of printed pamphlets), BN Salle de Réserve, Yc. 932, No. 43 [dated 1696].

Petit, Louis. *In ortum Delphini.* Paris, 1729. Bibliothèque Nationale.

Petrarca, Francesco, *Opera omnia,* Basel, 1554 (Toronto) ; Oporinus, 71-139 (Bodleian) ; Neri, F. (and others), *Francesco Petrarca: Rime, Trionfi, e poesie latine,* Milan 1951 (Toronto) ; F. de' Rossetti, *F. Petrarchae Carmina minora,* Milan, 1829 (2 volumes). Harvard.

Petremot, François, *Alcon,* Paris MS anc. fonds lat. 8404. Bibliothèque Nationale.

Philomusus. *See* Chigi.

Piat, Nicolas. *Daphnis ecloga.* [Paris, 1725]. Bibliothèque Nationale.

Pigna. *See* Nicolucci.

Pinicianus, Johannes. *Virtus et Voluptas.* Vienna, 1512. Harvard.

Place, Claude de la, *Magi* [Paris?], n.d. (Bibliothèque Nationale); *Pastores* [Paris?], 1634. Bibliothèque Nationale.

Pontano, Giovanni, Oporinus, 51-70 (Bodleian); Oescher, Johannes, *Pontani Carmina*, Bari, 1948 (Harvard); Soldati, *Pontani Carmina*, Naples, 1902, 2 volumes (Harvard); Elaine J. Harper, "The Eclogues . . ." (Unpublished Ph.D. Dissertation, University of Indiana, 1957).

Praetorius, Bernardus, *Del. poet. Germ.*, V, 245-403. Harvard.

Quarengo, Antonio, *Ecloga Almon* ["Alcon" in the text], Padua, 1566. Bibliothèque Nationale.

Quatrario, Giovanni, in Giovanni Pansa, *Giovanni Quatrario di Sulmona: Contributo alla storia dell'umanesimo*. Sulmona, 1912. Harvard.

Raiius, Flaminius (Tommaso Raggio), *CIPI*, VIII, 39-44. Harvard.

Rapin, René, *Selecta patrum, etc.*, 1-10. Bibliothèque Nationale.

Ravasini, Tommaso. *Amores Parthenii*. Parma, 1697. Harvard.

Regnier, Jean, Oporinus, 709-24. Bodleian.

Remmius, Abraham (Ravaud). *Poemata*. Paris, 1645. Harvard.

Rena, Andrea della, *Andreae Ammonii Carmina omnia* (ed. Clemente Pizzi), Florence, 1958 (Harvard); Oporinus, 725-33. Bodleian.

Rheder, Martin. *Ecloga de vita beata*. Wittenberg, 1578. Bibliothèque Nationale.

Roillet (Rouillet), Claude. *Varia poemata*. Paris, 1556. Bibliothèque Nationale.

Roscius, Julius, *Lusus pastorales*, Vat. MS Barb. lat. 1967. Pius XII Memorial.

Rossi, Francesco de' (Cecco di Mileto), *CIPI*, VI, 315-18. Harvard.

Rota, Bernardino, *CIPI*, VIII, 172-75. Harvard.

Rotondus, Petrus, *Ecloga*, Vat. MS Ferraj. 587. Pius XII Memorial.

Sabinus, Georg, Oporinus, 784-89 (Bodleian); *Poemata*, Leipzig, 1558. Harvard.

Sainte-Marthe, Abel I. *Poemata*. Paris, 1597. Bibliothèque Nationale.

Sainte-Marthe, Scévole. *Poemata*. Paris, 1606. Bibliothèque Nationale.

Salutati, Coluccio. *See* the *Epistolario* (ed. Francesco Novati), I, 150-55, 156-57; 167-72 (Harvard); E. Carrara in Volume LV of *Giorn. stor.*, pp. 453 ff. Harvard.

Sannazaro, Giacopo, *Opera omnia*. Venice, 1535 (Bodleian); Oporinus, 440-60 (Bodleian); *Opera* (ed. Broukhusius), Amsterdam, 1689 and 1728 (Bodleian); *Opera omnia* (ed. Giovanni Antonio Volpi), Bassano, 1782. Bodleian.

Santeul, J. B. de. *Santolii Victorini Opera poetica*. Paris, 1695. Bibliothéque Nationale.

Scaliger, J. C. *Poemata omnia*. Paris, 1621. Harvard.

Scheffer, Sebastian. *Poemata*. Frankfort, 1572. Harvard.

Schneider, Joseph. *Carminum libri viii*. Trieste, 1878. Harvard.

Schoonhoven, Floris van. *Poemata.* Leyden, 1613 (Harvard); *Del. poet. Belg.,* IV, 88-122. Harvard.

Schosser, Johann. *Poemata.* Leipzig, 1560. Harvard.

Schryver, Cornelius de. *Sacrorum bucolicorum Aeglogae tres.* Antwerp, 1536. Harvard.

Secundus. *See* Everaerts.

Seidel, Johann. *Ecloga de nuptiali Lucae Cononis.* Wittenberg, 1554. Harvard.

Sepin, Gervais, *Del. poet. Gall.,* III, 743-829. Harvard.

Silvestri, Domenico, *Consolatio pastoralis,* Florence MS Laur. plut. XC, inf., cod. 13. Biblioteca Lorenziana.

Simonius, Johannes, *Del. poet. Germ.,* VI, 221-28. Harvard.

Sluyper, Jakob de. *Sluperii Herzelensis Poemata.* Antwerp, 1575 (Harvard); *Del. poet. Belg.,* IV, 352-54. Harvard.

Sousa, João de Mello de, *CIPL,* II, 349-56. Harvard.

Souvigny, Guy de, *Ecloga ad Urbanum viii,* Vat. MS Barb. lat. 2129. Pius XII Memorial.

Spagnuoli, Giambattista ("Mantuan"), Oporinus, 140-215 (Bodleian); *Opera omnia,* Bologna, 1502 (Bodleian); *Opera omnia,* Antwerp, 1576, 2 volumes (Bodleian); *The Eclogues of Mantuan,* Baltimore, 1911 (ed. W. P. Mustard). Harvard.

Stenius, Simon, *Del. poet. Germ.,* VI, 312-15. Harvard.

Stiblinus, Caspar, in *Olympiae Moratae Opera omnia.* Basel, 1570. Bodleian.

Stigel, Johann, Oporinus, 776-82. Bodleian.

Stoius, Matthias, *Del. poet. Germ.,* VI, 574-78. Harvard.

Stratenius, Petrus. *Venus Zelandia et alia poemata.* The Hague, 1641. Harvard.

Strozzi, Tito Vespasiano, *Strozii poetae, pater et filius,* Venice, 1513 (Bodleian); Fógel, J., and L. Juhász, *Titus Vespasianus Strozza: Borsias, Bucolicon liber,* Leipzig, 1933. Bodleian.

Sussanneau (or Susannet), Hubert. *Annotationes.* 2nd ed. Paris, 1543. Bibliothèque Nationale.

Synesius, Eucharius, Oporinus, 765-71. Bodleian.

Taglietti, Giovanni Antonio, *CIPI,* IX, 212-23. Harvard.

Tassus, Christophorus, *Ecloga,* MS Vat. lat. 6285. Pius XII Memorial.

Tilesio, A. *A. Thylesii Consentini Carmina.* Naples, 1766. Harvard.

Tillier, François. *In obitum Caroli IX.* Paris, 1574. Bibliothèque Nationale.

Tirimbocchi, Gaspare de' (Tribrachus), in Bertoni, G., and E. P. Vicini, "Gli studi di grammatica," *Atti e memorie della Deputazione di storia patria per la provincia Modenese,* 1905. Bibliothèque Nationale.

Tizio, Roberto, *CIPI,* IX, 268-71. Harvard.

Tomitano, Bernardino. *Thetis.* Venice, 1574. Bibliothèque Nationale.

Urceo, Antonio, Oporinus, 47-51 (Bodleian) ; [*Codri Opera*], Bologna, 1502. Bodleian.

Valentini, Giambattista. *Cantalycii epigrammatum liber.* Venice, 1493. Bodleian.

Vallongnes, Pierre de, *In obitu Francisci Fouquet,* n.p., n.d. Bibliothèque Nationale.

Varadier, Gaspard. *Juvenilia.* Arles, 1679. Bibliothèque Nationale.

Verardus, Marcellinus, *Ecloga unica,* MS Vat. lat. 10806. Pius XII Memorial.

Verdier, Claude du. *Peripetasis epigrammatum; ecloga Aphtarques* [*sic*]. Paris, 1581. Bibliothèque Nationale.

Verdizzoti, Giovanni Mario. *Damon.* Venice, 1570. Harvard.

Vida, Girolamo, Oporinus, 477-86 (Bodleian) ; *Carmina minora,* Basel, 1534 (Bodleian) ; *Carmen pastorale,* [Rome, 1513] (Bodleian) ; *Poemata,* London, 1732. Bodleian.

Vinta, Francesco, *CIPI,* XI, 249-52 (Harvard) ; *Carmina quinque,* etc., 82-86. Harvard.

Virgilio, Giovanni del, *CIPI,* XI, 362-72. Harvard.

Visdomini, Antonio, Oporinus, 215-19. Bodleian.

Vita, Petrus, *Ecloga Poemon* [*sic*], MS Vat. lat. 6285. Pius XII Memorial.

Vitel, Jean de. *Les premiers exercices poétiques.* Paris, 1588 (Bibliothèque Nationale) ; also ed. C.-A. de Robillard de Beaurepaire, Rouen, 1904. Bibliothèque Nationale.

Volpi, Giovanni Antonio. *Carminum libri iii.* Padua, 1725. Harvard.

Wake [Jones], Samuel, and Thomas Chester, *Musae Anglicanae,* II, 144-48. Bodleian.

Walle, Jakob van der. *Poematum libri ix.* 3rd ed. Antwerp, 1669. Harvard.

Weydenbram, Friedrich. *De veteri politia judaica et de regno Christi.* Wittenberg, 1554. Bibliothèque Nationale.

Yvelin, Nicolas. *Ecloga recens edita in Gymnasio Plessaeo.* Paris, 1587. Bibliothèque Nationale.

Zanchi, Basilio (Pietro). *Poemata.* Bergamo, 1547 (Bodleian) ; *Poemata,* Rome, 1550. Bodleian.

INDEX